Eugene O'Neill and the American Critic

A Summary and Bibliographical Checklist

JORDAN Y. MILLER

HAMDEN   ARCHON BOOKS   LONDON
1962

67-6988

Library of Congress Catalog Card No.: 62-8014
Printed in The United States of America

PREFACE

The twenty-two year disappearance of Eugene O'Neill as an active participant in the modern American theatre, save for the brief flurry of excitement attending *THE ICEMAN COMETH* in 1946, and the resurgence of interest in the man and his plays after his death have been a phenomenon unique in our dramatic history. The almost complete oblivion of this writer who contributed so heavily to the emergence of American drama as a world leader in stage literature after World War I, and his subsequent posthumous return to prominence raise many interesting questions. Why did he cease writing so abruptly? Why was he so completely forgotten for two decades? What has caused the current interest in his admittedly heavy and somber plays? And how permanent will he become in our literary heritage?

When this study was originally undertaken shortly after the death of Eugene O'Neill, its purpose was to determine only the reasons for his long absence from the theatre and the apparent lack of interest in him at the time of his death. Major critics like Brooks Atkinson and John Mason Brown deplored the disinterest in the passing of this "giant" who had "dropped from the earth," as Atkinson put it, but surprisingly little note of the event was taken by the public in general or the theatre in particular. As the work progressed, it became clear that certain patterns could be traced through the large bulk of critical material that had been written about O'Neill and, indirectly by way of this opinion, through O'Neill's own life. In the midst of the investigation, the O'Neill revival began with the off-Broadway production of *THE ICEMAN COMETH* and the sensation of *LONG DAY'S JOURNEY INTO NIGHT* in 1956. For about three years O'Neill was once again the center of attention in the theatre world; public and critics again found him worthy of serious and extended discussion.

The final achievement of the original idea has been twofold: First, the assembling of all important published items concerning Eugene O'Neill from his earliest successes through the posthumous revival up to the end of 1959 in a bibliography

designed to guide the student of the American drama and of
Eugene O'Neill to the location of this material and to its contents, for whatever further purpose may be desired. Second,
the writing of a brief summary of the four major points which
contributed to O'Neill's long absence and the subsequent revival, which manifested themselves in the careful reading of
all the assembled material. Some of the many questions about
O'Neill's past and possible future have thus been tentatively
answered, and information about the great volume of O'Neill
criticism and biography has been assembled, again tentatively,
in a comprehensive, usable form.

This investigation has relied entirely upon published critical and biographical material available through the major
library collections in the New York Public Library, at Yale
and Columbia Universities, and at Dartmouth College. It is
not based upon personal interviews nor upon any study of
manuscript material except a few autograph letters available
in the Landauer collection at Dartmouth. It is intended solely
as a broad review of the public reception accorded Eugene
O'Neill as seen through the eyes of the professional critics
and essayists who saw and studied his plays, and who knew
the man as a business acquaintance or personal friend.

Because of the scope of the task and because of certain
physical limitations, there are possibly some gaps in the bibliography which can be filled at a later date; likewise, there
may be unintentional errors which future revisions will correct.
It is with these facts in mind that this work is regarded as
"tentative." Those who make use of it, however, will find it
as complete and comprehensive as possible, within the limits
explained in the introductory remarks preceding each major
section.

In addition to the summarizing essay and the bibliography
proper, considerable factual material concerning O'Neill and
his plays has been included. There is a chronology of his life,
a listing of the order of composition and publication of all the
plays, and a chronology of major productions including casts
and other production information. An index is appended to
assist in locating specific material as needed.

There are many to whom I owe my sincerest thanks and
appreciation for their help on this project. In its original form

it was my doctoral thesis presented to the graduate faculties of Columbia University. The encouragement and the patience of Prof. Lewis Leary, Prof. Oscar James Campbell and Prof. Maurice Valency, who comprised my major committee, were of vital importance in its completion. In the field of the mechanics of research my gratitude is extended to the New York Public Library and its many departments whose cordial assistants were always ready to help. Particularly I wish to thank the curators of the Theatre Collection and the Newspaper Room for the time they expended on my behalf. I owe thanks as well to Mr. E. C. Lathem of Baker Library, Dartmouth, for allowing me the full facilities of the Treasure Room during my stay there. It is also pleasant to remember the brief moments with the late Mrs. Bella Landauer in Hanover as we discussed her collection of O'Neill programs and letters. To Prof. Kenneth Macgowan go my thanks for the pleasant interview I had with him and the helpful points he made in correcting certain portions of my chronology. Especial thanks must be extended to Mr. Donald Gallup, Curator of the Collection of American Literature at Yale, who extended the full facilities of his office to me during the summer months I spent in New Haven, and who encouraged and assisted me in seeing this effort brought to publication. To my student assistants, Mrs. Judy Grossman and Mrs. Laurel Johnson, goes much sincere appreciation for their careful aid in proofreading.

And finally to my wife and children who endured the heat of two New York summers with me and who sat out a cold rainy season on a Connecticut beach while I pored over assorted library collections I owe more than can here be expressed.

JORDAN Y. MILLER

Manhattan, Kansas
1962

SPECIAL NOTE

Except for a limited number of significant references included herein as ADDENDA, this bibliographic checklist carries only to the end of 1959. In 1960 and 1961 no important book, either biographical or critical, was published about O'Neill, but in 1962 three major publications appeared within a very few months of each other. Significant as biography is *O'Neill*, by Arthur and Barbara Gelb. As of now, their large volume is definitive biography, containing detailed information based on a vast amount of research on O'Neill and his family. Hence, certain statements contained in the introductory chapters, in the life chronology, and in the bibliographic annotations of this book may seem to be obvious and unnecessary discrepancies. However, they must be understood to antedate not only the Gelbs' book, but *The Tempering of Eugene O'Neill*, by Doris Alexander, and *O'Neill and His Plays*, by Oscar Cargill and others.

July, 1962   J.Y.M.

TABLE OF CONTENTS

EUGENE O'NEILL AND
THE AMERICAN CRITIC

PROLOGUE

In February 1956 the simultaneous Stockholm production and American publication of Eugene O'Neill's LONG DAY'S JOURNEY INTO NIGHT brought renewed acclaim to the man who, nearly four decades earlier, had begun an artistic career destined to bring international fame to himself and world recognition to American drama. Then, in November of the same year, the New York premiere gave American newspaper and magazine critics an opportunity to write something they had written only once in over twenty years — an opening night review of a new play by Eugene O'Neill.

The reports of this historic occasion sounded with a familiar ring. A new theatre-going generation read critical passages little altered from the days when the appearance of an O'Neill play was a normal and exciting part of a full Broadway season. The drama was one of "helpless grief and hopeless loss," making its journey "on the usual square wheels of O'Neill's style." It represented once more the "tragedy of alienation," and the characters displayed the "moral schizophrenia" common to O'Neill's work. It was often "barbarously written" and in bad need of editing. Its uncertain value as permanent literature was estimated as O'Neill's most significant contribution to our stage, or as inferior to his previous successes. But one decision seemed unanimous; the play was a profound theatrical experience of "tremendously powerful" effect. As usual, O'Neill made other modern writers "seem miniscule" and gave the current theatre "size and power."

With the continuing success of José Quintero's revival of THE ICEMAN COMETH at the Circle-in-the-Square added to the public's enthusiastic reception of LONG DAY'S JOURNEY, O'Neill was suddenly as much alive on the American theatrical scene as any actively contributing playwright of mid-century. Within the next two years there was a substantial O'Neill revival of international scope. Stockholm continued to stage hitherto unproduced plays; A TOUCH OF THE POET appeared in 1957, HUGHIE in 1958, and MORE STATELY MANSIONS, in its sprawling, unedited form, was under consideration in 1959. New York at last saw *A MOON FOR THE MISBEGOTTEN* in 1957 after its abortive road tryouts of 1947, and *A TOUCH OF THE POET*, both in print and on stage, the following year. The Yale University Press, O'Neill's posthumous publishers, brought out *HUGHIE* in 1959, the same year the Phoenix Theatre revived *THE GREAT GOD BROWN* at the Coronet Theatre, soon rechristened the Eugene O'Neill. Hollywood issued a gloomy, ponderous *DESIRE UNDER THE ELMS*. The musical stage saw Anna Christie sing and dance in *New Girl in Town* and watched television's Jackie Gleason dominate *AH, WILDERNESS!* in the successful creation called *Take Me Along*.

Moreover, the name O'Neill now seemed to be attractive offstage as well, and as many as eighteen different books about his life and works were reported by the New York *Times* as "in progress" simultaneously. In 1958 Doris Falk traced the theme of tragedy through all of O'Neill's plays in *Eugene O'Neill and the Tragic Tension*. The same year Agnes Boulton, the playwright's second wife and mother of his two surviving children, wrote *Part of a Long Story* to tell of their early years of life and love. In 1959 Croswell Bowen, seeking the help of Shane O'Neill, the derelict disinherited second son, wrote "A Tale of the House of O'Neill" called *The Curse of the Misbegotten*, an attempt to recreate the image of the doomed, isolated artist who more and more withdrew from public and family to become a legend years before his death. Critics began to analyze the "O'Neill renaissance" and to determine whether or not our theatre and its literature were about to accept, permanently and with high position, the works of this largely unknown but unquestionably famous composer of plays. Nobody was quite sure then. Nobody, even now, can tell.

By 1960 the rush to O'Neill had subsided. It was clear that after *HUGHIE* there were to be no more new plays. Only a handful of the long list of proposed books had been published. The true test was beginning. Could O'Neill survive this "second coming" and establish himself as a classic, or would he recede into the relative obscurity of classroom and textbook, to remain only as a famous name in the American theatre which he almost single-handedly changed into a world leader of provocative and stimulating dramatic entertainment?

The still recent surge of popularity and the present indecision concerning O'Neill's final artistic position have sharply emphasized the lack of interest in him which had become evident during the preceding twenty years. This lack of appeal becomes all the more pertinent in the 1960's because of the logical question, "Will it be repeated, and this time for good?" The privilege of witnessing hitherto unseen O'Neill plays, those created late in life, at a time when his artistic powers seemed to be heading toward the creation of a project of overwhelming scope and towering magnificence in the proposed mighty epic of eleven plays, could have indicated a renewed Age of O'Neill, with subject matter and theme achieving a maturity and wisdom that would remove these last plays a broad distance from the journeyman works of his first twenty active years. The hopes and the promise of newer, greater things did not materialize. The plays that did appear were mostly welcomed as substantial pieces of theatre art, but as in the case of *LONG DAY'S JOURNEY*, the comments reflected the oft-repeated O'Neill weaknesses of length and verbosity in his retelling of the frustrations of the struggle against life's many disillusions and delusions. What is more, the actual output of plays had been drastically limited because of the ill health which prevented O'Neill's yet active mind from transposing onto paper the thoughts it generated. With the positive knowledge that most of the fabulous "cycle" had been destroyed by his own hands and that what did survive in manuscript was nearly beyond salvage, it was keenly apparent that there was to be no new "Age." Indeed, there would not be, even in a limited sense, a "new" O'Neill to differentiate from the one whose major contributions to the active theatre had ceased, with one isolated post-war exception, in 1934.

Whatever O'Neill's permanent reputation may ultimately be, it will be impossible to base it on the four plays since 1934 to the exclusion of, say, *DESIRE UNDER THE ELMS, THE GREAT GOD BROWN, STRANGE INTERLUDE,* or *MOURNING BECOMES ELECTRA.* Only *THE ICEMAN COMETH* and *LONG DAY'S JOURNEY INTO NIGHT* seem destined to endure as latter-day exponents of O'Neill's perennial theme of love-hate, reality-illusion, and the search for life's meaning. *A MOON FOR THE MISBEGOTTEN,* hardly a success even on its second try, and *A TOUCH OF THE POET*, too obviously part of the unfinished larger work of the "cycle," are acknowledged second-rate efforts. Conversely, no lasting evaluation can rest solely upon the O'Neill who had withdrawn from public view after the failure of *DAYS WITHOUT END* over twenty-five years earlier. The tremendous power of the last plays, with their agonizing revelation of family sin and sorrow and their plainly evident compassion for entrapped human beings, are vitally important extensions of the same artistic philosophy. The entire canon must be considered.

If the works of Eugene O'Neill are to survive as more than interesting historical segments of our literary heritage, they must surmont four difficulties that have always prevented their unqualified acceptance as dramatic art and have always stepped between their creator and his critical recognition as a dramatic artist.

1. The most immediate cause for O'Neill's disappearance from public interest during his lifetime lay in his personality which, at all times, remained almost completely unknown even to his friends. This is not to say that the writer must be known to appreciate or even understand his works, any more than we must know Shakespeare before we can accurately evaluate the literary and dramatic qualities of his plays. But in O'Neill's case there is something a bit different, particularly in view of the intense personal quality of *LONG DAY'S JOURNEY*. Although there is the constant danger that a play like this may be taken too literally as autobiography, there can be no question but that O'Neill transposed to the stage a picture of his own life and the image of his mother, father and brother, which must be regarded as a reflection of a good portion of the real thing. With this play in mind one realizes that almost nothing was ever known about the "real" O'Neill while he lived, and we are prompted into a further revaluation of his works. If a late play, like this one, is so intensely personal, what of others?

Because of the tantalizing aspect of wanting to know more about him, of wanting to place other plays in some position perhaps more closely allied with his own experiences, or finding more of an autobiographical nature in them than we already know exists, we are left somewhat uncertain, still a little at sea, hesitating to place O'Neill's better works into a permanent niche of collective greatness. The discovery of O'Neill, the real man, will not change our attitude toward the literary value of most of his plays. Nevertheless, because he did inject into his dramas so much straight from his own life, it becomes almost impossible to distinguish between artist and man. He has, in a way, failed satisfactorily to separate the personal elements from the artistic, and at the same time has deprived us of a complete understanding of where one begins and the other ends, to the possible detriment of his ultimate critical position.

2. O'Neill's most obvious trademark, the unexpected theatrical device or dramatic effect, brought him widespread attention and made him the subject of international praise as well as condemnation. Here, too, he often failed, not only in the inability of the device to communicate what he often thought was an obvious message, but because he was unable to develop more fully the effects which he had so marvelously created. Furthermore, he was unable to lead new writers toward a similar style. He may have opened doors and encouraged the technical and thematic innovator to step forward more readily, but he himself started no school, was followed by no movement. Through lavish overuse of his rich inventiveness he became an ultimate failure by neglecting to maintain the kind of artistically original drama he sought to develop. The techniques of THE EMPEROR JONES or THE HAIRY APE have become dated; the race theme of ALL GOD'S CHILLUN GOT WINGS and the raw sex of DESIRE UNDER THE ELMS no longer cause thrill seekers to rush for tickets (or censors to rush for their blue pencils!). Masks, spoken asides, interminable speeches, and six-hour plays, all products of a great O'Neill past, must face acceptance as valid theatre in the future in order to establish artistic permanence. Judging from the experience of the 1959 revival of THE GREAT GOD BROWN, O'Neill's techniques have not yet passed the true test of lasting quality, and the dangers that they may not are still present.

3. O'Neill's avowed artistic purpose was to explore the mystic relationships between man and God. Audiences and critics could not always successfully follow his patterns of reasoning as he consistently failed to write in the spirit of the

age in which he lived. Distorted by civil censors and misunderstood by the audiences, his themes, like his physical techniques, frequently could not convey what O'Neill positively regarded as the clearly stated message. Now, with the writer no longer alive to explain his meaning, as he once did with *THE GREAT GOD BROWN*, still forcing upon his audiences long, garrulous dramas soaked in alcohol and inhabited by disillusioned dreamers, the question can be asked, "Has O'Neill, in spite of this, established himself as a permanent American classic? Or, as in his lifetime, has he written apart from the spirit of the age and thereby failed to establish the universality of a permanent literature?"

4. In his early career O'Neill worked steadily against the stuffy, suffocating romanticism which dominated the American théatre before World War I. In his sea plays and early longer plays he received wide praise as the breaker of the ancient barriers in his use of earthy language, believably realistic situations, and unconventionally unromanticized, or "unhappy," last acts. In fact, it seemed that he had set out to destroy the romantic ideal, for those of his characters who did live by such a code were invariably destroyed in the harsh realities of a world which did not care. None the less, he was continually heading toward an ultimate surrender to the very romantic outlook which he initially set out to oppose. By the end of his first twenty years, O'Neill had returned to "conventional" Christianity in *DAYS WITHOUT END* and the sentimentalities of early-century Connecticut small town life in *AH, WILDERNESS!*, confounding friend and critic alike. The return to "realism" of *THE ICEMAN COMETH* and *LONG DAY'S JOURNEY* reversed this reversal, only to prove that the very basis of romanticism — the eternal look at life through the distorting lens of "pipe dreams" and illusions — lies at the heart of existence. Without it, all perish. What, then, is the "real" O'Neill in artistic theme and philosophy? Will we be forced to say that for all his impact as the dramatic and theatrical iconoclast, O'Neill ultimately surrendered to a conventional romanticism that prevents his achievement of a permanent high place in American dramatic literature?

I — THE UNKNOWN MAN

The task of clearly establishing the identity of the "real" or "true" O'Neill was exasperatingly difficult to his friends and almost completely impossible to others. With the great amount of material written about him, it is logical to assume that a pattern would evolve from which to construct a clear picture. Instead, rather than being parts of a single puzzle, the random pieces appear as a mixture cut from different stock, painted by varied hands, and rarely meshing to form a coherent portrait. Although he was the subject of more printed discussion than many of his greatest contemporaries, Eugene O'Neill as a man lived and died one of the most inaccessible and unknown American literary artists ever to achieve international recognition. The scarcity of accurate information about him and his own adamant refusal to express himself outside his plays became one of the main factors in his failure to maintain his reputation during his lifetime. Even today, this difficulty imposes severe limits upon our understanding of him.

The source material for discovering the "inner" O'Neill (or, as will develop, for failing to discover it) can be arranged in five general categories. They are:

1. O'Neill himself, revealed in his own words and deeds.
2. The biographer, concentrating on a specific study of the man and his plays.
3. The personal acquaintance, able to speak or write from first-hand knowledge.
4. The interviewing journalist from newspaper or magazine, always seeking the new approach.
5. The dramatic historian, writing in text or reference book, balancing and evaluating the subject's place in history.

The following material, grouped under these five headings, represents a careful selection from the best sources and the most representative reports. None of it exhibits in any sense an intimate knowledge of the individual personality known as Eugene O'Neill. The friends who knew him longest after fame and success had been achieved were uniformly reluctant to say, "I knew Eugene O'Neill well." O'Neill commanded the most complete respect for his privacy, and that privacy was never violated. Wherever the search is made, the same conclusion is always reached: Eugene O'Neill was, both in life and after death, an almost unknown man.

1. O'Neill Himself

Eugene O'Neill was first and foremost a *dramatist*. "Tomorrow," his only published short story, appeared in *The Seven Arts* in 1917 and was generally ignored. He wrote another containing the germ of *THE HAIRY APE*, but it was never printed. His poetry column in the New London, Conn., *Telegraph*, edited and kept going through his own efforts as contributor in 1912, saw his attempts at verse breathe and collapse permanently, though infrequent contributions to the left wing New York *Call* and *The Masses*, and to Franklin P. Adams' "Conning Tower" kept it briefly alive. He once consented to write an introduction to an obscure book of poetry by his very good friend, Benjamin De Casseres. The book fell stillborn from the press; the introductory essay died with it. O'Neill refused ever again to undertake such a task, although in 1931 he was personally requested by Horace Liveright, his publisher, to write the introduction for the Sanborn and Clark bibliography of his works. When asked, on rare occasions, to appear in public, he declined with thanks, and with force.

O'Neill did publish a small number of critical remarks. For the *Provincetown Playbill No. 1*, Season 1923-1924, he wrote "Strindberg and Our Theatre," which showed his admiration for the Swedish dramatist and the expressionistic style in general. On *Playbill No. 1*, Season 1925-1926, appeared "Are the Actors to Blame?" in which he pleaded for good acting and good writing through repertory theatre. In 1932 and 1933 he placed at least three other items in the short-lived *American Spectator* which he helped to organize and edit, along with Theodore Dreiser, George Jean Nathan, Ernest Boyd and James Branch Cabell. First was "Memoranda on Masks," a somewhat impractical plea for more masked drama to help convey true inner psychological forces; next, "Second Thoughts," showing how most of his important plays might be improved by masks;

and finally, "A Dramatist's Notebook," expressing confidence that further use of masks could aid the "imaginative" theatre and improve acting technique.

O'Neill explained points about his current plays in an occasional communication to the editor of the New York *Times*, but these letters were rare enough to be called a part of his "works" and to be listed in Barrett Clark's biblography. He declined to reply to adversely critical letters from others, sometimes terming them mere "yapping" of "dullards" and "morons." He made no effort to sell his own viewpoints, told his friends that a flop was a flop and that he had no intention of gnashing his teeth. When he did make one serious attempt to clarify THE GREAT GOD BROWN in a widely reprinted newspaper article in 1926, his "explanation regarding this explanation" resulted in deeper obscurity for the average reader. His notebook kept during the composition of MOURNING BECOMES ELECTRA, also reproduced in part in several publications, will be considered later.

There is practically nothing else. To Eugene O'Neill, the play *was* the thing, and our final judgment of his contribution to our literature and stage tradition must rest solely thereon.

The only other sources of information about the "real" O'Neill from his own hand are his personal papers and the plays. Like so many whose inclination is literary, he was a voluminous letter writer. He may never have spoken in public utterance, but his friendly pen could move delightfully, with agility, and at quantity-output speed. There is no doubt that the O'Neill letters, properly collected and edited, would reveal a clearer picture than exists today. This task remains impossible until the large accumulation of letters, papers, manuscripts and other personal material at Yale is released for investigation. Fortunately, there are several volumes of biography and personal reminiscences, plus a few dramatic histories, that reproduce a number of letters. Barrett H. Clark's *Man and His Plays* series contains several as does Isaac Goldberg's *The World of George Jean Nathan*. Lawrence Langner's *The Magic Curtain* reproduces various excerpts connected with the Theatre Guild's production of O'Neill's plays. O'Neill collections in the libraries at Dartmouth and Princeton contain a modest number of originals. From these sources can be gained a reliable impression of O'Neill as a correspondent. All letters are cordial, detailed, sometimes argumentative; never are they dull, pedantic, overbearing, or foolish. They reveal a man faithful to his friends, helpful to strangers (no letter was ever curt; all were friendly and informal), happy to set down his views on any subject.

The plays have often been studied for their revelation of O'Neill's character, and the autobiographical qualities of the later ones have prompted some thoughtful analysis and wild guesswork in an attempt to find more of the same in the plays up to 1934. Before *LONG DAY'S JOURNEY* and the recently published biographies, any estimate of the personal aspects of O'Neill's work was on uncertain ground for lack of a satisfactory starting place. *JOURNEY* provides the starting line, but it also offers an opportunity to be misled by too close an analysis of the earlier plays.

The one-act sea plays are based directly upon O'Neill's maritime experiences and a large number of the characters are straight from life. Smitty of *MOON OF THE CARIBBEES* and *IN THE ZONE* has often been identified with the author. It is not beyond credibility to assign Smitty's melancholy and brooding upon a disastrous love to O'Neill's own unfortunate first marriage and subsequent attempt at suicide. Smitty's physical and intellectual qualities are rather pointedly O'Neill's, but there is a legitimate question about the plays being true "autobiography." Smitty is, after all, a minor character who becomes lost in the noisy activities of the *Glencairn's* rowdy crew. The sensitive misdirected Robert of *BEYOND THE HORIZON*, like Smitty, reflects O'Neill himself, but the tragedy that develops is hard to place directly in O'Neill's own life.

THE STRAW is a direct transcription of life in a tuberculosis sanitorium, with the young reporter, Stephen Murray, very like O'Neill. Eileen Carmody is based upon an actual acquaintance and the incidents are often close to reality. There does not seem to have been a love affair in O'Neill's experience as the play develops it, and, on the whole, the story is not really autobiography. Discordant marital relations in *WELDED* can be regarded as reflections of the writer's own experiences and his view of marriage bonds as seen in his own family. *THE FIRST MAN*, reversing the usual male attitude, portrays a father enraged and resentful at the impending birth of a child. O'Neill's own indifference to and often seeming dislike for his two younger children seem a definite part of this unpleasant and unsuccessful play, even though its date is early. The attitudes, evident later in real life, are clearly there. The esthete, Dion Anthony in THE GREAT GOD BROWN, represents the artist in O'Neill, and the brief but effective opening scene with the parents reflects the young O'Neill's inability to communicate with his own father. It has occasionally been pointed out that Dion and Brown speak with each other in a manner suggesting O'Neill's relationship with his much older brother, James, Jr.

Ephraim Cabot of DESIRE UNDER THE ELMS physically and emotionally bears marked resemblances to James O'Neill himself, and the often violent antagonisms between crude parent and sensitive son, with the underlying mutual admiration, is not unlike the attitudes of Eugene O'Neill toward his actor father. The whole picture of family loves and hates, of the distances separating husband, wife, son and lover in STRANGE INTERLUDE grows out of O'Neill's own experiences. AH, WILDERNESS!, hailed widely at its first appearance as a recollection of O'Neill's childhood, is known to be an idealized portrait of a situation that did not exist, but the rebellious Richard, who was supposed to be the central character as O'Neill first conceived the play, is surely O'Neill the young dissenter. The characters which surround him have often been accurately equated to people O'Neill knew in New London. Muriel, though younger and more naive, has been identified as one of O'Neill's romantic interests during his summers in Connecticut. DAYS WITHOUT END summarizes many of O'Neill's past transgressions, but the return to conventional religion is far from autobiography. In fact, as those who knew the original plans for the play can verify, O'Neill at one time made his priest a Protestant minister, refuting the argument that the playwright had returned to the church of his fathers. THE ICEMAN COMETH is inhabited by men and women O'Neill knew intimately, several of them only moderately disguised. Larry Slade, sitting in the midst of them, drinking, observing, philosophizing, is once more O'Neill.

Still, all of this is more of a deliberate searching for evidence and an unsatisfactory equating of biography with the artist's ideas and themes, merely based on personal experience. To say each is a part of an autobiography is a dangerous generalization. Not until the very last plays can such be found, and even then the changes and omissions are obvious. *A MOON FOR THE MISBEGOTTEN* is, of course, based on the true story of James O'Neill, Jr.'s, return to New London with the body of his mother. How much of the rest of the story is related to the truth is mostly speculation. The incident of the hogs was, we know from *LONG DAY'S JOURNEY*, a family joke. But what of brother James' position otherwise? From whence comes Josie, the redeeming freakish virgin? And *LONG DAY'S JOURNEY*, as close as it is to O'Neill's life, omits and alters at will. Time is compressed; events we would like to know more of are not followed through; and others are not touched at all.

Clearly the plays do not offer the portrait we seek, no matter how hard the search. They help create an image, but if the whole story is available, it must be sought elsewhere.

2. The Biographer

There is no completely satisfactory biography of Eugene O'Neill. A competent one by a person outside the O'Neill family cannot be forthcoming until the Yale collection is released for study. We must rely on other sources for the time being.

Barrett H. Clark was the first to regard the young playwright as a worthy subject for biography. From 1926 to 1946 he issued a series of volumes entitled *Eugene O'Neill: The Man and His Plays*. They discuss O'Neill's successes, his failures, artistic ideas and philosophies as expressed in personal letters and conversations. As biography the books are a disappointment. They suffer from the same limitations found so frequently elsewhere in placing judgment too closely on the plays alone.

O'Neill supplied Clark with a summary of his own early history, but both O'Neill's report and Clark's interpolations are remarkably deficient in precise date and detailed fact. Of the man, we learn little. The obvious vagueness did not displease O'Neill. He had given Clark his permission to write the original book, but had stated bluntly that he felt there was "too damn

much of that premature sort of thing being done." He regarded books about young writers with their major literary
accomplishments still ahead of them as quite unnecessary.
When Clark revised the book in 1933 and sought clarification
of certain anecdotes, Mrs. O'Neill suggested that her husband
assist him in getting the stories straight. O'Neill replied "Non-
sense!" — the further from the truth they were, the more privacy
he would have, "like a mask."

The one other early volume approaching biography is
Richard Dana Skinner's *Eugene O'Neill: A Poet's Quest* of 1935.
Its value is significant but limited. As critic of the Catholic
weekly, *Commonweal,* Skinner frequently reviewed and often
praised O'Neill's plays. In his book, he chose to explore them
in terms of his own concept that O'Neill was a poet on a quest
similar to the quests of Catholic saints who sought truth and
meaning in life and man's relationship to God. O'Neill sent
Skinner the most important section of the book, a chronology
of composition of every major play. In wishing Skinner successful hunting, he admitted that the undertaking could well
reveal aspects unknown to himself.

Skinner hunted, and found much, but the discoveries and
revelations presumed acceptance of Catholic doctrine and its
attitudes toward saintly behavior. Critics reviewing the book
warned that Skinner's "intense partisanship" must be taken
into consideration and his belief that *AH, WILDERNESS!* and
DAYS WITHOUT END, especially the latter, represented a
positive arrival in artistic accomplishment was not a sound conclusion. Skinner's comparison with the saintly pilgrimage was
certainly original and did represent a new approach to O'Neill
criticism, although the protests that the character of the writer
cannot be judged by the plays alone were, and still are, valid.

Most of the other full-length books before 1958 cannot be
counted as biography. Sophus Keith Winther's *Eugene O'Neill:
A Critical Study,* 1934, is an excellent discussion of the plays
without biographical emphasis. It is weakened, as well, by Winther's inclination to find the entire O'Neill canon successful in one
way or another. A similar point can be made against *Six Plays
of Eugene O'Neill* by Alan D. Mickle, 1929, who ranks O'Neill
with Shakespeare, Ibsen and Goethe. Edwin Engel's *The
Haunted Heroes of Eugene O'Neill*, 1953, considers the plays

critically, with extended plot resumes, and the man almost none at all. Doris Falk's *Eugene O'Neill and the Tragic Tension* of 1958 comes closest to biography through its criticism, tracing the development of O'Neill's tragic theme through all the plays as the reflection of the "lifelong torment of a mind in conflict." It becomes, however, an artistic interpretation rather than a direct account of the writer's life.

Of all the proposed books awaited during the O'Neill revival only two are purely biographical. The first, Agnes Boulton's *Part of a Long Story* fits more properly into the category of recollections by a personal acquaintance, and is therefore treated later. The other, by journalist Croswell Bowen, assisted by Shane O'Neill, is the most complete and accurate that we yet have. Both, however, have their limitations.

Bowen's *The Curse of the Misbegotten*, 1959, does more than any other single volume to pinpoint names, dates, times and places, and is a major contribution to our knowledge of O'Neill, the man. For the first time we can begin to form a coherent picture of the artist's life and the ideas and philosophies that grew into the written play. The impression that emerges is one of a man who searched his entire life for happiness and security, but who was never able to find it long enough at one time or in one place to remove the sense of pursuit by a relentless fate. Simultaneously, the book evokes tremendous respect for the man's intense desire to be left alone and for the remarkable body of work which emerged.

Bowen's effort is, on the other hand, of limited value. The side we see of O'Neill, particularly his relationship with his wives and children, must necessarily come from Bowen's close work with Shane O'Neill, whose life in so many ways paralleled the aimlessness of his father's youth. The almost cruel neglect and calloused indifference of O'Neill toward his family must be taken as a fairly one-sided interpretation. Almost certainly there is another viewpoint we have not yet been allowed to see. Also, Bowen pauses far too long to evaluate the individual plays as they appeared in O'Neill's lifetime. The book loses interest as biography while contributing nothing of significance to O'Neill criticism.

A "fictionalized" biography appeared in 1959 with Max Wylie's *Trouble in the Flesh*, but the portrait of O'Neill in this invention, though recognizable at first, becomes so completely distorted and without basis in fact that the book cannot be seriously regarded as any form of O'Neill biography.

This, with Miss Boulton's book, completes the list. It is a gradually growing library, but it needs more solid contributions to fill it out completely. Perhaps the next decade will provide them.

3. The Personal Acquaintance

O'Neill's personal friends supply little of additional biographical value. The reasons are not difficult to find. O'Neill was never a person who could easily welcome anyone into his confidence. The requirement for intimate friendship was a willingness to be a friend on his own terms, which presumed unconditional acceptance of and adaptation to the O'Neill mode of life. While this could include a long and difficult journey over the Provincetown sands by foot or on horseback, a hair-raising trip in a powerful car on narrow French roads with O'Neill at the wheel, or a fish-like devotion to the water in nearly all seasons, more than anything else it involved a respect for O'Neill's strongest wish: a single-minded, unalterable desire to be alone and to be left alone.

Nevertheless, O'Neill fostered some very unusual friendships. These might include the Hudson Dusters, a decaying underworld gang of his Greenwich Village days, who welcomed the somber, mysterious young man so far removed from their own kind, but who could drink many of them under the table. Or it could be the small band of intellectuals led by George Cram Cook and wife, Susan Glaspell, whose Provincetown Players started O'Neill on his way, as he, equally, started them. Noted among others are the names of H. L. Mencken and George Jean Nathan. Their *Smart Set* magazine published and praised the early efforts of the young writer, and Nathan's criticism in its whiplash fashion stung playwright and public alike. Kenneth Macgowan, producer, critic, and later college professor, worked closely with him; Robert Edmond Jones was his devoted designer and one-time producing partner; and we have already mentioned Clark and De Casseres.

a. Before Provincetown

After his emergence as a successful writer O'Neill seldom encountered those who had drunk, sailed, or lived with him in the years before. He did not pointedly avoid his old friends, but his way of living became so different and his contacts so remote from his earlier acquaintances that there was no common ground for intercourse. The world of Mencken, Nathan, Jones, Macgowan and the Theatre Guild was far different from that of the Hudson Dusters, Honduras and the forecastle. There is no indication that O'Neill himself avoided his erstwhile companions because of any changed attitudes of his own; rather it was their avoidance which marked the separation, for there was the feeling by some that "Gene" had risen above them.

LONG DAY'S JOURNEY INTO NIGHT provides many clues to the reasons for the meager documentation of O'Neill's childhood and youth. The continual traveling of the parents and the sort of "second-class" position which they held in New London society during the summers prevented the establishment of close and friendly contacts. We are given a picture of a household into which friends never dropped, callers never came. Of O'Neill's personal behavior, Judge Frederick P. Latimer, under whom O'Neill had worked on the New London Telegraph in 1912, once said that he was the most "stubborn and irreconcilable social rebel" the Judge had ever met. Clayton Hamilton, well-known critic and author, was a close friend of the family, but unfortunately he wrote almost nothing about this wild young boy he must have known so well. In one series of lectures, later published, he did mention that it was mostly his own urging which led the elder O'Neill to finance the publication of THIRST and Other One Act Plays and to place Eugene in Harvard. Gladys Hamilton, his wife, has recalled the inarticulate young man whose eyes seemed to speak what his tongue could not.

Of O'Neill's friends and cronies on his many voyages we know almost nothing. Certain of his acquaintances became characters in his early plays, but none of them were literate enough to write any informative articles after O'Neill achieved his fame. Nearly all that we do know about the seagoing adventures comes from O'Neill himself.

The best comments by O'Neill's pre-Provincetown friends come from those who knew him in George Pierce Baker's playwriting class at Harvard. John V. A. Weaver wrote one of the most detailed reports of this period in an item for the New York *World* in 1926. O'Neill, according to Weaver, stood out in the class "like an oyster in a lunchroom stew." He would squirm in his chair and give the appearance of "delightful anarchy" in his attitudes. His withdrawal from the group and reluctance to speak prevented for some time his expression of opinion about the classroom studies, but once he spoke, suggesting that the piece under discussion might, with a few tunes, become "sure-fire burley-cue," he became more of a member of the crowd in their drinking, bull sessions, and other activities. Weaver also relates that O'Neill's attractiveness to women was apparently irresistible.

Although O'Neill never completed much work during his stay in the class, his companions, according to Weaver, marveled at the outpouring of ideas, including plans for two of the *Glencairn* cycle; *THE SNIPER; THE SECOND ENGINEER;* a "lovely little fantasy about abortion"; and a play about a man who was always hoping to get away from his environment to go beyond the horizon. The class was appalled at O'Neill's "savage radicalism," but all were confident that he would some day be America's greatest playwright. When O'Neill did go on to his fame, Weaver felt that the swashbuckling charm had departed and that plays like *THE GREAT GOD BROWN, ALL GOD'S CHILLUN GOT WINGS, DESIRE UNDER THE ELMS,* and *WELDED* were "rungs down the ladder to sterility."

The only other item relating to the Harvard experience was a composite article published in the New York *Herald-Tribune* under the title "Fellow Student Thought O'Neill 'Very Likeable,'" in 1927. It included, first, a statement from Barrett Clark, quoting a letter by George Pierce Baker, which found O'Neill a steady worker, able to write one-act plays, but no good in three acts. He seemed aloof, but a nice person when you knew him. Next was a statement by O'Neill, who said that most of his own stuff was "terrible" and that he received far more from Baker personally than from the class. The last part, from an unnamed "fellow student," remembered *THE DEAR DOCTOR,* a bad one-act farce written for the class, and *THE*

SECOND ENGINEER, a labored and stiff attempt. He recalled that O'Neill trembled, as if trying to keep from stuttering, but was likeable enough.

b. After Provincetown

From the start of O'Neill's fame in Provincetown until his death, his many friends contributed extensively to our knowledge of O'Neill as a person, and they have equally strengthened our awareness of what we do not know. Over and over again the point is reiterated that it was virtually impossible to become, in the generally accepted sense, a "close" friend of Eugene O'Neill.

First, what is learned from the partners of his work — those of Provincetown and of the later producing companies? A good starting point is Helen Deutsch and Stella Hanau's interesting volume, *The Provincetown*, telling the story of the Provincetown Players. The book does not dwell on O'Neill and his place in the expanding fortunes of the Players any more than it does the other members, but it provides the only complete account of the famous group's development and O'Neill's entry into it. O'Neill was never a close member of the Players and seldom appeared on the scene except during rehearsals of his own plays. When the organization lost the services of its president and guiding angel, George Cram Cook, O'Neill, always unsuited for any executive position, was never one of those considered as a possible replacement.

In *Theatre* magazine in 1930, poet Harry Kemp, an early Provincetowner by way of Kansas, recalls that his first impression of O'Neill reminded him of Edgar Allan Poe, dressed like a sailor who had jumped ship. He relates how O'Neill would write his plays in bed, covered with blankets, warming his fingers over an oil stove in a Provincetown flat over a grocery. In the days at the Golden Swan (the Hell Hole) among the Hudson Dusters, O'Neill could fight and hold his own, but never picked a quarrel. His magnificent independence constantly asserted itself, as on the occasion when David Belasco sent a message that he wished to talk with O'Neill at the Belasco studio. O'Neill replied that *his* studio was the third back room of the Hell Hole if Belasco wanted to see him. The interview never took place. Always convinced that he knew what was best for his own plays, O'Neill would bluntly say so, and turned away from Cook to hire Arthur Hopkins to direct *THE EMPEROR JONES*. The play was a sensation, O'Neill was on his way, and from then on he and the Provincetown Players gradually lost touch.

Also writing in 1930 for the Boston *Transcript*, Montiville Morris Hansford, although a frequent lengthy house guest of O'Neill during the composition of *THE GREAT GOD BROWN*, *STRANGE INTERLUDE* and *LAZARUS LAUGHED*, admits the impossibility of putting the man down in print. O'Neill, says Hansford, was aloof, had an elusive mind, and always conveyed the feeling of great distance, appearing almost anti-social. He nevertheless welcomed those who had something to say or were doing something worthwhile, but intensely dis-liked any discussion which did not have a definite point or reach a conclusion. He was completely unable to find his way through conventional social banter; in the midst of a conversa-tion he might get up from his chair, and immediately become absorbed in a book. He had a sort of physical helplessness, not knowing what to do with his body, and would flit from mood to mood in a manner at times almost comic. In a group of his closest friends, however, he could be entirely at ease, but would seldom discuss his own plays, preferring sports and current events. Those who knew him had the constant feeling that he was never at home with anybody and nobody was quite at home with him.

There are other scattered reports of the "real" O'Neill, among them accounts by Harold de Polo and David Karsner, both of whom spent fishing holidays with O'Neill and family in the Maine woods in 1926. Theresa Helburn of the Theatre Guild has likened O'Neill to Lindbergh, a "lone eagle" in the drama, with courage and intense conviction and the same kind of desire for privacy. Lawrence Langner, patent attorney and leading light in the Theatre Guild, wrote his own biography, *The Magic Curtain*, in 1951. Entire chapters are devoted to O'Neill and his contacts with the Guild during that organiza-tion's tenure as his Broadway producer. The picture Langner paints is no different and no more complete than any other. He describes the restless, peripatetic author who refused to attend his own plays, could seldom be moved to change what he had already written, and remained adamant in his belief that he alone knew what was best for his own plays. Generous portions of the extended correspondence between O'Neill and Langner reinforce the impression of warm, informal friendliness gained from similar examples elsewhere.

A second group, those who did not work directly with O'Neill in the staging of his plays, have also written a substantial volume of interesting comment. Outstanding was the poet and journalist, Benjamin De Casseres. So enthusiastic were his feelings for the playwright that many of his articles between 1927 and 1930 must be read with a good deal of caution. The genius of O'Neill headed "into the light of eternal cosmic and human laws" and could be mentioned only in companionship with Shakespeare, Strindberg, Ibsen and Pirandello. O'Neill smashed through the morons and brought mountains to Mohamet, always the dissenter, the outsider, the "enemy of social convention" which only the strong Dionysiac could get away from. O'Neill, said De Casseres, was beyond good and evil, as inexorable as Sophocles or Hardy, storming and conquering life. When this flow of ecstatic praise has been penetrated, one can find some biographical facts from De Casseres' reports, particularly the account of their first meeting in a theatre. He had gone to a rehearsal of *ANNA CHRISTIE* with the assignment to "get a page for Sunday" for the New York *Times Magazine*. He was not prepared for the personality he was to encounter. The "volcanic black eyes" seemed to say, "Excuse me for not being nice, but I've just returned from Hell." O'Neill's personality was marked "No Thoroughfare — and stop lying to me."

George Jean Nathan was an equally devoted friend, but not given to excessive eulogy. His portrait offers much more information about O'Neill's true character, although Nathan's vigorous style often seems to be working for an effect, rather than for truly objective reporting. Only once, says Nathan, did he ever hear O'Neill laugh out loud. (De Casseres had described O'Neill's smile as "lightning across a black cloud.") When his indignation was aroused, he would avoid speaking, even to his friends. He was fond of writing long letters in reply to almost any question, but, paradoxically, the best way to lose his friendship was to ask him, face to face, for a direct opinion on something. His outward appearance was cold, even icy, but to those who knew him, he displayed a "naturally boyish quality" and an innocent artlessness. Contrary to the popular impression that he was completely withdrawn into a dark, sunless and tortured world, Nathan emphasizes O'Neill's delight in light detective fiction, Damon Runyon, the sports column, swimming, prize fighting, garden work, his nickelodeon piano Rosie, and the latest music hall jokes.

There are other personal reminiscences, some long, some brief, each presenting a genuine friend but a constantly distant companion. Russell Crouse, Pierre Loving, Alfred Kreymborg, Kenneth Macgowan, Mary Heaton Vorse — friends, companions, co-workers — all have described, as best they can, the strange and enigmatic man who walked among them. Few could penetrate the mask of the dark, brooding face, but all saw in their friendship something unique and valuable.

Perhaps it is not accurate to include Agnes Boulton's *Part of a Long Story* as the writing of a "personal acquaintance," but because it is not, strictly speaking, "biography," and because it came from one who, above all, should have been best "acquainted," it seems to fit. When one has finished her absorbing story, there is the same impression that strikes the reader of the items by those who knew him less intimately: Eugene O'Neill remained impossible to fathom, and his distance, whether in an alcoholic haze, submerged in his writing, or as a husband and parent, was always just beyond one's ability to cross and reach the true man.

Part of a Long Story, engrossing as it is, remains a curiously unsatisfactory report of the early years of acquaintance and marriage. Its signal value is, of course, its intimate portrait unavailable from any other source. The strange young man seated in the dingy Hell Hole back room, declaiming poetry to bum and streetwalker — and commanding a fascinated audience; the restrained, uncommunicative, temperamental artist, shy to an almost pathological degree, but on occasion loud, compelling, and violent, often without warning; the heavy drinker whose alcoholic binges became legendary; the dedicated writer who let nothing, not wife, friend, or drink, interfere with his steady intense concentration; the lover and husband whose affection bore a casual off-handedness that hid the sincere and serious need for love and understanding from others; all of these faces of the Eugene O'Neill of Provincetown and Greenwich Village stand forward in a unique collection of reminiscences told with unemotional compassion and without recrimination. The picture they form of life with a genius emerges best described as nightmarish. The book is one of mood, more than of fact, as was probably Miss Boulton's original intent. Its disappointing lack of exact date and time, its distressingly casual "I don't remember" attitude toward important matters, and its often repeated hour-by-hour recounting of a week-long drinking spree become disturbing. Yet it must be read as one of the most vital links in our very weak chain of O'Neill's personal history. O'Neill's brother James, his parents, the habitues of the Provincetown theatres, the Hell Hole and elsewhere, those of both sexes who sincerely loved O'Neill for all his exasperating inconsistencies and unpredictable temperament are all here, each treated with fairness and equality. Perhaps it is best that Miss Boulton leaves us only with a mood, for certainly her ten year life with this man must stand out in her own mind not as one of a series of orderly events, clearly placed in time, but as a decade spent in an ultimately fruitless attempt to reach out to an agonized soul that searched for, but eventually rejected, the kind of love she had to offer.

4. The Interviewing Journalist

Magazine and newspaper articles, complete with illustrations, began to appear regularly as early as 1918, while O'Neill was still considered little more than an effective writer of one-act plays. The accumulation of these reports from professional journalists is much greater than from those who knew him as a personal friend. They lack the intimacy of the others, and at the same time fail to contribute any more significant information.

In 1922 O'Neill was already a legend of sorts, and there was a demand to know just who the "real" person was. Oliver M. Sayler, a frequent critic of the plays, wrote "The Real Eugene O'Neill" for *Century* in January 1922. He discussed O'Neill's lack of interest in public reaction to the plays and noted the "inner fire" in this intense, reticent young man with the piercing eyes and quiet sense of humor. His harshness, said Sayler, came from lack of maturity instead of striving for effect, but it may be softened in the future. The same month Malcolm Mollan of the Philadelphia *Public Ledger* printed a widely requoted newspaper interview entitled "Making Plays with a Tragic End: An Intimate Interview with Eugene O'Neill Who Tells Why He Does It." O'Neill will write of life as he sees it, said Mollan, providing a "conventional" happy ending only when necessary and in keeping with the individual play. Until that time, he would be forced to create something which audiences insisted on calling "unhappy" because his personal views permitted of nothing else. As an explanation of O'Neill's dramatic philosophy, the article remains of considerable value even today. Mary B. Mullet's "The Extraordinary Story of Eugene O'Neill" appeared in *The American Magazine* for November 1922, a long factual report containing information now common knowledge. In 1923, Charles Merrill, interviewing O'Neill at his Cape Cod home, waxed extremely sentimental with a picture of cozy domesticity and peaceful isolation from the world.

By 1924, when plays were appearing at the rate of two or three a year, Carol Bird wrote about "Eugene O'Neill: The Inner Man" in *Theatre* for June. O'Neill was described as taciturn, laconic, reserved, shy, compassionate, with one outstanding feature, the somber, tender, melancholy eyes. As so many were to do, Miss Bird discovered O'Neill's hatred of superficial veneer. His silences were the product of genius. He was a man who was able to project the thoughts of those who hear in the silences. In 1928 Walter Prichard Eaton, acknowledging O'Neill's "irreconcilable rebellion," could not, however, find his personal behavior arrogant. Living in his own imaginative world and putting it in dramatic form, he increased the dignity of the dramatist's craft in this country. Like Emerson and Thoreau he retired to his Cape Cod dune home where he found "night stars are more important . . . than night clubs." By 1933 O'Neill was, to Brooks Atkinson, more relaxed than he had previously been, more human, capable of laughing "without brilliant provocation," somewhat released from his absorption with the tragic as he rehearsed *AH, WILDERNESS!*. To *Newsweek* he was still the "shy, dark boy."

Except for some brief reports during the excitement of the 1936 Nobel Prize award, no important O'Neill interview occurred between 1934 and 1946. When he emerged from "retirement" with the production of THE ICEMAN COMETH, he had to be introduced to an almost entirely new generation of playgoers. A new O'Neill play was almost like something out of a distant historical past; in fact, it seemed downright anachronistic.

One of the notable events of his return to New York was a press conference, something O'Neill had never before attempted. It was held in June 1946 in the offices of the Theatre Guild. O'Neill discussed his much-heralded but unseen "cycle" and his belief that the United States was at once the greatest success and the greatest failure as a nation in the world. Typical reports were by Robert Sylvester in the New York Daily News and by Muriel Band in Mayfair. Both described O'Neill's increased gauntness, his palsy, the piercing eyes, and underlying humor. His cordiality was universally acknowledged. Kyle Crichton of Collier's later gained a personal interview in O'Neill's apartment. He looked less like a ghost than one might imagine, said Crichton, and possessed a "sense of humor that will make a monkey out of you if you don't keep your guard up." Informed of Crichton's surprise at this sense of humor, O'Neill replied, "Oh, yes — some days. Other days, other moods."

Edith Isaacs in Theatre Arts wrote one of the best articles during the ICEMAN period. She realized that O'Neill created a legend about himself with the help of no publicity agent or outside assistance. Nobody was so well loved and liked by his friends, a man who always remained above little spites and prejudices. She described him to the new generation viewing THE ICEMAN COMETH as shy, high strung, nervous and thoughtful, "a man driven by an unnamed force toward an unseen goal."

The most complete picture of O'Neill at this time was drawn by Hamilton Basso in his New Yorker "profile" of February and March 1948. Typical of that magazine's biographical sketches, it was long, interestingly written and comprehensive. It offered a late summary of most of the facts of public interest, plus a review of many points about which others had once written, but which now existed in widely scattered sources, unavailable to the average reader. Part I was completely historical and, because of accurate factual detail, far better as biography than Clark's *Man and His Plays* volumes. There was no suggestion anywhere of the background of his youth at home, so horrifyingly portrayed in *LONG DAY'S JOURNEY*, except one quotation about his father, whom he regarded as a primary example of "the tragedy of success." Part II was mostly about the plays, with some suggestion of their initial critical reception, and some of O'Neill's remarks about Strindberg. Part III discussed various opinions about O'Neill as a man, from the pejorative term "black Irishman" to the highest artistic praise, and added O'Neill's own opinion of himself as a seaman who had taken up writing, rather than a writer who had been to sea. Then, near the closing page, Basso dropped the explosive news that all of the "cycle" had been destroyed except *A TOUCH OF THE POET*, because O'Neill felt he had become stale.

5. The Dramatic Historian

Dramatic and theatrical histories are poor assistance in analyzing the personality of Eugene O'Neill because of the obvious need of such works to speak on broad general terms. The following selected examples, taken from books which devote considerable space to O'Neill, show how little additional information can be gained from them.

Joseph Wood Krutch in *The American Drama Since 1918* wrote that "in late years" (*i.e.*, since *DAYS WITHOUT END*) he [O'Neill] had lived almost as a hermit, refusing to attend his own first nights and showing, externally at least, no interest in anything other than his immediate work. Remarking on O'Neill's inability to express himself precisely, Krutch pointed out the writer's difficulties in thinking in abstract terms and his inability to communicate clearly. Krutch saw O'Neill as truly a mystic, concerned with the fundamentals of conflict between good and evil, which he continually inserted into his plays.

Arthur Hobson Quinn gave O'Neill an entire chapter, "Eugene O'Neill: Poet and Mystic," in his *History of the American Drama from the Civil War to the Present Day*, 1936. He asserted that to know the plays we must understand the man, but his chapter remains mostly historical. Quinn saw O'Neill primarily as a poet, but also as a playwright, and a great dramatist because he was "more than a dramatist." His "profound imaginative interpretation" of struggling, aspiring humanity was one of his great artistic contributions. John Gassner's excellent *Masters of the Drama* called this unique personality "a veritable seismograph of the ideas, viewpoints, and promptings of the new age" who reflected the younger generation's discontent with a materialistic America.

Other historians contribute very little more which could guide us beyond what we already know. There is always the feeling, as Quinn indicates, that to know the plays one must know the man, but no carefully thinking critic or historian will ever restrict the enjoyment of the collected works of any literary artist to an understanding of the writer's life. O'Neill's case is no different, but because of his isolation as an artist of the tragic theme and because of the admitted autobiographical nature of *LONG DAY'S JOURNEY*, the search for more meaning in the interrelationship of man, artist and plays will continue. So far, the search has not brought its expected reward; there is no way of knowing if it ever will.

II — THE DRY WELL

In 1947 Edmund Gagey, Barrett Clark and others were confident that Eugene O'Neill had a strong future before him. Nobody would yet offer an estimate of his final place in American stage literature until his work was complete, and in 1947 it appeared far from done. The production or active preparation of at least three new O'Neill plays was familiar theatrical news. THE ICEMAN COMETH had already been staged; A MOON FOR THE MISBEGOTTEN was on its tryout tour; A TOUCH OF THE POET was to be produced "soon." The evidence was plain that the life work of Eugene O'Neill had not yet ended.

Nobody, therefore, could have suspected that O'Neill's writing career actually was finished. Each of the "new" plays had been written at least three years previously. ICEMAN was ready in 1939; POET was done by 1940; MISBEGOTTEN was complete in 1943; and LONG DAY'S JOURNEY had been an anniversary gift to Mrs. O'Neill in 1942. The future which Gagey and Clark hopefully awaited had already passed. None of these plays restored the reputation which had begun to suffer more than ten years earlier. As THE ICEMAN closed, MISBEGOTTEN suspended production indefinitely without ever reaching New York, and POET was abandoned, O'Neill faded as quickly as he had reappeared. The lapse of another decade between the first New York production of ICEMAN and LONG DAY'S JOURNEY did not change the fact that for over twenty years Eugene O'Neill disappeared from the professional American theatre. His last plays had shown nothing new. The rich vein of dramatic and theatrical technique, which had served him well during his career, had finally become so diluted that its immediate market value was of little worth.

After 1956 the product seemed to find a market. ICEMAN commanded an off-Broadway audience and critical acclaim it could not attract ten years earlier. The power of LONG DAY'S JOURNEY overcame its lugubrious style to become one of the all-time O'Neill successes. The excellent production and fine cast of A TOUCH OF THE POET, now resurrected, ran out the season. *A MOON FOR THE MISBEGOTTEN* finally made New York. Then nothing more. Was this the start of that future once so strongly hoped for, or the last rush of a one-time strong dramatic force, a kind of shout from the grave, before its final disappearance? No suggestion of impending growth was, of course, possible, for Eugene O'Neill was dead. But perhaps there was, in these last plays, something new in dramatic style and theme which would exert some kind of guiding influence upon the theatre of the moment, would emerge from the deep reservoir of O'Neill's many and varied skills to point a new and better way. The truth is that no such thing happened, and the indication is that if O'Neill is to survive in our active stage literature it will probably be in spite of, and not because of, the technical contributions of these or any other of his plays. There was really nothing new. Only two plays had previously been unseen, and they showed nothing beyond extreme length (this was old hat) and heavy-handed "realism" (an early O'Neill trademark). Even the grotesque dimensions of Josie in *MISBEGOTTEN* had been trimmed to manageable size. The plays proved, if they proved anything, that the latter day O'Neill had exhausted the deep well of genuine originality which at one time had sustained him; stylistically there was nothing new.

*   *   *   *   *   *

Consistency in style was never a part of O'Neill's strength. Critics were always seeking the proper niche for his permanent mounting, but they were continually unable to find it. With the early sea plays, including *ANNA CHRISTIE* and *BEYOND THE HORIZON*, they fashioned for him a pedestal of "stark realism" that soon melted in the steaming jungle of *THE EMPEROR JONES* and the stoke hole of *THE HAIRY APE;* it was replaced by expressionism, in turn moulded into naturalism, and subsequently nicked and scarred with romantic and classical symbolism, all hastily patched from time to time with mysticism. Masks, half-houses, thirteen acts, and spoken thoughts brought playgoers and critics through a labyrinth of stage effects. None of these, in writing or production, ever solidified or developed into a specific "O'Neill style." Nevertheless, this very unpredictability in itself became a style, forcing critic and audience to play a continual game of guessing what he would employ next.

In an artist's development from his apprentice to his master works, varied experimentation along the way can be expected. O'Neill was aware of this, and defined his own nascent art as "mere groping" in a letter to George Jean Nathan in 1920. His definition can excuse the uncertainties of his approach before 1925, during his trials with intensely grim irony, realistic melodrama, and expressionism. The groping, unfortunately, never ceased, and a cogent philosophy never evolved. By the middle of the decade some sort of levelling off in idea or style should have been forthcoming. Instead, O'Neill subjected the playgoer to more bewilderment and novelty as each play brought a fresh approach.

If O'Neill was groping, he was simultaneously attempting to overcome this disadvantage through his intimate knowledge of what constituted good theatre. Although he forced upon the producer some extraordinary tasks in design, direction and acting, responsible critics never accused him of using trickery for its own sake. They knew he employed whatever medium he felt to be most appropriate for what he had to say with no appeal to the box office or public feelings in mind. But there were warnings, at this middle period in his career, that O'Neill must emerge with something more substantial. The dangers were too apparent that the theatricality which so often threatened to engulf him would prevent his achieving the artistic strength of which he seemed capable. St. John Ervine, one of O'Neill's most astute English critics, sounded this note of caution. O'Neill, he asserted, was too fond of making experiments. Because he had a lot to say, he should have stuck to a single approach, along a steady path. Showing a kind of "wilful extravagance" and a refusal to use his material with any kind of economy, O'Neill dissipated his strength, despite the astonishing fertility and high imagination exhibited in the plays. All this was becoming a perversion of his talents, said Ervine, and he should get away from being the faddist and get down to being an accomplished dramatist.

There is no need to discuss in detail the well-known O'Neill surprises of beating drums, masks and soliloquies. It is revealing, however, to trace them in certain patterns in order to indicate the continuing uncertainty of the viewing critic, and to show their eventual permanent disadvantage to the playwright.

1. Critical Response
Early Plays, 1917-1924

Critical reaction during the first eight years of O'Neill's career forms the first pattern. As the one-act plays appeared in the Greenwich Village "art" theatres, O'Neill was greeted as the new realist on the American stage, the challenger of the trite sentimentalists and romanticists, unafraid to face life as he saw it. Critical confusion entered with the longer plays after 1920, when O'Neill occasionally diverged from his expected path, but the professional reviewers readily accepted his position as a vivid, forceful creator of stage realism. The significant factor is that the reviewers themselves placed O'Neill in this position and were unable to realize that his aberrations were the beginnings of the overt theatricality that became his medium of expression after 1925.

Opinion of the permanent value of O'Neill's first plays was varied, but there was consistent agreement about his strength and style. The early sea plays received almost uniform comment from the daily press and various national magazines. They were as realistically effective as Conrad, tense, grim, with the sense of tragedy. They were almost brutal, made audiences gasp with their impact, displayed "rugged craftsmanship" and hard, virile pathos. BEYOND THE HORIZON gave the professional critics their first opportunity to judge O'Neill as a writer of full-length plays suitable for the more sophisticated uptown theatres. They were further convinced of their first judgment. Here was great power, the essence of tragedy, a digging at emotional roots of real people in a real play. Terms like "greatest American drama within recent memory" were not uncommon. The names of Ibsen, Synge and Chekhov were used to describe this unusual new writer.

THE EMPEROR JONES introduced a temporary roadblock. The critics were careful what they wrote, and remained restrained in comment, and few assumed that O'Neill would continue in this unusual vein. It was an "extraordinary drama of imagination," admirable in its craftsmanship. While finding it "highly interesting" one newspaper commentator questioned if O'Neill was actually better than George M. Cohan or Eugene Walter. It was, to another, "possibly" a profound piece of work. Charles Gilpin, the first Negro in a leading dramatic role in New York, drew far more extravagant praise and commanded more column space than the play itself.

The "realistic" plays continued to dominate O'Neill's early writing. *DIFF'RENT*, the first play after *JONES*, opened in late December 1920, lasting 100 performances in the Village and uptown, where it failed to capitalize on *JONES'* successful invasion. It was frequently compared to the unusual *JONES*, and there was difficulty in assessing its worth. The antithetical opinions that grew commonplace in later years now began to appear. Said the New York *Clipper:* "far superior" to *JONES*, which was merely "stagey." In contrast, Heywood Broun stated that O'Neill obviously did not know what he was writing about. Another found the hero suffered and died of "O'Neillitis," the instinct for violent death; *Variety* said the play should never have been written and that O'Neill ought not be produced again until he gains restraint. Oliver M. Sayler, who was to review many O'Neill plays, said it was one of his best, a great "naturalistic" play.

GOLD, in June 1921, brought the critics no closer together. The unsuccessful tale of madness was a thrilling yarn of adventure and crime, or it was feeble, crude melodrama. In some ways it was O'Neill's most impressive, but it had too many "chunks of gloom." It was *ANNA CHRISTIE* in November of the same year that brought back O'Neill's "realistic power," but even this Pulitzer Prize winner kept the critics reserved in their praise. The *Sun* called it merely an unconventional play that "dwindled" to a conventional ending. The *Herald* found there was too much "realism" and the sea a fantastic protagonist, while Burns Mantle in the *Mail* decided the "sheer realism" was all to the good. O'Neill himself could lay permanent claim to fame on this play alone, or, depending on the paper one read at the time, he displayed only "great promise." The next two plays helped in no way to decide in which direction lay the critical consensus. *THE STRAW*, also November 1921, was preferred for its optimism, had "one of the most thrilling" of last acts in our native theatre. It was, on the other hand, "a parody of a play," unbearable, strangely beautiful, lugubrious, depressing, and vital. *THE FIRST MAN* in March 1922 was painful and morbid, a "keen satire," one of O'Neill's best. There was "no glory here," no excuse for this revolting and abhorrent treatment of gestation. The majority, in this case, were disheartened by the grimness and despair and the too-strong "naturalistic" tendencies.

In the two years from *BEYOND THE HORIZON* to *THE FIRST MAN*, O'Neill had produced eight plays. Two Pulitzer Prizes had not eliminated the critical reluctance to welcome him as the complete answer to American dramatic prayers. It was beginning to be a case of damnation through lack of praise, rather than condemnation through adverse opinion. When reviewing *THE FIRST MAN*, the *Tribune's* anonymous critic had called it "murky" and stated, "The name of Eugene O'Neill's star is Wormwood." Certainly that nova which was O'Neill of the one-act sea plays was rapidly burning out, and the resulting haziness was beginning to obscure some erstwhile promising talent.

Then in March 1922, O'Neill finally drilled straight into the strong vein of imagination from which he was to draw for the next ten years. With *THE HAIRY APE* he proved that *JONES* had not been a fluke and that the same general style, more fully developed, could be successfully repeated. The play also evoked sensation and violent response as no other O'Neill play had thus far done.

The uneven critical reaction remained, but it becomes more interesting because of the confusion. Convinced that O'Neill was a firm realist who only slightly dabbled in foreign expressionistic techniques, some writers were almost completely blinded by what they saw. The *World* said it was not as good as *JONES* because it was less articulate; Burns Mantle said it was better because of more intimate contact with the modern world. Maida Castellun in the leftish *Call* found it one of O'Neill's finest achievements, powerful and shattering; J. Ranken Towse, in the conservative *Post*, dismissed it as juvenile appeal to ignorance and passion, ominous of O'Neill's future and a worthless play. The inability to recognize the style was evident when Arthur Pollock of the Brooklyn *Eagle* found enough realism to make Belasco weep, and Brock Pemberton in the *Globe* said the similarities between this and Toller's expressionistic *Masse Mensch* were uncanny. Others were confused by the shift from the "realism" of the first half to the "fantasy" of the second, but did not realize that O'Neill never intended a single part of the play to be realistic in any sense whatever.

Those the furthest removed from comprehending O'Neill's intent were critics like R. Robbins of *Industrial Solidarity*, a labor periodical, and Patterson James of *Billboard*. Robbins praised this defense of the I.W.W. and saw O'Neill as painting the "inner tragedy of the proletarian soul." James wrote the most violent and vitriolic attack against any O'Neill play of that or any later time. He compared the drama's "realism" to swill wagons and slaughter houses. He could find no place on the stage for such a play and determined that it was the lowest point of modern drama in its vile language and revolting subject matter. These two commentators were joined by the New York city fathers in their failure to comprehend O'Neill's purpose. *THE HAIRY APE* was the first of O'Neill's plays to meet threats of official censorship, although the accusations against it did not reach the peak to come with later plays.

There was one more unsuccessful try at the old-style realism in *WELDED*, presented in March 1924. This portrayal of the war between men and women survived only twenty-four performances and has been almost completely ignored ever since. Outside of *LONG DAY'S JOURNEY*, which is heavily autobiographical, O'Neill never again attempted anything of its type. Critical response found it wearisome, prodigiously dull, garrulous, uneventful, morbid, without normal human experience.

2. Transition, 1924-1925

In May and November 1924, O'Neill produced two plays which marked the transition between the realism of his early successes and the dismal failures, and the unconventional techniques so clearly identified in his mature work. Professional criticism, twice jolted by *JONES* and *THE HAIRY APE*, still was uncertain, but the words "Greek" and "genuine tragedy" were beginning to appear more regularly.

The first of those plays, *ALL GOD'S CHILLUN GOT WINGS*, employed a stylized, almost expressionistic, setting, with color, space and stage properties designed to symbolize the impenetrable line drawn between the Negro boy and white girl. In dialogue and characterization, however, it was severely realistic. The cross between this "stark realism" and symbolism led critics once more into disparate reactions as they sought meaning in the social problem of miscegenation which O'Neill always insisted was secondary to the tragedy of lost souls he thought he had created. Heywood Broun saw it as a downstroke in O'Neill's uneven career, and Alexander Woollcott agreed that it was "lesser O'Neill." Edmund Wilson in the *New Republic* thought it one of the best things about race prejudice yet written, and hence one of the best of O'Neill; Ernest Gruening in *Theatre Arts* thought the race issue should be more clear-cut. Ludwig Lewisohn, *Nation*, added that the transcendency of character was almost Greek.[1]

In the second play, *DESIRE UNDER THE ELMS*, O'Neill demanded the utmost from his scene designer as he combined some of his best realistic writing (if the dialect, which most critics found strained and unreal, is disregarded) with a setting that became not only a symbol but a vital part of the play itself. The actors did not perform *against* this setting but directly *within* it. The walls of the entire front of the two-story house could be removed from scene to scene, and the many areas and levels of the four interior rooms plus the surrounding farmyard permitted some strikingly effective stage pictures. Even when the curtain descended, the audience was confronted with a somber stone wall jutting out beyond the proscenium, continually symbolizing the rocky hardness of the land and the people's lives. For the first time O'Neill had fused theatrical technique and literary form so completely that to

---

[1]A completely atypical venture into historical romance with *THE FOUNTAIN* in December 1925 will not be considered. It was the only play of its kind that O'Neill attempted and it failed in twenty-four performances. Practically every critic found it a ponderous, boring play, a "trial by scenery," according to Gilbert Gabriel, *Sun*.

have eliminated the required visual pattern would have cancelled the play's intended effect.

This impressive departure in stage mechanics, though praised, did not receive the attention which critics paid to the dramatic theme itself. There was violent dissent, an expected part of the increasing quantity of O'Neill criticism, but the critic who sought for what O'Neill said, more than for what he did, began to discover the first indications of greatness in his tragic approach:

> Gilbert Gabriel, *Telegram:* Some vivid and great moments, such as the bedroom scene, slumping into repugnance in the last two scenes.
>
> Fred Niblo, Jr., *Telegraph:* Gruesome, morbid, as real to life as a sewer, one that "anyone who cares anything about the theatre cannot approve . . . or disapprove in silence."
>
> Stark Young, *Times:* O'Neill has written nothing with more qualities of realism, poetry and terror than this.
>
> Burns Mantle, *News:* Should be seen by all who praise foreign drama, and by all students of drama.
>
> Richard Dana Skinner, *Independent and Weekly Review:* Not a tragedy because nobody is on a height to fall. Everybody is on one level and rots there.
>
> Louis Bromfield, *Bookman:* On fine level of Greek tragedy.

Except for the one-act plays, abandoned as an art form after 1919, the only conventional works which brought O'Neill any kind of consistently favorable reception during his initial decade were *BEYOND THE HORIZON* of 1920 and *ANNA CHRISTIE* of 1921. Once he had ventured into the realm of experimentation and unusual staging, except for *AH, WILDERNESS!* near the end of his active career, he never again was able to fashion a success in an "ordinary" manner. An O'Neill play came to mean an *unusual* play, creating an immediate audience sensation with new stage devices. The turning point had been reached, and the third pattern emerged suddenly and completely, preceded by warnings that can now be seen as ample, but which were not always entirely understood.

3. Theatricality, 1926-1931

After the production of DESIRE UNDER THE ELMS, the rush of three and four plays a year abruptly ceased. For the next six years, O'Neill wrote an average of only one play per year, but they all fit into the third pattern of overt theatricality. Critical reports almost never reached any point of agreement regarding either his aim or achievement, and O'Neill himself was sometimes disappointed in the accomplishments of his own devices. The theatre for which he wrote was often unable to do him the justice he wanted; at the same time, he could not adjust his work to the facilities which the theatre could offer him. The following discussion will not only indicate reasons for this failure, but will show that the richness of a particular innovation in style, once successfully used, could not be employed again. Being forced to abandon each style in its turn and to strive anew, O'Neill finally exhausted the technical possibilities. Then, when the stage effect and the message both failed, O'Neill, as an artist, rapidly declined.

a. The Mask

The first outstanding element was the mask. The Fifth Avenue promenaders in THE HAIRY APE had worn masks, and the Congo mask on the Harris' wall in ALL GOD'S CHILLUN had achieved symbolic importance. In THE GREAT GOD BROWN, however, the use of masks became an integral part of the message. Although this use became awkward in certain intimate scenes, no thoughtful critic condemned the play on the basis of this fault alone.

Brooks Atkinson refused to be bothered by the lack of clarity which all critics found to a degree, especially with the transfer of the Dion personality to Brown. He found more important what O'Neill did, rather that what he did not do, admiring the fine shades of beauty, nuances of truth, and passionate qualities of emotion. Gilbert Gabriel admired O'Neill's writing for posterity instead of popularity, and offered his high but troubled admiration for this "most poetic and penetrating play." R. W. Osborn stated that the unexpected was

introduced "as usual," but there was a certain symbolic running away at the last. Richard Watts regarded it as eloquent
and stirring, except that the whole remained a fascinating
"half-mad" enigma with a trick last act which showed a reading
of Strindberg with more care than wisdom. Alexander Woollcott, liking some of it, called other portions "pure undiluted
blah!" Others found fault with the purely physical device of
the masks, or praised them as an important part of the whole
thematic design. Protests of the dissenters who used terms
such as "glorious confusion," "pretentious," and "jerkily written"
went mostly unheeded. Audiences supported the play and it
ran out the season.

For all the praise and satisfying public reception of this
difficult play, O'Neill's theatrical technique was not placed
on any more stable ground. The instability and uncertainty
of what he was doing was evident in a letter O'Neill himself
sent to Benjamin De Casseres in June 1927, in which he acknowledged that the simple double-personality conveyed by
the masks was not what he had intended. He felt that the production had not satisfactorily developed them; the "right" masks
would have become mystic instead of confusing, would have
shown "the abstract drama of the forces behind the people."
He was confident that a re-reading of the play would clarify
the original intent — a dangerous assertion to make, and a discouraging one in view of the fact that no play should have to
be *read* to be understood by an audience. O'Neill's own explanation in writing was published in many newspapers in
February 1926, and reprinted in later books. This same line
of reasoning was used to show what the play had been designed
to do, and before he was through, he had to make use of an
"explanation of this explanation" only to further complicate
the whole thing.

Complete loss of theatrical perspective occurred in 1927
with *LAZARUS LAUGHED,* the only important play that
O'Neill never saw professionally produced. Again to De Casseres, he stated that "of course" the play was better for reading
than it ever could be for acting, since it was impossible to do
on any stage of today. The "imaginative theatre" for which
he wrote it did not exist.

A reading of *LAZARUS* will quickly show that the fairly simple "abstract forces" of *BROWN* were not enough. O'Neill describes massed performers representing the "seven periods" of life such as childhood, youth, middle and old age, each group further represented by seven types such as simple, ignorant, proud, servile, revengeful and so on. There were forty-nine different combinations in the varied groups which Lazarus encountered — Jews, Romans, or Greeks — all broken down in the same way. The accumulation of masks reached into hundreds. Amidst it all, Lazarus, unmasked, became younger and younger, while Miriam, his wife, became older and older. There were, in addition, half-masks for Caligula and other more important characters.

The Pasadena Community Playhouse in California undertook the only full-scale production of *LAZARUS LAUGHED* in 1928. The few professional critics who saw it praised the effort of the many volunteer hands that had created what O'Neill demanded. Students at Fordham University attempted a revival in 1948, but those who attended found it far beyond the ability of undergraduates. Brooks Atkinson termed it shallow, sophomoric, hortatory, overwrought; *Variety* labeled it an ordeal in the theatre. It was, to others, tedious, verbose, pretentious and, in one dismissal, O'Neill's "biggest lemon," worth forgetting immediately.

If O'Neill had attempted to refine his use of the mask so that audiences, willing and eager to listen and watch, might see the facets of his philosophy, perhaps he would have developed an ancient technique as an important and successful part of modern drama. But instead of careful reworking of a potentially great dramatic effect, he chose *LAZARUS LAUGHED* and leaped into a whirlpool of fantastic shapes and figures which drowned out any chance of more refined subtlety. Furthermore, in his typical fashion of misjudging his own talents, he regarded it as his finest piece of writing.

The plays that followed made no attempt to reintroduce the mask either in the style of *BROWN* or *LAZARUS*. Except for the weird hybrid of *DAYS WITHOUT END*, O'Neill permanently abandoned this particular technique.

b. The Monologue-Soliloquy

In *THE EMPEROR JONES*, O'Neill had experimented with what was essentially a monologue. Except for the opening scene and the brief closing dialogue, the entire play was a recitation of Jones' mounting terror. It was effective theatre, and as such was never severely criticized. *THE HAIRY APE* further developed the style, as Yank gradually lost contact with reality and concluded the play by talking to himself and to an inarticulate gorilla. Expressionistic staging, with its attendant attractions and distractions, welcomed the long, soliloquizing speech as part of its own style. A few of O'Neill's more realistic attempts, such as *WELDED*, had conveyed outwardly the expression of an inner thought which would not normally have been uttered aloud, but this was accepted as legitimate dramatic license. Then, without previous warning, almost as in the case of *BROWN'S* fully grown but underdeveloped masks, *STRANGE INTERLUDE'S* stream-of-consciousness, expressed-thought, monologue-soliloquy style exploded the bomb which was to be the dramatic sensation of the 1928 spring season, and, to be sure, for many seasons to come.

Critics hastened to assure their readers that this was nothing new, that the Greeks had long had the word for it, and that the Elizabethans could write it far better. They then equally assured everyone that it was an astounding new technique, and that new dramatic vistas had been presented by O'Neill, the genius of the age, who had done the impossible.

> Brooks Atkinson, *Times:* The technique of experiment is more important than the story; the asides at times are "the very stuff" of drama.
> Gilbert Gabriel, *American:* "A magnificent venture," one which "cleaves the skyline of tomorrow."
> Robert Littell, *Post:* All future conventional plays will seem flat and two dimensional.
> Dudley Nichols, *World:* Perhaps the most important event in the modern American theatre.
> Percy Hammond, *Herald-Tribune:* "O'Neill has broken the drama's shackles."

Other prominent critics such as Joseph Wood Krutch and Stark Young approved this "overwhelming milestone" in the theatre. The *Literary Digest* summarized this "body blow" to realism, and Arthur Hornblow's staid *Theatre Magazine* saw a return to the great days of the drama and reverence for the theatre.

Dissenters like David Carb, *Vogue*, did not like the contrivances, which were both irritating and depressing; he warned that if O'Neill so continued, there would be calamity for him and the American theatre. Gilbert Seldes, *Dial*, agreed, because he regarded O'Neill as too good a dramatist to have to employ the asides, a "technical felicity" which spoiled the play.

It is interesting, knowing not only what followed in O'Neill's own career but in the development of American drama as a whole, to see how much closer to the truth David Carb spoke than the lyric singers who saw the vistas of drama so much greater. The "aside" influenced only one other play, also by O'Neill. Like the mask, the system could not be re-employed for the reason that the ultimate had already unknowingly been reached. A reflection of the technique back upon itself was fatal. No other writer would dare undertake it, for he would be immediately, and probably unfavorably, compared to O'Neill. Again, like the mask, there had been no gradual build-up, no series of plays in which it was perfected, but a sudden explosive and sensational birth of a theatrical effect in full form. Anything which followed would be anticlimax.

DYNAMO, also in 1928, was therefore certain to fail. Its collection of O'Neill stage felicities brought no strength, but, instead, resembled a kind of junk heap of tricks. Foremost were the "interludisms," already worn out, which hung heavily in the air, saying nothing, contributing no inner revelations. Their style merely got in the way. The cut-away house of *DESIRE UNDER THE ELMS*, unequalled in its scenes of seduction, passion and murder, reappeared as two constructivist houses, completely lacking the vitality of the earlier form. In disturbing contrast, the final scenes took place against a setting designed to portary in sight and sound the Belascoesque realism of a humming Connecticut powerhouse.[2] But no longer was

[2]See Lee Simonson's *The Stage is Set* (New York, 1946) pp. 117, 120, for a reprint of Simonson's memorandum from O'Neill explicitly explaining his strong opinions about the necessity for this setting and its accompanying sound effects.

realism a forte. Johnny-the-Priest's went out with *THE LONG VOYAGE HOME*, and the bar and barge disappeared with *ANNA CHRISTIE*.

Critics and public alike refused to support *DYNAMO*. The asides were a crutch rather than an inspiration; the play was ludicrous and "frequently raving," sleazy and quick, of no importance. Charles Brackett's comment in the *New Yorker* summarized all attitudes well. Said he: "Pretentious rant."

c. Five-hour Theatre

The tremendous length of *STRANGE INTERLUDE* was novel enough in itself, but the multi-act marathon approach was yet to reach its climax in the gigantic attempt of *MOURNING BECOMES ELECTRA*. O'Neill traced the development of the play in a series of published notes which can be read in the files of various newspapers and in Barrett Clark's *European Theories of the Drama*.

Nearly a year after beginning the play and keeping detailed notes about attempting to reach the Greek classic design in a modern play, O'Neill began his struggles with technique. In March 1930 he was seeking the best way to show the increasing sense of fate hanging over his characters and thought that half-masks and asides might do it. In seeking more distance and perspective, he envisioned his approach as a display of "unrealistic truth, wearing the mask of lying reality" and hoped he could catch the effect. By July he considered dropping the asides, warning himself that he must be suspicious of "hangover inclinations" from *STRANGE INTERLUDE*, the ruin of *DYNAMO*. A later notation the same month expressed dislike for the half-mask and it was eliminated the next day. By September he acknowledged that the omission of the asides helped "enormously" and he soon had dropped all soliloquies of any kind because they "get in the way." Not long thereafter all masks disappeared and stage makeup replaced them to show the family resemblances and the presence of fate.

On 26 October 1931 the audience once more entered the theatre in the middle of the afternoon and departed toward midnight, with the *INTERLUDE* race for dinner in between. Those present did not know that practically everything in the O'Neill cupboard had been tried and abandoned, but they fully realized they were undergoing a unique theatrical experience. What the audience saw in *MOURNING BECOMES ELECTRA* was something never before attempted on the American stage by an American writer. Here was a conscientious and sincere attempt to bring to the contemporary stage a modern psychological sense of fate in a classic form, closely paralleling the dramatic pattern of the Greek original. It could not be taken lightly. It refused to be shunted aside as the rant of *DYNAMO* had been dismissed. The major critics looked at it this way:

> Brooks Atkinson, *Times:* A cause for great rejoicing by O'Neill, the Guild, and the drama in general.
>
> John Anderson, *Journal:* A masterpiece, putting the flesh of modern psychology on the bare bones of impersonal Greek tragedy. A mark of "enduring greatness."
>
> John Mason Brown, *Post:* Proves that the theatre is very much alive. The play stands above the present day theatre like the Empire State Building.
>
> Gilbert Gabriel, *American:* One of the dramatic masterpieces of the world today.
>
> Richard Lockridge, *Sun:* Marks O'Neill's emergence as an artist of the theatre.

The recurring problem of important O'Neill plays again appeared, such praise as this notwithstanding. Once accomplished, the format of the play could not be repeated. The trilogy, like the *INTERLUDE* asides, had to be relinquished in the future. O'Neill's eventual plan, as we know, was to go far beyond a three-play series into the eleven plays of the cycle, *A TALE OF POSSESSORS SELF-DISPOSSESSED,* an overwhelming effort that never came close to completion. Length and compounded stories were a dead issue as a valid theatrical technique.

4. Unsuccessful Repetition, 1934-1947

Although the Theatre Guild produced *AH, WILDERNESS!* in 1933 and *DAYS WITHOUT END* in 1934, O'Neill's long absence as a creative force in the American drama might as well have begun immediately after *MOURNING BECOMES*

ELECTRA. The structure of the ensuing plays was uninspired, and the stylistic repetitions were discouraging to critics and public alike. Not until the skilled treatment given *THE ICE-MAN COMETH* and *LONG DAY'S JOURNEY INTO NIGHT* twenty-five years later was there cause for enthusiastic response.

The dismal stumbling of *DAYS WITHOUT END* brought out most of the worst of the formerly successful O'Neill techniques.[3] It was almost completely static, presenting the least action of any O'Neill play. *STRANGE INTERLUDE* had been mostly talk, but there was no improvement at all in *DAYS WITHOUT END*, whose talk was of no particularly original quality and of considerable quantity. The characters got nowhere as they sat in an office, pondering over the fake "novel" which the hero said he was writing, or arguing over the many philosophies of life and death which the protagonist had tried and abandoned during his lifetime. "Confusing, florid, ornamentally phony," said John Anderson; O'Neill's error was in making faith an intellectual process that could be touched through words. Robert Garland found it all sophomoric (a favorite term of many critics toward O'Neill's plays), told in the most awkward manner possible. It was little better than a high school debate, said *Newsweek*. Most reviewers agreed that it was one of the dullest things O'Neill ever wrote.

What of the monstrosity called Loving, who pranced and hissed through the entire play under a hideous mask? He uttered the "interludisms" for John, the "live" protagonist, in the person of an alter-ego, but there was none of the subtlety of the changing masks in *THE GREAT GOD BROWN*, or the appeal of the personal asides in *STRANGE INTERLUDE*. Bernard Sobel observed that the poignancy and novelty of the masks had been lost by now, and although others like Percy Hammond could find it "theatrically effective" it never achieved the over-all powerful effect it was designed to create. John Mason Brown thought it was one of O'Neill's most feeble plays. Everybody pretty well agreed that the sex problem, the male-female struggle, the mask, the aside, the double personality were all tossed together in an agglomeration which the general public could not accept. It was all old, and every aspect of the

---

[3] *AH, WILDERNESS!* that "strange interlude in the midst of a world of tragedy," as Sophus Winther termed it, will be discussed later.

play's technique was forced into unfavorable comparison with each attempt in the past.

The twelve year gap between DAYS WITHOUT END and THE ICEMAN COMETH brought a Nobel prize, reports of the growth of the cycle from three to eleven plays, and many rumors about new Broadway productions. When THE ICEMAN was finally staged in 1946, seven years after it had been written, it displayed little of technical appeal. For the third time O'Neill demanded that his audience break the evening with a meal, and the audience responded. This time, however, the length did not find compensation in some outstanding dramatic technique. Praise for strength of character, tragic awareness, compassion and beauty was continually tempered with a plea that O'Neill stop letting the volume of words interfere with what he had to say. The play had no strong and enthralling Nina and her three men, and it lacked the force of a Greek-style trilogy. Instead of accepting the length as incidental, the observer became uncomfortably aware of the deadening pressure of a very loquacious assemblage on the stage in front of him.

Criticism of this over-extension was frequent, and many writers made a special point of discussing the play's effectiveness in spite of its length. Brooks Atkinson, praising it as one of O'Neill's best, still termed it "over long and garrulous." Ward Morehouse termed it "long winded" but agreed that the imaginative theatre was still alive in the power and intensity of the writing. Robert Garland could not find why O'Neill felt called to write this combination of The Lower Depths and old-time vaudeville, while Sterling North stated bluntly "action draggeth, dialogue reeketh, play stinketh," wondering how this "turkey" ever got produced or published. Nowhere were the size and the style of production regarded as assets.

There was more to come during O'Neill's lifetime: the debacle of A MOON FOR THE MISBEGOTTEN. Its collapse on the road in 1947 and the publication in 1952 with O'Neill's own brief preface explaining his decision to give it to the public with no prospects of New York production, put a final inglorious touch on a once tremendous technique. In its original form, if one is to follow the specific directions, it is not difficult to see why the play did not reach New York. O'Neill had still failed to learn the lesson of practicality. Now, instead of demanding the utmost in the skills of designer or technician, he required in his heroine, Josie, something which nature herself had to supply. She was to be five feet eleven in stocking feet, weigh one hundred eighty pounds, and to be "almost a freak." She was to be stronger than any but exceptionally strong men, to be able to do the work of two "ordinary" men, but with no mannish quality about her. She is, said O'Neill, "all woman." In addition, as if to show the complete deterioration from the rock-hard God and the sturdy farm house of *DESIRE UNDER THE ELMS*, the Connecticut homestead, once more with movable walls, displayed its collapsing dismal form of broken windows, peeling paint and tar paper.

The fate of *A MOON FOR THE MISBEGOTTEN* represented a full swing of the pendulum, for the play followed closely and ironically the same path to obscurity of O'Neill's first printed work, *THIRST and Other One-Act Plays*, thirty-eight years before. It did not specify shark fins circling around a stage raft, as in *THIRST*, or floating icebergs, helpless lifeboats, and dead children crying, as in *FOG*, but it did require a woman who was "almost a freak." Moreover, as it returned on that path, *MISBEGOTTEN* touched a familiar spot in O'Neill's technique, asking the audience to see what writing could not express, and acting could not interpret. There may have been no attempt to convey through mask or stylized makeup any "death-in-life" motives or "return to death-birth-peace" yearnings, but as the huge girl held a no-good drunkard close to her powerful body for a night of blissful death-like sleep over which she watched, unsleeping, madonna-like, she strove to save his soul through a return to the "womb of Infinity." And all characters, their habits of speech unaltered in over thirty years, still uttered "Nuts with that sin bunk" as if Yank himself were again treading the stage.

5. Revival, 1956-1959

The three year revival of public interest in O'Neill cannot be assigned to any appeal of his technical novelties from the past, or to anything which he might have created during his many years of silence. Only two new plays, not counting

HUGHIE, as yet unstaged in America, appeared. Of the seven plays to receive widespread attention during this period, two were revivals, two were musical comedy versions, and one was a motion picture. Only *LONG DAY'S JOURNEY* and *A TOUCH OF THE POET* had never been seen before. Both, interestingly enough, were successful.

All of the plays, it must be remembered, were completed by 1943. Nothing in the O'Neill revival represents anything composed more than seven or eight years after the last play to appear in New York, *DAYS WITHOUT END*. None of them contain a single new device, and the four legitimate productions (excluding the musicals and the film) rely on much that audiences had already seen, praised, and aften simply endured, as far back as 1926.

First came José Quintero's revival of *THE ICEMAN COMETH*, late in 1956. Its astounding success must have been a pleasant surprise, considering the reservations given it at its first appearance and the limited success of its run. Everything was still there; no changes of consequence were made, except the single important one of placing the setting in the intimacy of theatre in the round, instead of a large Broadway house, and compelling the small audience of less than two hundred to surround the acting area. Somehow, the play's whole effect was radically changed. The same critics who ten years earlier had seen the original still felt that O'Neill stated and restated the obvious to a far greater degree than needed, but this time the extraordinary length did not interfere with the mood and the theme that O'Neill conceived. The intimacy of the audience, for one thing, seemed highly in the play's favor, for now there was a feeling of being a part of the experience, rather than a distant observer of it. Others felt that the length, already known, could be ignored and the play's message sought with greater ease. Perhaps the play was on a level that communicated more directly a decade later than its original time. Whatever occurred, press and public alike were suddenly aware that O'Neill could become alive as much in the 1950's as in the 1930's, but they found this awareness through nothing technically new. Indeed, it was in spite of the cumbersome techniques still visible.

LONG DAY'S JOURNEY INTO NIGHT brought with it

only length, and was a kind of genetic throwback to the "sordid realism" of the earliest plays. Once more, there was nothing new in technique. Audiences were carried into the midst of *BEYOND THE HORIZON* (Edmund's continual wish to get away and his recollections of life aboard the windjammer); *THE STRAW* (the continual reference to tuberculosis); *WELDED* (husband and wife in a deadly fight, unable to live together or apart); *THE FIRST MAN* (inability of the family to understand or appreciate the talents and interests of other members) and so on. It was all from a distant O'Neill past, and, like the revived *ICEMAN*, telling its story in spite of a heavy hand.

A *MOON FOR THE MISBEGOTTEN* did not succeed, even with the talents of normal-sized Wendy Hiller interpreting, somewhat freely, the physical dimensions of Josie. Lacking the strength of *JOURNEY* and the intimacy of the new *ICE-MAN*, it was too much a part of the technical decline of years before. Brooks Atkinson wrote that no production could solve the problems O'Neill introduced, evident from the first time it was tried out, because it was prolix, uneventful, a tired work. Walter Kerr called the first half "rattled and blathered." There was praise, to be sure, because O'Neill's familiar fierce qualities brought a "shattering" experience to the theatre. But it proved that it had nothing to offer now, any more than it did before, and it showed that O'Neill's last play was, sadly enough, an exhausted work.

A *TOUCH OF THE POET* had nothing to offer technically. With small cast, conventional length and typically O'Neill theme, it gave only the smallest inkling of what the eleven plays in the *POSSESSORS* cycle might be like. There was no critical reaction particularly firm about any aspect of the play. The strongest debate involved matters of casting, with the choice of Helen Hayes regarded as everything from perfect to grotesquely inappropriate. Descriptive terms were monotonously familiar: "overwritten" and "garrulous" equated with "powerful" and "strong."

The only echo from the far past was the Phoenix Theatre's revival of *THE GREAT GOD BROWN* in October 1959. The critical attitude toward the technique of the masks was no more enthusiastic than it had been when the play first appeared.

No strong stand was taken, one way or another, and the luke-warm reception for the entire production did not encourage a long run. Brooks Atkinson regarded this thirty-six-year-old play exactly as "avante garde" as anything by Beckett or Ionesco. Thomas Dash felt these same contemporaries were "rank amateurs" in comparison. John Chapman used the term "curio"; to Walter Kerr the whole thing seemed dry as sand; John McClain called it "a mess of dried shaving cream." There was no more appreciation of O'Neill's experiments on the occasion of revival than when Dion Anthony and Billy Brown first donned their papier-mache faces.

*   *   *   *   *   *

There may have been many areas into which the inventive and highly imaginative mind of Eugene O'Neill could have entered. He never indicated where they might have been. The eleven play *TALE OF POSSESSORS* would have been unconventional enough in its size and scope alone, but its destruction, because of O'Neill's fear that he was becoming stale, established his own recognition of his approaching failure. His careful outline of the energy devoted to *MOURNING BECOMES ELECTRA* virtually admitted that he had given his all. He seemed to know that what he now used was old and tiresome. Agreeing with him, the critics more than ever begged that he apply a heavier hand on the obliterating blue pencil.

O'Neill was not a writer who flooded the stage with queer effects and sensational tricks for their own sake, thereby removing himself from the norm as an eccentric of little worth. None of his significant innovations were summarily dismissed; all of them were discussed, argued, and debated. They knew no language barrier, and in translated versions evoked comparable response in every country in which they appeared. His mastery of what made good technical theatre was almost never questioned as long as each innovation was effectively handled.

The impact of O'Neill's plays *in the theatre* — always fascinating, frequently electrifying — is part of a rare phenomenon in dramatic history: a man whose extraordinary skill and frequent success completely failed to influence others or to induce them to follow in any manner resembling his own. His trail was never followed, and no new school of theatre ensued. O'Neill may have shown those who came after him that they need not fear the unexplored territory of experimentation and unconventional style, and that the sloughs and entanglements of a deadening and well-established tradition could be successfully overcome. Nevertheless, he was unable to guide them.

There was continual hope that O'Neill could tap new sources in his deep well of inventiveness, but his lavish use of the product had exhausted the vein. Other writers appeared with new commodities to sell, which they successfully marketed, and O'Neill disappeared as a dominant theatrical force.

III — THE ISOLATED ARTIST

From the days when he traveled as an infant with his father's roving troupes to the last years of his life, Eugene O'Neill never "belonged" anywhere. Because James O'Neill always wanted his wife with him, the young Eugene was boarded out in a series of private schools when he did not himself accompany his parents. As a child, deprived of making permanent friends with playmates, and with a brother ten years his senior, O'Neill never knew an actual home, even taking into consideration the large New London summer residence used as the setting for *LONG DAY'S JOURNEY INTO NIGHT*. The aimless wanderings of his sea voyages are a familiar story. In later years, more and more aloof, O'Neill often increased his distance from friends and associates by many hundred miles. From Provincetown to Bermuda, wrote George Jean Nathan in 1932, every place O'Neill resided was always the "best" and "only" place he could ever work and live. His life, like Yank's, could never discover its own place in the world.

Had O'Neill's isolation resulted in successfully created dramatic themes, or had the "purity of thought" which he strove to achieve by removing himself from close association with the Broadway area brought his plays any widespread understanding, his personal distance would not be a matter of concern. The unfortunate truth is that Eugene O'Neill was an isolated artist as well. What he often conceived as an obvious messaged frequently became blurred or obscure as he repeatedly failed to communicate with his audience on the levels he had carefully planned. He was a playwright devoted to the artistry of his profession but unable to formulate and maintain a consistent dramatic approach which could successfully identify his artistic style and at the same time bring to the audience the desired message.

His aims were prevented in these three ways:
1. An indecisive thematic approach before *THE GREAT GOD BROWN* in 1925.
2. A series of unfortunate encounters with the censor.
3. The failure of his later plays to speak a language

appropriate to the audiences and the times for which he wrote.

Since O'Neill's death, only the third item is pertinent to his lasting position in our stage literature, but a study of all three will help to show the cause for his temporary eclipse, and at the same time indicate certain elements that must be overcome to achieve that permanent place.

1. Thirteen Steps To Man And God

"What are you trying to do," asked James O'Neill, after he had seen BEYOND THE HORIZON a few months before his death, "send the audience home to commit suicide?" To him, the theatre was a place for pleasant entertainment. To the young Eugene, the theatre was a place for the expression of art. Audiences could, of course, find entertainment in what they saw. But O'Neill, a dedicated dramatic artist, believed that they could find much more. He wholly accepted the criterion that great serious drama, to become great art, must seek meaning in the passions and troubled lives of human beings. In a widely quoted statement, he once explained his own refinement of this approach when he said, "Most modern plays are concerned with the relation between man and man, but that does not interest me at all. I am interested only in the relation between man and God."

Recognizing his intent, critical opinion seldom opposed him; recognizing his limitations, that same opinion repeatedly warned him to take care. Through the reckless tossing about and uncontrolled treatment of his subject matter in the phenomenal successes and abysmal failures which followed each other month by month, O'Neill had delineated no thematic pattern. The divergence of his approach, like the varied theatricality, became in itself an uncertain style — quicksilvery, incapable of being firmly grasped. In 1922 J. Ranken Towse of the New York *Post* pointed to three plays running at one time — *THE FIRST MAN, THE HAIRY APE* and *THE STRAW* — and implored O'Neill not to let himself give way to the broad and easy "path of sensationalism" or to make use of the unique and abnormal merely to point out well-known general propositions. He hoped that the young man's ability would keep him from destroying himself.

O'Neill did not "destroy" himself, but for a period of five years he wrote and produced thirteen plays of uneven quality and uncertain direction, only half of which rose toward the high plane of his own affirmed motif. They broke into two distinct thematic classifications. One was, without question, Man-to-God. The other two must be labeled, despite O'Neill's professed eschewal, Man-to-Man.

Written		Produced
	Man-to-Man Theme	
1919	*THE STRAW*	1921
1920	*DIFF'RENT*	1920
	GOLD	1921
	ANNA CHRISTIE	1921
1921	*THE FIRST MAN*	1922
1922	*WELDED*	1924
	Man-to-God Theme	
1918	*BEYOND THE HORIZON*	1920
1920	*THE EMPEROR JONES*	1920
1921	*THE HAIRY APE*	1922
1922	*THE FOUNTAIN*	1925
1923	*ALL GOD'S CHILLUN GOT WINGS*	1924
1924	*MARCO MILLIONS (first version)*	1928
	DESIRE UNDER THE ELMS	1924

In neither of these groups did O'Neill achieve his desired communication with his audiences. In the first six, unable to go beyond the assertion that men and women are often trapped in snares of their own design, O'Neill brought no original dramatic idea which could mark him as a thinker of consequence. With the single exception of *ANNA CHRISTIE*, these six had no commercial or critical success, and O'Neill personally rejected each of them when Horace Liveright asked him to choose his best plays for a one-volume edition. He preferred to regard even the prize-winning *ANNA CHRISTIE* as one of his lesser accomplishments.

In view of O'Neill's later achievements and his own stated

intent as a dramatic artist, it is not difficult to show how the
six plays in the man-to-man category never became more
than a discussion of man's duties to his fellow man. In *THE
STRAW*, Eileen Carmody, conscientious, hard working, no
longer had any personal responsibility toward her family after
the onset of her disease, while theirs toward her began. They
were unable to recognize their duty and were glad to be rid of
her. Once confined, Eileen's health was measured in terms of
her love for Murray, another inmate. He reciprocated first as
his duty to a dying woman, and then in a genuine emotion, but
neither he nor she lived or loved in relation to anything beyond their own human ideals. Isaiah Bartlett's madness destroyed himself and family (and the unfortunate shipmates) in
GOLD. But his responsibilities were to himself as an individual
and as head of a family, besides those as captain of a ship
whose crew he treated unmercifully. His refusal to face reality
was a very human trait. "We're all poor nuts," was Anna's
estimate of the human position, and although Chris spoke of
his "ole davil" enough to suggest a supernatural being, nowhere in *ANNA CHRISTIE* was the responsibility of man to
God clearly drawn. The responsibilities were those of Chris
to his daughter, Burke to Anna, and Anna to them both. And
so with all the rest: Emma toward Caleb in *DIFF'RENT;*
Curtis Jayson toward his wife and child in *THE FIRST MAN;*
and the Capes, of *WELDED*, toward each other. The direct
responsibility of man for man (or woman), regardless of implied overtones otherwise, was all that one could successfully
find in these plays.

These six plays had not supplied O'Neill a method by
which he could adequately communicate his turbulent yet
vigorous thoughts. As Towse had indicated, they were strained
presentations of over-simplified situations. All were realistically
conceived in technique, treating basic human passions of love,
lust, greed and selfishness. All were straightforward, non-mysti-
cal, easy to understand; they were earthy, often highly melodramatic, and at times unattractively "authentic," as in the
birth scene of *THE FIRST MAN* and the sanitorium background
of *THE STRAW*. In trying to break the stranglehold of conventionality, O'Neill had created a tubercular heroine, a mad
sea captain, a sexually frustrated old maid, and a philosophical

strumpet, each of whom had literary ancestors of much higher quality, none of whom had anything to say worth the trouble of their creation.

Happily for his future, O'Neill was simultaneously proceeding with plays of a more clearly articulated man-to-God theme. The "God" of the second group of plays cannot be defined concretely, for O'Neill never intended that his statement be interpreted as an attitude toward any specific deity of any specific faith. It must be separately defined for each play, but it will uniformly represent an abstract quality of spirituality, involving the characters' relationship to an essence which dwelt within themselves, or was present in the universe in which they moved. The protagonists displayed actions which were not so much counter to their personal responsibilities toward others in society as against themselves and their make-up as human beings.

In *BEYOND THE HORIZON* Robert's fatal decision to remain home conformed to the wishes of his family. He did not destroy himself and ruin the loves of others because of his lack of responsibility toward human society, but because of his failure to respond to what was within his own soul. He possessed no insane delusions like Isaiah Bartlett's, nor false standards of pristine delicacy such as drove Emma Crosby to her doom. Instead, he offended the sensitive, romantic soul which his maker had created. Brutus Jones, madly circling the forest, looked straight at Brutus Jones in each succeeding vision, and it was Brutus Jones who destroyed him. The silver bullets of the natives only administered a welcome *coup de grace.* Jones was his own god, and he found it was a false one. He hysterically abandaoned it in a frantic plea to the "real" one, by then incapable of saving him. Yank, of *THE HAIRY APE,* could not find himself. His old god — force, fire, coal, sweat — had left him helpless, and he could not apply the principles of his faith to the new and strange world into which he was introduced. His was the story of a lost soul seeking to belong somewhere, and it was only superficially a tale of a beaten proletarian victim of capitalism. Ponce de Leon of *THE FOUNTAIN* came to the realization that his prescribed Catholic God never meant man to survive forever, and the eternal cycles of life, love and death must continue in defiance of man's fervent prayers for their ending. Jim Harris in *ALL GOD'S CHIL-LUN* would play right up to the gates of Heaven with his "Painty Face," reduced to childish imbecility, and he could not understand how God could forgive Himself for what He had done. The problem was not that of human beings defying a social code, but of man's relationship to the God that had created him in different colors. The God of Marco Polo may have been one neatly defined by a church and represented on earth by the authority of a Pope, and the God of Kukachin may have been labeled "heathen" by the pious Polos, but Marco, incapable of understanding the meaning of any god, ignored the beautiful princess who pleaded with him to find the soul within himself and her love for him. He could not, for his god of material wealth deluded him, and Kukachin died. Finally, the hard God of Ephraim Cabot in *DESIRE UNDER THE ELMS* was everywhere in evidence. It was Cabot's im-movable relationship with that rigid, artificially created God of rocks and stones which saved him, while his son and his own wife, who had flung themselves against that God, were taken away to a punishment far greater than that which society itself would give them.

In significant contrast to the man-to-man group with its lone success, *ANNA CHRISTIE*, only one of these man-to-God plays, *THE FOUNTAIN*, was a failure. They generally stood far above the routine offerings of other playwrights then holding the stage. Alexander Woollcott, in a statement which could be applied to each of the seven, said that *BEYOND THE HORI-ZON* was "so full of meat" that the rest of the season's offerings looked like "so much meringue."

The critics agreed that O'Neill said considerably more in these plays than in his others, but they did not, even then, fully comprehend all that he had conceived. *BEYOND THE HORIZON*, accepted universally as a moving tragedy, did not convey the abstractions of the "longing and loss" which O'Neill carefully planned in the rhythmic pattern of alternating ex-terior and interior scenes. Heywood Broun thought the con-struction was clumsy; J. Ranken Towse found it "shambling." Many critics felt O'Neill had not yet mastered his trade. The sensational theatricality of *JONES* and Gilpin's performance far overshadowed the universality of the message. Some opinions accused the playwright of dwelling too much on Negro psychology; others found fault with the "visions" which lost their effect through too careful "selection." *THE FOUNTAIN* suffocated under the weight of its own exotic trappings and the unimpressive attempt at poetic diction. The heavy-handed satire of MARCO MILLIONS was not even produced during the wave of anti-Babbitt sentiment when it was written; it was already out of date when the Theatre Guild presented it. But most discouraging of all was the distortion three of the plays received in their encounter with the law.

2. The Interposing Censor

Playwrights in New York have seldom encountered organized resistance from official or private censorship bodies. "Banned in Boston" is a familiar phrase, and England's Lord Chamberlain still controls with absolute, although somewhat relaxed, power. Political dictators, religious leaders and citizens' leagues everywhere in the world have jointly or independently succeeded at one time or another in keeping from the public the plays judged contrary to the common good. In New York, however, stage censorship has seldom been a problem acute enough to cause alarm. Violent critical reaction and loud individual protests have always been heard, but the intervention of civic officials has been rare.

Unfortunately, Eugene O'Neill wrote three plays before 1925, all of them within his man-to-God category, which appeared at a time when the manners and morals of the stage were under careful scrutiny. As he tried to develop his dramatic philosophy in *THE HAIRY APE, ALL GOD'S CHILLUN GOT WINGS* and *DESIRE UNDER THE ELMS,* he met with confused, bungling, often ridiculous attempts at censorship which all critics and serious-minded playgoers deplored. The result was the complete distortion of O'Neill's artistic aims, whereby his fundamentally serious psychological studies were twisted into lewd and obscene trash.

O'Neill could possibly have compromised some of the difficulties, but his attitude toward his work refused to let him. His own sincerity forced him to give his characters an appropriate milieu in which to operate, and he was unable to soften it. That milieu was the truth as he saw it, with no attempt at disguise or portrayal in veiled form. The truth involved strong sounding (but actually unreal) language, including many damns, Gods, Jesuses, hells, tarts, bulls, whores and guts; and a head-on encounter with social taboos such as miscegenation, incest, abortion and prostitution. The use of this truth, with no emphasis on its unpleasantries for their own sake, aroused in those conscious of public "morals" a sudden awareness that here was a lawless pervert daring to put into action before a defenseless public such shameful, degrading spectacles. O'Neill quickly became associated with the lowest category of bedroom farce and cheap burlesque smut.

After *THE HAIRY APE* had run unmolested for two months, the police, according to the New York *Times* of 19 May 1922, charged it with being "obscene, indecent, and impure." A copy of the play was forwarded to Chief Magistrate William G. McAdoo for his appropriate action. McAdoo, as quoted by the newspapers, denied he had any intention of taking action. The whole affair looked like a press agent's idea, according to one comment. Nobody was ever quite sure who started it, and official procrastination gave the papers an excellent opportunity to ridicule the absurdities of police censorship that suddenly found a play "indecent" after nearly 75 performances. The storm subsided almost as quickly as it had risen, but the damage had been done. The effectiveness of O'Neill's message, hidden as it was behind the confused critical reaction in the first place, became all but lost in the argument about "impurity." O'Neill himself had this to say in reply to a telegram from the *World:* "Such an idiotic attempt to suppress will bring only ridicule to the poor dolts who started it."

Two years later, New York's Mayor John Hylan took a personal interest in *ALL GOD'S CHILLUN GOT WINGS*, already published but not yet produced. Regardless of O'Neill's insistence that it was a tragedy far beyond a mere discussion of miscegenation, it was generally regarded as another social "problem play." The "problem" became so over emphasized by production time that Mayor Hylan intervened in an attempt to prevent the staging of a play that would dare to show a white woman kissing a Negro's hand. The *Times* first reported his

protests in early March 1924, and the production was post-
poned, bringing an immediate denial from Kenneth Macgowan
that official threats had been the cause.

The play finally opened in the Village on 15 May with
Hylan still adamant. The mayor's attempt at censorship had
taken a somewhat unconventional method: refusal to permit
children to appear in the first scene because they were too young.
Nevertheless, the curtains parted as scheduled, and James Light,
the producer, read the first scene to the audience. The play
thereupon continued as written. Insurrections and race riots did
not materialize, and younger children with heavier parts in
uptown theatres performed their nightly roles in freedom. The
publicity only increased public interest in the play. The uproar,
inevitable in such squabbles, drowned out the statement of
O'Neill's tragic theme. The play never became the great work
O'Neill had hoped for. He was sure that CHILLUN, one of
his "most misunderstood" plays, would some day come into
its own.

As a dramatic piece, DESIRE UNDER THE ELMS, if
left alone, could have remained a play of debatable tragic
merit and possibly noble aspirations, with a limited audience
and a modest level of popularity. A few critics could not break
through O'Neill's crude New England dialect, surface Freudian-
ism and violence to discover any meaning, although the play
was widely regarded as O'Neill's first important step toward
greatness. But once more the heavy hand of officialdom made
the play something it was never designed to be — a sex drama
full of suggestiveness and sensual sin.

New York District Attorney Joab Banton, incited by a
crusading New York *World*, was determined to clean the filth
from the current drama. As he viewed the scene from City
Hall he spied, along with questionable third-rate plays long
since forgotten, an O'Neill play in which a step-mother seduced
her step-son while in her nightgown. He ordered it closed. In
February 1925 producer Kenneth Macgowan refused to be impressed by threats of jail and defied the order. A complex
system of judgment by play juries finally evolved after weeks
of haggling and the O'Neill tragedy received unanimous ac-
quittal on 13 March. The result was a sharp upswing in at-
tendance. The spectators came to see just what had so violently

agitated the censors. The audience became a vulgar one, seeking an illicit thrill, snickering at the nightgown and the seduction. Others, hearing it was a "decent" play after all, came to see its deep moral lesson, and were also forced to depart without the effect for which they came. On both a critical and popular level, the play had failed to communicate, its great impetus lost amid the trampling of public guardians and their camp followers.

In the spring of 1926 a Los Angeles police officer, offended at the floor-length nightdress, arrested the entire cast for presenting an obscene play. The case dragged on through months of litigation. A full production was staged before judge and jury, while the prosecutor loudly protested that it had been illegally expurgated. A hung jury in April ended the case, with the play continuing before capacity audiences whose morals were, supposedly, nightly corrupted. In England the Lord Chamberlain refused to permit a production of this work "abhorrent to English audiences" until January 1940.

Through his insistence on veracity of scene and type as an instrument in his communication, O'Neill often lost contact with his audiences when they took that instrument as the primary dramatic object. These misunderstandings worried him, but he could never alter his serious intent in order to conform with "safe" procedures. Then, as other plays like the cursing, blaspheming *What Price Glory?* raised howls of delight and gasps of disbelief, the barriers which had confronted O'Neill for the first years of his career completely broke down. No longer was such elemental behavior new. It was accepted as dramatically viable. Thereafter, save in Boston, O'Neill had no difficulty, and the adulteries, abortions, fornications and incests of his later works brought no threat of padlock or arrest. The public had grown up to O'Neill's standard. Now he should be able to communicate on a level common to both.[4]

---

[4]Troubles with censors in Detroit and elsewhere contributed materially to the failure of *A MOON FOR THE MISBEGOTTEN* to survive its road tryouts and enter New York in 1947. There was never any difficulty with the play in New York itself.

3. Departure From The Spirit Of The Age

After he acquired a firm and consistent attitude in the man-to-God theme, O'Neill gained a certain strength which he had badly dissipated in the thirteen earlier, unsteadier plays. With censors ridiculed and scoffed into silence and audiences attending the plays for their own values, instead of those falsely implied and exaggerated, O'Neill had every chance to develop into the greatest playwright in the language. He had the desire and the temperament. He had the inspiration and the material. He had the public and the producers. But he failed even then to reach the greatness so may serious critics prayed he would. He continually fell short, and the value of his communication was never appreciated to the degree worthy of the attempt. He wrote of his discouragement in 1925 to Arthur Hobson Quinn, convinced that "most of my critics don't want to see what I'm trying to do or how I'm trying to do it."

Joseph Wood Krutch made some interesting remarks on this subject of communication. He observed that recent literary criticism had shown that men like Poe, James, Adams, Thoreau, Melville and Hawthorne were great literary artists and also lonely men whose public did not readily welcome what they wrote because of the failure to "participate in the spirit of the age." O'Neill, attempting to communicate something entirely different from what other playwrights tried, wrote "tragedy with a capital T," as he introduced a world of which the audience was afraid. He wrote his plays during a period of cheerful confidence. They did not attack Main Street and Babbittry as others did, but were absorbed with primitive passions and dark Gods. Most people, then, could not understand what he was trying to say. Krutch pointed out that the characters in an O'Neill play were in the grip of strong and primitive passions that the spectator could not believe possible. Because O'Neill's intent was serious, and his tragedy was *meant* to be tragedy, it was impossible successfully to "explain away" the plays. They had to be taken with the seriousness with which they were created.

From 1925 until the middle of 1929, the entire nation was exhilarated by a booming prosperity of seemingly unquestioned permanence. It was a time of mounting riches, Fords by the millions, Rotarians by the clubful, and God blessing the manufacturer. Any person who doubted the future and the prosperous life it represented by writing serious tragedy could not, certainly, be understood. Writers might worry about the decline of morals, the racketeering of the bootleg era, and the irresponsible young generation with coonskin coats and flapper styles, but nobody was concerned with "tragedy with a capital T." In the face of this attitude, Eugene O'Neill, the dramatic artist, attempted to arouse that concern. He still followed no pattern; he continued to vary his approach from play to play with hardly a repetition. But he knew that he could no longer treat man's relation to God in plays which were too easily confused with soap box social criticism. The violence of interracial marriage or of labor's helpless wandering in capital's glittering world must not interefere with his direct statement that mankind was in serious trouble. The Great God Business was faulty, destroying alike the souls of the artistic sensitive dreamer and the practical hard-headed business man, compensating them both with a prostitute for a guardian angel. The strange interlude in God's electrical display was terrifying, as it presented the emancipated modern woman with lovers uncounted and a final old age of forty-five in which to rot in peace. The love-lit eyes of a beautiful Oriental princess were interpreted as signs of a cold by a completely unvisionary Marco Polo, welcomed home from his worldly success without a soul, but with a frumpish fat and forty sweetheart. Values were lost, were transvalued. From his Bermuda manor house, Eugene O'Neill saw a "sickness of today" and it worried him.

At the height of this era when money conquered all and dollars flowed from stocks, bonds and John D. Rockefeller, O'Neill analyzed the sickness of today in a resounding failure, *DYNAMO.* Presented in February 1929, when the market began its last mad lurch for the top, this play showed several mentally unstable men and women on a search for a "new God to replace the old one." Atheist, unbending Puritan, sensual daughter, monomaniac son, all clashed in a furious encounter involving murder, beatings, dynamo worship and electrical suicide. It solved little, but it displayed the deep disturbances within the writer. A new god was needed, because the old God was assumed to be dead. The result was nothingness, and critics were hard put to discover the salvation often suggested, if unachieved by the protagonists, in O'Neill's earlier plays.

O'Neill always felt that *DYNAMO* was "right." Although he made no public statements, he defended it in letters to his friends. One letter to Benjamin De Casseres, written in March 1929, was outstanding in its muddled confusion, and it bears comparison with the widely reprinted explanation for *THE GREAT GOD BROWN*. These two plays were the most openly direct attacks O'Neill ever made on the false gods of modern business and industrial life; in both of them he remained much farther away from his audiences than he wished.

O'Neill began his explanation of *BROWN* by recognizing that an "open-faced avowal" of the underlying abstract theme could not be made by the play itself, because of the nature of the hidden theme. It was therefore up to him as author to confess the "mystical pattern" which was the play's overtone. This was to by "mystically within and behind" the characters, forcing them to an expression in "mysterious words, symbols, actions" that they themselves do not understand. Similarities in the plea for *DYNAMO* are obvious. O'Neill asked that one not be blinded by the "general theme" because it was actuallly of secondary value. The psychological struggle of the protagonist was three-fourths of the play which "not one damn single person" seemed to have discovered. O'Neill feared most people sought a much shallower symbolism than what he himself felt important, but he did admit that perhaps it was all his own fault in giving the audience a "wrong steer" anyway. He was sure ("unless I'm stark nuts") that the repudiation of old gods, the mother's drag on her son from her grave, the position of the dynamo as a mother, and the electrocution of Father Gods stood out like red paint. Some day, he was sure, the play would come into its own. As in the case of *ALL GOD'S CHILLUN*, nothing of the sort happened. To write a play with the general theme secondary and the secondary theme important, as seemed to be the case in *DYNAMO* as well as in *BROWN*, showed a positive failure to communicate. Unfortunately, O'Neill was never one to admit that the red paint might not be there if he insisted it was.

Still in the seclusion of a far-off retreat, this time in France, O'Neill devoted almost the whole of two years, 1929-1931, to the creation of his "grand opus," *MOURNING BECOMES ELECTRA*. Without making the positive and damning assumption that the play bulged with symbolic references and allegorical meanings, one may discern generalities which reflected the temper of an artist who took the headlong destruction of Man as his own personal affair. O'Neill attacked the bigoted narrowness of a decadent Puritanism and clannish living, and the blind social acceptance of prestige and power founded on stained souls. In thirteen acts of violence O'Neill revealed a civilization rotten and collapsing. Could it be significant that, as he wrote and produced this climactic effort, the society whose sickness he feared was tumbling into Hell and taking with it the lives and livelihood of those at one time most devoted to it? Contemporary comment and the available O'Neill letters and notebooks have not produced a satisfactory answer, but the O'Neill student cannot summarily dismiss a parallel between the writer's awareness of the catastrophe and the resulting creation of *ELECTRA*.

The original Aeschylean trilogy was written by a thinker who questioned the ethics of a polytheistic society or the eccentricities of gods possessed of most of the human failings and a few of the assets. From *Prometheus* to the *Oresteia* a powerful Zeus, untempered by wisdom and mercy, grew into a god who brought justice to both heaven and earth. The old social order of blood for blood, apparent in the heinous crimes of the *Agamemnon* and *Choephoroi* must change. Orestes and his deeds became only the instrument for elevated debate in *The Eumenides*, which established law and order, allowed justice to prevail, and moved the reconciled Furies to higher form. In their general lines, the first two plays of both trilogies were similar: the decaying society, blood for blood, the god of wrath and hell fire. In close comparison, the society of O'Neill's own age was sick and soulless, led by a capricious god of money and quick riches who put Al Capones in control of cities' destinies, and held out the offer of eternal salvation on the stock market, whose whims brought sudden and complete damnation. A new order had to come. The destruction of the old was inevitable.

The parallel vanished in the final play, *The Haunted*, counterpart of *The Eumenides*, as O'Neill brought his concluding acts around to more direct relationship to modern attitudes. Orestes became, in Orin, a secondary figure, but Electra, in Lavinia, emerged. Instead of emerging with her as a changed, bettered deity, the "old god," as in *DYNAMO*, died. Lavinia had to punish herself; the Puritan god of wrath was incapable of proper function or of alteration. A new god, also one of destruction, as in *DYNAMO's* electric generator, seemed the only one left. But it, too, failed. What was left? A living with the past which was possible only behind closed shutters and locked doors. Outside were ignorant townspeople, Peters and Hazels, conventional, conforming, unchanging. Their social leaders were destroyed. Who would replace them was yet unknown. A sterile vacuum existed. The next step could not be predicted, but until some force of equal strength arose, one could only look back at the Mannon vacuities with the resolution that in the future a better leadership would evolve. The opening night of *MOURNING BECOMES ELECTRA*, 26 October 1931, was almost to the day the second anniversary of 1929's wild downward skid. The old god was surely dead; the Mannons became dust in grave or airless mansion. No Erinnyes into Eumenides; no Zeus of thunderbolts into Zeus of peace and prosperity. The thread of modern fate, drawn uncertainly from William Brown's disastrous assumption of Dion Anthony's mask, became firmly spun in Nina's sexless, rotting peace, and was finally clipped as Lavinia disappeared behind the cold pillars of her living tomb.

Although *ELECTRA* ran for nearly six months, it is logical to assume that most of the spectators did not begin to fathom what O'Neill was trying to communicate. The ordinary viewer lacked the scholarly knowledge of Greek tragedy and its sense of fate necessary to interpret the play on the level which O'Neill contemplated. The "Tired Business Man," said *Vanity Fair's* reviewer, could find nothing to amuse him in this display of violence. Robert Benchley saw it only as a grand, stupendous thriller, with the melodramatic hand of Monte Cristo much in evidence. The New York *Times*, speaking editorially, begged that poor old New England be left alone in its struggles with the depression instead of accusing it of such horrors as in this play. Joseph Wood Krutch thought that the play did not *mean* anything any more than *Hamlet meant* anything. Agreement with each or all of these views was quite possible, but none of them grasped what O'Neill had in mind. The play was never intended to amuse tired business men, and reading O'Neill's notes proves that a *Monte Cristo* melodrama was never his aim. He was accusing New England of no horrors, and he wished the play to mean far more than Mr. Krutch's analysis would give it. Once again O'Neill's failure to project exactly what he felt must be marked against him.

DAYS WITHOUT END, produced more than two years later, was O'Neill's most obvious affirmation of his man-to-God theme. It was welcomed by the religious press, both Catholic and Protestant, as a complete and wonderful surrender to Christ crucified. Once more there was widespread confusion of attitude and a loss of any solid value to the playgoer, who was almost never able to see the play without a preconceived conviction that it was a great and inspiring conversion of O'Neill the erstwhile unbeliever, or that it was only another ineffectual repetition of what O'Neill had said many times over. Instead of attracting wider understanding, the popular symbol of the Cross enraptured the churchman far beyond the play's merits, and dismayed the layman at so conventional and cheap a trick.

DAYS WITHOUT END received a successful Boston try-out and came into New York in January 1934. It was almost completely condemned by the New York press:

John Anderson, *Journal:* Confusing, florid, ornamentally phony.

John Mason Brown, *Post:* Tedious and artificial, one of O'Neill's feeblest.

Brooks Atkinson, *Times:* Written as if O'Neill had never written before; a bad play.

Gilbert Gabriel, *American:* The real miracle is that it was done at all; nothing can make it a good play.

Robert Garland, *World-Telegram:* Shoddy specimen of "holy-hokum."

These opinions brought some vigorous and often hysterical counterattacks in the clerical press, accusing the lay reviewers of bigotry and prejudice, afraid of ridicule in case they dared praise this important play. An editorial in *Catholic World* was among the most even tempered. It felt the professional lay critics could not in justice be called upon to evaluate something as deep in meaning as a religious conversion.

The solution of the play, to Joseph Wood Krutch, showed that the "primitive religious instinct" was still working, be it Catholic, Protestant, Hebrew, or other. It is easy to agree with this opinion, because O'Neill had failed to show any new outlook. The almost pagan treatment of the man-to-God theme in *LAZARUS LAUGHED*, in which the Dionysiac laughter of the protagonist affirmed the eternal life in "Yes" and sent all who encountered it into a kind of orgiastic frenzy, was at least original with O'Neill. In *DAYS WITHOUT END*, weakly echoing the theme of *LAZARUS* with a statement about life laughing with love, O'Neill plodded through a very unexciting play to an embarrassingly routine conversion and "miracle." Static, obvious, heavy, it was a new O'Neill, for it communicated directly, simply, and by means of material which did nothing to elevate him above the routinely successful play maker. Paradoxically, that same directness, obvious as it was, prevented any uniform understanding among those who saw it. "O'Neill's greatness has begun. May they be Days without End," wrote Fred Eastman of *Christian Century*. "Magnificently Catholic; O'Neill is heading toward the light," said the Rev. Gerard B. Donnell, S.J., in *America*. "Dull, pedestrian, unconvincing in every respect," said Edith Isaacs in *Theatre Arts*. "Morbid inspection of the human soul; spiritual indigestion," complained Cy Caldwell of *New Outlook*.

❖   ❖   ❖   ❖   ❖   ❖

The isolation of Eugene O'Neill the artist had become almost complete with the failure of *DAYS WITHOUT END*, and there ensued the dozen years' silence broken by *THE ICEMAN COMETH* in 1946. Just before and during that long period a number of thoughtful articles appeared concerning O'Neill's artistic future. All were reluctant to give him "permanent" evaluation, because O'Neill was still young (forty-four at the time of *ELECTRA*) and known to be hard at work on the "cycle" and other plays. Nevertheless, certain outstanding scholars regretted the change of O'Neill's approach to his work. At least four important critics, writing within a five year period between 1932 and 1938, not privileged to know what was yet to come, sensed the presence or the imminent approach of a surrender, and realized that the O'Neill of the past decade was in all probability gone.

First: John Mason Brown, "The Present Day Dilemma of Eugene O'Neill," New York *Post*, 19 November 1932. In reply to O'Neill's *American Spectator* article, "Memoranda on Masks," Brown feared that O'Neill's concern for the importance of masks boded ill for the future, being symptomatic of the isolation which greatness had thrust upon him. Brown preferred O'Neill the emotionalist to O'Neill the thinker, the realist to symbolist, seaman to Freudian, and straight-hitting dramatist to brave but self-conscious experimenter with tricky forms. Preoccupied with form rather than content, O'Neill could no longer mingle with men and had become a recluse apart from life. Instead of gaining from his fame and contact with the crowd, he suffered and was defeated by his victory. Brown took note of Casa Genotta, O'Neill's Sea Island, Georgia, home, terming it ironic that he had a house fixed up like Shaw's Captain Shotover's of *Heartbreak House*, to the cabin of which he climbed to read his Jung and Freud and to defend masks. Brown found it just as sad as any of the plays, and just as ironic.

Second: Montrose J. Moses, "The 'New' Eugene O'Neill," *North American Review*, December 1933. Moses suspected that we had not been quite right in viewing O'Neill as the dark, wild, morose rebel of legend, for *AH, WILDERNESS!* compelled us to pause and question. This play did not mean that O'Neill was in smoother, calmer waters, but it did indicate that the portrait of the "wild sojourner in tortured souls, the morbidly resentful, brooding on social injustice" was challenged. Often in the past O'Neill had been violent and untutored in his thinking aloud, giving a sort of nervous reaction to his audience, and letting the plays disintegrate in anti-climaxes following climaxes, but now the "sustained simplicity" of *AH, WILDERNESS!* showed signs of being over sweet, of overdoing the opposite extreme. Because he had walked before us in such great steps and had projected most of his plays upon such a great canvas, we were struck by this unexpected dramatic atmosphere. Being basically curious about a man of whom we had known so little, and whose close friends had offered little assistance, we had been made even more so by this play. What will this "tremendous showmanship" do next? asked Moses.

Third: Hiram Motherwell, "O'Neill: What Next?" *Stage,* August 1935. After a year's silence, articles began to appear discussing the possibilities of what was to come. Motherwell found it surprising that O'Neill had been taken seriously in the first place. Since the plays could be regarded as "at once absurd and deeply true" this public acceptance was something of a compliment. It took great courage for O'Neill to write the kind of gloom he did, over and over again, and still convince his audiences that *STRANGE INTERLUDE* was not ridiculous but "part of the every day truth of modern psychology."

Now, with *AH, WILDERNESS!* and *DAYS WITHOUT END*, said Motherwell, O'Neill had come to a parting of the ways, for his plays were neither tragedy nor comedy. He speculated that future plays would probably lie somewhere in between, and he seemed to agree with others that O'Neill would not return to what he once was. Perhaps the new approach would not be so much about Man and God as about Man and the social system. Could the protagonist be the individual in struggle with the social order, or would it be the social order itself? Provided O'Neill's indignation at the fate of the down and outs, as shown in the early plays, could be transferred into an attack on social systems beyond mortal control, he might flower again with the same power of ten years previously. O'Neill, concluded Motherwell, had been the ruthless pathologist of the individual. Was he perhaps to become its diagnostician and prophet?

Fourth: Lionel Trilling, "Eugene O'Neill: A Revaluation," *New Republic,* 23 September 1938. This is one of the best essays published when O'Neill was still considered active. In fact, it is one of the best of any essays about O'Neill and his work. It was written by a scholar not normally considered a dramatic critic. Unlike Atkinson or Brown, Nathan or Krutch, Trilling brought what could almost be termed a neutral approach.

Trilling first asked that we recognize O'Neill's genius. In this light, he also asked to remember that whatever the atmosphere in which something was originally written, it is later read in light of the *force* with which it is presented (as Sophocles and Aeschylus, for example, are now read), not to find the right answer, but to experience the strength of the attack on life and the "moral complexities." This is what we do with O'Neill, despite his many failures. In contrast to John Mason Brown's disappointment at O'Neill's results when he began to "think," Trilling pointed out that there had always been "thought" in O'Neill's works which permitted many people, Catholic as well as Communist, to find something of worth. O'Neill was always trying to solve life, doing it better in the non-realistic plays than the realistic. Through symbol and myth, O'Neill was always moving toward some kind of finality promised by religion and philosophy. The world is continually one of plus and minus, and O'Neill's work "an algebraic attempt" at the solution.

O'Neill's force came from the upheaval and breaking of taboos as in *THE GREAT GOD BROWN*, where both the ideals of the business man and the poet alike destroyed each other. He solved the problem of evil by the tragic "affirmation of life in the face of individual defeat." But, said Trilling, unable to live in a world that is a tragic universe, O'Neill turned from man's strength of intellect and emotion to his oldest weakness: blind faith. *DAYS WITHOUT END* had to come to the Cross to find peace, but this, in turn, made it one of his weakest plays, because Life Eternal banished life itself. "O'Neill has crept into the dark womb of the mother church and pulled the universe in with him," concluded Trilling. It was a far cry from the statement in *THE GREAT GOD BROWN*: "It isn't enough to be life's creature. You've got to create her, or she requires you to destroy yourself."

✻　✻　✻　✻　✻　✻

By the time this series of articles began, O'Neill had been an active member of the American theatre and a contributor to its dramatic literature for over fifteen years. He was still unknown as a man, and in technique and subject matter had been unable to establish any recognizable and critically acceptable consistency. Thus, by 1933, John Mason Brown had expressed the O'Neill paradox of increased success and mounting lack of communication, an almost complete defeat from his own victory. Montrose Moses, two years later, waited for the "real" O'Neill to emerge. Hiram Motherwell sensed a change of great value toward a better dramatic form that did not develop. Lionel Trilling, five years after Brown, discovered only a turn toward a blind faith and a departure from the previous courageous affirmation of life.

The artist, "pulling the universe in with him," isolated in his California estate, worked on a mysterious "cycle" which he must have known could never be produced. Refusing to allow the release of any new play until the world returned to sanity, he became further and further removed from his countrymen, and the return to Broadway in 1946 was unable to reinstate him. The revival of a decade later was therefore a remarkable phenomenon in the face of this seeming permanent disappearance. The lasting qualities of O'Neill's work, if it is to remain as part of our literature, must be those aspects which now, even more than before, communicate in the spirit of the age.

Probably *A MOON FOR THE MISBEGOTTEN* can most easily be dismissed among the plays produced during the three years up to 1960. Generally accepted as a "tired" work, the effort of a dying, or at least exhausted, man, the play had failed miserably on its initial tryout and fared little better once it did arrive on the New York stage. Reviews found only a "ghost" of O'Neill's other plays, failing to reach the pinnacle of tragedy with a definite limitation to its "alcoholic values." As Woolcott Gibbs observed in the *New Yorker*, for all his verbosity elsewhere, O'Neill had something to say; here he does not. The theme of the giant virgin, a kind of grotesque extension of the earth-mother Cybel in *BROWN*, "redeeming" the pathetic alcoholic shell of a man by her night-long vigil, brought little message to today's audiences.

LONG DAY'S JOURNEY and *A TOUCH OF THE POET*, both far more successful in the theatre, can more easily be placed within today's social and spiritual framework and emerge with something more closely communicating with the spirit of the age. The autobiographical qualities of the former must, in this instance, be dismissed. Over and above the personal history, the play did have a message about the sensitive soul in the midst of a society which would not, or could not, understand it. Lacking the often exasperating O'Neill devices that so frequently stood between author and audience, and void of the florid mysticism of such plays as *DAYS WITHOUT END*, or even *GREAT GOD BROWN*, *LONG DAY'S JOURNEY* talked fairly plainly about the need of all mankind, however grim his fortunes or however self-created his existing unfortunate situation, for love and understanding. Brooks Atkinson found it had "obvious truths" about the tensions and loyalties of family life which transcended the personal story. Clerical as well as lay press welcomed it for the picture it showed of tragic fate, understandable in today's terms. *Christian Century* saw an artistic stature coming from the consistent view of human nature, and *Commonweal* described a "seamless pattern of time, suffering and nobility" typical of tragedy. By stripping himself and his family bare, O'Neill did the same for humanity in general, and for all the hell through which his characters are sent, they have his continual love and compassion.

A TOUCH OF THE POET, the last full-length play we will probably ever see, can be judged by standards far more "typical" than many others. Robert Coleman in the *Mirror* discovered something missing in most of O'Neill's other plays — humor, along with the love and compassion. Richard Watts of the *Post* could also find enormous power and compassion quite typical of O'Neill. The *Hudson Review* thought O'Neill was improving as a dramatic craftsman with an authentic tragic theme. Dissension about the play rested mainly on the same complaints of all O'Neill's plays: repetition, overwriting and lack of focus. There were, however, few who could condemn the play for its lack of communication or its departure from the spirit of the age.

We cannot rely on these last plays to provide O'Neill's final position in our literature. They do, however, indicate the possibility of a changed attitude toward the whole collection of O'Neill's works. The pipe dreams of *THE ICEMAN COMETH*, the illusions, self-delusions and bitter disappointments of wasted lives are universal, not of any one time. When they came upon the stage at the end of a global conflict, when life held promise of extended peace and goodwill, the inmates of Harry Hope's bar did not communicate. Perhaps now they do. While the

Williamses, Ionescos, Becketts, Genets and others of the contemporary theatre find a permanent sickness and a meaninglessness in life associated with piles of chairs, life in ashcans and endless waitings for Godots, O'Neill stands forth in towering strength and impact with a message that reveals a strong faith in the grandness of mankind capable of asserting the tragic affirmation of life in the face of death. Although not a commercial success, *THE GREAT GOD BROWN* of 1959, in a society far from that of 1929, still speaks of the organization man in the grey flannel suit, the conformist, the suppressed artist who dare not be himself, and dare be nothing else. There is a message, and it communicates.

Will this message communicate in the future? Will the Lavinia Mannons who shut themselves into dark houses, the Ninas who decay in peace at 45, and the Ephraim Cabots who defy their fates and embrace their rock-hard Gods, still speak in the spirit of the age in the universal permanence of great literature? If so, O'Neill has achieved the artistry for which he struggled. If not, he has ultimately failed to communicate in the spirit of any age.

IV — ROMANTIC SURRENDER

M. M. Morrill, after a visit to O'Neill's Cape Cod home in 1930, was convinced that "he must be uncomfortable to be content; he must be lonely to be compassioned; he must suffer to be happy; he must defy life to find its harmony." Morrill's soaring rhetorical ecstacy placed O'Neill against the elemental forces, surrounded by the "same dynamic power" that swept naked and dangerous through the plays. "God! what a stark, terrible, solitary place for a soul to be — a sane soul — this Cape Cod shack of Eugene O'Neill's!" he cried.

By Morrill's account this "shack" would seem to be the ultimate in desolate isolation, a sort of Hellmouth itself, from which spewed the consuming fire of O'Neill's inspiration. In reality it was nothing of the sort. Eugene O'Neill, in all his defiance of tradition and conventionality, never regarded himself as a suffering, sorrowing artist destined to fight the ocean's very waves for his survival. After the commercial success of *ANNA CHRISTIE* in 1921 O'Neill never lacked material comforts. Other successful plays, phenomenal sales of published versions, and wise investments brought a considerable fortune that placed him far beyond the want and stress so commonly associated with the brooding artist. He was able to provide himself and his family with personal luxuries and magnificent homes throughout the last thirty years of his life.

In both his manner of living and in his plays O'Neill continually reflected a strain always inherent in his nature which, for lack of a better term, we shall call "romanticism." The facts concerning his homes will speak for themselves, but in the case of the plays a more subjective analysis will be required, supported from time to time by professional reviews and critical opinion.

Romanticism is an elusive term. A single, successful definition of it probably does not exist. Historically, there is little argument that the freedom of imagination and artistic fancy of romantic drama separates it from the severe limits of classicism, but just what constitutes the "romantic" play today is open to an assortment of interpretations. Because it is impossible to consider O'Neill in the light of any single "movement," it would be erroneous arbitrarily to classify him in any way, as so many critics discovered during his active career. We cannot, for example, identify him as a "romanticist" in terms of the broad expanse of nineteenth century romanticism. It is best, then, to develop a definition for our own purposes, perhaps arbitrary in certain respects, but reflecting enough of the popular concept to be accepted as a recognizable term, applicable to Eugene O'Neill.

The romanticist, developing what he *feels*, is removed from the immediate world of the realist, who would recreate precisely what he *sees*. The romanticist is able to maintain a strong faith in the goodness of things, turning to human inspiration, untrammeled, unmolested, as the source of human success. He is the advocate of individuality and personal freedom, for no ideal is reached through outer conformity, but through inner independence. Man's development is a matter not of direct concern with other men, in artificial societies, but with himself, his own soul.

Although the romanticist recognizes that evil exists and he must often endure the oppressive forces upon which the realist may dwell, he has faith in powers that the realist or the naturalist cannot accept. Pure love may conquer and redeem all. Two hearts beating as one can stand unflinchingly against fate, even though it may be violently destructive. The power of dreams is great; life without its visions is useless. Nature has a beauty of its own, and the power to inspire awe. The fog is clean, white, purifying. The pounding surf is invigoratingly musical; the howling wind strong and inspirational. Man and nature in combination are grand. All of this can lead toward a kind of optimism, a confidence in the future of man, because the great things of the past have been inspired and accomplished by the same forces the romanticist admires. It can also lead toward sentimentality, with its delight in beauty, adventure and love for the sake of emotional pleasure.

The theatre into which O'Neill entered had long been dominated by many trite conventions and artificial complications which never failed to progress toward the properly happy ending. So violent, even savage, were O'Neill's early attacks on the conventional stage romanticism that critics and public

never doubted his extreme distaste for anything hearkening of
its contrived or saccharine implausibilities. His reputation as
a "grim realist" was so strong that by the time of THE GREAT
GOD BROWN his audience was unable, or perhaps unwilling,
to recognize that he was creating dramatic characters whose
romantic make up was designed to evoke sympathy.

It is not difficult to trace the evolution of O'Neill's romanticism in the terms just defined. By the end of his career,
O'Neill had completely surrendered to this romantic concept
in both character and atmosphere, but instead of marking a
final plateau of achievement, it served only to emphasize his
weakness. The same trouble afflicted him in this respect as in
all other facets of his development as an artist. Having come
from no well-planned progression of artistic style, this romanticism seemed artificial, over sentimental and derivative.

With the exception of BOUND EAST FOR CARDIFF in
1914, O'Neill's best short plays were composed from 1916 to
1918, the years of his acquaintance with the Greenwich Village
radicals, the Hudson Dusters and those who summered on the
uncommercialized Provincetown sands. Wherever the romantic
ideal appeared in these plays it was ironically twisted, or used
to destroy a character. O'Neill's open revolt against the restricted traditional theatre was everywhere apparent in the
Glencairn cycle. The sultry, sensuous atmosphere of moonlight
in the Caribbean, the crooning chant of native song drifting
over the water, the ship idling at anchor in the bay, were in
ironic contrast to the lustful brawling climax of the motley
crew's free-for-all. Critical expression praised the authentic tang
of the sea which this "Conrad of playwrights" inserted into
his realistic portrayal of life afloat. O'Neill's unromantic interpretation was strongly reinforced by his treatment of all characters whose romantic feeling persisted in the face of these unfavorable surroundings and impossible odds. None were allowed to survive. Smitty, the misfit, preferring to remain isolated
with his memories of a shattered romantic life, was branded
as an object of suspicion and fear by both the native girls and
his own unsentimental forecastle mates. He had no place
among them, and they inflicted a final ignominy before his
helpless face, reading the letters which had spelled his doom.
Yank's dying vision of land and a home of his own mocked

him as he perished in agony from a mortal wound inflicted by the sea, while the ship plodded steadily, unheedingly toward Cardiff. And Olson, dreaming of home, mother and the farm in a highly sentimental re-creation of the projected return of the prodigal, found an unromantic, anti-sentimental world slugging him in the guts with a "mickey."

The three other plays published with the *Glencairn* cycle pursued the same unrelenting destruction of the romanticist. Mrs. Keeney, of *ILE*, boarded her husband's whaler with typical romantic images of the sea, but found only monotony, mutiny and madness, in that order. In *THE ROPE*, Abraham Bentley prepared to welcome back his worthless son, Luke, not with a fatted calf but with a fortune, provided that the son would recognize his sins by offering to take his own life. Bentley's weirdly distorted attempt at reconciliation resulted in Luke's further determination to find the money by torturing it out of the "old skunk," unaware that the feeble-minded Mary had already found it and was tossing the gold piece by piece into the sea. Finally, Isaiah Bartlett's mad romanticism in *WHERE THE CROSS IS MADE* brought hallucinations which killed him and drove his son insane.

"No modern writer," wrote Sophus K. Winther in 1934, "has attacked [the romantic ideal] more consistently or more bitterly than Eugene O'Neill." The six plays of the man-to-man theme probably owed much of their limited popular appeal to the lack of any subtlety in this anti-romantic attitude. The antiseptic atmosphere of *THE STRAW* was largely unromantic, and although O'Neill suggested hope through the old standby of the regenerative power of love, in which the romanticist believes, he plainly told his audience that there was none. Anna Christie was "redeemed" by the love of a bumbling romantic Irishman in a plot line going directly to Marguerite Gauthier and beyond, but O'Neill, holding Chris' "ole davil" ready to strike at any time, did not admit of any romantic happiness-ever-after. Among the other plays the romantic ideal was also ruthlessly destroyed. Determined to have a man who was "diff'rent," who met the perfection of her own romantic standards, Emma Crosby was turned into a disgusting picture of a sexually frustrated, desperate old maid. Married love in *THE FIRST MAN* merely produced an unwanted child for Curtis

Jayson and killed his wife. In *WELDED*, the Capes, bonded to each other by the erotic attractions of sex, were destined to a series of violent squabbles and jealousies which had no connection with romantic concepts of marriage. They did not die, but as individuals with souls of their own they were destroyed.

As a whole, the man-to-man plays were too strong in their attempt to destroy the romantic ideal. They shocked and repulsed, without any compensating attitudes. The audiences still hoped that the final curtain meant better things for the central characters, but the hope was vain. The spectators grasped the same straw that Eileen Carmody grasped; against better judgment, they hoped for and thought they saw happiness for Anna and Matt. Michael and Ellen Cape were, after all, reunited, and Curtis Jayson finally welcomed his son. But most of these were not good plays, and, except for *ANNA CHRISTIE*, none deserved or received serious consideration.

In the man-to-God plays, more expert and appealing in character creation and technical skills, those who showed symptoms of conventional romance were almost viciously eliminated. The striking fact, however, is O'Neill's failure successfully to convince his audiences that the destruction was inevitable because of that romanticism. In nearly every case the denial of the romantic experience, not its accomplishment, resulted in the final catastrophe.

For instance, Robert Mayo was destroyed by deliberately turning *from* his chance to fulfill his romantic dreams beyond the horizon. The "incurable romanticist" within him prevented any success with the practical realities of running a farm, but how much more convincing the "destructive power of the romantic ideal" would have been had O'Neill permitted Robert to sail with his uncle to the exotic ports of which he dreamed. Romantic yearning may destroy when frustrated, which only proves its tremendous holding power. If it destroys when practiced, then the point is successfully made.

Yank, in *THE HAIRY APE*, wallowing in the filth of the stokehole, romanticized far beyond its true value his own contribution toward making the ship go. O'Neill could have destroyed him within that framework had he shown Yank's automatic stokers or diesel engines which would eventually failure to realize his own insignificance against the onrush of part. But Yank, like Robert, was destroyed out of his proper environment. He could no more fit into society than Robert could run a farm. He died, seeking a place for himself, which, in reality, he possessed all along, exactly as Robert belonged aboard his uncle's ship.

In *DESIRE UNDER THE ELMS* Eben Cabot, far removed from the rock-hard father and his God, replaced the overly-romanticized picture of his dead mother with the living, sensuous Abbie. As the two lovers were led away to probable death, they were together, in a completely romantic union, in which their love for each other would conquer and be greater than their heinous deeds for which they must suffer. The romantic ideal, apparently destroying them, had succeeded only in elevating them to a stature which many critical reviews felt approached the tragic.

The thirteen plays written before *THE GREAT GOD BROWN* all drove their leading characters to an often horrible fate. But instead of proving the destructive power of an over-developed sensitivity to the romantic ideal, many of them demanded further sympathy toward the sufferer. Under proper circumstances, plainly possible within the world in which they lived, the protagonists could have survived in peace and contentment. In his early plays, O'Neill had apparently erected a strong fortress against the romantic ideal, but it was jerry-built and eventually gave way. His final surrender was therefore not surprising, but a logical consequence.

✿   ✿   ✿   ✿   ✿   ✿

O'Neill could have found the isolation he wished for his work in many spots in New York, but instead he chose his old haunt, Provincetown, about as far out in the sea as one can get and still remain on mainland America, and again as far out on the sand as that narrow neck of peninsula permits. After his 1918 marriage to Agnes Boulton, he purchased the abandoned Coast Guard lifesaving station at Peaked Hill Bars and remodeled it as a home. It was accessible only on foot or horseback and then by the firmest determination. Because Morrill journeyed to the "shack," as he insisted on calling it, less than replace the hand-fired furnaces of which he was such a vital a year before it disappeared into the sea in a violent Cape Cod storm, and because O'Neill had gone to Bermuda and abandoned the place as a home, his reaction to its stark loneliness is perhaps understandable. More pertinent to the conditions under which O'Neill lived was the description published by J. M. Breese in *Country Life in America* in November 1923. Some excellent photographs of both the exterior and interior prove that the building was far from being a mere "shack."

Though condemned as a Coast Guard structure, it was as sound as most of the construction in the vicinity. The interior was tastefully and appropriately furnished: mat rugs on the floors and mat hangings on the walls, a convenient and comfortable kitchen and dining area in the old galley, bedrooms meant for restful and breeze-fanned sleeping, and a sort of patio-terrace effect on the end, with huge fireplace. The large front room, made over from the boat room, still contained the hooks which suspended the rescue craft from the ceiling beams, above the thick-planked floors where many a drenched body had been laid out for identification. From the sandpocked windows could be seen the surf into which O'Neill loved to swim and row his kayak. On the roof, where he was often photographed, smiling, tanned, content, was the lookout station, a frequented spot, reached by a steep staircase from below. Here he lived through the summers with his family. Walter Prichard Eaton refused to see discomfort in this type of life and compared O'Neill to Thoreau, who most certainly did not suffer in order to be happy. Mary Heaton Vorse, whose wharf first housed the commercial ventures of the Provincetown Players, noted that the collapse of the cottage, as she more appropriately called it, marked the end of a chapter, for it was here that O'Neill composed most of his early successes, beginning with *THE EMPEROR JONES*. The house was a shrine for friends, she said, who could always find a warm welcome.

This was the first of the many homes Eugene O'Neill chose for himself. In this isolation there was no sign of hardship and suffering, but a desire to be comfortable. He could have been the gay Bohemian in Greenwich Village, the personification of artiness in Washington Square, or the suave young idol of Broadway. He preferred the sand against his bedroom window, while the ghosts of the dead victims and the courageous heroes from the Coast Guard station walked in the night. It was the atmosphere of the true romanticist at heart.

❖   ❖   ❖   ❖   ❖   ❖

THE GREAT GOD BROWN, marking the turn from earlier disorder to the concentrated man-to-God thesis, also showed that the makeshift anti-romantic battlements had weakened. The romantic ideal could still destroy, and the dreamy, artistic, misunderstood Dion Anthony was defeated in a society which could find no place for him except as a prostituted talent sold under the name of William Brown. The real Dion, completely sublimated, died, while the Dion of the public eye continued in Billy Brown. O'Neill knew, however, that without romance and sentiment, without joy of living for its own sake, life was without meaning. Brown was subsequently destroyed by his inability to realize that Dion's inner romantic self had made the mask live and work in a hostile society where Dion's own commonplace, conventional wife could not recognize him. The anti-romantic, anti-sentimental society, bent on its own personal achievements in cash and architectural monuments, was destroying its few saving graces.

The strange perversions of Nina Leeds still fascinate students of drama who discuss *STRANGE INTERLUDE* as a tragedy, a psychopathic study, or the erotic biography of a nymphomaniac. Her fanatic idolizing of the dead Gordon, conceived in her mind as the perfect romantic image, prevented any normal life, and could easily be taken as a positive indication of the hideous destructive power of the romantic ideal. The fact is, however, that O'Neill once more denied his protagonist the privilege of fulfillment of a romantic dream. By allowing social taboos and moral teachings to keep Nina from her lover, and then by killing him, O'Neill sent Nina to her own destruction. Her distorted attempt to atone for her error by surrendering herself to nameless and numberless veterans in a hospital failed to remove her frustration, so she proceeded to marry without love and to undertake a purely "scientific" experiment in eugenics in an ironic attempt to maintain the front of a conventional happy home. The experiment succeeded, but with the sudden revival of a romantic impulse that she

had presumed completely dead, she was unable to cope with
the situation and brought ruin not only to herself, old and decaying at forty-five, but to her "three men" — husband, lover
and "father," all of whom, in their own ways, had been her
romantic slaves. We must presume that had Nina's love with
Gordon been consummated, illicitly or otherwise, things would
have been much different: for the better, because there was
little that could have been worse.

In *MOURNING BECOMES ELECTRA* the House of Man-
non began its frightful course downward as a result of an earlier
concept of romance with Marie Brantome. Likewise, Christine's
desire for the love of a dashing romantic sea captain caused
her personal downfall. Still, O'Neill held up the romantic ideal
as the human and preferable course of life. The "affair Brantome"
was illicit and destructive, but it was based on a kind of romantic attitude which the Mannons were incapable of expressing within their own narrow clan and which, by human nature
itself, they were forced to seek. Christine came to her marriage
bed wanting the tenderness of the romantic lovemaker. When
it was denied, the marriage was destroyed, *not* by her clandes-
tine affair with Adam Brant, but by the husband who sickened
her and who, much too late, sought to recover the ground he
had lost. Lavinia still had the way open and knew that obeying
the romantic call of the South Seas would save her. O'Neill
showed her the way, then took it from her as she called out
in romantic passion "Adam!" to unsuspecting, unromantic Peter
Niles. O'Neill let us know that without romance she could
not live.

In his last two plays before the twenty year eclipse O'Neill
suddenly, dramatically and without apology, surrendered to
the romantic ideal he had apparently fought for so many years.
At the time, the sudden reversal was surprising and shocking,
but in retrospect it appears more logical.

We have already discussed the surrender to conventional
religion which marked the romantic turn of *DAYS WITHOUT
END*. The other play, the successful *AH, WILDERNESS!*,
made a strong impression in its abrupt and complete change of
view and its clearly comic intent. Gilbert Gabriel felt it was
a comedy of recantation as well as recollection and hence very
pleasing. Richard Lockridge was glad to see that O'Neill was

"just plain folks" after all, and Brooks Atkinson was happy to see O'Neill on a level where he could talk to all of us. Others saw the play as O'Neill's own "personal revolution" affirming a new positive attitude toward life. Hope was expressed, however, that this "new" O'Neill did not become ordinary and conventional and permanently remove from the stage one of the most exciting reasons for going to the theatre. Joseph Wood Krutch was afraid that O'Neill would now be compared with other "sentimental" writers. It was difficult not to make this comparison, and the picture of a summer night in a small Connecticut town, screen doors flapping, lovers and parents happily embracing, nostalgic atmosphere everywhere, showed plainly enough that simple sentiment had replaced passion.

It is interesting, and somewhat disturbing, to observe how readily most writers leaped at this very ordinary play to prove that O'Neill was, after all, a human being. Regardless of the praise he had elicited for all his daring experiments of the past, and regardless of the welcome he received as the hewer of new paths, nobody had really understood him until he wrote, in six weeks time, a play which George Cohan himself could have done as easily. He was then welcomed as a member of the human race with all past sins forgiven.

*   *   *   *   *   *

After writing *DESIRE UNDER THE ELMS* and beginning *MARCO MILLIONS*, O'Neill moved to Bermuda in 1925, for about a three year stay. Here, far from the increasing madness of Coolidge prosperity, he sat on the sands near his spacious manor house, Spithead, and wrote of the laughter of a Dionysian Lazarus and the annihilating possessiveness of Nina. While Billy Brown was being destroyed and the artist Dion Anthony neglected, their creator lacked none of the comforts of life, in surroundings bearing no resemblance to the more primitive coziness of Peaked Hill Bars. Perhaps he gained a certain perspective for the plays he was writing, but he was beginning to move further away from the direct contact with his subject matter that any other writer of less strength would certainly have needed.

In December of 1928 O'Neill added further romance to

his own myth by attempting to travel incognito through the Orient. Further interest was supplied by rumors that it was part of a triangle involving a love affair with a beautiful actress and the impending divorce suit of his wife. Then in July 1929, after Agnes Boulton secured a Reno divorce and he married Carlotta Monterey, O'Neill took a thirteen year lease on the Chateau de Plessis in the south of France. It was an isolated spot, in spite of its size, reached only by considerable driving. It was perfect for the necessary quiet thinking as he labored on *MOURNING BECOMES ELECTRA*, but we learn that the man who struggled through the dunes of Cape Cod was to install a swimming pool, a roof garden and a gymnasium.

In 1933, from his home at Sea Island Beach, off the coast of Georgia, O'Neill sent the Theatre Guild his last two plays before the long silence. He had returned to America after less than three of the projected thirteen years in France. He was still adamant about his refusal to join the Broadway crowd, and found an obscure location in the small dot of land reached by causeway from the mainland. By so doing, he removed himself from the world more completely and was unable to regain the touch with reality and real people which he had shown in the plays from Provincetown, or even Bermuda and France. As the nation watched the quick and decisive, though at times bold and irregular, steps of the new administration and the Depression waters lapped at more and more households, the saccharine pleasantries of *AH, WILDERNESS!* and the religious sentiment of *DAYS WITHOUT END* bespoke much of O'Neill's permanent surrender.

"Judge the man's house and you judge him," wrote the anonymous commentator in *House and Garden* for January 1934, whose article, "O'Neill Goes Mildly Pirate," presented in text and excellent photography a report of O'Neill's Georgia home. What appeared was not a "shack" once inhabited by rugged Coastguardsmen. It was not even a chateau of centuries age. It had been constructed less than two years before, designed by its present owners. It sprawled among rustling palm trees, behind a sturdy stone wall, its ancient Cuban tile roof glistening. It could have been, in its isolation, a pirate lair, a den for smugglers, a hideout for spies and traitors. It was, instead, a private home, "a combination of the early Majorcan peasant-house of the 16th Century tinctured with a flavor of the 15th Century monastery." The outstanding exterior feature was a series of windows above the outside double door, boldly resembling the stern of a Spanish galleon. Through the entrance hall, past African wizard masks and Japanese No masks on the thick walls, and up the tiled stairs, the camera entered, to nobody's surprise, the kind of Captain's cabin which Sir Francis Drake might have occupied. The tilted bank of windows looked out onto the white-capped ocean beyond the spray-washed beach. Huge hand-adzed timbers formed the wall and ceiling supports, practically creaking with the roll of the ship that had seemingly been boarded. Nautical gadgets, a clock that rang ship's bells, a portion of a mast with marlin-spikes set 'round.

The name of this spot, so removed from all reality, so lost in romance of pirate seas? "Casa Genotta" — the Castle of Gene and Carlotta. The essence of romance.

In less than five years, O'Neill departed from Sea Island to gain more "atmosphere" in the Pacific Northwest for his projected multi-play cycle. He became enthusiastic about California and the Far West and decided to remain there. He finally built a Chinese-style mansion called Tao House in Contra Costa County, California. There were continual reports of plays almost ready. He told Barrett Clark in 1941 that he had finished two plays outside the cycle, was still enthusiastic about the whole idea, but preferred to wait until sanity returned to the world. By 1943 A MOON FOR THE MISBEGOTTEN was complete and A TOUCH OF THE POET rewritten. He mentioned a cycle of eight one-act plays and said that LONG DAY'S JOURNEY INTO NIGHT and THE ICEMAN COMETH were the best he had ever done. There was also a shortened version of LAZARUS LAUGHED which he hoped to see produced in college theatres. He consistently refused, nevertheless, to take interest in the production of any of the plays, and it was not long until the press was almost completely uninterested. From 1940 to 1945 there was virtually nothing about him.

❖   ❖   ❖   ❖   ❖   ❖

When THE ICEMAN COMETH at last appeared in 1946, what did it have to say? On the surface it said something about

pipe dreams, and it said it many times. It presented something
of the old O'Neill power and sincerity which could not be
evaded. Critics often remarked on its thematic resemblance to
Gorki's *The Lower Depths* or Ibsen's *The Wild Duck.* The romantic ideal brought destruction here, too, but the actual death
in this case came to an innocent party, Hickey's Ellen, who,
loving, believing, faithful, had to be destroyed through no
fault except her own perfect goodness. She, certainly, was the
unseen tragic heroine. Hickey's revelation was terrifying, piti-
ful and revolting, but the play still said one important thing:
mankind cannot live without a certain kind of romantic idealism.
Although it killed Ellen, it also demonstrated that up to her
death she could not have lived without it, for her own life
would have been destroyed with the admission of the realities
of Hickey's faithlessness and debauchery. She had the biggest
pipe dream of all; it both sustained and killed her. And yet,
living is impossible without these dreams; death is the only
logical result if we lose them. The derelicts who returned to
their booze in Harry's bar were deliriously happy that reality
had passed them by in what they could dismiss as a crazy
phase of Hickey's last hours. No more did they need to face
the reality that would soon kill them all. O'Neill said all this
long ago, and, it appeared at the time, better and more skilfully.

Eric Bentley, reviewing *A MOON FOR THE MISBEGOT-
TEN* in the *New Republic,* found that the play would do little
to change anybody's view, as it was neither O'Neill's best nor
worst. He thought it was better than some recent plays, which
was so much the worse for recent plays. Opinions from others,
as we know, were not enthusiastic. The play was an almost
complete surrender to the romantic ideal in the grotesque
creation of Josie, the giant virgin. Her virginity was great, and it
was powerful, as she herself was a great and powerful good
woman. She could redeem, madonna-like, the sins and sufferings
of little, insignificant, snivelling mankind who slept, as in death,
on her great bosom all night through. The morning had to be
beautiful to wake him, said Josie to her astonished father, and
she waited for the proper instant before she roused Tyrone
from his innocent sleep. The message of *A MOON FOR THE
MISBEGOTTEN* was neither that of *THE GREAT GOD
BROWN* nor of *DAYS WITHOUT END,* and at the same time

it had neither the dramatic quality of one or the sectarian attraction of the other. Perhaps, like Anna Christie, Josie, giant that she was, was just a "poor nut," and maybe her life, too, was just part of the strange interlude in the electrical display of God the Father. To have returned with vigor and new energy to the theatre after the very-near nihilistic message of *THE ICEMAN COMETH*, O'Neill would have had to come forth with more than the limited appeal and message of *A MOON FOR THE MISBEGOTTEN*.

Now, seven years beyond his death, the possibility of recouping much of O'Neill's reputation from the past and establishing his plays as permanent, important parts of our national dramatic literature is distinctly possible. While the "romantic surrender" seemed to reduce the forceful impact of O'Neill's pen during the last years of his creative life, causing head-shaking doubts among the critics who viewed the output, it may well be that it has been the saving grace which will now, and in the future, give universal appeal to the plays. Faced with the possibility of the annihilation of society in the miscalculations that could bring a final global war, and witnessing on all sides the writers who see mankind awash in a senseless world of sickness, perversion and vast meaninglessness, we can turn to the plays of Eugene O'Neill and find a far different outlook. Here is tragedy written, as Joseph Wood Krutch has often said, with a capital T, and the world it portrays is not a happy one. But because of O'Neill's continual faith in mankind and his realization that he must maintain the romantic ideal to survive with any dignity at all, the plays avoid the blank outlook of so many who view our day as an empty space. O'Neill's characters are not perverse; they are not "sick." They are, to be sure, deluded and disillusioned. They can become obnoxious and bullying, or pitifully decayed. They are not, however, depraved. Their tragedy is their inability to maintain their romantic dreams in the face of a world unsympathetic to them.

O'Neill's permanence will not rest upon the complete surrender to the romantic sentimentalities of a bad play like *DAYS WITHOUT END*. It will not possibly survive upon the trappings of the suffocatingly lush *THE FOUNTAIN* or, for that matter, the exotic *MARCO MILLIONS*. It probably will not rely heavily upon Nina's distortions of romantic love in *STRANGE INTERLUDE*, nor upon Josie's freakish virginity. The hopeful message that does survive is that somewhere the human life must have the romantic outlook upon which to draw strength, or face the entombment of a tragic heroine like Lavinia Mannon, or the spiritual death of Cornelius Melody, whose beautiful mare lies slaughtered along with his dreams. Somewhere there must be a meeting, a compromise between, the qualities of Dion Anthony and Billy Brown, both of whom die under the sympathetic, comprehending eye of the prostitute Cybel, who can see them as the suffering individuals they are.

The "practical" Melody of *A TOUCH OF THE POET* is an empty man, just as the inhabitants of Harry Hope's bar are hollow men revealed for what they truly are when they face up to reality. Edmund Tyrone of *LONG DAY'S JOURNEY* can best survive when he leaves the sordid quarrels of family behind, realizing he should have been created a bird, capable of soaring into a romantic world far above this one. These are not depressing, discouraging, nor disgusting men, for this was not O'Neill's purpose in creating them. They, and others of the plays that see the need for the romantic, and ponder its position in the world that men have created for themselves, may enable Eugene O'Neill to achieve the permanence and the esteem that he at one time seemed so near to grasping, but which, while he lived, continually avoided him.

A CHRONOLOGY OF THE LIFE OF EUGENE O'NEILL

This is a composite from many sources, because no single reference can supply all the information we would like to have. O'Neill strongly preferred to keep all details hazy and vague so that they could offer protection, "like a mask," to the personal life which he steadfastly maintained was his own business.

Most of the source material, therefore, is discouragingly indefinite. Hamilton Basso's *New Yorker* profile, "The Tragic Sense," of 1948 (No. 170) contributes a substantial quantity of information about the early years, and Barrett Clark's *Man and His Plays* series (No. 21) has been helpful. Agnes Boulton's *Part of a Long Story*, 1958 (No. 7) and Croswell Bowen's *The Curse of the Misbegotten*, 1959 (No. 8) are the latest and most completely detailed sources, but even they, especially Miss Boulton's account of the early years of her marriage, are frequently distressingly imprecise.

It is, none the less, possible to gather a substantial amount of interesting information that can supply a significant outline of the events in the life of this individual who remained, while living and in many ways after death, a fascinating enigma.

16 Oct. 1888.   Born on third floor of Barrett House, Times Square, New York. (Site now marked by bronze plaque on corner of 43rd and Broadway.) Father: Irish-born James O'Neill, born 1846, Thomastown, Kilkenny County, famous throughout America in title role of *Count of Monte Cristo*. Mother: Ellen (or Ella) Quinlan O'Neill, quiet, beautiful, artistic, born in New Haven, Conn., 1857, convent-bred in South Bend, Indiana.

1888-1895.   Traveled with parents on road tours to important cities all over the United States. Until age seven, under care of Scotch nurse who regaled him with tales of murder and terror.

1896-1900.   Attended   Mount   St.   Vincent-on-Hudson

boarding school, Riverdale, New York, operated by Sisters of Charity.

1900-1902.   Attended De La Salle Military Institute, New York, as day student and boarder.

Sept. 1902-June 1906.   Attended and graduated from Betts Academy, Stamford, Conn. (no longer in existence), considered one of better preparatory schools. Summers spent with family at New London, Conn., home, on Pequot Ave.

Sept. 1906.   Entered Princeton as freshman, class of 1910.

Spring 1907.   Sometime after two week suspension (and subsequent reinstatement) voluntarily left Princeton without completing first year's requirements. Cause of discipline, according to Bowen, was breaking glass insulators on telegraph poles along trolley line from Trenton. O'Neill's own tale of throwing bottle through Pres. Wilson's window later firmly denied. Whole episode has reached minor legendary proportions, may never be accurately explained.

1907-1908.   Lived on West 58th Street, New York, in apartment with Frank Best. Became "secretary to the president" of the New York-Chicago Supply Co., third-rate mail order house dealing in cheap jewelry, in which James O'Neill had financial interest. Meanwhile "did the town" with brother James, ten years his senior, and eager tutor in ways of the worldly.

Summer 1909.   Introduced by Frank Best to beautiful Kathleen Jenkins, non-Catholic, daughter of once wealthy New York family. Impulsively married in Hoboken, New Jersey, they lived together only a few days. (One source indicates marriage was compulsory.) Both families violently disapproved. (Bowen speaks only of Mrs. Jenkins, divorced, but Boulton, quoting O'Neill, continually speaks of "her parents.")

Oct. 1909.   Soon after 21st birthday, upon arrangement (virtually an order) by father, hoping to break up marriage, departed with Earl C. Stevens on gold prospecting tour to

Honduras. Contracted malaria, found no gold. Boulton reports return home in "three or four months"; Bowen says six.

5 May 1910. Birth of son, Eugene Gladstone, Jr. Father and son did not meet until after child's eleventh birthday. One story, perhaps apocryphal, relates O'Neill did see him some weeks after birth at Kathleen's home.

Summer 1910. Became assistant stage manager of father's road company, *The White Sister.* Toured three months, St. Louis to Boston. Main task was to watch ticket takers to prevent unauthorized admissions.

Fall 1910-Summer 1911. Refusing to remain with father's acting company, shipped from Boston on Norwegian square-rigged barque, among last of active sailing vessels. After voyage of 65-85 days (reports disagree) jumped ship in Buenos Aires, took jobs with Westinghouse posing as draftsman, Swift and Company sorting hides, and Singer Sewing Machine as salesman. Was fired by (or quit) each in succession within a matter of weeks. Subsequently shipped as seaman on cattle boat to Durban, South Africa, returning to South America and living nearly destitute along waterfront. Later admitted that at one time he almost turned to robbery for money to live on.

Fall 1911. Returned to New York as ordinary seaman aboard British tramp steamer, from which came many ideas for *Glencairn* cycle and other sea plays.

Dec. 1911. Consented to give Kathleen divorce on grounds of adultery.

Winter 1911-1912. Lived in destitution (room rent, $3.00 a month) at Jimmy the Priest's waterfront dive, New York, surviving on whisky, free lunch, and allowances from father. Life here was later reflected in *ANNA CHRISTIE* and *ICEMAN.* Sometime during this period apparently attempted suicide with veronal but saved by quick action of friends and insufficient dosage. Bowen, quoting others, says summer of 1910, soon after seeing infant son. Boulton, quoting O'Neill, reports "a year or so later" after return from Honduras. Kenneth Macgowan reinforces this version; both state suicide attempt was caused by distress over marriage difficulties.

Spring and Summer 1912. Shipped as able seaman to Liverpool and back. Wages $27.50 a month. After wild New York party, took train to New Orleans and encountered father's *Monte Cristo* company. Joined and toured 15 weeks through Far West. Acting ability condemned by father and himself.

Aug. 1912. Lived with family at New London summer home. Worked short while (variously reported from four to six months) as cub reporter on *The Telegraph* under Judge Frederick P. Latimer, who first felt O'Neill had talent. (Bowen says work began in May, which does not account for time spent on ship or with *Monte Cristo* company.) Ran column of poetry, often maintained by his own contributions, 24 of which were signed by various cryptic pseudonyms. Contributed limited number of verses to left wing New York *Call, The Masses,* and Franklin P. Adams' "Conning Tower." Main interest was swimming and boating, rather than journalism. Apparently courted several "nice" girls in town, including anonymous young lady who appears later as Muriel in *AH, WILDERNESS!*

11 Oct. 1912. Final divorce decree from Kathleen Jenkins on grounds of adultery. No alimony sought or received; support of child left entirely to the mother.

1 Nov. 1912. Ill health compelled resignation from *Telegraph.*

24 Dec. 1912. Health broken, entered Gaylord Farm tuberculosis sanitorium, Wallingford, Conn. While a patient began serious interest in reading plays, especially Strindberg. (*THE STRAW* is based directly on experiences as patient.)

24 May 1913. Discharged as an arrested case.

Summer-Winter 1913-1914. Lived 15-16 months at Mrs. Rippin's New London boarding house overlooking Long Island

Sound. Became expert swimmer while health mended completely. Began serious playwriting. Rippin daughters typed and mailed plays regularly to New York producers who never produced them. *THE WEB* apparently the first, followed by eleven short plays and two longer ones. Most have been destroyed, although a few survive in *Lost Plays of Eugene O'Neill*, 1950 (see Chronology of Publication).

Spring 1914. Wrote *BOUND EAST FOR CARDIFF*, to be his first produced play.

16 July 1914. At urging of Clayton Hamilton, critic, author, family friend, applied for admittance to George Pierce Baker's English 47, Dramatic Composition, at Harvard, stating avowed purpose of becoming "an artist or nothing."

Aug. 1914. The Gorham Press, Boston, published *THIRST and Other One Act Plays* at personal expense ($1000) of James O'Neill. Book had no success whatever, is now valuable collector's item. O'Neill later disowned it, prevented its reissue during lifetime. Hamilton, who had insisted it be published, was the only critic to review it (No. 1726).

Sept. 1914-May 1915. Attended Baker's class. Was known by classmates, all younger and less experienced in worldly matters, as nervous, shy, reserved, restless.

Summer 1915. Took room at 38 Washington Square West, Greenwich Village, and began to be a "regular" at John Wallace's Golden Swan bar, popularly known as "The Hell Hole" and immortalized in *THE ICEMAN COMETH*. Return visit to New London ended romance with "Muriel."

Winter 1915-1916. On income ($10 weekly) supplied by father, lived at Hell Hole. Became friend of political radicals, I.W.W.'s, and gang of underworld characters known as Hudson Dusters, many of whom he could drink under the table. Never became a member of any one group, but was always welcomed as fine drinking companion, entertaining all comers with memorized renditions of Francis Thompson's "The Hound of Heaven."

Had little actual contact with typical struggling artists and writers of the Village. Although his alcoholic sprees were wild and could last for days, most evidence proves what Boulton says later: all drinking stopped completely whenever work was undertaken. Did not write anything while intoxicated, and never took drugs of any kind.

Summer 1916. Resided in friend's shack in Provincetown, Mass., haven for artists and not yet popular tourist attraction. Continued to write short plays. Newly formed Provincetown Players, headed by George Cram Cook and wife, Susan Glaspell, auditioned *BOUND EAST FOR CARDIFF*. Production undertaken in Mary Heaton Vorse's 50 x 100 ft. Wharf Playhouse, where success was immediate.

Fall 1916. Lived over John Francis' Provincetown store, continually writing short plays. Favorite writing position was in bed. One story relates he affixed a sign on his door stating bluntly: "Go to hell."

Nov. 1916. First bills by Provincetown Players at Playwrights' Theatre, converted brownstone house, 139 Macdougal Street, Greenwich Village. *BOUND EAST FOR CARDIFF*, *BEFORE BREAKFAST, FOG* and *THE SNIPER* all produced. No apparent evidence that any New York newspapers reviewed any of O'Neill's plays.

10 Dec. 1916. In the earliest known newspaper reference, New York *World* reported "the son of James O'Neill" had been involved with a group of Provincetowners somehow connected with the "flight" of Richard Mansfield, Jr. Details remain obscure.

29 Mar. 1917. Arrested in Provincetown with friend Harold De Polo, on suspicions of vagrancy. Released without charge, although for some time thereafter, because of habit of roaming Provincetown sands, was carefully observed by authorities on suspicion of wartime "spying."

Summer 1917. Turned down by Navy, claimed Army

exemption as arrested tubercular case. Returned to Provincetown and wrote short story, apparently destroyed, forming
nucleus of later play *THE HAIRY APE*.

June 1917. "Tomorrow," his only published short story,
appeared in *The Seven Arts*. Contained elements later found in
ICEMAN. Received first important royalties: $50.00.

Oct. 1917. *THE LONG VOYAGE HOME* appeared in
The Smart Set, the first publication of a play outside *Thirst*.
Royalties: $75.00. Met Agnes Boulton, handsome 24-year old
widow, author of short stories and pulp fiction, from Connecticut.

Winter 1917-1918. *THE LONG VOYAGE HOME* and
ILE produced at Playwrights' Theatre, now in converted stable,
133 Macdougal St. *IN THE ZONE*, first O'Neill play to be presented by Washington Square Players, reviewed by major newspaper critics. Although an active contributor to Provincetown
productions, still preferred Hell Hole gang. Returned to
Provincetown; lived with Agnes Boulton in rented studio. Income still provided by father's allowance.

12 Apr. 1918. Married Agnes Boulton in Provincetown.

Spring 1918. First steady and substantial income from
IN THE ZONE, sold as vaudeville piece for $50.00 per week.
Producer John D. Williams took six-month option on first full-
length play, *BEYOND THE HORIZON*.

Summer 1918. Lived in flat over a Provincetown store,
writing more one-act plays and first drafts of *CHRIS*, the original *ANNA CHRISTIE*. Brother James a permanent house guest.

Nov. 1918. Returned to New York for rehearsals. First
meeting between Agnes and elder O'Neills at Prince George
Hotel.

Winter 1918-1919. Resided at Agnes' former home, Old
House, West Point Pleasant, New Jersey, within easy commuting
distance of New York. Wrote *CHRIS* and *THE STRAW*.

May 1919. Boni and Liveright published first important play collection, *THE MOON OF THE CARIBBEES and Six Other Plays of the Sea*. First meeting with George Jean Nathan, then editor on *The Smart Set*, who had arranged for first publication of *LONG VOYAGE HOME*. Their acquaintance became permament close friendship.

Summer 1919. Moved into remodeled former Coast Guard station on Peaked Hill Bars, Provincetown, purchased by James O'Neill and given to his son and family as a gift. House so remote from town could be reached only on foot or horseback over dunes.

30 Oct. 1919. Birth of son, Shane, in Provincetown.

2 Feb. 1920. John D. Williams produced *BEYOND THE HORIZON* at Morosco Theatre. First shown at special matinees; eventually given permament run of 111 performances. Only one of his son's plays that James O'Neill ever saw. Disapproved of its serious realism.

June 1920. Pulitzer Prize awarded to *BEYOND THE HORIZON*.

10 Aug. 1920. Death of James O'Neill after long period of decline. Left estate of $165,000.

Fall-Spring 1920-1921. Resided at Peaked Hill Bars and in rented Provincetown house during bad weather, writing *EMPEROR JONES* and other long plays. Despite success of *HORIZON*, family remained in close financial straits.

3 Nov. 1920. Opening at Playwrights' Theatre of *EMPEROR JONES* to much acclaim.

Fall and Winter 1921-1922. Lived in New York during rehearsals of *ANNA CHRISTIE*, which opened 2 Nov. 1921. Returned to Provincetown to write *HAIRY APE*. In early 1922 met Eugene, Jr., nearly 12, only recently informed of his true parentage. O'Neill immediately took over cost of his private school education.

28 Feb. 1922. Death of Ellen Quinlan O'Neill in Los Angeles, where she and James, Jr., had gone to sell certain properties. Left estate approximately $112,000. Her death and James' drunken return to New London with the body form basis of *MOON FOR THE MISBEGOTTEN.*

May 1922. Pulitzer Prize awarded to *ANNA CHRISTIE.* Weekly royalties (about $850 according to Bowen) permanently removed all financial difficulties.

Fall 1922. Purchased Brook Farm, Ridgefield, Conn., as winter home. Peaked Hill Bars still used as summer home.

Winter 1922-1923. Breakup of original Provincetown group. O'Neill with Robert Edmond Jones and Kenneth Macgowan organized The Greenwich Village Theatre.

Feb. 1923. Elected to National Institute of Arts & Letters and awarded gold medal for drama.

8 Nov. 1923. Death of brother James at age 45. Left estate over $73,000.

March-May 1924. First encounter with the law in censorship difficulties with *ALL GOD'S CHILLUN.* New York Mayor Hylan, trying to prevent production of drama of miscegenation, forbade use of children in opening scene, on grounds they were too young. Play opened, without children and without difficulty, on 15 May.

Dec. 1924. Moved to Campsea, Paget West, Bermuda. Worked on *GREAT GOD BROWN.*

Feb.-Mar. 1925. *DESIRE UNDER THE ELMS,* accused of "obscenity," cleared by New York "play jury."

13 May 1925. Daughter, Oona, born at Campsea.

Summer-Fall 1925. Family moved to Nantucket Island, Mass. Barrett H. Clark received permission to write first of his biographies (No. 21).

Dec. 1925. O'Neill listed as contributing editor, along with Carl Sandburg, Maxwell Anderson, and others, to *The New Masses*, radical left-wing magazine supporting international labor movement.

Winter 1925. Rented Bellevue, large mansion in Bermuda, while negotiating for purchase of 19th century 13-acre estate, Spithead. Worked on *STRANGE INTERLUDE*.

Feb.-Apr. 1926. Cast of Los Angeles production of *DESIRE UNDER THE ELMS* arrested for presenting obscene play. Brought to trial, cast produced play in court and trial ended with hung jury. Case dropped; play continued.

23 June 1926. Awarded honorary Litt. D. from Yale at annual commencement.

Summer 1926. Resided with family at Belgrade Lakes, Maine. Acquaintance begun with Carlotta Monterey, who had appeared in a production of *HAIRY APE*.

Fall and Winter 1926-1927. Resided at Brook Farm, then returned to Spithead, Bermuda, completing *STRANGE INTERLUDE*. Left family to attend rehearsals of *MARCO MILLIONS* and *INTERLUDE* and never returned. Resumed acquaintance with Carlotta Monterey.

30 Jan. 1928. Opening of *STRANGE INTERLUDE*.

Feb. 1928. Left for Europe on 3-year exile from United States.

May 1928. Pulitzer Prize awarded to *STRANGE INTERLUDE*.

Sept. 1928. Eugene, Jr., entered Yale as freshman, class of 1932.

Oct.-Dec. 1928. Embarked on a "round the world trip." Reasons obscure, but probably based on decision to leave family for Miss Monterey. Details of entire venture are garbled. Clippings from New York *Times* and other sources tell of serious but undefined illness in Shanghai and certain unsuccessful attempts at disguise. Did not return to Europe until January.

Jan. 1929. Took up residence at Villa Mimosa, Cap d'Ail, France.

May 1929. Sued by Georges Lewys (Gladys Adelina Lewis) for plagiarism of her novel *The Temple of Pallas Athene* in *STRANGE INTERLUDE*.

2 July 1929. Agnes Boulton granted Reno divorce on grounds of desertion; terms of settlement kept secret.

22 July 1929. Married Carlotta Monterey.

27 July 1929-May 1931. Resided at Chateau de Plessis, Sainte Antoine du Roches, France, under 13-year lease. Completed *MOURNING BECOMES ELECTRA*.

16 Sept. 1929. *STRANGE INTERLUDE* banned in Boston; played to packed houses in nearby Quincy.

6 Jan. 1931. Peaked Hill Bars home destroyed in Cape Cod storm.

Apr. 1931. Plagiarism suit dismissed as "preposterous." Georges Lewys ordered to pay costs of $17,500.

17 May 1931. Left France permanently; returned to New York.

Summer 1931. Resided at Northport, Long Island.

26 Oct. 1931. Opening of *MOURNING BECOMES ELECTRA*, last of the great tragedies before 12-year semi-retirement.

14 Nov. 1931. In special ceremonies at Yale, bust executed by Edmond Quinn presented to Department of Drama.

Winter 1931-1932.   Resided in Park Avenue apartment.

June 1932.   Eugene, Jr., graduated from Yale, winner of three important prizes in classical scholarship. Married a year, received teaching appointment at Yale and started work on PhD.

Summer 1932-Fall 1936.   Lived in Casa Genotta (the Castle of Gene and Carlotta) built to specifications on Sea Island, Georgia. Noted for its study, built to resemble sailing ship captain's study. Here wrote *DAYS WITHOUT END* and *AH, WILDERNESS!* Overwork brought on near-breakdown in 1934, which compelled several months' rest.

Sept. 1932.   Announced as editor of *The American Spectator,* along with Theodore Dreiser, George Jean Nathan, James Branch Cabell. Eventually wrote three articles (see Non-Dramatic O'Neill) before *Spectator* folded.

19 Sept. 1932.   Made associate member of Irish Academy of Letters.

9 Nov. 1933. Elected member of American Academy of Arts and Letters.

8 Jan. 1934.   *DAYS WITHOUT END* opened in New York, last play to appear on stage until 1946.

Fall 1934.   Shane entered Florida Military Academy, St. Petersburg, which he attended four years.

3 Nov. 1936.   Having put Casa Genotta up for sale, arrived in Seattle, Wash.; rented house on Puget Sound. Hoped to get material for proposed play cycle, *A TALE OF POSSESSORS SELF-DISPOSSESSED.*

Nov. 1936.   Awarded Nobel Prize for Literature.

Dec. 1936.   To avoid further public contact over Nobel Prize, fled to San Francisco.

26 Dec. 1936. Appendicitis operation in Oakland. While a hospital patient, received Nobel Prize from representative of Swedish government.

28 Jan. 1937. Casa Genotta sold.

Dec. 1937-Dec. 1943. Lived in Tao House, Chinese-style mansion built to specifications, on 158-acre estate in Contra Costa County, California. Completed last plays, *ICE-MAN, LONG DAY'S JOURNEY, MOON FOR THE MISBE-GOTTEN, TOUCH OF THE POET*. Began other parts of *A TALE OF POSSESSORS*.

Dec. 1941-Fall 1943. Shane enlisted and served in American merchant marine.

Spring 1942. Oona graduated from exclusive Brearly girls' school. Named New York Debutante of the Year, 1942-1943. Moved as popular member of young society.

16 July 1943. Marriage of Oona to famed film comedian Charlie Chaplin, his fourth wife. Her age, 18; his, same as O'Neill, 54. Her mother, according to New York *Times,* was very pleased. O'Neill never forgave her and eventually disinherited her, along with Shane, and all their issue.

Jan. 1944. Tao House sold, moved to Nob Hill apartment, San Francisco.

1944-1945. Suffered permanently injurious paralytic stroke. Eugene, Jr., having left Yale, now in radio in Hartford, Conn. Shane in Greenwich Village, still without steady employment, drifting toward drug addiction.

31 July 1944. Marriage of Shane to Cathy Givens, Norwalk, Conn.

Oct. 1945. Moved to New York from San Francisco, living in various hotels and apartments.

19 Nov. 1945.   Birth of Eugene O'Neill, III, to Shane and Cathy O'Neill. Died in infancy, February, from "accidental suffocation."

Spring 1946-Spring 1948.   Lived in remodeled New York apartment on East 84th, former home of playwright Edward Sheldon.

June 1946.   Before opening of *ICEMAN* held first and only press conference in offices of Theatre Guild.

9 Oct. 1946.   Opening of *THE ICEMAN COMETH*, final play to be presented in New York during lifetime.

20 Feb. 1947.   Opening of *A MOON FOR THE MISBEGOTTEN* in Columbus, Ohio, last play to open anywhere during lifetime. Tryout tour abandoned; play never entered New York.

1947.   Resided in New York; ill health prevented any further writing.

28 Jan. 1948.   Slipped and broke an arm in New York apartment; became patient in Doctors' Hospital.

Apr. 1948.   Left New York for Boston, for treatment in Lahey Clinic.

10 Aug. 1948.   Shane arrested for possession of heroin.

23 Aug. 1948.   At suggestion of Judge Harold Medina, Shane sent to Lexington hospital for treatment of drug addiction.

Summer 1948.   Moved to Marblehead, Mass., and purchased shore home. Joined Euthanasia Society of America, eventually became member of its American Advisory Council.

1948-1950.   Although health seemed improved, unable to work consistently. Lived in virtual seclusion in Marblehead.

25 Sept. 1950. Eugene, Jr., committed suicide, Wood-stock, New Jersey, after many marital difficulties and unsuccessful life as classics teacher at Yale and Princeton, lecturer, television panelist, and stage actor. Death a profound shock to O'Neill.

1 Feb. 1951. "Cruel and abusive treatment" charged by Carlotta Monterey O'Neill.

5 Feb. 1951. Admitted to Salem, Mass., hospital with broken right knee. Wife admitted to McLean Hospital, Belmont, Mass., after breakdown.

Mar. 1951. Signed petition stating wife unable to take care of herself.

31 Mar. 1951. Arrived at Doctors' Hospital, New York, for further treatment of knee.

Apr. 1951. Charges and counter-charges dropped; reconciled with wife.

May 1951-Nov. 1953. Left New York, disposed of Marblehead home, and moved to Hotel Shelton, Boston. During this period destroyed most of remaining plays or portions of plays and virtually all of proposed *DISPOSSESSED* cycle. Treated for brief while in 1951 in Boston hospital for severe nervous trembling.

27 Nov. 1953. Died in Boston. Official cause: bronchial pneumonia. Age: just past 65.

2 Dec. 1953. Interred in Forest Hills Cemetery, Boston.

CHRONOLOGY OF COMPOSITION, COPYRIGHT AND DOMESTIC PUBLICATION

This is a chronological list of all important facts relating to the composition, copyright, or publication of various editions of all of O'Neill's plays. It does not, however, include those published in general anthologies.

Few people realize the great number of apprentice works which O'Neill poured into the Copyright Office and never published, or which he wrote but never copyrighted. The unauthorized publication of *Lost Plays* by New Fathoms Press in 1950 called brief atention to a few of these early plays. O'Neill himself thought he had destroyed them, and never wished them to be made public. If we are to judge the quality of those destroyed by the appearance of those which New Fathoms resurrected, we can say that their loss was of minor consequence to American drama.

Sources for this Part are varied. The primary text is Sanborn and Clark's *Bibliography of the Works of Eugene O'Neill*, published in 1931 (No. 115), which is the only detailed collation of O'Neill's plays. The second source is the U.S. Copyright List of the Government Printing Office. The Greenwich Theatre Playbill No. 3, Season 1925-1926 for *THE FOUNTAIN*, contains a list of all the plays noted below as destroyed. Other source material is indicated where appropriate.

The Chronology is arranged in the following pattern:

1. Title of play in *ITALIC CAPITAL LETTERS*. In a few cases the play may comprise part of a more complete book title and will appear in this fashion: *MOON OF THE CARIBBEES and Six Other Plays of the Sea*.

2. Pertinent information concerning the play. Those plays which O'Neill copyrighted but never published, or those that he copyrighted himself before they were published, are described by information from the copyright record, including number of acts, type of play, and number of pages. Plays never copyrighted and known or presumed to be destroyed are listed

with whatever information is available. Publication data, including city, publisher, and date, are shown if known.

3.   Other information of interest.

4.   Entry number in Sanborn and Clark's *Bibliography*. (This information is occasionally included in the material under 2 and 3 above.)

All entries are as close as practicable to actual chronology.

1913

WIFE FOR A LIFE
One act. Typewritten; copyrighted 15 Aug.

The earliest recorded O'Neill play, although *THE WEB* is often considered his first play. Contents remained unknown until the publication of *Lost Plays*.

1914

BREAD AND BUTTER
Four acts. Typewritten; copyrighted 2 May.

CHILDREN OF THE SEA
One act; 13 pages. Typewritten; copyrighted 14 May.

ABORTION
One act. Typewritten; copyrighted 19 May.

Apparently O'Neill worked on this play in Baker's 47 Workshop at Harvard, because it is mentioned in some of the published reminiscences of his classmates. Contents unknown until publication of *Lost Plays*.

THE MOVIE MAN
One act comedy; 11 pages. Typewritten; copyrighted 1 July. Later published in *Lost Plays*.

THIRST and Other One Act Plays
Boston, Gorham Press, August 1914. Published as part of "American Dramatists Series."

This is O'Neill's first published book, an issue of 1000 copies which, during his lifetime, he insisted would never be republished. It fell almost stillborn from the press; today it commands a high price as a collector's item, available only in large libraries. The entire project was financed by O'Neill's father.

Contents: *FOG, RECKLESSNESS, THIRST, THE WEB, WARNINGS.* None of these plays have been found under any other copyright date. Their date of composition is uncertain. *THE WEB* is often considered the first play O'Neill ever wrote, probably very close to *WIFE FOR A LIFE.*

Sanborn and Clark, No. 4.

SERVITUDE

Three acts. Typewritten; copyrighted 23 Sept. Eventually published in *Lost Plays.*

BOUND EAST FOR CARDIFF

O'Neill says this was written before he attended Harvard, and various authorities place its writing as spring of 1914. It was apparently first copyrighted in Frank Shay's first series of *The Provincetown Plays,* 1916.

1915

THE SNIPER

One act. Typewritten; copyrighted 13 May.

BELSHAZZAR

Six scenes, biblical. Never copyrighted; destroyed.

A KNOCK AT THE DOOR

One act, comedy. Never copyrighted; destroyed.

THE PERSONAL EQUATION

Four acts. Never copyrighted; destroyed.

Begun in Prof. Baker's Harvard 47 Workshop as *THE SECOND ENGINEER.* Deutsch and Hanau (No. 29) refer to a reading which O'Neill gave of the first act before the Provincetown group, but it was never considered for production.

*From this point forward, this Chronology will list the
dates of copyright or composition of those plays known
either to have been destroyed or omitted from publication. Other plays will be listed by publication (or copyright, if different) date and no attempt will be made to
place them in their year of composition. O'Neill spent
many months, and even years, on his later plays, so
the attempt to pinpoint the writing would be un-
rewarding.*

1916

BOUND EAST FOR CARDIFF
In *The Provincetown Plays,* First Series, edited by Frank
Shay, N.Y., November, 1916.
This volume contains the first published version of a major
O'Neill play. 1200 copies were printed, mainly for friends and
patrons of the Playwrights' Theatre. Some were sold at the
door during intermissions. The book is not as rare as *THIRST,*
etc., and can be found in many libraries.
Sanborn and Clark, No. 6.

BEFORE BREAKFAST
In *The Provincetown Plays,* Third Series, edited by Frank
Shay, N.Y., December, 1916.
The first printing was 500 copies and others were made
later without Shay's editing.
Sanborn and Clark, No. 7.

BEFORE BREAKFAST
New York, Frank Shay, December, 1916.
Prepared from the original text and type of the Province-
town Third Series above. A rare volume; available in Special
Collections, Butler Library, Columbia, and in American Litera-
ture Collection, Sterling Library, Yale.
Sanborn and Clark, No. 8.

ATROCITY
One act; pantomime. Never copyrighted; destroyed.

THE G.A.N. (Also reported as THE G.A.M.)
One act; farce-comedy. Never copyrighted; destroyed.
Greenwich Village Playbill dates it 1916; Kenneth Mac-
gowan in *Vanity Fair*, April 1922, dates it 1917.

1917

NOW I ASK YOU
Three acts, prologue and epilogue; 98 pages. Typewritten;
copyrighted 23 May.

THE LONG VOYAGE HOME
In *The Smart Set*, 53 (October 1917) 83-94.
H. L. Mencken and George Jean Nathan were among the
very first to recognize O'Neill's importance. O'Neill was extremely grateful to them for their assistance and criticism, and
in a letter to Nathan expressed his surprise and pleasure at the
publication particularly because he had submitted them only
for comment. This is the first appearance of one of O'Neill's
plays in a periodical.
Sanborn and Clark, No. 11.

1918

ILE
In *The Smart Set*, 55 (May 1918) 89-100. Sanborn and
Clark, No. 12. Also issued in printed wrappers extracted from
Smart Set, as part of the Flying Stag plays for the little theatre.

BEYOND THE HORIZON
Three acts; 128 pages. Typewritten; copyrighted 7 June.
Three acts; 121 pages. Typewritten; copyrighted 5 Aug.

THE MOON OF THE CARIBBEES
In *The Smart Set*, 55 (Aug. 1918) 73-86.
Sanborn and Clark, No. 13.

TILL WE MEET
One act. Never copyrighted; destroyed

1919

CHRIS CHRISTOPHERSON
Three acts, six scenes; 111 pages. Typewritten; copyrighted 5 June.

This play appeared on the stage in 1920 as *CHRIS* in an unsuccessful tryout run in Atlantic City and Philadelphia. After its withdrawal and rewriting, it emerged as *ANNA CHRISTIE*. It never appeared in print in either of its "Chris" forms, and is not included in the Sanborn and Clark bibliography.

MOON OF THE CARIBBEES and Six Other Plays of the Sea
New York, Boni and Liveright, June 1919.

It is No. 14 in Sanborn and Clark which notes differences in various printings. The dialogue is "rougher" than in *The Smart Set*. This first printing of important O'Neill plays consisted of 1200 copies.

Contents: *THE MOON OF THE CARIBBEES; BOUND EAST FOR CARDIFF; THE LONG VOYAGE HOME; IN THE ZONE; ILE; WHERE THE CROSS IS MADE; THE ROPE.*

THE STRAW
Three acts, five scenes; 121 pages. Typewritten; copyrighted 19 Nov.

EXORCISM
One act. Apparently copyrighted sometime in 1919, although exact date is not known. It was never published and was given one production by the Provincetown Players. It is not noted by Sanborn and Clark.

HONOR AMONG THE BRADLEYS
One act. Never copyrighted; destroyed.

THE TRUMPETS
One act; comedy. Never copyrighted; destroyed.

1920

THE DREAMY KID
In *Theatre Arts Magazine*, 4 (Jan. 1920) 41-56.
Sanborn and Clark, No. 16.

BEYOND THE HORIZON
New York, Boni and Liveright, March 1920.
O'Neill's first publication of a long play. No. 18 in Sanborn and Clark, who point out minor differences in the second printing of 1923.

GOLD
Four acts; 101 pages. Typewritten; copyrighted 27 July.

THE OLE DEVIL
Four acts; 119 pages. Typewritten; copyrighted 29 Nov.
Never published, and not noted in Sanborn and Clark. Apparently elements of this were combined with *CHRIS* to become the final *ANNA CHRISTIE*.

1921

THE EMPEROR JONES
In *Theatre Arts Magazine*, 5 (Jan. 1921) 29-59.
The first publication of this play. The text, with many incidental editorial changes, was used later in Stewart Kidd edition below. Boni and Liveright used text prepared by O'Neill. (Information from Sanborn and Clark, in which this is No. 22.)

THE EMPEROR JONES, DIFF'RENT, THE STRAW
New York, Boni and Liveright, April 1921.
This is the first of several series of O'Neill's plays published both before and after stage production and using two or more play titles. Published earlier than the Stewart Kidd edition of *JONES*. Slight differences in physical appearance of the printings are noted by Sanborn and Clark, in which this is No. 23. 2200 copies were printed — 1000 more than the one act plays of 1919, above.

THE EMPEROR JONES
Cincinnati, Stewart Kidd Co., Sept. 1921. Edited by Frank Shay.

Adapted from *Theatre Arts* version, above, and the first separate edition of this play. Printed under general title of "Stewart Kidd Modern Plays" and later reprinted as one of "Appleton Modern Plays."

Sanborn and Clark, No. 25.

GOLD
New York, Boni and Liveright, Sept. 1921.

Uniform with *MOON OF THE CARIBBEES, etc.*

Sanborn and Clark, No. 28.

THE FOUNTAIN
Nine scenes, prologue; 115 pages. Typewritten; copyrighted 13 Oct.

THE OLDEST MAN
Four acts; 119 pages. Typewritten; copyrighted 13 Oct.

The original title of *THE FIRST MAN*.

1922

THE HAIRY APE, ANNA CHRISTIE, THE FIRST MAN
New York, Boni and Liveright, July 1922.

Uniform with other Boni and Liveright editions.

Sanborn and Clark, No. 29.

THE DREAMY KID
In *Contemporary One-act Plays of 1921 (American)*.

Selected and edited by Frank Shay. Cincinnati, Stewart Kidd, Oct. 1922.

Text editorially changed from *Theatre Arts* edition, 1920, above. The first appearance of this play outside a magazine.

Sanborn and Clark, No. 17.

1923

WELDED
Three acts; 73 pages. Typewritten; copyrighted 2 May.

THE MOON OF THE CARIBBEES and Six Other Plays of the Sea.
New York, Boni and Liveright, 1923. Introduction by George Jean Nathan.

"The Modern Library of the World's Best Books" — the first of the Modern Library reprints of O'Neill's plays. Merely a re-issue of 1919 edition plus introduction. Not noted in Sanborn and Clark.

THE ANCIENT MARINER
One act, 7 parts. Never copyrighted. Not actually a play, but an adaptation of Coleridge's poem to a kind of stage pantomime. No definite composition date has been established. Not noted in Sanborn and Clark. (See below, 1960.)

1924

ALL GOD'S CHILLUN GOT WINGS
In *The American Mercury*, 1 (Feb. 1924) 129-148.

Mencken and Nathan, after the demise of *The Smart Set* and their founding of the *Mercury*, continued their interest in the fast developing O'Neill. This controversial play was published nearly three months before its production.

Sanborn and Clark, No. 37.

ALL GOD'S CHILLUN GOT WINGS and WELDED
New York, Boni and Liveright, April 1924.

A few minor variations from the *Mercury* version above. Uniform with previous editions in this series. By now O'Neill is selling well enough to call for a first printing of 3200 copies.

Sanborn and Clark, No. 38.

DESIRE UNDER THE ELMS
Three parts; 156 pages. Typewritten; copyrighted 29 Aug.

1925

MARCO'S [sic] MILLIONS
8 acts and epilogue; 217 pages. Typewritten; copyrighted 28 Jan.

The title appears thus in the copyright list. O'Neill always insisted that the play as produced should be called MARCO MILLIONS, the second term being meant as a surname rather than an indication of Marco's actual wealth. The copyright title is probably in error.

The Complete Works of Eugene O'Neill
New York, Boni and Liveright, Jan. 1925 (actually copyrighted 1924).

These two volumes, limited to 1200 sets, contain the first printing of DESIRE.

Contents: Vol. I — ANNA CHRISTIE; BEYOND THE HORIZON; THE FIRST MAN; DIFF'RENT; GOLD; THE MOON OF THE CARIBBEES; BOUND EAST FOR CARDIFF; THE LONG VOYAGE HOME; IN THE ZONE; ILE.

Vol. II — THE EMPEROR JONES; THE HAIRY APE; ALL GOD'S CHILLUN; DESIRE UNDER THE ELMS; WELDED; THE STRAW; THE ROPE; THE DREAMY KID; WHERE THE CROSS IS MADE; BEFORE BREAKFAST.

Sanborn and Clark, Nos. 42 and 43.

DESIRE UNDER THE ELMS
New York, Boni and Liveright, April 1925.

"The Provincetown-Greenwich Plays." The first separate edition of this play. Apparently reprinted from the Complete Works, above.

Sanborn and Clark, No. 44.

THE GREAT GOD BROWN
Five acts. Copyrighted 2 July 1926.

The Works of Eugene O'Neill.
New York, Boni and Liveright, July 1925.
In four volumes. Differs from *Complete Works* above in omission of the sea plays. Sanborn and Clark (Nos. 45, 46, 47, 48) note several minor changes. This is the "trade" edition.
Contents: Vol. I — *ANNA CHRISTIE; ALL GOD'S CHILLUN; DIFF'RENT.*
Vol. II — *BEYOND THE HORIZON; THE STRAW; BEFORE BREAKFAST.*
Vol. III — *DESIRE UNDER THE ELMS; THE HAIRY APE; WELDED.*
Vol. IV — *THE EMPEROR JONES; GOLD; THE FIRST MAN; THE DREAMY KID.*

1926

THE GREAT GOD BROWN, THE FOUNTAIN, THE MOON
OF THE CARIBBEES and other Plays.
New York, Boni and Liveright, March 1926.
Uniform with 1925 four volume "Works." 5000 copies were printed.
Contents, in addition to those in title: *BOUND EAST FOR CARDIFF; THE LONG VOYAGE HOME; ILE; WHERE THE CROSS IS MADE; THE ROPE.*
Sanborn and Clark, No. 53.

THE EMPEROR JONES
"Reading version" in *Everybody's Magazine*, 54 (April 1926) 134-148.

THE EMPEROR JONES
In *Golden Book*, 3 (April 1926) 517-530.

LAZARUS LAUGHED
Eight scenes. Copyrighted 23 June.

1927

MARCO MILLIONS

New York, Boni and Liveright, April 1927.

Uniform with 1925 and 1926 "Works" series above. The first publication of a single long play before presentation, although some of the others had already been published before production. Even unproduced, the play was considered worth 7000 copies.

Sanborn and Clark, No. 58.

MARCO MILLIONS

New York, Boni and Liveright, May 1927.

Limited edition, 450 copies signed by the author, of which 440 were for sale. Sanborn and Clark (No. 60) note it is the same as the trade edition, same errors, pagination, etc.

STRANGE INTERLUDE

Nine acts. Copyrighted 1 July.

LAZARUS LAUGHED

First act only, in *The American Caravan*, edited by Van Wyck Brooks, Lewis Mumford, Alfred Kreymborg, and Paul Rosenfeld. New York, The Macaulay Co., September 1927.

This is the first published version of any part of this play, and is much different from the later complete edition. It was, according to Sanborn and Clark, submitted at the personal request of the editors.

Sanborn and Clark, No. 62.

LAZARUS LAUGHED, A Play for an Imaginative Theatre

New York, Boni and Liveright, 12 Nov. 1927.

The first publication of the entire play.

Sanborn and Clark, No. 63.

LAZARUS LAUGHED, etc.

New York, Boni and Liveright, 26 Nov. 1927.

A separate edition of 775 copies, 750 offered for sale. Apparently follows the precedent established by the limited edition of *MARCO*.

Sanborn and Clark, No. 64.

1928

THE EMPEROR JONES and THE STRAW

New York, The Modern Library, 1928. With an introduction by Dudley Nichols.

Not noted in Sanborn and Clark. This edition found in *Publishers Trades List Annual*. Apparently an unsuccessful Modern Library edition, for *JONES* is generally included in other collections. This has not been found in any library consulted.

A play, STRANGE INTERLUDE

New York, Boni and Liveright, Feb. 1928.

Uniform with others of this series of "Works" starting in 1925. O'Neill is popular enough to risk an initial printing of 20,000 copies.

Sanborn and Clark, No. 65.

STRANGE INTERLUDE

New York, Boni and Liveright, March 1928.

Limited edition, 775 copies, 750 for sale. Identical text with February printing, but text is in blue and black inks for ease in distinguishing between speech and thoughts.

Sanborn and Clark, No. 66.

THE EMPEROR JONES

New York, Boni and Liveright, July 1928. With 8 illustrations by Alexander King.

Special limited edition of 775 copies, 750 for sale.

Sanborn and Clark, No. 27.

DYNAMO

Three parts. Copyrighted 4 Oct.

1929

ILE

In *Golden Book*, 9 (February 1929) 87-93.

THE HAIRY APE

New York, Horace Liveright, April 1929. With 9 illustrations by Alexander King.

Another limited edition of 775 copies, 750 for sale. Uniform with *JONES*, 1928.

Sanborn and Clark, No. 32.

The Strange Interlude

During the height of the controversy in Boston, when the play was banned, a pamphlet appeared under this title containing excerpts to prove the play was "obscene." It was employed widely to support the censorship, but it was also vigorously attacked for its inclusion of a long list of passages out of context and hence meaningless. The publisher is unidentified. The New York Public Library has a copy.

Sanborn and Clark, No. 68.

DYNAMO

New York, Horace Liveright, October 1929.

Uniform with the four-volume trade edition of 1925 and subsequent volumes of "Works" series. Sanborn and Clark (noted as No. 71) state this is the third version. The first was the form presented by the Guild, the second went to the English publisher, and this is still another. There seem to be substantial differences among all of them.

DYNAMO

New York, Horace Liveright, December 1929.

Limited edition, 775 copies, 750 for sale.

Sanborn and Clark, No. 73.

1930

ANNA CHRISTIE

New York, Horace Liveright, November 1930. With illustrations by Alexander King.

Limited edition, 775 copies, 750 for sale. Uniform with *JONES* and *APE* in this illustrated series.

Sanborn and Clark, No. 33.

1931

MOURNING BECOMES ELECTRA
A trilogy. Copyrighted 12 May.

MOURNING BECOMES ELECTRA
New York, Horace Liveright, November 1931.
The regular trade edition.

MOURNING BECOMES ELECTRA
New York, Horace Liveright, December 1931.
Special edition of 500 copies signed by the author.

Inscription to MOURNING BECOMES ELECTRA
A broadside 28 x 43 cm. was issued reproducing in facsimile
O'Neill's inscription to the final longhand manuscript of the play.
50 copies were printed.

1932

BEFORE BREAKFAST
In *Golden Book*, 15 (February 1932) 151-156.

Nine Plays, selected by the author.
New York, Horace Liveright, December 1932. With an
introduction by Joseph Wood Krutch.
Contents: *THE EMPEROR JONES; THE HAIRY APE;
ALL GOD'S CHILLUN; DESIRE UNDER THE ELMS;
MARCO MILLIONS; THE GREAT GOD BROWN; LAZARUS
LAUGHED; STRANGE INTERLUDE; MOURNING BE-
COMES ELECTRA.*
This later becomes the Modern Library Giant.

Representative Plays by Eugene O'Neill.
New York, Liveright, Inc., 1932.
Contents: *MARCO MILLIONS; EMPEROR JONES; ANNA
CHRISTIE; WHERE THE CROSS IS MADE; MOON OF
THE CARIBBEES.*

STRANGE INTERLUDE
New York, Horace Liveright, 1932.
The "Black and Gold Library."

1933

DAYS WITHOUT END
Four acts. Copyrighted 20 July.

AH, WILDERNESS!
Four acts. Copyrighted 8 Aug.

AH, WILDERNESS!
New York, Random House, October 1933.

AH, WILDERNESS!
New York, Random House, November 1933.
Limited edition of 325 copies, autographed, bound in leather.
Published simultaneously by Macmillan in Toronto.

1934

DAYS WITHOUT END; A Drama of Religious Faith.
New York, Random House, January 1934.
The Yale Library catalogues an "uncorrected page proof"
of this play, with some errors corrected by an unidentified hand,
which is one of 25 copies bound in paper wrappers. The College
Library, Columbia, also catalogues one of these. It is dated 1934.

DAYS WITHOUT END; A Play.
New York, Random House, February 1934.
Limited edition of 325 copies, autographed, bound in leather.

THE EMPEROR JONES
New York, Appleton-Century, 1934. With a study guide
for screen version by W. Levin and M. J. Herzberg.
Published in "Appleton Modern Plays."

1934-1935

The Plays of Eugene O'Neill
New York, Charles Scribner's Sons, 1934-1935.

The Wilderness Edition, a 12-volume set, with illustrative plates and portrait, limited to 770 copies, signed by the author, with 750 for sale. Copyrighted as follows: Vols. 1 & 2, Nov. 1934; Vols. 3 & 4, Dec. 1934; Vols. 5, 6, & 7, Jan. 1935; Vols. 8 & 9, Mar. 1935; Vols. 10 & 11, May 1935; Vol. 12, June 1935.

Contents: Vol. 1 — *STRANGE INTERLUDE.*

Vol. 2 — *MOURNING BECOMES ELECTRA.*

Vol. 3 — *THE EMPEROR JONES; AH, WILDERNESS!*

Vol. 4 — *ALL GOD'S CHILLUN GOT WINGS; LAZARUS LAUGHED.*

Vol. 5 — *MARCO MILLIONS; THE HAIRY APE.*

Vol. 6 — *BEYOND THE HORIZON; WELDED.*

Vol. 7 — *DYNAMO; DIFF'RENT.*

Vol. 8 — *THE STRAW; THE FIRST MAN.*

Vol. 9 — *DAYS WITHOUT END; GOLD.*

Vol. 10 — *THE GREAT GOD BROWN; ANNA CHRISTIE.*

Vol. 11 — *DESIRE UNDER THE ELMS; THE FOUNTAIN.*

Vol. 12 — The *Glencairn* plays; *WHERE THE CROSS IS MADE; THE ROPE; THE DREAMY KID; BEFORE BREAKFAST; ILE.*

1936

ILE
In *Scholastic Magazine*, 38 (15 February 1936) 4-6.

Nine Plays by Eugene O'Neill.
New York, Random House, 1936. Introduction by Joseph Wood Krutch.

Same as 1932 edition by Liveright, but issued as "Nobel Prize Edition."

AH, WILDERNESS!
New York, Samuel French.
"French's Standard Library" edition. *Drury's Guide to Best*

Plays lists the date as 1936. The Yale Library indexes a copy as 1933, labels it "Sinclair Lewis' copy" (he once played the role in summer stock in 1940). The later date would seem more correct, since the play was having its initial run in 1933-1934 season, during which time French would probably not bring out such a version.

1937

THE EMPEROR JONES, ANNA CHRISTIE, THE HAIRY APE
New York, The Modern Library, March 1937. Introduction by Lionel Trilling. Published simultaneously by Macmillan, Toronto.

1939

During 1939 Dramatists Play Service, New York, issued the following O'Neill plays:
BEYOND THE HORIZON
THE EMPEROR JONES
ILE
IN THE ZONE
WHERE THE CROSS IS MADE

1940

THE ICEMAN COMETH
Four acts. Copyrighted 12 Feb.

During 1940 The Sun Dial Press, New York, issued the following volumes:
AH, WILDERNESS!
ANNA CHRISTIE; ALL GOD'S CHILLUN;
    DIFF'RENT
DAYS WITHOUT END
DESIRE UNDER THE ELMS; THE HAIRY APE;
    WELDED

DYNAMO
THE EMPEROR JONES; THE FIRST MAN; THE
    DREAMY KID
THE GREAT GOD BROWN; THE FOUNTAIN; THE
    MOON OF THE CARIBBEES and Other Plays
LAZARUS LAUGHED
MARCO MILLIONS
MOURNING BECOMES ELECTRA
STRANGE INTERLUDE

THE LONG VOYAGE HOME; 7 Plays of the Sea.
New York, The Modern Library (Random House).
Merely a re-issue of the familiar *THE MOON OF THE CARIBBEES etc.*, noted frequently above, which capitalizes on the successful motion picture, *The Long Voyage Home.*

Nine Plays by Eugene O'Neill.
New York, Garden City Publishing Company. Introduction by J. W. Krutch.
A "deluxe edition" of the same volume issued in 1934 and 1936, above.

1941

Nine Plays by Eugene O'Neill.
New York, The Modern Library (Random House). Introduction by Joseph Wood Krutch.
First printing of the Modern Library Giant.

Plays of Eugene O'Neill
New York, Random House.
A three-volume boxed edition of O'Neill's plays; not a Modern Library series, and not considered "complete" because of omission of certain early one-acters.
Contents: Vol. 1 — *STRANGE INTERLUDE; DESIRE UNDER THE ELMS; LAZARUS LAUGHED; THE FOUNTAIN;* The *Glencairn* Series; *ILE; WHERE THE CROSS IS MADE; THE ROPE; THE DREAMY KID; BEFORE BREAKFAST.*

Vol. 2 — *MOURNING BECOMES ELECTRA; AH, WIL-DERNESS!; ALL GOD'S CHILLUN GOT WINGS; MARCO MILLIONS; WELDED; DIFF'RENT; THE FIRST MAN; GOLD.*

Vol. 3 — *ANNA CHRISTIE; BEYOND THE HORIZON; THE EMPEROR JONES; THE HAIRY APE; THE GREAT GOD BROWN; THE STRAW; DYNAMO; DAYS WITHOUT END.*

1946

A TOUCH OF THE POET
Four acts. Copyrighted 4 Jan.

THE ICEMAN COMETH
New York, Random House, October 1946.
The first publication of this play, copyrighted in 1940.

1948

BEYOND THE HORIZON
New York, Dramatists Play Service. "Acting edition."

1949

THE EMPEROR JONES, ANNA CHRISTIE, THE HAIRY APE
New York, The Modern Library (Random House). Intro-duction by Lionel Trilling.
A new edition, but same volume, as 1937 issue.

1950

Lost Plays of Eugene O'Neill
New York, New Fathoms Press.
An unauthorized edition of five of O'Neill's earliest plays, "found" (with the copyright expired) in the Library of Congress.

O'Neill at first prepared to fight the publication, but his health was in a period of rapid decline and, feeling the struggle pointless, he dropped his action. The volume met with a varied, but generally unenthusiastic, reception, calling down the ire of most critics for the publisher's attempt to make capital on obviously inferior works at the expense of their creator. The book is available in most libraries, but as far as is known, it gained New Fathoms Press little if any cash, and no prestige whatever.

Contents: *ABORTION; THE MOVIE MAN; THE SNIPER; SERVITUDE; WIFE FOR A LIFE.*

1951

Plays of Eugene O'Neill
New York, Random House.
"Random House Lifetime Library." A new edition of 1941 set, above, still in three volumes, but including *THE ICEMAN* in Vol. 3.

1952

A MOON FOR THE MISBEGOTTEN
New York, Random House.
Unable to secure New York production, and the play a catastrophe on the road in its tryouts in Columbus, Pittsburgh, and Detroit, O'Neill submitted this play to the publishers exactly as he had written it, prefaced by his own brief remarks. It was the last publication during his lifetime, and the last by Random House.

1955

LONG DAY'S JOURNEY INTO NIGHT
Copyrighted as an unpublished work by Carlotta Monterey O'Neill.

1956

LONG DAY'S JOURNEY INTO NIGHT
New Haven, Yale University Press, February 1956.

O'Neill originally desired that this play not be published or produced until twenty-five years after his death because of its intense personal nature. He had given it to his wife in its original script as a wedding anniversary gift on 22 July 1941, written, as he said, "in tears and blood." Before he died, however, he expressed willingness to allow the Royal Dramatic Theatre in Stockholm to produce it. Mrs. O'Neill requested Random House, in whose safekeeping O'Neill had deposited a sealed script, to publish the play. Although legally entitled to do so at Mrs. O'Neill's request as estate executrix, Random House declined, but the Yale Press accepted the work. Royalties from the publication are returned to Yale to help preserve the O'Neill collection and maintain the O'Neill scholarships at the School of Drama.

THE ICEMAN COMETH
New York, Random House.

A reprinting of the 1946 edition but including pictures from the production at the Circle-in-the-Square.

1957

A TOUCH OF THE POET
New Haven, Yale University Press.

The only surviving play from the projected cycle, A TALE OF POSSESSORS SELF-DISPOSSESSED. Published in America during the Stockholm production and before the 1958 staging in America.

1958

Lost Plays of Eugene O'Neill.
New York, The Citadel Press.

A subsequent printing of the 1950 publication by New Fathoms Press.

1959

HUGHIE

New Haven, Yale University Press.

The only surviving play from a projected cycle of one-act "monologues" to be called *BY WAY OF OBIT*. The play was produced in Stockholm but by the end of 1960 had not been done in the United States.

1960

THE ANCIENT MARINER

In *Yale University Library Gazette*, 35 (October 1960) 61-68.

Reprinted, with appropriate introductory comments by Donald Gallup, Curator of the Yale Collection of American Literature, with the permission of Carlotta Monterey O'Neill.

The Two Projected Cycles

O'Neill worked for some time on two multi-play cycles, most of which were destroyed before his death. Details about them are indefinite and often conflicting, but Mr. Donald Gallup, of the Yale Collection of American Literature, in which the O'Neill papers are preserved, has supplied some very helpful information concerning the over-all plan of the cycles and the plays contained within them.

A TALE OF POSSESSORS SELF-DISPOSSESSED

As early as February 1932 the New York *Times* reported that O'Neill planned three plays in a series to cover American life from 1776 to the present day. At the time of the Pittsburgh tryout of *AH, WILDERNESS!* newspaper accounts mentioned four plays "based on the Gold Rush," calling it a "monumental" work which would take years to complete and several nights to produce. In 1935 the total had reached seven, to begin with 1829 in New England and encompass five generations. This "marathon drama," said one wire service release, made him the "Wagner of playwrights." The first plays were to be ready for the 1936-1937 season. By October 1935 the Guild was said to have announced that "eight separate dramas" had been completed, covering 125 years, and that one or more were soon to be forthcoming.

During 1936 conflicting reports about the status of this "octology" appeared frequently; some said the plays were nearly ready, others said they were far from finished with no prospect of early production. Early in 1937 the Guild was to do two of the eight per season, and the following December the number had increased to nine. Said the New York *Times*, mentioning that Walter Huston and Rosalind Russell might be cast in the leading roles, and that there was nothing "tricky" about the cycle: "It is just an old fashioned 4½ years' run, at the rate of two plays per season." During the next few years predictions of all kinds appeared concerning possible production, and the total number finally reached eleven.

Barret H. Clark's final edition of *Eugene O'Neill: The Man and His Plays* reported in 1947 that O'Neill intended to go back to his old vein of ironic tragedy. From Mr. Gallup's information, the whole series was to begin in 1776 and carry down to at least 1932, tracing the history of an Irish family in America. As far as can be determined, these are the intended plays:

Title: A TALE OF POSSESSORS SELF-DISPOSSESSED (originally entitled: *A TOUCH OF THE POET*)
PLAY I. *(THE) GREED OF THE MEEK.* 1776-1793.
PLAY II. *AND GIVE ME (US) DEATH.* 1806-1807.
According to Mr. Gallup these first two plays at one time were inverted in order. O'Neill discovered that they were too long for single plays, and faced with the necessity of dividing them in two, finally destroyed both. The cycle then would have had the reported eleven plays, although only nine titles are known.
PLAY III. *A TOUCH OF THE POET.* 1828. (Originally *(THE) HAIR OF THE DOG.*)
This is the only play to survive in condition to produce and is the only one ever published. Mr. Gallup states it was the first of the cycle to be completed.

PLAY IV. *MORE STATELY MANSIONS.* 1837-1842 (or later).

This play survives in draft form, far too incomplete to be produced as it stands. The Royal Dramatic Theatre in Stockholm has considered editing it for staging.

PLAY V. *THE CALMS OF CAPRICORN.* 1857.

PLAY VI. *THE EARTH'S THE LIMIT.* 1858-1860.

PLAY VII. *NOTHING LOST SAVE HONOR.* 1862-1870.

PLAY VIII. *(THE) MAN ON IRON HORSEBACK.* 1876-1893.

PLAY IX. *(THE) HAIR OF THE DOG.* 1900-1932.

This last play was originally the title given the third play, which eventually became *A TOUCH OF THE POET.* Mr. Gallup reports that O'Neill himself seemed quite uncertain about a title for the last play, and originally had considered *TWILIGHT OF THE POSSESSORS.* In 1934 O'Neill was reported at work on a play called *THE LIFE OF BESSIE BOWEN (BROWN, BOLEN)* which Mr. Gallup states finally became incorporated into the ninth play, *HAIR OF THE DOG.* Karl-Ragnar Gierow, director of the Royal Dramatic Theatre of Stockholm, reports in *World Theatre,* Spring 1958, that *BESSIE BOWEN* was to be about the motor car industry. He also mentions another play, *THE LAST CONQUEST* or *THE THIRTEENTH APOSTLE* which was to include Christ and Satan as characters. Gallup states that *BESSIE BOWEN* was finally destroyed in 1947. Mrs. O'Neill has reported that all others were destroyed by O'Neill and herself, torn and burned page by page. Unable to complete them, the playwright did not want any other hand to touch them.

BY WAY OF OBIT

In 1939 O'Neill was reported at work on a play entitled *BY WAY OF OBIT,* but details were lacking. Mr. Gallup reports that this was to be another cycle of eight one-act plays, or, more accurately, monologues. One play survives, *HUGHIE,* written probably in 1940. It has been produced by the Royal Dramatic Theatre in Stockholm, and published in America by the Yale University Press. The over-all plan of this cycle remains uncertain.

MAJOR PRODUCTIONS OF EUGENE O'NEILL'S PLAYS

This is a chronological list of all important *domestic* productions of O'Neill's plays. Most of them opened "cold" in New York because of O'Neill's reluctance to permit road tryouts in the traditional manner. In two cases, *CHRIS* and *A MOON FOR THE MISBEGOTTEN*, the original productions never reached Broadway. Others, like *DAYS WITHOUT END* and *AH, WILDERNESS!* opened with the same company which had appeared on limited out of town runs. This list includes data concerning the few road tryouts, with appropriate explanations where necessary. No attempt has been made to include any productions outside the United States. Also omitted are the touring companies which went on the road after the New York openings.

Sources are varied. The greater part of the information comes from the Burns Mantle yearbooks. The early Provincetown data is taken from Deutsch and Hanau's *The Provincetown*. Other material is from newspapers and magazines, playbills of various sorts, and other miscellaneous sources found in library collections.

1916

BOUND EAST FOR CARDIFF

Presented Summer, second bill, Wharf Theatre, Provincetown.

Cast

Yank	George Cram Cook
Captain	David Carb
First Mate	Eugene O'Neill

The first production anywhere of a play by Eugene O'Neill. Mary Heaton Vorse owned the tiny wharf where the newly formed group produced its plays. This second season displayed the talents of the young man who had recently joined them, "dressed like Edgar Allan Poe who had just jumped ship." Only about 60 spectators could crowd into the theatre, but all reports speak of the play as a tremendous experience. The exact date is uncertain; all sources merely say "Summer, 1916." This is one of the few appearances of O'Neill as an actor. His stage fright was considerable.

THIRST

Presented Summer, fourth bill, Wharf Theatre, Provincetown.

The three-man cast included O'Neill in the part of the mulatto sailor. There is no record of a second production at any time, nor any record of the play having been reviewed.

BOUND EAST FOR CARDIFF

Presented November, first bill, Playwrights' Theatre, 139 MacDougal Street, New York.

Cast

Yank	George Cram Cook
Driscoll	William Stewart
Cocky	Edw. J. Ballantine
Davis	Harry Kemp
Scotty	Frank Shay
Olson	Bion Nordfelt
Smitty	Lew Parrish
Ivan	Francis Buzzell
Captain	Henry Marion Hall
First Mate	Eugene O'Neill

The first New York production at the newly established theatre in Greenwich Village. The cast probably represents many from the original Wharf production. The performance attracted little attention and New York newspapers ignored it completely.

BEFORE BREAKFAST

Presented 1 December, third bill, Playwrights' Theatre.

Cast

Mrs. Rowland .... Mary Pyne
Alfred, her husband (unseen) .... Eugene O'Neill

The last appearance of O'Neill on any stage. His appearance consisted of the insertion of his hand onto the set, and a subsequent offstage groan.

1917

FOG

Presented January, fifth bill, Playwrights' Theatre.
This is apparently the only production the play ever received. The details of the production are unavailable.

THE SNIPER

Presented 16 February, seventh bill, Playwrights' Theatre.

Cast

Rougon .... George Cram Cook
Priest .... Donald Corley
German Captain .... Theron M. Bamberger
Private of Regiment .... Morton Stafford
Another private .... Robert Montcarr
Jean .... Ida Rauh

Another of the very early works tried by the Provincetown group. It has never received any other production. It was also ignored by the press.

IN THE ZONE

Presented 31 October, first bill, Washington Square Players, Comedy Theater, New York.
The first O'Neill play presented by this group. Neither the

New York *Times* nor the Burns Mantle volume gives individual casts, but among the actors appear such names as William Gillette (not *the* William Gillette), Arthur E. Hohl, Robert Strange, Frederick Roland, Jay Strong, Rienzi de Cordova and Harry Ehlers. This play became a favorite vaudeville skit, and brought O'Neill some of his earliest steady royalties. This performance is the first O'Neill play listed by Burns Mantle (1909-1919), who does not include the Provincetown productions of that decade.

THE LONG VOYAGE HOME

Presented 2 November, first bill, Playwrights' Theatre.

Cast

Bartender	George Cram Cook
Olson	Ira Remson
Driscoll	Hutchinson Collins
Cocky	O. K. Liveright
First girl	Ida Rauh
Second girl	Alice MacDougal

ILE

Presented 30 November, second bill, Playwrights' Theatre. Directed by Nina Moise.

Cast

Ben	Everett Glass
Steward	Robert Edwards
Capt. Keeney	Hutchinson Collins
Mr. Slocum	Ira Remson
Mrs. Keeney	Clara Savage
Joe	Louis B. Ell

1918

ILE

Presented 18 April, Greenwich Village Players, Greenwich Village Theatre, New York.

Cast

Ben	Everett Glass
Steward	Francis McDonald
Capt. Keeney	Joseph Macaulay
Mr. Slocum	Harold Meltzer
Mrs. Keeney	Margaret Fareleigh
Joe	John Ahearn

THE ROPE

Presented 26 April, seventh bill, Playwrights' Theatre. Directed by Nina Moise.

Cast

Abraham Bentley	O. K. Liveright
Annie	Dorothy Upjohn
Pat Sweeney	H. B. Tisdale
Mary	Edna Smith
Luke Bentley	Charles Ellis

THE ROPE

Presented 13 May, Washington Square Players, Comedy Theatre.

Cast

Abraham Bentley	Whitford Kane
Annie	Josephine A. Meyer
Pat Sweeney	Robert Strange
Mary	Kate Morgan
Luke Bentley	Effington Pinto

WHERE THE CROSS IS MADE

Presented 22 November, first bill, Playwrights' Theatre.
Directed by Ida Rauh.

Cast

Nat Bartlett .... James Light
Dr. Higgins .... O. K. Liveright
Sue Bartlett .... Ida Rauh
Capt. Bartlett .... Hutchinson Collins

THE MOON OF THE CARIBBEES

Presented 20 December, second bill, Playwrights' Theatre.
Directed by Thomas Mitchell.

Cast

Yank .... Harry Winston
Driscoll .... Hutchinson Collins
Olson .... Wm. Forster Batterham
Davis .... W. Clay Hill
Cocky .... O. K. Liveright
Smitty .... Charles Ellis
Paul .... Percy Winner
Lamps .... Phil Lyons
Chips .... Fred Booth
Old Tom .... William Stuart
First Mate .... Louis B. Ell
Bella .... Jean Hobb
Susie .... Bernice Abbott
Pearl .... Ruth Collins Allen

1919

THE DREAMY KID

Presented 31 October, first bill, Playwrights' Theatre.
Directed by Ida Rauh.
Settings by Glenn Coleman.

Cast

Mammy Saunders	Ruth Anderson
Coely Ann	Leathe Colvert
Irene	Margaret Rhodes
The Dreamy Kid	Harold Simmelkjaer

1920

BEYOND THE HORIZON

Presented 2 February, Morosco Theatre.
Produced by John D. Williams.
Moved to Criterion Theatre, 23 February; Little Theatre, 9 March.

Cast

Robert Mayo	Richard Bennett
Andrew Mayo	Robert Kelly
Ruth Atkins	Elsie Rizer
Capt. Dick Scott	Sidney Macy
Mrs. Kate Mayo	Mary Jeffery
Mrs. Atkins	Louise Closser Hale
James Mayo	Erville Alderson
Mary	Elfin Finn
Ben	George Hadden
Dr. Fawcett	George Riddell

The first "uptown" production of an O'Neill play, undertaken on an experimental basis by John Williams. It was produced at special matinees, using cast members already committed to regular evening performances elsewhere. The critics welcomed the play and its popularity increased until it finally received, after two subsequent moves, a regularly scheduled run. It brought O'Neill his first Pulitzer Prize.

Total performances: 111

CHRIS

Presented 8 March by George C. Tyler in Atlantic City, N.J.

Cast

Chris Christopherson .... Emmett Corrigan
Anna .... Lynn Fontanne
The Mate .... Arthur Ashley

This was the abortive road tryout of the first version of *ANNA CHRISTIE*. The newspaper reception was only luke-warm, and after a week in Atlantic City the play moved to Philadelphia where it died an unmourned death. O'Neill never permitted its publication and no existing script is known. After this failure O'Neill waited four years before permitting another out of town tryout.

EXORCISM

Presented 26 March, fifth bill, Playwrights' Theatre.

Cast

Ned Malloy .... Jasper Deeter
Jimmy .... M. A. McAteer
Maj. Andrews .... William Dunbar
Mr. Malloy .... Remo Bufano
Nordstrom .... Lawrence Vail

Listed as "a play of anti-climax" and never again produced. The director was Edward Goodman. It was never reviewed.

THE EMPEROR JONES

Presented 1 November, Provincetown Players.
Burns Mantle says "Neighborhood Playhouse" but Genevra Herndon in her dissertation says "Playwrights' Theatre."
Moved to Selwyn Theatre 27 December; Princess Theatre 29 January 1921.

Cast

Brutus Jones .... Charles Gilpin
Harry Smithers .... Jasper Deeter
Native woman .... Christine Ell
Lem .... Charles Ellis

The sensational success which brought the public crowding up to the tiny Provincetown box office demanding to become members in order to witness this phenomenal play. Thereafter the small theatre in Greenwich Village was never the same. This also marks the first major role for a Negro in the American theatre. Gilpin's tremendous interpretation extended through the season and carried him throughout the nation on an extended tour.

Total performances: 204

DIFF'RENT

Presented 27 December, Provincetown Players.

First performances listed at Playwrights' Theatre, then a transfer uptown on matinee schedule to Selwyn Theatre, 21 January. Later transfers, giving it regular run, to Times Square, 4 February, and Princess, 7 February.

Cast

Capt. Caleb Williams	James Light
Emma Crosby	Mary Blair
Jack Crosby	Eugene Lincoln
Capt. John Crosby	Alan MacAteer
Mrs. Crosby	Alice Rostetter
Harriet Williams	Elizabeth Brown
Alfred Rogers	Iden Thompson
Benny Rogers	Charles Ellis

This was probably a case of pushing good luck too far. The play was given a moderate welcome by the few critics who first saw it. Mary Blair was generally felt to be a more than competent Emma. Because of the apparent success downtown, the transfer was made to capitalize on the fortunes of the *HORIZON* matinees and the *JONES* regular performances. The move was a bad one, and the public would not come. Perhaps a longer run at the smaller theatre would have been more successful, but the play generally is not deemed worthy of much attention anyway.

Total performances: 100

1921

GOLD

Presented 1 June, Frazee Theatre, New York.
Produced by John D. Williams.
Staged by Homer Saint-Taudens.

Cast

Abel	Ashley Buck
Butler	George Marion
Capt. Isaiah Bartlett	Willard Mack
Silas Horne	J. Fred Holloway
Ben Cates	Charles D. Brown
Jimmy Kanaka	T. Tamanoto
Mrs. Bartlett	Katherine Grey
Sue Bartlett	Geraldine O'Brien
Danny Drew	Charles Francis
Nat Bartlett	E. J. Ballantine
Dr. Berry	Scott Cooper

This is generally regarded as the "expanded" version of the one-act *WHERE THE CROSS IS MADE*, but O'Neill always maintained that the longer play came first. The fourth and final act of *GOLD* provided most of the material for the more popular shorter piece. *GOLD* was not a success and quickly closed, although Willard Mack received some interesting notices for his portrayal of the mad captain.

Total performances: 13

ANNA CHRISTIE

Presented 2 November, Vanderbilt Theatre, New York.
Produced by Arthur Hopkins.
Settings by Robert Edmond Jones.

Cast

Johnny-the-Priest	James C. Mack
Chris Christopherson	George Marion

Marthy Owen .... Eugenie Blair
Anna .... Pauline Lord
Mat Burke .... Frank Shannon

The first production of one of O'Neill's busiest seasons, in which four of his full length plays were produced both uptown and down. This rewrite of *CHRIS* won wide critical acclaim both for the writer and the star. It won another Pulitzer Prize and has become one of the most familiar of O'Neill's plays. Many felt the "happy ending" was poor, although O'Neill denied that it was happy. He never liked the play, and did not include it in his own choice of his best plays.

Total performances: 177

THE STRAW

Presented 10 November, Greenwich Village Theatre.
Produced by George C. Tyler.

Cast

Bill Carmody .... Harry Harwood
Nora .... Viola Ormonde
Tom .... Richard Ross
Billy .... Norris Millington
Dr. Gaynor .... George Woodward
Fred Nicholls .... Robert Strange
Eileen Carmody .... Margalo Gilmore
Stephen Murray .... Otto Kruger
Dr. Stanton .... George Farren

Most critics thought this second production of the season was a touching, well-written play, in spite of the distasteful subject of tuberculosis, but that its tragic qualities were debatable. Margalo Gilmore, to star later in *MARCO MILLIONS*, was approved as a warm and charming heroine, but Otto Kruger met unenthusiastic response. The direction of the play was not particularly good and the whole production, which had far more to offer than other of O'Neill's failures, was ineffectively handled and terminated after a disappointing run. For many

O'Neill students, however, it has remained one of his better, although less known, plays.

Total performances: 20

1922

THE FIRST MAN

Presented 4 March, Neighborhood Playhouse, New York.
Produced by Augustin Duncan.

Cast

Curtis Jayson	Augustin Duncan
Martha	Margaret Mower
John Jayson	Harry Andrews
John, Jr.	Gordon Burby
Richard	Alan Bunce
Esther	Margherita Sargent
Lily	Marjorie Vonnegut
Mrs. Davidson	Marie L. Day
Mark Sheffield	Eugene Powers
Emily	Eva Carder
Richard Bigelow	Frederic Burt

Originally "The Oldest Man." The birth scene and its screams offended most critics, although many caught the humor of the satire of a close-knit family.

Total performances: 27

THE HAIRY APE

Presented 9 March, Playwrights' Theatre.
Produced by the Provincetown Players.

Cast

Yank	Louis Wolheim
Paddy	Henry O'Neill
Long	Harold West
Mildred Douglas	Mary Blair

Her Aunt .... Eleanor Hutchinson
Second Engineer .... Jack Gude

The sensation of this play's style and subject matter, and the acting of Louis Wolheim, rivalled the furor over *JONES* and the performance of Charles Gilpin. Theatre crowds once more came downtown in such large numbers that the play was forced to move to the Plymouth on 17 April. There were strong reactions from the District Attorney's office, which threatened to close it as obscene for its shocking, jolting language, but it continued on through the season unmolested.

Total performances: 127

1924

WELDED

Presented 17 March, Thirty-ninth Street Theatre, New York. Produced by Eugene O'Neill, Kenneth Macgowan, and Robert Edmond Jones in association with the Selwyns.

Cast

Eleanor Owen .... Doris Keane
Michael Cape .... Jacob Ben-Ami
John Darnton .... Curtis Cooksey
A Woman .... Catherine Collins

The first of the productions by the newly formed company of O'Neill, Macgowan, and Jones, which broke away from the now disintegrating original Provincetown group. The play, which had tried out in Baltimore to unenthusiastic notices, was a distinct failure. Few critics could find any pleasure or point of view in the sordid, heavily Strindbergian battle of the sexes. Some praise for individual performances could not save it.

Total performances: 24

THE ANCIENT MARINER

Presented 6 April, Provincetown Playhouse (no longer Playwrights').
Directed by Robert Edmond Jones and James Light.
Settings by Robert Edmond Jones.
Masks by James Light.

Cast

Ancient Mariner .... E. J. Ballantine
First Wedding Guest .... James Shute
Second Wedding Guest .... H. L. Rothschild
Third Wedding Guest .... Charles Ellis
Helmsman .... James Meighan
Bride .... Rosalind Fuller
Bridegroom .... Gerald Stopp

An attempt at a pantomimic dramatization of the Coleridge poem. Using both original directions and those contained in the poem, and with a combined system of actions and readings of the verse, O'Neill attempted to interpret the story. It was not a success, and most critics felt O'Neill was far away from his element.

Total performances: 29

ALL GOD'S CHILLUN GOT WINGS

Presented 15 May, Provincetown Playhouse.
Directed by James Light.
Settings by Cleon Throckmorton.

Cast

Jim Harris, child .... William Davis
Ella Downey, child .... Virginia Wilson
Shorty, child .... George Finley
Jim Harris, adult .... Paul Robeson
Ella Downey, adult .... Mary Blair
Mrs. Harris .... Lillian Greene
Hattie Harris .... Flora Cole

Shorty, adult	Charles Ellis
Joe	Frank Wilson
Mickey	James Martin

Because of muddled censorship attempts from City Hall, offended by the theme of miscegenation, the play was denied the use of children in the opening scene, ostensibly because they were too young. This did not halt production, because James Light, the director, read the passage to the audience, after which the play proceeded without incident. O'Neill always felt the work was badly misunderstood and would some day come into its own among his important plays.

S. S. GLENCAIRN

Presented originally 14 August by Barnstormer's Barn, in Provincetown, Massachusetts. Then in New York as follows:

3 November at the Provincetown Playhouse, directed by James Light.

16 December at the Punch and Judy.

12 January 1925 at the Princess.

Cast

Yank	Sidney Machet
Driscoll	Lawrence Cecil
Olson	Walter Abel
Davis	Howard McGee
Cocky	Walter Kingsford
Smitty	E. J Ballantine
Ivan	James Meighan
Swanson	Samuel Selden
Scotty	Archie Sinclair
Paul	Abraham Krainis
Lamps	Clement O'Loghlen
Old Tom	Stanley Howlett
Big Frank	William Stahl
Paddy	H. L. Remsten
Captain	Edgar Stehli

First Mate .... Lewis Barrington
Bella .... Mary Johns
Joe .... Stanley Jowlett
Nick .... Edgar Stehli
Freda .... Helen Freeman

The first attempt to bring the four *Glencairn* plays together. It met with considerable critical success and has since been revived many times.

Total performances: 99

DESIRE UNDER THE ELMS

Presented 11 November, Greenwich Village Theatre.
Produced by the Provincetown Players.
Moved to Earl Carrol, 12 January; George M. Cohan, 1 June; Daly's 63rd Street, 28 September.

Cast

Simeon Cabot .... Allen Nagle
Peter Cabot .... Perry Ivins
Eben Cabot .... Charles Ellis
Ephraim Cabot .... Walter Huston
Abbie Putnam .... Mary Morris

A success while in the village, this play moved uptown, where it prospered on its notoriety. A campaign was at the time in full swing to "clean up" New York plays by eliminating so much "sex." The long run can in part be attributed to thrill-seekers (most of them keenly disappointed at the lack of "filth" they came to see), but the play did have its merits that were widely recognized by others. It has often been regarded as the nearest O'Neill ever came to establishing the feeling of Greek tragedy. Many still think it is his best play.

Total performances: 208

1925

THE FOUNTAIN

Presented 10 December, Greenwich Village Theatre.
Produced by Kenneth Macgowan, Robert Edmond Jones and Eugene O'Neill.
Designed by Robert Edmond Jones.
Musical setting by Macklin Morrow.

Cast

Ibnu Aswad	Stanley Berry
Juan Ponce de Leon	Walter Huston
Pedro	William Stahl
Maria de Cordova	Pauline Moore
Luis de Alvaredo	Egon Brecher
Christopher Columbus	Henry O'Neill
Beatriz de Cordova	Rosalind Fuller
Diego Menendez	Crane Wilbur
Nano	Curtis Cooksey

This does not let one visualize the entire cast, or the overwhelming scenery which Jones designed, much to the critics' admiration and to the plays complete suffocation. This attempt at poetic romance and interpretation of history did not succeed any more than some of the heavily "realistic" plays of earlier years.

Total performances: 24

1926

THE GREAT GOD BROWN

Presented 23 January, Greenwich Village Theatre.
Produced by Kenneth Macgowan, Robert Edmond Jones, Eugene O'Neill.
Staged by Robert Edmond Jones.
Moved to Garrick Theatre, 1 March; Klaw Theatre, 10 May.

Cast

William A. Brown	William Harrigan
His Father	Milano Tilden
His Mother	Clifford Sellers
Dion Anthony	Robert Keith
His Father	Hugh Kidder
His Mother	Eleanor Wesselhoeft
Margaret	Leona Hogarth
Cybel	Anne Shoemaker

Despite the complete mystification of the average audience, many critics and a good part of the public found this play thoughtful and somewhat profound. The use of masks was confusing, but did not hinder the viewer's pleasure. The play marked O'Neill's turning point away from the realism of the past and showed the beginnings of the mysticism that was to dominate future plays. It was also one of the few times when O'Neill felt obliged to explain his play's meaning, which he did by a widely reprinted article for the press.

Total performances: 283

THE EMPEROR JONES

Revived at the Provincetown Theatre, 16 February.
Staged by James Light.

Cast

Brutus Jones	Charles Gilpin
Harry Smithers	Harold McGee
Old native woman	Barbara Benedict
Lem	William Stahl

Revived 10 November, Mayfair Theatre.
Produced by Mayfair Productions.

Cast

Brutus Jones	Charles Gilpin
Harry Smithers	Moss Hart
Old native woman	Hazel Mason
Lem	Arthur Ames

Total performances, second revival: 61

The 10 November Mayfair production is described by Moss Hart in *Act One*.

BEYOND THE HORIZON

Revived 30 November, Mansfield Theatre.
Produced by The Actors Theatre.

Cast

James Mayo	Malcolm Williams
Kate Mayo	Judith Lowry
Capt. Scott	Albert Tavernier
Andrew Mayo	Thomas Chalmers
Robert Mayo	Robert Keith
Ruth Atkins	Aline MacMahon
Mrs. Atkins	Eleanor Wesselhoeft
Mary	Elaine Koch
Ben	Victor Kilian
Dr. Fawcett	Joseph McInerney

The revival was widely praised by the critics. The performance of Aline MacMahon as Ruth was outstanding.
Total performances: 79

1928

MARCO MILLIONS

Presented 9 January, Guild Theatre, by the Theatre Guild.
Staged by Rouben Mamoulian.
Settings by Robert Edmond Jones.

Cast

Marco Polo	Alfred Lunt
Donata	Natalie Browning
Tedaldo	Morris Carnovsky
Nicolo	Henry Travers
Maffeo	Ernest Cossart
Kublai, the Great Kaan	Baliol Holloway

Chu-Yin .... Dudley Digges
Kukachin .... Margalo Gillmore

The Guild's first O'Neill, staged lavishly, and moderately successfully. Many felt the Babbitt in oriental dress from Renaissance Italy was not very amusing at this late date, but others saw its merits. It ran concurrently with the sensational *STRANGE INTERLUDE*.

Total performances: 92

STRANGE INTERLUDE

Presented 30 January, John Golden Theatre.
Produced by The Theatre Guild.
Staged by Philip Moeller.

Cast

Charles Marsden .... Tom Powers
Prof. Leeds .... Philip Leigh
Nina Leeds .... Lynn Fontanne
Sam Evans .... Earl Larimore
Edmund Darrell .... Glenn Anders
Mrs. Evans .... Helen Westley
Gordon, a boy .... Charles Walters
Madeline Arnold .... Ethel Westley
Gordon, a man .... John J. Burns

The first of O'Neill's over-length plays and, from all angles, the most successful of his works up to this time. It brought his third Pulitzer Prize and was heralded as the beginning of new and wonderful things in the modern drama. Its wide popular support and long run, the longest of any O'Neill play before the 1956 revival of *ICEMAN*, never failed to amaze even O'Neill's most ardent enthusiasts.

Total performances: 426

LAZARUS LAUGHED

Presented 9 April, by the Pasadena, California, Community Playhouse.

This "play for an imaginative theatre" was rumored in production by the Provincetown group, but the Pasadena performance is the only large-scale staging it ever received. The production was lavish, complete with all costumes and masks as directed, and was enthusiastically received. The cast was entirely local, and all work was voluntary.

Total performances: 28

1929

S. S. *GLENCAIRN*

Revived at the Provincetown Theatre, 9 January.

Cast

Yank	Lionel J. Stander
Driscoll	Byron Russell
Olson	Walter Abel
Davis	Harold McGee
Cocky	George Tawde
Smitty	E. J. Ballantine
Ivan	George Tobias
Scotty	Archie Sinclair
Paul	Richard Gaines
Paddy	H. L. Remsten
Captain	Robert Lucius Cook
First Mate	Max Essin
Bella	Mary Johns
Joe	Robert Lucius Cook
Nick	A. Montague Ash
Freda	Dorothee Nolan

Total performances: 90

DYNAMO

Presented 11 February, Martin Beck Theatre.
Staged by Philip Moeller.
Produced by the Theatre Guild.
Designed by Lee Simonson.

Cast

Rev. Light	George Gaul
Mrs. Light	Helen Westley
Reuben Light	Glenn Anders
Ramsay Fife	Dudley Digges
May Fife	Catherine Doucet
Ada Fife	Claudette Colbert

The first of the proposed trilogy exploring "the sickness of today." O'Neill was unhappy that he had announced a coming trilogy, for many critics reserved judgment until the other two had been produced. The original plan was never carried through. O'Neill also objected to the leggy display of the heroine, who continually detracted from the play's effectiveness. He always felt the play was terribly misunderstood, along with *ALL GOD'S CHILLUN*.

Total performances: 50

BEFORE BREAKFAST

Revived at the Provincetown Theatre, 5 March.

Cast

Mrs. Rowland	Mary Blair

Presented along with Vergil Geddes' *The Earth Between*. An interesting event for two reasons. First, Geddes, in his 1934 pamphlet, *The Melodramadness of Eugene O'Neill*, was to be one of O'Neill's strongest critics. Second, the star of Geddes' piece was hailed as one of great promise. Her name was Bette Davis. Neither play in this bill was very well received.

Total performances: 27

1930

MARCO MILLIONS

Revived by the Theatre Guild, Liberty Theatre, 3 March.

Cast

Marco Polo	Earl Larimore
Donata	Helen Tilden
Nicolo	Frederick Roland
Maffeo	Harry Mestayer
Kublai	Sydney Greenstreet
Chu-Yin	Henry Travers
Kukachin	Sylvia Field

Total performances: 8

1931

MOURNING BECOMES ELECTRA

Presented 26 October, by The Theatre Guild, Guild Theatre. Staged by Philip Moeller.

Cast

Seth Beckwith	Arthur Hughes
Christine	Alla Nazimova
Lavinia	Alice Brady
Peter Niles	Philip Foster
Hazel Niles	Mary Arbenz
Ezra Mannon	Lee Baker
Adam Brant	Thomas Chalmers
Orin	Earl Larimore

This trilogy which ran for many hours and many acts was commonly regarded as O'Neill's masterpiece and the climax of his career. It did have its violent detractors, but probably no more than many other of his plays. O'Neill's published notes report over three years of careful thought and planning, during which time he included and then rejected many of his previous stage effects such as spoken thoughts and masks.

Total performances: 150

1932

MOURNING BECOMES ELECTRA

Revived by the Theatre Guild, 9 May.

Cast

Lavinia	Judith Anderson
Orin	Walter Abel
Christine	Florence Reed
Adam Brant	Crane Wilbur

The road company returned for a brief engagement. Most critics found the play still effective, although the loss of Brady and Nazimova was acutely felt.

Total performances: 16

1933

AH, WILDERNESS!

First performed at Nixon Theatre, Pittsburgh, 25 Sept. Presented 2 October, by The Theatre Guild, Guild Theatre.
Staged by Philip Moeller.
Settings by Robert Edmond Jones.

Cast

Nat Miller	George M. Cohan
Essie	Marjorie Marquis
Arthur	William Post, Jr.
Richard	Elisha Cook, Jr.
Mildred	Adelaide Bean
Tommy	Walter Vonnegut, Jr.
Sid	Gene Lockhart
Lily	Eda Heinemann
David McComber	Richard Sterling
Muriel	Ruth Gilbert
Belle	Ruth Holden

The "new" O'Neill emerged in this play, amazing his friends and critics alike with a nostalgic comedy of "recollection." It was the first time an actor received top billing in an O'Neill play. The name of George M. Cohan appeared on the marquee lights along with O'Neill's. This is undoubtedly the most popular O'Neill play, and is constantly revived. It is a favorite with little theatre and college groups.

Total performances: 289

1934

DAYS WITHOUT END

First performed at Plymouth Theatre, Boston, 27 Dec. Presented 8 January, by The Theatre Guild, Henry Miller Theatre.

Staged by Philip Moeller.

Settings by Lee Simonson.

Cast

John	Earl Larimore
Loving	Stanley Ridges
William Elliot	Richard Barbee
Father Baird	Robert Loraine
Elsa	Selena Royle
Lucy	Ilka Chase

The "return to the Cross" signified, for many critics, the "arrival" of Eugene O'Neill. For others it meant the worst play he had ever written. The reviewers in various religious publications, both Catholic and Protestant, overwhelmingly praised it; other critics almost universally condemned it.

Total performances: 57

1937

S. S. GLENCAIRN

Revived by the WPA Federal Theatre Project at the Lafayette Theatre, 29 October.

Staged by William Challee.

Settings by Perry Watkins.

This revival was presented by an all-Negro cast, none of whom achieved fame except Canada Lee, who played Yank. The critics praised O'Neill for having made all his plays available to the Federal Theatre Project, but in the case of the *Glencairn* cycle, it was difficult to adjust to the colored cast in such a variety of national roles.

Total performances: 68

1938

DIFF'RENT

Revived by Charles Hopkins for the WPA New York State Federal Theatre Project at the Maxine Elliott Theatre, 25 January.

Setting and costumes by Ben Edwards.

Lighting by Feder.

Cast

Capt. Caleb Williams	Erford Gage
Emma Crosby	Lennore Sorsby
Capt. John Crosby	Gene Webber
Mrs. Crosby	Rose Morison
Jack Crosby	Douglas Campbell
Harriet Williams	Irene Taylor
Alfred Rogers	Jay Velie
Benny Rogers	Frank Daly

1941

AH, WILDERNESS!

Revived by the Theatre Guild, at the Guild Theatre, 2 October.

Staged by Eva Le Gallienne.

Produced by Theresa Helburn, Lawrence Langner, Eva Le Gallienne.

Settings by Watson Barratt.

Cast

Nat Miller	Harry Carey
Essie	Ann Shoemaker
Arthur	Victor Chapin
Richard	William Prince
Mildred	Virginia Kaye
Tommy	Tommy Lewis
Sid	Tom Tully
Lily	Enid Markey
David McComber	Hale Norcross
Muriel	Dorothy Littlejohn
Belle	Dennie Moore

The critics found Harry Carey a pleasing replacement for Cohan but the play was now less of a starring piece.
Total performances: 29

1946

THE ICEMAN COMETH

Presented 9 October, Martin Beck Theatre.
Produced by Theatre Guild in association with Armina Marshall.
Staged by Eddie Dowling.
Supervised by Theresa Helburn and Lawrence Langner.
Settings and lighting by Robert Edmond Jones.

Cast

Harry Hope	Dudley Digges
Ed Mosher	Morton L. Stevens
Pat McGloin	Al McGranary
William Oban	E. G. Marshall
Joe Mott	John Marriott
Piet Wetjoen	Frank Tweddell
Cecil Lewis	Nicholas Joy
James Cameron	Russell Collins
Hugo Kalmar	Leo Chalzel
Larry Slade	Carl Benton Reid

Rocky Pioggi	Tom Pedi
Dan Parritt	Paul Crabtree
Pearl	Ruth Gilbert
Margie	Jeanne Cagney
Cora	Marcella Markham
Chuck Morello	Joe Marr
Theodore Hickman	James Barton
Moran	Michael Wyler
Lieb	Charles Hart

The twelve-year drought was broken by this third long play demanding a dinner hour break. Press conferences, advance publicity, and O'Neill's return to New York made headlines throughout the country. It was to be his greatest effort, said George Jean Nathan. Reception, however, was mixed. It clearly did not herald the long awaited New Age of O'Neill on the Broadway stage. It was also the last new play presented in New York during O'Neill's lifetime.

Total performances: 136

1947

A MOON FOR THE MISBEGOTTEN

Presented 20 February by the Theatre Guild at the Hartman Theatre, Columbus, Ohio.

Cast

Phil Hogan	J. M. Kerrigan
Josie Hogan	Mary Welch
Mike Hogan	J. Joseph Donnelly
James Tyrone, Jr.	James Dunn
T. Stedman Harder	Lex Lindsay

This was the official tryout opening of the last new O'Neill play to see production before his death. It ran its original week in Columbus and journeyed to Pittsburgh and Detroit, where it ran into considerable difficulty with censors. "Casting trouble" finally caused its withdrawal. Of conventional length, it was published with O'Neill's own brief preface, the last to be printed during his lifetime.

1948

S. S. GLENCAIRN

Revived by the New York City Theatre Company, at the New York City Center, 20 May.
Produced by José Ferrer.

Cast: (principals only)

Yank	Richard Coogan
Driscoll	George Mathews
Olson	Ralph Roberts
Cocky	Kenneth Treseder
Smitty	Robert Carrol
Ivan	Harold J. Stone
Bella	Juanita Hall
Captain	Ralph Sumpter
Fat Joe	José Ferrer
Nick	Victor Beecroft
Freda	Nan McFarland

Total performances: 14

1951

ANNA CHRISTIE

Revived by the New York City Theatre Company, at the City Center of Music and Drama, 9 January.
Staged by Michael Gordon.
Sets and costumes by Emeline Roche.
Production Manager, Billy Matthews.

Cast

Johnny-the-Priest	Frank Rowan
Chris Christopherson	Art Smith
Marthy Owen	Grace Valentine
Anna	Celeste Holm
Mat Burke	Kevin McCarthy

A generally welcomed revival, with main criticism against Miss Holm's interpretation. The play was moved to the Lyceum Theatre for an extended run, but interest suddenly fell and it closed quickly.

Total performances: 29

1952

DESIRE UNDER THE ELMS

Revived by the American National Theatre and Academy at the ANTA Playhouse, 16 January.

Staged by Harold Clurman.

Set by Mordecai Gorelik.

Costumes by Ben Edwards.

Cast

Eben Cabot	Douglas Watson
Simeon Cabot	Lou Polan
Peter Cabot	George Mitchell
Ephraim Cabot	Karl Malden
Abbie Putnam	Carol Stone

Another highly praised revival which had more success than the *ANNA CHRISTIE* of City Center, yet was unable to maintain a sustained run. Malden's Cabot was considered to be very powerful.

Total performances: 46

1956

THE ICEMAN COMETH

Presented 8 May at Circle-in-the-Square, New York.

Staged by José Quintero.

Scenery and lighting by David Hays.

Costumes by Deidre Cartier.

Revival supervised by Leigh Connell, Theodore Mann, and Jose Quintero.

Cast

Harry Hope	Farrell Pelly
Ed Mosher	Phil Pheffer
Pat McGloin	Albert Lewis
Willie Oban	Addison Powell
Joe Mott	William Edmonson
Piet Wetjoen	Richard Abbott
Cecil Lewis	Richard Bowler
James Cameron	James Greene
Hugo Kalmar	Paul Andor
Larry Slade	Conrad Bain
Rocky Pioggi	Peter Falk
Don Parritt	Larry Robinson
Pearl	Patricia Brooks
Margie	Gloria Scott Backe
Cora	Dolly Jonah
Chuck Morello	Joe Marr
Hickey	Jason Robards, Jr.
Moran	Mal Throne
Lieb	Charles Hamilton

This tiny Greenwich Village theatre made theatrical history by undertaking this play. Its large cast and extreme length plus its unsuccessful stage history were enough to discourage any producer. The revival, presented in arena style, was none the less an immediate success. Most critics found the production superior to the original in nearly every way. The intimate atmosphere of the theatre itself and the excellent casting and direction all contributed to the powerful impact. Mrs. O'Neill was so pleased with the entire undertaking that she asked Quintero to produce *LONG DAY'S JOURNEY*.

Total performances: 565

LONG DAY'S JOURNEY INTO NIGHT

Produced 7 November at the Helen Hayes Theatre, New York.

Staged by José Quintero.

Settings by David Hays.

Lighting by Tharon Muser.
Costumes by Motley.
Production supervised by Leigh Connell, Theodore Mann, and José Quintero.

Cast

James Tyrone	Frederic March
Mary Tyrone	Florence Eldridge
James Tyrone, Jr.	Jason Robards, Jr.
Edmund Tyrone	Bradford Tillman
Cathleen	Katherine Ross

The immediate success of the Stockholm production and the praise given the published version in February, 1956, prompted a demand for a New York production. The play had been planned for release 25 years after O'Neill's death, but Mrs. O'Neill has revealed that her husband anticipated release much earlier, and always wanted the Royal Dramatic Theatre in Stockholm to do the play. The tremendous success of Quintero's *ICEMAN* at the Circle-in-the-Square prompted Mrs. O'Neill to ask him to stage this play on Broadway. It was highly praised by the critics.

Total performances: 390

1957

A MOON FOR THE MISBEGOTTEN

Produced 2 May at the Bijou Theatre, New York.
Staged by Carmen Capalbo.
Settings by William Pitkin.
Lighting by Lee Watson.
Costumes by Ruth Morley.
Production supervised by Carmen Capalbo and Stanley Chase.

Cast

Josie Hogan	Wendy Hiller
Mike Hogan	Glenn Cannon

Phil Hogan .... Cyril Cusack
James Tyrone, Jr. .... Franchot Tone
T. Stedman Harder .... William Woodson

Ten years after the Guild failed to bring the first company into New York following its tryout failures, Carmen Capalbo independently staged O'Neill's last play to somewhat reserved critical reception which generally found Wendy Hiller's interpretation of Josie the best aspect of the production.

Total performances: 68

1958

A TOUCH OF THE POET

Produced 2 October at the Helen Hayes Theatre.
Directed by Harold Clurman.
Designed by Ben Edwards.
Produced by Robert Whitehead.

Cast

Mickey Maloy .... Tom Clancy
Jamie Cregan .... Curt Conway
Sara Melody .... Kim Stanley
Nora Melody .... Helen Hayes
Cornelius Melody .... Eric Portman
Dan Roche .... John Call
Patty O'Dowd .... Art Smith
Patch Riley .... Farrell Pelly
Deborah .... Betty Field
Nicholas Gadsby .... Luis Van Rooten

Once again Stockholm witnessed this only surviving portion of the many-play cycle, *A TALE OF POSSESSORS SELF-DISPOSSESSED* before it arrived in New York. Despite its obvious fragmentary nature as part of a much larger concept, the production was enthusiastically received.

Total performances: 284

1959

THE GREAT GOD BROWN

Revived by the Phoenix Theatre at the Coronet Theatre, 6 October 1959.
Directed by Stuart Vaughan.
Settings and costumes by Will Steven Armstrong.
Lighting by Tharon Musser.

Cast

Mrs. Brown	Sasha Von Scherler
Mr. Brown	Patrick Hines
Billy Brown	Robert Lansing
Mrs. Anthony	Patricia Ripley
Mr. Anthony	J. D. Cannon
Dion	Fritz Weaver
Margaret	Nan Martin
Cybel	Gerry Jedd

Total performances: 32

THE NON-DRAMATIC O'NEILL

O'Neill wrote nothing of permanent significance other than his plays. Before he entered Harvard in 1914, he edited a poetry column in the New London, Connecticut, *Telegraph*, but he was often forced to keep it going by his own contributions. Some of the poems he signed; others he designated by various cryptic signatures, such as an "O" on one day, an "N" the next, an "E" the following day, and so on through his name. The left wing New York *Call* and F.P.A.'s "Conning Tower" printed some of his poems, and Sanborn and Clark (over O'Neill's friendly protest) reprinted several in their 1931 *Bibliography of the Works of Eugene O'Neill* (No. 115).

The list below includes the very few items other than the poems which O'Neill wrote in addition to his plays. Until the entire Yale collection of manuscripts is opened for investigation, this list represents a virtually complete report of O'Neill's non-dramatic writings.

Entries are chronological.

1917

"Tomorrow." *The Seven Arts*, June, pp. 147-170.

O'Neill's only published short story. He told Richard Dana Skinner that he once wrote another story containing the germ of *THE HAIRY APE*, but it was never published. (Reported in Skinner's *Eugene O'Neill: A Poet's Quest* No. 123.)

1920

"A letter from O'Neill." NY *Times*, 11 Apr., VI, 2.

Noted as No. 20 in Sanborn and Clark's bibliography. It is O'Neill's own explanation of the origin of *HORI-*

ZON through his acquaintance with an old sea dog who continually cursed his foolishness for running away to sea 20 years before.

1921

"Eugene O'Neill's credo and his reasons for his faith." NY *Tribune,* 13 Feb., 1:4, 6:5.

O'Neill's written defense of *DIFF'RENT,* which attempts to show that the characters are ordinary human beings.

Letter to the editor. NY *Times,* 18 Dec., VI, 1:8.

Dated Provincetown, 12 Dec. Attempts to show that the ending of *ANNA CHRISTIE* is neither happy nor unhappy. Only the immediate crisis is solved; the problem continues. Sanborn and Clark, No. 21.

1924

"Strindberg and our theatre." *Provincetown Playbill* No. 1, Season 1923-1924. Also in NY *Times,* 6 Jan., VII, 1:1 [Reprinted in Deutsch and Hanau, *The Provincetown,* NY, Farrar & Rinehart, 1931 (No. 29).]

A widely quoted article in which O'Neill states his debt to Strindberg and his belief in the Swedish dramatist's importance in world theatre.

1925

"Playwright and critic: The record of a stimulating correspondence." Boston *Transcript,* 31 Oct., III, 8.

Letters from O'Neill to George Jean Nathan. They also appear in Isaac Goldberg's *The Theatre of George Jean Nathan* (No. 52).

"Are the actors to blame?" *Provincetown Playbill* No. 1, Season 1925-1926. Also in NY *Times* 8 Nov., VIII, 2:1 [Reprinted in Deutsch and Hanau, *The Provincetown*, NY, Farrar & Rinehart, 1931 (No. 29).]

A plea for repertory acting, which O'Neill feels will enable the modern actor to break the restrictions of type casting and give the playwright, director and designer something to work with. Sanborn and Clark, No. 36.

"The Fountain." Greenwich Village Theatre program, No. 3, Season 1924-1925.

O'Neill explains that this play represents his ideas of what prompted Ponce de Leon to seek the Fountain of Youth. O'Neill takes a solemn oath that the play is not "morbid realism." Sanborn and Clark, No. 41. (This Program also contains a valuable list of O'Neill's destroyed plays.)

1926

"The playwright explains." NY *Times*, 14 Feb., VIII, 2:1 and other newspapers of 13 & 14 Feb. [Reprinted in Quinn, A. H., *The American drama from the Civil War to the present day*, NY, Crofts, 1936 (No. 110); and Durham and Dodds, eds., *British and American plays, 1830-1945*, NY, Oxford, 1947 (No. 34).]

O'Neill's explanation of the meanings behind the characters in *BROWN*. It is not always clear, and his "explanation of this explanation" almost needs further clarification. Sanborn and Clark No. 50.

Letter on *Goat Song*. NY *Times*, 7 Mar., VIII, 2:8.

> O'Neill writes his praise for one of the most stimulating evenings ever spent in the theatre.

1928

Foreword to *Anathema: Litanies of negation*, by Benjamin De Casseres. NY, Gotham Book Mart.

> O'Neill wrote the foreword to this book at the request of his very good friend, De Casseres. It was his first and last contribution of this type, and after its publication he consistently refused to undertake anything else like it for any purpose whatever. This book of poetry, limited to 1250 copies, was not a success. Perhaps O'Neill's almost vicious attack on the public for their ignorance of De Casseres was no help.

1931

"O'Neill's own story of Electra in the making." NY *Her-Trib.* Th. Sec., 8 Nov., p. 2. Frequently reprinted elsewhere. Appears in Clark's *European theories of the drama*, NY, Brown, 1946, pp. 529-536 (No. 22).

> Revealing excerpts from O'Neill's working diary for *MOURNING BECOMES ELECTRA*.

1932

"O'Neill says Soviet stage has realized his dreams." NY *Her-Trib.*, 19 June.

Excerpts from an O'Neill letter to the Kamerny Theatre, praising the performance of *CHILLUN* and *DESIRE* which he saw in Paris. This refers to one of the few occasions when O'Neill attended the theatre himself. He almost never saw a production of his own plays, here or abroad.

"Memoranda on masks." *American Spectator*, 1 (Nov.) 3.

O'Neill's plea for a masked drama to indicate true inner psychological forces, both in modern and classical drama. Only with masks can we see the true meanings as in Hamlet, etc.

"Second thoughts." *American Spectator*, 1 (Dec) 2.

O'Neill states that he wishes to add many more masks to all his plays, including all those which originally contained them.

1933

"A dramatist's notebook." *American Spectator* 1 (Jan.) 2.

A further defense of masks for stage crowd effects, an aid to the "imaginative" theatre and an improvement for acting techniques.

1935

"Prof. George Pierce Baker." NY *Times*, 13 Jan., IX, 1:2.

O'Neill's brief tribute to his teacher upon Baker's death. He says Baker's inspiration and encouragement made him believe in himself and his work.

"We owe him all the finest we have." *Emerson Quarterly,* (Emerson College of Oratory, Boston) 15 (Jan.) 1-2.

Brief tribute to the inspiration Baker supplied.

1936

Brown, John Mason. "Eugene O'Neill salutes Mr. Anderson's Winterset." NY *Post,* 6 Apr.

Reprints O'Neill's letter to Drama Critics' Circle praising their choice for annual prize.

1939

"Prof. G. P. Baker, a note and some communications." In *George Pierce Baker: A memorial.* NY, Dramatists Play Service.

O'Neill's contribution to this volume praises his erstwhile teacher.

1956

"The last will and testament of Silverdene Emblem O'Neill." New Haven, Yale University Library, 1956.

This is the will which O'Neill wrote on the death of a favorite dog. It was published by the Yale Library and presented to Mrs. O'Neill upon the publication of *LONG DAY'S JOURNEY.*

A CRITICAL BIBLIOGRAPHY

CRITICAL BIBLIOGRAPHY

GENERAL INTRODUCTION

This Bibliography is designed as a comprehensive guide to the critical reception given Eugene O'Neill in this country from his earliest days as a contributing dramatist until the end of 1959, and to the limited but valuable biographical material found in American books and periodicals. It is arranged in the following three main divisions, each with its own individual pattern explained by an appropriate introduction:

BOOKS. All references from individually published volumes, other than periodicals.

PERIODICALS. All general references from any form of periodical, as distinct from reviews and criticism of individual plays.

INDIVIDUAL PLAYS. All references, whatever the source, to produced and published versions of the separate plays.

Each main entry is briefly annotated. In most cases these notes do not criticize the reference material but merely give a short summary of each writer's central idea, so that the user may estimate its value without first having to seek it out.

No bibliography of this type can hope to be absolutely "complete" by the inclusion of all available material. Limits must be set and lines must be drawn if the end product is to have practical *use* in an easily *usable* form. Furthermore, there are bound to be omissions because of unavailability of sources, or simply because of unintentional oversight. When these gaps do exist, it is hoped that any future revisions will be able to fill them.

The following restrictions apply:

1. Only those items relating directly to Eugene O'Neill have been included. This embraces all material about his life and plays: critical, biographical, or merely informational. It eliminates all comments upon this material by other critics. For example, books of criticism, like Richard Dana Skinner's widely quoted *Eugene O'Neill: A Poet's Quest*, or biographies

by Barrett Clark and others, are listed. Subsequent criticisms of the books by other reviewers are not.

2. O'Neill did not write for the screen or the musical stage; all motion picture and musical versions of his works were the products of other hands. Consequently, only those reviews and opinions dealing with his plays are included. This eliminates comments on the filmed *STRANGE INTERLUDE, MOURNING BECOMES ELECTRA, DESIRE UNDER THE ELMS*, and others. It also eliminates the opera version of *THE EMPEROR JONES*, as well as *New Girl in Town (ANNA CHRISTIE)* and *Take Me Along (AH, WILDERNESS!)*.

3. With isolated exception, no foreign references, save those few items written by English or European critics especially for publication in this country, have been listed. Prof. Horst Frenz of Indiana University has made a study of O'Neill's European reputation, and his forthcoming work on this subject will fill this important gap. Meanwhile, Prof. Frenz's several articles on the subject may be consulted with reward.

4. Although several of O'Neill's plays, such as *DESIRE UNDER THE ELMS, ALL GOD'S CHILLUN GOT WINGS, STRANGE INTERLUDE* and others, have encountered censorship difficulties, and a suit was instituted against *STRANGE INTERLUDE* for plagiarism, no factual news items about these events are included. Most facts of this nature and all important information concerning O'Neill's private life are placed in the Life Chronology (p. 91).

For ease in cross reference and indexing, entries are numbered consecutively straight through the entire bibliography.

Consult the introduction to each of the three main divisions for further explanation of the limitations and arrangements of the material it contains.

ABBREVIATIONS USED IN THIS BIBLIOGRAPHY

Amer. — American
Am. Lit. — American Literature
Am. Mag. — American Magazine
Am. Merc. — American Mercury
Am. Quar. — American Quarterly
Am. Rev. — American Review
Am. Schol. — American Scholar
Am. Speech — American Speech
Ariz. Quar. — Arizona Quarterly
Arts & Dec. — Arts and Decoration

Bk. — Book
Brook. — Brooklyn

Cath. Wld. — Catholic World
Ch. — Chapter
Christ. Cent. — Christian Century—
Class. Jour. — Classical Journal
Coll. Eng. — College English
Comp. Lit. — Compartive
  Literature
Contemp. Rev. — Contemporary
  Review
Cur. Op. — Current Opinion

Dram. Mir. — Dramatic Mirror

ed. — editor; edition
Ed. Th. Jour. — Educational
  Theatre Journal
Eng. Jour. — English Journal
Eng. Rev. — English Review
Eng. Stud. — English Studies

Her-Trib. — Herald-Tribune

illus. — illustrated
Ind. & Week. R. — Independent
  and Weekly Review
Ind. Quar. for Bookmen — Indiana
  Quarterly for Bookmen

Jour. — Journal
Jour-Am. — Journal American
Jour. Comm. — Journal of Commerce

Ky. For. Lang. Quar. — Kentucky
  Foreign Language Quarterly

Lit. D. — Literary Digest
Lit. Supp. — Literary Supplement
Liv. Age — Living Age

mag. — magazine
Mich. Alum. Quar. Rev. — Michigan
  Alumni Quarterly Review
Mod. Dr. — Modern Drama
Mod. Lang. Notes — Modern
  Language Notes
Mod. Lang. Q. — Modern Languages
  Quarterly

New Rep. — New Republic
New States. — New Statesman
No. — Number
North Am. Rev. — North American
  Review
ns — new series
NY — New York
NYPL — New York Public Library

p. — page
pp. — pages
Phila. — Philadelphia
Pitt. — Pittsburgh
PMLA — Publication of the Modern
  Language Association
prod. — production
pub. — publishing; publisher

quar. — quarterly
Quar. Jour. Sp. — Quarterly Journal
  of Speech

Rev. — Review
rev. ed. — revised edition
Rev. of Rev. — Review of Reviews

Sat. R. Lit. — Saturday Review of
  Literature. Also indicated as Sat.
  R. after magazine dropped the
  "literature."
sec. — section
South Atl. Quar. — South Atlantic
  Quarterly
South Sp. Jour. — Southern Speech
  Journal

Theatre — Theatre Magazine
Th. Arts — Theatre Arts, including
  all of its many titles such as
  Theatre Arts Magazine, Theatre
  Arts Monthly, etc.
Th. Guild Mag. — Theatre Guild
  Magazine

Th. World — Theatre World
Tulane Dr. Rev. — Tulane Drama
  Review

Univ. — University
Univ. of Cal. Chron. — University of
  California Chronicle

v. — volume

Va. Quar. Rev. — Virginia Quarterly
  Review
Van. F. — Vanity Fair
vol. — volume

Week End R. — Week End Review
Weekly Rev. — Weekly Review
Wor-Tel. — World-Telegram
W. W. Daily — Women's Wear Daily

GENERAL REFERENCES — BOOKS

INTRODUCTION

It is virtually impossible to discuss contemporary drama without mention of Eugene O'Neill, and his name receives extended consideration in nearly every kind of dramatic history. References are also frequent in the broader literary histories, in collections of essays, books of literary criticism, and in similar volumes. There is also a limited but important library devoted exclusively to O'Neill as man and artist. This portion of the bibliography is a compilation of these references, arranged as explained below.

I. CONTENTS. Certain restrictions have been made in the type and treatment of the material.

1. No item has been entered unless it has been considered worthy of the effort to seek it out. This eliminates a considerable number of merely passing references to O'Neill contained in a wide variety of books.

2. As a general rule, introductions to plays contained in standard drama anthologies have been omitted. Most of them, even in the finer collections, are so short and routine that they contribute nothing to O'Neill scholarship. Only a few of these prefaces are important enough for inclusion.

3. Articles in other anthologies are listed independently, or under the title of the volume that includes them, depending upon the type of book, the familiarity of its editor, or the importance of the original author. For instance, the introduction by Joseph Wood Krutch to the familiar Modern Library *Nine Plays by Eugene O'Neill* is listed under "Krutch." The book itself is not listed. On the other hand, an essay by Alan Reynolds Thompson published in a collection by Norman Foerster appears twice, under Thompson and Foerster, because of the reputation of each man. In all cases, cross references are included, but annotations appear only with the main entry.

4. All items *reprinted* from other sources are handled in this manner:

a. Essays from other books are included without annotation under the title of the volume in which they are reprinted if the book's author and/or the title are of recognizable importance. Again, Krutch's "Introduction" is an appropriate example. It appears not only by itself under "Krutch," but is also listed under Moses and Brown's *The American Drama as Seen by Its Critics*, a well-known collection of critical essays. Cross references are included, but all items receive full annotation only under their main entry.

b. Reprints of essays of a general nature (excluding individual play reviews) which first appeared in periodicals or newspapers are listed without comment under the title of the volume in which they appeared, with appropriate cross reference to the main entry included under Periodicals.

c. Reprints of individual play reviews are listed without annotation under the title of the volume in which they appear, with appropriate cross references to the main entry under Individual Plays.

II. MECHANICS. This biblography is patterned after standard bibliographic practices, but departs on occasion as shown below. The order of information for each entry is as follows:

1. Author or editor in alphabetical order. Title is used if author is unknown; no entry appears under "Anonymous."

2. Book title, in *italics*. Library of Congress catalogue card procedure is followed by capitalizing only first words and proper nouns.

3. City of publication (New York is NY throughout); publisher's name, abbreviated but easily recognizable; publication year. Pertinent information about all subsequent editions follows immediately.

4. Specific chapter or page reference to those sections dealing with American drama and/or O'Neill, if separate from main body of book.

5. Information, included in brackets [ ], concerning all subsequent reprintings of the material in other publications.

6. Brief annotation, primarily designed to furnish a concise picture of the contents of each entry. Occasionally,

significant references will be criticized or evaluated in the accompanying note.

NOTE: Entries of more than routine interest or of special significance are marked with an asterisk (*) at the left margin. All of O'Neill's plays are spelled out in *CAPITAL LETTERS*. An abbreviated form is often used to save space; *e.g.*, *ICEMAN* for *THE ICEMAN COMETH*; *DESIRE* for *DESIRE UNDER THE ELMS*, and so on.

1. Angoff, Charles, ed. *The world of George Jean Nathan*. NY, Knopf, 1952.
Reprints the following essays by Nathan:
"Eugene O'Neill," from *Intimate Notebooks* (No. 96), pp. 30-42.
Review of *ICEMAN*, from *Theatre Book of the Year 1946-1947* (No. 100), pp. 395-411.

2. Atkinson, Brooks. *Broadway scrapbook*. NY, Theatre Arts, 1947.
Reprints these two essays:
"O'Neill gets the Nobel prize," originally, "Ennobel-ing O'Neill," NY *Times*, 22 Nov. 1936 (No. 159), pp. 52-55.
"The Iceman Cometh," originally, "Four-hour O'Neill," NY *Times*, 20 Oct. 1946 (No. 1169), pp. 241-246.

* 3. Bentley, Eric. *In search of theater*. NY, Knopf, 1953; Vintage, 1954. Part Two, No. 9, "Trying to like O'Neill."
The opening chapter, "The Broadway Intelligentsia," discusses the inferiority of *ICEMAN*. The essay "Trying to Like O'Neill" was originally published in *Kenyon Review*, July 1952 (No. 172).

* 4. — — — —. *The playwright as thinker*. NY, Reynal & Hitchcock, 1946; Harcourt, Brace, 1949; London, R. Hale, 1949.
Chapter Two, "Tragedy in Modern Dress," discusses the new *genre* of the tragedy of modern life. Section V and appended notes discuss Wedekind and O'Neill as representative of the aftermath of Ibsenesque bourgeois tragedy, of which *ELECTRA*

is a "grotesque" example. O'Neill's seeming profundity turns into "silliness," says Bentley, taking issue with Krutch's attitudes (Nos. 68 & 69). The "melodramadness" school of Geddes (No. 47) and others will applaud Bentley, while those who side with Skinner (No. 122) and Krutch may be offended. Bentley's well-founded comments, however, must be seriously considered.

5. Blankenship, Russell. *American literature as an expression of the national mind.* NY, Holt, 1931. "Eugene O'Neill," pp. 710-717.

Mostly facts about the plays. The criticism finds *LAZARUS* and *BROWN* at top of O'Neill's works.

6. Block, Anita. *The changing world in plays and theatre.* Boston, Little, Brown, 1939, pp. 137-193.

Plot detail and dialogue passages from all of O'Neill's plays. Miss Block considers O'Neill a great genius and has only praise for his work. Interesting comparison can be made with Eleanor Flexner's left wing approach (No. 40).

*   7. Boulton, Agnes. *Part of a long story.* NY, Doubleday, 1958.

This is the first half of a proposed two volume account of O'Neill's eleven-year marriage to Miss Boulton. It begins with her arrival in New York and first meeting with the 29-year old playwright in 1917 and carries through the birth of their first child, Shane, in October, 1919. The story is told without emotion or recrimination as a romance between two lonely people seeking desperately to find themselves amid their hard drinking, hard living Bohemian friends. It is curiously erratic in precise detail. Many important dates and other facts we would like to know are frequently omitted or noted as "forgotten"; yet it is filled with minute descriptions of long alcoholic binges or the items of food at a particular meal. None the less, it is a rewarding book. For instance, it reveals O'Neill's own version of his first marriage and his suicide attempt as told to his wife, and there is considerable opportunity to become acquainted with the elder brother, James. More important, perhaps, is Miss Boulton's recreation of O'Neill's early struggles for artistic recognition in Greenwich Village and Provincetown while submitting periodically to complete alcoholic paralysis. The entire story seems to emerge from an atmosphere that can only be termed nightmarish. Even if Miss Boulton does not complete her second volume, the student of O'Neill will find much to be grateful for in this short work.

* 8. Bowen, Croswell, assisted by Shane O'Neill. *The curse of the misbegotten: A tale of the house of O'Neill.* NY, McGraw-Hill, 1959.
Extensively assisted by O'Neill's younger son, Bowen has attempted to tell the story of O'Neill's life and artistic career in terms of the apparent "curse" upon the "house"; namely, the inability of its members successfully to communicate to each other their deep capacity for love, with the resulting doom to a lonely isolated life in the midst of material and artistic plenty. It is not, however, merely a book of critical analysis or philosophical interpretation, but is by far the most complete factual account of O'Neill's personal history to be published through 1959. Its early chapters provide specific detail helpfully supplementing Miss Boulton's account (No. 7), and the entire volume gives more insight into O'Neill's vastly complex inner nature and outer character manifestations than any other work up to this time. Still, it is not a true biography; it is, as Bowen states, a "tale" — highly readable, vastly interesting, and, like Miss Boulton's report, terrifying in the darkness it reveals but cannot successfully explain. Its major drawback is Bowen's many pauses to discuss the merits of individual plays as they appeared, thus slowing down the interesting story he is telling.

9. Boyd, Alice K. *The interchange of plays between London and New York, 1910-1939.* NY, King's Crown Press, 1948.
This detailed study of plays that crossed the Atlantic discusses the comparative success and failure of each. Includes all of O'Neill's plays staged in England, with complete statistical data. An extremely valuable document for a comparative study of British and American writers and audiences.

10. Brooks, Cleanth, and Robert B. Heilman. *Understanding drama: Twelve plays.* NY, Holt, 1948.
Appendix A compares the *Oresteia* with *ELECTRA.*

11. Brooks, Van Wyck. *The confident years.* NY, Dutton, 1952. "Eugene O'Neill: Harlem," pp. 539-553.

Brooks reviews O'Neill's plays and career, with emphasis upon treatment of the Negro. He determines that perhaps O'Neill is "all the more American because he was uncertain, tentative, puzzling, and groping."

12. Brown, John Mason. *Letters from greenroom ghosts.* NY, Viking, 1934. "Christopher Marlowe to Eugene O'Neill," pp. 69-116.

An original and clever book, incorporating much of Brown's dramatic criticism in the form of letters from great artists of the past. Marlowe finds similarity between himself and O'Neill and praises the tragic view, but warns that O'Neill is beyond himself in Freud. Having come this far, he is expected to go further, and mere recollection, as in *AH, WILDERNESS!*, will not suffice.

13. — — — —. *Seeing more things.* NY, Whittlesey House, 1948. "Moaning at the bar," pp. 257-265.

Reprint of "All O'Neilling," review of *ICEMAN, Sat. R. Lit.,* 19 Oct. 1946 (Nos. 183 & 1174).

14. — — — —. *Still seeing things.* NY, McGraw-Hill, 1950.

Reprints "American tragedy," *Sat. R. Lit.,* 6 Aug. 1949 (No. 184), pp. 185-195.

15. — — — —. *Two on the aisle.* NY, Norton, 1938. "Mr. O'Neill's Mourning Becomes Electra," pp. 136-142.

Reprint of review in NY *Post,* 27 Oct. 1931 (No. 1455).

16. — — — —. *Upstage: The American theatre in performance.* NY, Norton, 1930. "Eugene O'Neill," pp. 60-77.

O'Neill is ironic instead of tragic, says Brown. *DESIRE* is the nearest approach to Thebes. Brown finds O'Neill an "unsatisfactory genius" whose plays are "peaked with greatness rather than sustained by it"; his mysticism may be his undoing.

17. Canby, Henry Seidel. *Seven years' harvest: Notes on contemporary literature.* NY, Farrar and Rinehart, 1936. "Scarlet becomes crimson," pp. 139-146.

Reprint of Canby's article on *ELECTRA, Sat. R. Lit.*, 7 Nov. 1931 (No. 1469).

18. Cargill, Oscar. *Intellectual America: Ideas on the march.* NY, Macmillan, 1941. Ch. IV, "The primitivists," pp. 332-340; Ch. VI, "The Freudians," pp. 685-720.

O'Neill is treated in two categories. The early works of *JONES, APE* and others are regarded as "primitivist," *INTERLUDE* and *ELECTRA* as Freudian. Good analysis of most of the plays, finding *ELECTRA* in many ways superior to the Greek.

19. Carpenter, Frederic I. *American literature and the dream.* NY, Philosophical Library, 1955. "The romantic tragedy of Eugene O'Neill," pp. 133-143.

A review of the more important plays in terms of their dramatizing O'Neill's contrast between dream and reality. Carpenter feels that O'Neill has always known the impossibility of achieving the romantic dream, and feels the result is resignation and quiescence.

20. Cheney, Sheldon. *The art theatre.* NY, Knopf, 1925.

This book is not about plays but about the development of art theatres. Some excellent illustrations include pictures of the Guild Theatre, Neighborhood Playhouse, and Pasadena Playhouse, all directly associated with major O'Neill plays. O'Neill is mentioned only in connection with the Provincetown and other groups.

* 21. Clark, Barrett H. *Eugene O'Neill.* NY, Robt. M. McBride, 1926. Subsequent editions entitled *Eugene O'Neill: The man and his plays,* NY, McBride, 1929; London, Jonathan Cape, 1933; NY, McBride, 1936; Dover, 1947. [Excerpts printed in *Theatre Arts,* May 1926, pp. 325-326.]

The 1926 edition was the first book published anywhere to be devoted entirely to Eugene O'Neill. The same general plan of the original was maintained in all subsequent editions: a brief life history and a short analysis of each play from *WIFE FOR A LIFE* to date of publication. Each edition contains passages from letters and articles by O'Neill, plus various bibliographical material. O'Neill never quite understood Clark's motives for writing the book in the first place; but, while expressing his plain disapproval, never interfered. The 1947 edition is, of course, the most valuable of all and includes *MOON FOR THE MISBEGOTTEN*. Although it is the best single book about O'Neill up to 1947, it is not a complete biography nor a detailed criticism. The material, however, still has its place on any reference shelf.

*   22. – – – –. *European theories of the drama, with a supplement on the American drama*. NY, Crown, 1947, pp. 529-536.

Prints excerpts from O'Neill's working diary for *ELECTRA*. (See Non-Dramatic O'Neill, 1931.)

23. – – – –. *A study of the modern drama*. NY, Appleton, 1925, 1928, 1936, 1938, pp. 404-410 (same in all editions).

Statistics and data on O'Neill's life and plays; appropriately changed with each new edition.

24. – – – –, and George Freedly, eds. *A history of modern drama*. NY, Appleton-Century, 1947. Ch. XIII, "Eugene O'Neill," pp. 682-691.

General review of O'Neill life and works. The book itself is dedicated to O'Neill.

25. Clurman, Harold. *Lies like truth*. NY, Macmillan, 1958. "Eugene O'Neill," pp. 24-33.

Three short essays on O'Neill's artistry, the published version of *MOON FOR THE MISBEGOTTEN* (No. 1410) and production of *LONG DAY'S JOURNEY* (No. 1309). Clurman finds O'Neill our greatest dramatist because of his consistent writing as an artist.

26. Combs, George H. *These amazing moderns*. St. Louis, The Bethany Press, 1933. "Eugene O'Neill," pp. 248-270.

A prejudiced view which finds ignorance of O'Neill's plays to be bliss, not loss. The critical comment makes no effort to go below O'Neill's surface violence.

27. Commager, Henry Steele. *The American mind: An in-*

terpretation of American thought and character since the 1800's.
New Haven, Yale, 1950, p. 110.

O'Neill discussed in connection with Faulkner, Hemingway, and Jeffers as spokesmen for a new determinism, taking away from the conscience of men the responsibility for social and human evils.

28. Cowley, Malcolm, ed. *After the genteel tradition: American writers since 1900.* NY, Norton, 1937.

Reprints Lionel Trilling's "Eugene O'Neill, a revaluation," *New Rep.*, 23 Sept. 1936 (No. 377), pp. 127-140.

* 29. Deutsch, Helen, and Stella Hanau. *The Provincetown: A study of the theatre.* NY, Farrar & Rinehart, 1931. [Pre-publication excerpts printed in *Theatre Guild Mag.*, Aug. 1930, pp. 20-21, and Sept. 1930, p. 30. Passages from Ch. 1 are in *Drama*, June 1931, p. 3.]

This informal and interesting history is the definitive text concerning the Provincetown Players. No study of O'Neill is complete without it. Contains a complete list of all productions, with casts, from 1915 through 17 Nov. 1929. Also valuable for its publication of O'Neill's two articles, "Are the Actors to Blame?" (See Non-Dramatic O'Neill, 1925.)

* 30. De Voto, Bernard. *Minority report.* Boston, Little, Brown, 1943. "Monte Cristo in modern dress," pp. 190-197.

Reprint of "Minority report," *Sat. R. Lit.*, 21 Nov. 1936 (No. 220).

* 31. Dickinson, Thomas H. *Playwrights of the new American theatre.* NY, Macmillan, 1925. "The playwright unbound," pp. 56-123.

The 67 pages of this essay represent the longest article about O'Neill in a book of criticism up to this time. It reviews each play in the light of O'Neill's creative vitality and imagination, unbound by the confines of criticism and definition.

32. Downer, Alan S. *Fifty years of American drama, 1900-1950.* Chicago, Regnery, 1951.

General review of American plays by type. O'Neill discussed in relation to his various contributions.

33. Dukes, Ashley. *Youngest drama: Studies of 50 dramatists.* London, Benn, 1923; Chicago, Charles H. Sergel, 1924, pp. 70-76.
A discussion of modern drama since Ibsen. Favorable comment on O'Neill plays through *ANNA CHRISTIE.*

34. Durham, Willard H., and John W. Dodds, eds. *British and American plays, 1830-1946.* NY, Oxford, 1947. "Eugene O'Neill," pp. 535-538, introducing *BROWN.*
The essay on O'Neill in this anthology is brief, but these two items are also reprinted:
O'Neill's own explanation of the play (See Non-Dramatic O'Neill, 1926.)
Brooks Atkinson's opening night review, NY *Times*, 25 Jan. 1926 (No. 1025).

35. Eastman, Fred. *Christ in the drama.* NY, Macmillan, 1947. "Eugene O'Neill," pp. 92-103.
Because of his lack of spiritual insight, O'Neill lacks the sense of tragedy found in Euripides, to whom Eastman compares O'Neill in *ELECTRA. DAYS WITHOUT END* shows O'Neill realizes redemption in God's grace.

36. Eaton, Walter Prichard. *The drama in English.* NY, Scribner's, 1930, pp. 331-343.
Brief discussion, mainly about O'Neill's experiments.

37. — — — —. *The theatre guild: The first 10 years.* NY, Brentano's, 1929.
Eaton's informal history of the Guild is interesting and valuable, but discussion of O'Neill, whom the Guild did not produce until 1928, is somewhat incidental. Includes some excellent pictures of Guild productions and the Guild Theatre itself, and a list of all casts of Guild plays for the first ten years. A good non-critical reference.

*   38. Engel, Edwin A. *The haunted heroes of Eugene O'Neill.* Cambridge, Mass., Harvard, 1953.

One of the most complete volumes devoted to a study of the entire O'Neill canon. It specifically avoids bibliography and biography, holding closely to the plays in a concentrated attempt to analyze them and to determine their over-all worth and central themes. Various sections, bearing interesting titles like "Only God's Chillun Got Wings," "Everywoman," and "Everymannon," discuss important items from all plays in chronological order. Engel feels that O'Neill's early plays, up to about 1925, are best, and will in the long run survive. The detailed synopses and the many excerpts from the plays can be legitimately criticized, but to anyone not familiar with O'Neill's works, they will be helpful and revealing.

* 39. Falk, Doris V. *Eugene O'Neill and the tragic tension.* New Brunswick, NJ, Rutgers Univ. Press, 1958.

A 200-page study, expanding a doctoral dissertation, which takes all of the plays in order of their appearance and carefully analyzes them as the cumulative development of a single theme — expressing and assuaging "the lifelong torment of a mind in conflict." A valuable companion to Engel's treatment (No. 38).

* 40. Flexner, Eleanor. *American playwrights, 1918-1938.* NY, Simon & Schuster, 1938. Ch. V, "Eugene O'Neill," pp. 130-197.

A left wing outlook which deplores O'Neill's insistence on dealing with man's relation to God instead of taking into account that the main trouble in society today is man's relation to man. Interesting, if biased, account, especially in the light of O'Neill's initial welcome from socialist groups.

41. Foerster, Norman, ed. *Humanism and America: Essays on the out-look of modern civilization.* NY, Farrar & Rinehart, 1930.

See Thompson, Alan Reynolds, "The dilemma of modern tragedy" (No. 134).

42. Gagey, Edmond M. *Revolution in American drama.* NY, Columbia, 1947. "Eugene O'Neill," pp. 39-70.

Brief review of each major play. Lists nine important contributions O'Neill has made to the stage. He is best remembered for plays which show "ideal fusion of realism and imagination."

43. Gassner, John. *Form and idea in modern theatre.* NY, Dryden, 1956.

Occasional mention of O'Neill in an excellent study of the structure of modern drama.

44. — — — —. *Masters of the drama.* NY, Random House, 1940; Dover, 1945, 1954. "The voyages of O'Neill."

One of the standard comprehensive histories of world drama. Its 16 pages on O'Neill review all the plays with plot outlines and fairly routine comment.

* 45. — — — —. *The theatre in our times.* NY, Crown, 1954. "O'Neill in our time," pp. 249-256; "The Electras of Giraudoux and O'Neill," pp. 257-266.

A major collection of essays on all phases of modern theatre by this tireless compiler of drama anthologies and theatre histories. An excellent companion to *Masters of the Drama* (No. 44). The two fairly brief articles on O'Neill are very good. The first, written before the revival of the mid-fifties, expresses concern for O'Neill's unwarranted neglect by the newer theatrical generation; the second compares and contrasts two modern interpretations of the perennial Electra theme. (Gassner erroneously calls O'Neill's Aegisthus "David Mannon" instead of the correct Adam Brant.) The frontespiece is Gorelik's design for *DESIRE UNDER THE ELMS.*

46. — — — —, ed. *A treasury of the theatre.*

First edition, 1935, and revised edition, 1940, were edited by Gassner together with Philo M. Buck, Jr., and H. S. Alberson. Subtitle: "An anthology of great plays from Ibsen to Odets." Gassner's brief essay, "Eugene O'Neill," pp. 245-248, precedes *ANNA CHRISTIE.* Publisher: Simon and Schuster. Distributor: The Dryden Press.

Next edition, 1950, edited by Gassner alone. Subtitle: "From Henrik Ibsen to Arthur Miller," but spine prints "Ghosts to Death of a Salesman." Two essays on O'Neill, pp. 786-789 and 817-818, precede *ANNA CHRISTIE* and *THE HAIRY APE.* Publisher: Simon and Schuster. Distributor: The Dryden Press.

Later edition, 1960, "Third College Edition," also by Gassner, bears subtitle on title page and spine, "From Henrik Ibsen to Eugene Ionesco." Includes the same plays by O'Neill and the essays bear same pagination. Publisher: Simon and Schuster. Distributor: Henry Holt.

The O'Neill essays are general summaries much in the same style as Gassner's discussion in *Masters of the Drama* (No. 44), but conclude that O'Neill's works are "surely the most Cyclopean dramatic enterprise in the English language."

* 47. Geddes, Virgil. *The melodramadness of Eugene O'Neill.* The Brookfield Pamphlets, No. 4, Brookfield, Conn., The Brookfield Players, Inc., 1934.

This 48-page pamphlet uses most of O'Neill's plays to prove that O'Neill is not truly a man of the theatre because he does not actually contribute to what the new American drama and theatre demand. He lacks a comic spirit, a realistic understanding of women, and a true art; his tragedy is more like melodrama, lacking any philosophy. Geddes' attack is not violent, like Salisbury's (No. 113), but it is heavily one-sided. As one of the few early books devoted to O'Neill alone, however, it is well worth reading.

48. ― ― ― ―. *The theatre of dreadful nights.* The Brookfield Pamphlets, No. 3. Brookfield, Conn., The Brookfield Players, Inc., 1934.

A somewhat violent attack on theatrical producers for their inability to present worthwhile plays. O'Neill is included among the writers which prove the point.

49. Gilder, Rosamond, and others, eds. *Theatre Arts anthology: A record and a prophecy.* NY, Theatre Arts Books, 1950.

Reprints the following from *Theatre Arts:*

Hutchens, John, "Greece to Broadway," Jan. 1932 (No. 1502), pp. 619-622.

Isaacs, Edith, "Meet Eugene O'Neill," Oct. 1926 (No. 278), pp. 168-176.

Macgowan, Kenneth, review of *JONES*, Jan. 1921 (No. 921), pp. 592-594.

50. Glaspell, Susan. *The road to the temple.* London, Benn, 1926; NY, Frederick A. Stokes, 1927.

This biography of George Cram Cook (Miss Glaspell's husband) recounts the development of the Provincetown Players, with the group's early realization of how important O'Neill was to become.

*   51. Goldberg, Isaac. *Drama of transition.* Cincinnati, Stewart Kidd, 1922. "Eugene O'Neill," pp. 457-471.

The first extended discussion of O'Neill in a book of criticism. Prints list of destroyed plays later to appear on Greenwich Village Playbill for *THE FOUNTAIN* (see Non-Dramatic O'Neill, 1925). Goldberg finds O'Neill unable to fuse his elements perfectly, with the "traps of melodrama" evident in his "realism."

*   52. — — — —. *The theatre of George Jean Nathan.* NY, Simon & Schuster, 1926. "Eugene O'Neill to George Jean Nathan," pp. 143-165.

Unique because of its fourteen letters from the young playwright to Nathan, revealing his own attitudes toward his work, the producers, and the critics. No other book has such a large group of letters.

53. Gorelik, Mordecai. *New theatres for old.* NY, Samuel French, 1940. "O'Neill," pp. 230-236.

This volume belongs on every drama reference shelf as the finest account of twentieth century stage techniques. Gorelik discusses O'Neill's "inherited weakness of the will," and other aspects, such as a lack of clear statement of purpose. He agrees with Shaw's opinion that O'Neill is "banshee Shakespeare."

54. Hamilton, Clayton. *Seen on the stage.* NY, Holt, 1920. Reprints review of *BEYOND THE HORIZON, Vogue,* 1 April 1920 (No. 635).

55. Hamilton, William Baskerville. *Fifty years of the South Atlantic Quarterly.* Durham, NC, Duke University Press, 1952. Reprints "Eugene O'Neill," by Homer E. Woodbridge, *South Atl. Quar.,* Jan. 1938 (No. 395), pp. 258-271.

* 56. Hewitt, Barnard. *Theatre USA, 1688 to 1957.* NY, McGraw-Hill, 1959.

A unique history tracing the development of American theatre and drama through contemporary critical opinion. Reprints the following:

Gassner, John, review of *ICEMAN*, *Ed. Th. Jour.*, Oct. 1956 (No. 1222), pp. 279-281.

Kerr, Walter, "Long Day's Journey into Night," NY *Her-Trib.*, 8 Nov. 1956 (No. 1302), pp. 481-482.

Krutch, Joseph Wood, "The god of stumps," *Nation*, 26 Nov. 1924 (No. 747), pp. 333-335.

— — — —, "The tragedy of masks," *Nation*, 10 Feb. 1926 (No. 1054), pp. 363-364.

Lewisohn, Ludwig, "An American tragedy," *Nation*, 21 Feb. 1920 (No. 639), pp. 332-333.

Macgowan, Kenneth, review of *ANNA CHRISTIE*, *Th. Arts*, Jan. 1922 (No. 568), pp. 337-338.

— — — —, review of *JONES*, *Th. Arts*, Jan. 1921 (No. 921), pp. 333-335.

Motherwell, Hiram, "Mourning Becomes Electra," *Th. Guild Mag.*, Dec. 1931 (No. 1481), pp. 387-390.

Seldes, Gilbert, "The Hairy Ape," *Dial*, May 1922 (No. 1141), pp. 338-340.

Skinner, Richard Dana, "Strange Interlude," *Commonweal*, 22 Feb. 1928 (No. 1653), pp. 371-374.

57. Hicks, Granville. *The great tradition: An interpretation of American literature since the Civil war.* Rev. ed., NY, Macmillan, 1935. Ch. VII, "Two roads," pp. 253-256.

O'Neill is treated briefly as one of the literary pessimists of his age.

58. Hoffman, Frederick J. *The twenties: American writing in the post-war decade.* NY, Viking, 1955.

An astute and original discussion of the various types of literary expression during this ten-year period. Each section uses some literary work of particular significance for its "text." O'Neill's inclusion is noteworthy because of its brevity. In "Forms of Experiment and Improvisation" he receives two pages (221-

223) only because of his innovations. He is then summarily dismissed as a failure because of the failure of expressionism itself.

59. Hughes, Glenn. *History of the American theatre, 1700-1950.* NY, Samuel French, 1951, pp. 399-402.

Quick review of O'Neill's career, which brought our dramatic literature to "maturity." A fact-crammed history of the American theatre with excellent pictures of theatres and actors.

60. Isaacs, Edith J. R. *The Negro in the American theatre.* NY, Theatre Arts, 1947. Ch. 5, "Bright lights on Broadway"; Ch. 6, "Plays and players."

Full page picture of Gilpin's Jones; *CHILLUN* regarded as unsuccessful.

61. Jones, Robert Edmond. *Dramatic imagination.* NY, Duell, Sloan & Pearce, 1941.

This outstanding book by the designer who worked as O'Neill's partner should be read by all serious students of the theatre, though there is little mention of O'Neill except *INTERLUDE*, a "brilliant exception" to Jones' generalization that the present theatre is essentially one of prose and journalism.

62. Karsner, David. *Sixteen authors to one.* NY, Lewis Copeland, 1928. Ch. VI, "Eugene O'Neill," pp. 101-122.

Karsner, who spent some time with O'Neill in the Maine woods (see his article in NY *Her-Trib.*, 8 Aug. 1926, No. 283), feels the playwright's mystic quality cannot be conveyed in words.

* 63. Kaucher, Dorothy J. *Modern dramatic structure.* Univ. of Missouri Studies, Columbia, Univ. of Missouri Press, 1 Oct. 1928. Ch. VI, "Eugene O'Neill," pp. 125-158.

A detailed study of the dramatic structure of Eugene O'Neill's major plays. Considerable dialogue and stage directions show the use of sound, action, etc., in the development of the individual play. The progress of insanity in *GOLD* is diagrammed by two interesting charts. This is a valuable contribution to O'Neill scholarship from the dramatic and theatrical point of view, rather than the critical. The entire work of 183 pages is well worth close study, as it represents an interesting if highly technical analysis of modern playwrights and their techniques. A better O'Neill play might have served more aptly for Miss Kaucher's elaborate graph, but otherwise she treats all the plays with equal emphasis.

64. Kenton, Edna. "Provincetown and Macdougal street." Preface to Cook, George Cram, *Greek coins,* NY, George H. Doran, 1925.

Miss Kenton's main tribute is to Cook's efforts with the Provincetown group in its formative days and his insistence that the world would some day know the plays of O'Neill. The rest of the volume is a collection of Cook's poetry.

65. Kerr, Walter. *Pieces at eight.* NY, Simon & Schuster, 1957, pp. 120-125.

Kerr reviews *LONG DAY'S JOURNEY* as an exorcism of O'Neill's past. In summary, he feels that for all O'Neill's many weaknesses, the great strength in the plays is an overwhelming sense of the melodramatic.

* 66. Kinne, Wisner Payne. *George Pierce Baker and the American theatre.* Cambridge, Mass., Harvard, 1954. Ch. XXXVII, "Beauty vs. Broadway — Enter Eugene O'Neill," pp. 191-198.

No student of the American theatre can neglect this book, which recounts the work of the man who "epitomized the lay forces at work in the evolution of twentieth-century American drama." O'Neill's name, of course, reappears constantly throughout the book, along with many illustrations of playbills and scenes from the O'Neill plays produced at Yale. The short chapter devoted to O'Neill is significant because it prints for the first time the letter to Baker in which O'Neill seeks admittance to the 47 Workshop at Harvard, stating "I want to be an artist or nothing."

67. Kreymborg, Alfred. *Troubadour: An autobiography.* NY, Boni & Liveright, 1925. "The Provincetown players," pp. 303-311.

A discussion of O'Neill's association with the Provincetown by one who was there.

* 68. Krutch, Joseph Wood. *The American drama since 1918.* NY, Random House, 1939; George Brazillier, 1957. Ch. III, "Tragedy: Eugene O'Neill," pp. 73-133, both editions.

This "Informal History" is the best single-volume treatment of the major aspects of modern American drama and those who wrote it. The essay on tragedy includes other dramatists, but O'Neill occupies the major position. Krutch consolidates several of his earlier comments, including his introduction to *Nine Plays* (No. 69) into a penetrating and lucid analysis of all of O'Neill's major works. Two central themes are O'Neill's sense of "belonging" and his attempt to bring the grandeur and elevation of tragedy into modern times and temper. This should be a standard reference in any American drama library, especially in its revised version.

* 69. — — — —. Introduction to O'Neill, Eugene, *Nine Plays*, NY, Horace Liveright, 1932; Random House, 1936, 1939 (as Modern Library Giant). [Reprinted in Moses and Brown, *The American theatre as seen by its critics*, NY, W. W. Norton, 1934 (No. 89); in Thorp and Thorp, *Modern writing*, NY, American Book Co., 1944; and in Oppenheimer, Louis, *The passionate playgoer*, NY, Viking, 1958, No. 107.]

Krutch sets forth his consistently held tenet that O'Neill's tragedy is modern in every sense, feeling the view of its audiences as did all great tragedies. The height and depth of passion puts them in the class of those plays that "purge" by pity and terror, despite our lack of clear definition of the phrase. O'Neill's large weakness is lack of great language to accompany his tragic approach.

70. — — — —. *Modernism in modern drama.* Ithaca, NY, Cornell, 1953.

A few general references to O'Neill's regard for tragedy and the man-God theme, which is seen as essentially anti-modernistic, along with views of Maxwell Anderson.

* 71. Lamm, Martin. *Modern drama.* Translated by Karlin Elliott. Oxford, Blackwell's, 1952; NY, Philosophical Library, 1953. "Eugene O'Neill," pp. 315-333.

The essay is mainly a routine review of O'Neill's life and plays, finding him a great writer, with faults, but certainly along with Synge the greatest in the twentieth century. This study of modern drama from the Scandinavian view is worth close attention.

*   72. Langner, Lawrence. *The magic curtain*. NY, Dutton, 1951.

This director of the Theatre Guild, O'Neill's major producer from *MARCO MILLIONS* through the unsuccessful *MOON FOR THE MISBEGOTTEN*, writes of his years in this distinguished producing group, including information about his many contacts as a personal friend of O'Neill. An important document in the study of O'Neill the man and artist.

*   73. Lawson, John Howard. *Theory and technique of playwriting*. NY, Putnam's, 1949. Part II, Ch. V., "Eugene O'Neill," pp. 75-120.

An interesting discourse on O'Neill's confused philosophy and his attempts to display it in later plays. Nina and Hedda help compare O'Neill's and Ibsen's last phases.

74. Lewisohn, Ludwig. *Expression in America*. NY, Harpers, 1932, pp. 543-553.

Strongly unfavorable review, concerned with O'Neill's faults. There is hope O'Neill may "amount to something" some day.

75. Luccock, Halford E. *Contemporary American literature and religion*. Chicago, Willet, Clark, 1934.

ELECTRA is a direct contrast to the ideas of Hebrew and Christian religions.

76. McCarthy, Mary T. *Sights and spectacles 1937-1956*. NY, Farrar and Strauss, 1956.

Reprints "Dry Ice," *Partisan Rev.*, Nov-Dec. 1946 (No. 1189), pp. 81-88.

77. McCole, C. John. *Lucifer at large*. NY, Longmans, Green, 1937, pp. 112-115.

In this somewhat narrow attack on modern literature's treatment of mankind as less than human, O'Neill is mentioned because of his insistence on Freudian interpretations.

78. Macgowan, Kenneth, and William Melnitz. *The living stage.* NY, Prentice Hall, 1955. "Eugene O'Neill — Dramatic pioneer," pp. 487-490.

A comprehensive stage history designed for popular reading. It is somewhat disappointing because of the cheapening effect of its illustrations, which are all drawings instead of plates or photographs. It is, however, a good text, edited by O'Neill's one-time producing partner. O'Neill's original sketches for the setting of *DESIRE* are included.

79. Mackay, Constance D'Arcy. *The little theatre in the United States.* NY, Holt, 1917. "The Provincetown players," pp. 46-53.

Written when O'Neill's plays had been appearing less than a year, this brief history of the Provincetown group mentions the "signal power" of its writers, among them O'Neill and his original themes.

80. Maier, Norman R., and H. Willard Reninger. *A psychological approach to literary criticism.* NY, Appleton, 1933, pp. 101-104.

This interesting book, devoted to a somewhat different approach to literary criticism, terms *INTERLUDE* successful because it follows a successful literary technique, *i.e.*, the direction of the reader is clearly indicated and the precise meaning attained.

81. Mantle, Burns. *Contemporary American playwrights.* NY, Dodd, Mead, 1938. "Eugene O'Neill," pp. 62-73.

Factual account of O'Neill's life and works, with play list.

82. Mayorga, Margaret. *A short history of the American drama.* NY, Dodd, Mead, 1932. "Eugene O'Neill," pp. 317-337.

While mainly discussing playwrights before 1920, Miss Mayorga does review most of O'Neill's plays. Her main criticism is O'Neill's lack of knowledge about the real behavior of obsessed characters.

* 83. Mickle, Alan D. *Six plays of Eugene O'Neill.* NY, Horace Liveright, 1929.

The title is misleading. The book reviews but does not re-print *CHRISTIE, APE, BROWN, FOUNTAIN, MARCO* and *INTERLUDE*. Its complete and unqualified praise of O'Neill places him with Shakespeare, Ibsen, Goethe and Blake. Amidst all of Mickle's assertions that O'Neill could do no wrong, the most remarkable point is his "proof" that all the characters in *STRANGE INTERLUDE* are perfectly normal. None of O'Neill's most avid supporters in America ever admitted this. The lyric adoration is interesting but of limited value, especially in view of the fact that Mickle bases all his criticism on having read but not seen the plays.

84. Middleton, George. *These things are mine: The auto-biography of a journeyman playwright*. NY, Macmillan, 1947, pp. 118-119.
Contains a letter from O'Neill replying to congratulations sent to him on the success of *HORIZON*.

85. Morehouse, Ward. *Just the other day*. NY, McGraw-Hill, 1953.
Random mention of O'Neill in connection with Morehouse's life as a New York dramatic critic. Brief discussion of his stay with O'Neill in France.

86. — — — —. *Matinee tomorrow*. NY, Whittlesey House, 1949. Ch. 11, "The drama's revolt — and O'Neill," pp. 180-193.
General discussion of the new drama and O'Neill's influence. This is a very interesting popular history of 50 years of American drama and theatre by one who witnessed and criticized much of it.

87. Morris, Lloyd R. *Postscript to yesterday. America: The last fifty years*. NY, Random House, 1947. "All man's blundering unhappiness," pp. 177-184.
A general review of O'Neill's major plays and their treatment of the "sickness of today" in a chapter devoted to American play-wrights from Fitch to Behrman.

88. Moses, Montrose J. *The American dramatist*. Boston,

Little, Brown, 1925. Ch. 20, "Eugene O'Neill and the new drama," pp. 415-434.

Moses views the early plays rather narrowly, especially *ALL GOD'S CHILLUN*, and finds O'Neill's view too dark and uncompromising.

89. — — — —, and John Mason Brown. *The American theatre as seen by its critics, 1752-1934.* NY, Norton, 1934.

Reprints the following articles:

Anderson, John, review of *DAYS WITHOUT END*, NY *Journal*, 9 Jan. 1934 (No. 678).

Benchley, Robert, review of *MOURNING BECOMES ELECTRA*, *New Yorker*, 7 Nov. 1931 (No. 1464).

Broun, Heywood, review of *BEYOND THE HORIZON*, NY *Tribune*, 4 Feb. 1920 (No. 610).

Krutch, Joseph Wood, Preface to *Nine Plays*, 1933 ed. (No. 69).

90. Muller, Henry J. *The spirit of tragedy.* NY, Knopf, 1956. "Tragedy in America: O'Neill," pp. 311-315.

In a volume devoted wholly to tragedy as a dramatic art from Greek to modern, O'Neill is seriously and "respectfully" treated as one who, like others, had great but unrealized tragic potential. *ELECTRA* briefly reviewed as his best play.

91. Myers, Henry Alonzo. *Tragedy: A view of life.* Ithaca, NY, Cornell, 1956. V. "Macbeth and the Iceman Cometh: Equivalence and ambivalence in tragedy," pp. 98-109.

O'Neill's tragic view of our time is the sickness of an age. While O'Neill is *ambivalent* in his finding mankind at once attractive and repulsive, Shakespeare shows *equivalence, i.e.,* joy and sorrow, guilt and remorse, and the justice of human destiny. An interesting and original approach to evaluating O'Neill's tragic idea.

92. Myers, J. Arthur. *Fighters of fate.* Baltimore, Williams & Wilkins, 1927. "Eugene O'Neill," pp. 306-318.

This book is subtitled, "A story of men and women who have achieved greatly despite the handicaps of the great white plague." It briefly reviews O'Neill's life and his accomplishments because of and despite his fight with tuberculosis.

93. Nathan, George Jean. *Art of the night.* NY, Knopf, 1928, pp. 160-164.

Nathan discusses O'Neill's sense of humor in *MARCO MIL-LIONS.* It is not a regular kind of humor, but is sardonic and bitter, and can be seen in most of O'Neill's plays.

94. — — — —. *Encyclopedia of the theatre.* NY, Knopf, 1940.

Not actually an "encyclopedia," but a series of items in alphabetical order showing Nathan's extensive theatre knowledge. Four pages on O'Neill recount Nathan's personal acquaintance with the man to whom he dedicated this book.

95. — — — —. *House of Satan.* NY, Knopf, 1926. "A few footnotes on O'Neill," pp. 199-207.

General discussion of what O'Neill has brought to the stage. Contains a number of interesting comments on the public reaction to *ALL GOD'S CHILLUN,* which Nathan sees basically as no different from many plays treating similar problems.

96. — — — —. *The intimate notebooks of George Jean Nathan.* NY, Knopf, 1932, pp. 21-38. [Reprinted in Van Doren, Carl, ed., *The Borzoi reader,* NY, Garden City Pub. Co., 1938, pp. 590-603 (No. 137); and in Angoff, Charles, ed., *The world of George Jean Nathan,* NY, Knopf, 1952, pp. 30-42 (No. 1)]

Intimate notes on O'Neill's personality, with interesting quotations from a letter in which O'Neill sums up his feelings on the completion of *ELECTRA.*

97. — — — —. *Materia critica.* NY, Knopf, 1924. "Certain dramatists," pp. 122-123.

Discussion of O'Neill's failure in Strindbergian drama like *WELDED* and *FIRST MAN.*

98. — — — —. *The morning after the first night.* NY, Knopf, 1938.

Chapter III discusses O'Neill and Anderson.

99. — — — —. *Passing judgments.* NY, Knopf. 1935. Ch. VIII, "O'Neill," pp 112-126.

General discussion; includes *AH, WILDERNESS!, DYNAMO, DAYS WITHOUT END.*

100. — — — —. *Theatre book of the year, 1946-1947.* NY, Knopf, 1947.
Reviews *ICEMAN*, pp. 93-111. Reprinted in Angoff, Charles, ed., *The World of George Jean Nathan* (No. 1).

101. — — — —. *The theatre in the fifties.* NY, Knopf, 1953.
Bits of personal reference here and there. Mentions some of O'Neill's ideas about newer playwrights.

* 102. — — — —. *The theatre of the moment.* NY, Knopf, 1936. Ch. XI, "The recluse of Sea Island," pp. 196-207. [Original article in *Redbook*, Aug. 1935, p. 34 (No. 329).]
Nathan was O'Neill's close personal friend and here tells some highly interesting "inside" stories, dispelling some of the previous misconceptions about his personality. These ten pages and the other "intimacies" of which Nathan writes elsewhere offer some of the best material obtainable on O'Neill the man.

103. — — — —. *The theatre, the drama, and the girls.* NY, Knopf, 1921. "Eugene O'Neill," pp. 181-185.
Nathan championed O'Neill's cause in *The Smart Set* and elsewhere as early as 1917 (see Chronology of Publication), but here mentions him in a book for the first time. Contains plot review of *HORIZON* and short discussion of "the most distinguished young man of the American theatre."

104. — — — —. *The world in falseface.* NY, Knopf, 1923, pp. 79-80; 141-143.
Two brief attacks on the shortsightedness of O'Neill criticism.

105. Nicoll, Allardyce. *World drama.* London, Harrap, 1949; NY, Harcourt, Brace, 1950. Ch. VIII, "Eugene O'Neill," pp. 880-893.
Concise review of each major play. O'Neill is the representative of American drama as a whole, full of vitality and strength, lacking refinements of greatness or sense of relationship with his times, but with no true literary ability. (Nicoll was Chairman

of the Department of Drama at Yale when the University awarded O'Neill an honorary LLD.)

106. O'Hara, Frank Hurburt. *Today in American drama.* Chicago, Univ. of Chicago Press, 1939.

This short review of modern American plays includes frequent references to O'Neill, but mainly discusses *APE* and its left-wing atmosphere.

107. Oppenhcimer, George. *The passionate playgoer.* NY, Viking, 1958.

Reprints the following:

Benchley, Robert, "Mourning Becomes Electra," (originally, "Top") from *The New Yorker*, 7 Nov. 1931 (No. 1464), p. 580.

Chapman, John, introduction to *LONG DAY'S JOURNEY* as originally printed in his 1957 *Broadway's Best*, p. 281.

Krutch, Joseph Wood, Introduction to *Nine Plays* (No. 69), p. 268.

108. Parks, Edd Winfield. *Segments of Southern thought.* Athens, Univ. of Georgia Press, 1938. Ch. XVI, "Eugene O'Neill's symbolism," pp. 293-313.

Broad discussion of O'Neill's symbols. Despite his apparent turn to the cross in *DAYS WITHOUT END*, says Parks, O'Neill is merely using another symbol to express the same thoughts he always has.

109. Pellizzi, Camillo. *English drama: The last great phase.* Translated by Rowan Williams, NY, Macmillan, 1936, pp. 253-262.

Whether or not he is aware of it, O'Neill is the Irish-Catholic rebel against Puritanism, very aware of the existence of evil and divine grace, according to this Italian critic.

* 110. Quinn, Arthur Hobson. *A history of the American drama from the Civil war to the present day.* NY, F. S. Crofts, 1927, 1936. Vol. II, Ch. XXI, "Eugene O'Neill, poet and mystic." [This chapter reprinted in *Scribner's*, ns, Oct. 1926, pp. 368-372.]

This standard history of the American drama has been updated to 1945 and published in a consolidated one volume edition with original volumes separately paginated. The essay on O'Neill has remained unchanged through the several editions and printings except for successive factual additions. Quinn finds his Celtic background has made O'Neill a mystic with the heart of a poet, and the analysis of the separate plays takes this central view. O'Neill's own explanation of *THE GREAT GOD BROWN,* which appeared in most New York newspapers in Feb., (see Non-Dramatic O'Neill, 1926) is reprinted in its entirety. There is also a personal letter from O'Neill, partly reproduced in facsimile, explaining his artistic philosophy. Although Quinn's book dwells heavily upon American drama before O'Neill, it is a popular and easy-reading history which is a basic reference text in any drama library.

111. — — — —. *The literature of the American people.* NY, Appleton-Century-Crofts, 1951. Ch. 49, "Vitalizers of the drama," pp. 928-934.

A few pages devoted to O'Neill's plays in this survey of American literature. The book is on a level with the three volumes by Spiller *et al* (No. 128), but bibliography is not as complete.

112. — — — —. *Representative American plays.* NY, Appleton-Century-Crofts, 1953. Seventh edition. "Beyond the Horizon," pp. 929-937.

This anthology has gone through seven editions, 1917, 1920, 1925, 1928, 1930, 1938, and 1953. It has always relied heavily on early American drama, and is not truly "representative" since 1918. *HORIZON* has always been the choice for O'Neill, and it has several pages of introduction in the last two editions.

*   113. Salisbury, William. *A dress suit becomes Hamlet. Why not, if Mourning Becomes Electra?* New Rochell, NY, The Independent Publishing Co., 1933.

Subtitle: "A dissertation upon the comedies of Eugene O'Neill, addressed to the author." This small pamphlet is a violently prejudiced attack upon all of O'Neill's major plays, full of ridicule based on superficialities of story form. Racial prejudice is injected without warrant in the form of vicious anti-Semitism; and there is name calling with no point. A low water mark in dramatic criticism.

114. Salzman, Maurice. *Plagiarism, the "art" of stealing literary material.* Los Angeles, Parker, Stone and Baird, 1931.
Includes a factual report of the Georges Lewys plagiarism case against O'Neill and *STRANGE INTERLUDE* (see Life Chronology).

* 115. Sanborn, Ralph, and Barrett H. Clark. *A bibliography of the works of Eugene O'Neill.* NY, Random House, 1931.
Careful collation of all texts to and including *DYNAMO*, with numerous plates illustrating variations. Contains limited references to periodical, newspaper, and book articles (including separate books on O'Neill) and also a collection of little-known poems which O'Neill reluctantly gave permission to publish.

116. Sayler, Oliver M. *Our American theatre.* NY, Brentano's, 1923. Ch. III, "Eugene O'Neill, the American playwright," pp. 27-43.
Sayler regards O'Neill as the personification of the current American drama. Brief life sketch and review of plays. Excerpts from Hugo von Hofmannsthal's widely quoted criticism (No. 277). Also includes O'Neill's own statement concerning his credo of leaving social ideas behind.

117. Sergeant, Elizabeth Shepley. "O'Neill: The man with a mask," in *Fire under the Andes*, NY, Knopf, 1927.
Reprinted from *New Rep.*, 16 March 1927 (No. 359).

* 118. Shipley, Joseph T. *The art of Eugene O'Neill.* Univ. of Washington Chapbooks, Seattle, Univ. of Washington Bookstore, 1928.
This 34-page pamphlet is the second small book (Clark's *Eugene O'Neill* (No. 21) was the first) devoted exclusively to O'Neill. Shipley finds that O'Neill's theme of life as a vale of tears is too restrictive. The booklet's value is limited by Shipley's emphasis on O'Neill's lack of humor.

119. — — — —. *Guide to great plays.* Washington, Public Affairs Press, 1956.
All important plays from sea plays of Glencairn cycle to *ICEMAN* (*DIFF'RENT* thrown in for some reason) are included

in this volume which reviews plots and some of the critical comments from the press.

* 120. Sievers, W. David. *Freud on Broadway*. NY, Hermitage House, 1955. Ch. VI, "Freud, Jung and O'Neill," pp. 97-133.

General review of O'Neill's plays in light of accepted and assumed influence of psychoanalysis. *A MOON FOR THE MISBEGOTTEN* is found to be one of the best. The entire book treats the Freudian theme in considerable detail as reflected on the New York stage during this century, often roaming far afield to include works one would normally not consider appropriate. An intriguing, if not always convincing, book.

* 121. Simonson, Lee. *The stage is set*. NY, Harcourt, Brace, 1932.

This excellent book treats most aspects of theatrical production from the viewpoint of one of our most successful designers. No specific section on O'Neill, but he is often mentioned, particularly in the very fine discussion of language and dramatic poetry. Simonson's hilarious parody of Hamlet's soliloquies as O'Neill would write them shows precisely what Krutch (Nos. 68 & 69) and others have meant in their deploring O'Neill's lack of poetic grandeur. *DYNAMO* is discussed in detail relative to its setting and O'Neill's emphasis upon sound effects.

122. Sinclair, Upton. *Money writes!* NY, A. & C. Boni, 1927. Ch. XXXV, "The springs of pessimism," pp. 175-177.

Sinclair's study of American literature from the economic point of view briefly mentions O'Neill, whose pessimism is regarded as part of the same disease afflicting art in a dying captialism.

* 123. Skinner, Richard Dana. *Eugene O'Neill: A poet's quest*. NY, Longmans, Green, 1935.

O'Neill's entire career is recreated as a poet's quest, comparable to a saint's pilgrimage. An interesting study, carefully drawn, but effective only if the reader accepts Catholic doctrine. Otherwise, an able discussion of the positions the plays occupy in O'Neill's life, based on a chronology of composition supplied by O'Neill himself. Although Skinner realizes other plays are yet to come, his conclusions would indicate O'Neill has "arrived" at the goal of his quest in *DAYS WITHOUT END*. The chronology, allowing for some inaccuracies in O'Neill's memory, is the most valuable item in the book.

124. — — — —. "A note on Eugene O'Neill," in Skillin, Edward S., ed., *The Commonweal reader*. NY, Harpers, 1949, pp. 80-83.
Reprints Skinner's review of *AH, WILDERNESS!*, *Commonweal*, 27 Oct. 1933 (No. 439).

125. — — — —. *Our changing theatre*. NY, Dial Press, 1931. Ch. III, "The song in tragedy," pp. 43-47; Ch. IV, "Tragedy without song," pp. 76-96.
Skinner believes that O'Neill will be a true poet of tragedy if he recaptures the vision of *BROWN*. The discussion of other plays, such as *INTERLUDE, DYNAMO, DESIRE*, forms the approach to Skinner's later book, *Eugene O'Neill: A Poet's Quest* (No. 122).

* 126. Slochower, Harry. *No voice is wholly lost: Writers and thinkers in war and peace*. NY, Creative Age Press, 1945. "In quest of everyman: Eugene O'Neill & James Joyce," pp. 248-254.
This book deals with various literary and artistic reactions to the social and cultural instability of today. The brief analysis of O'Neill is excellent, going to the center of his philosophy more directly than many other extensive treatments of the subject. Compare Slochower's essay with Krutch's opinion of O'Neill's tragic characters (Nos. 68 & 69), or Flexner's social viewpoint (No. 40).

127. Spiller, Robert E. *The cycle of American literature*. NY, Macmillan, 1955. Ch. XI, "Full circle: O'Neill and Hemingway," pp. 243-274.
O'Neill is discussed with Hemingway, Dos Passos, Wolfe, and others as part of the post-war generation literature of social protest, symbolism, and so on. O'Neill is clearly identified as apart from the "lost" generation.

*   128. — — — —, and others. *Literary history of the United States*. NY, Macmillan, 1949. Vol. II, No. 73, "Eugene O'Neill," by Joseph Wood Krutch, pp. 1237-1250.

This two-volume compendium and its third volume of bibliography (containing extended references to O'Neill) is the outstanding work in the field of American literary history. Krutch's essay again summarizes most of the views which he has expounded in other articles (Nos. 68 & 69). There is a brief account of the development of the little theatre movement and O'Neill's position therein. In discussing *DESIRE, BROWN, INTERLUDE*, and *ELECTRA*, Krutch considers that O'Neill's plays "are not so much summary of an era as a new mode and a new theme for the American stage."

129. Stark, Harold. *People you know*. NY, Boni and Liveright, 1923. "The hairy ape," pp. 244-247.

Interview between "Young Boswell" (Stark) and O'Neill, discussing O'Neill's basic dramatic theories.

*   130. Straumann, Heinrich. *American literature in the twentieth century*. London, Hutchinson's University Library, 1951. Ch. V, "The great conflict: The rise of American drama."

Written by a professor of English literature at University of Zurich. An interesting study which finds O'Neill the "most complete and powerful symbol" of the conflicts between determinism and pragmatism, and the acceptance of reality on the one hand and the search for values beyond the world of experience as an offshoot of the old moral and religious tradition on the other. This approach should certainly be considered in comparison with many domestic attitudes toward O'Neill's tragic view.

131. Stuart, Donald Clive. *The development of dramatic art*. NY, Appleton-Century, 1928, pp. 644-650.

LAZARUS and *BROWN* discussed as expressionism. *STRANGE INTERLUDE* as "super-naturalism."

132. Taylor, Walter F. *A history of American letters* Boston, American Book Co., 1936. Ch. V, "The rise of the drama: Eugene O'Neill," pp. 406-418.

O'Neill's work is divided into four categories called "Explora tions." *ELECTRA* does not suffer in comparison with *Lear* and *Macbeth*, though O'Neill is in the tradition of Webster and Ford, more than Shakespeare.

133. Thompson, Alan Reynolds. *The anatomy of drama.* Berkeley, Univ. of California Press, 1942, pp. 298-306; 1946, pp. 303-312.
Thompson downgrades O'Neill as a romanticist relying too heavily upon psychopathology.

❋   134. — — — —. "The dilemma of modern tragedy," in Foerster, Norman, ed., *Humanism and America: Essays on the outlook of modern civilization.* NY, Farrar & Rinehart, 1930, pp. 127-148.
The dilemma: a modern naturalist poet cannot be both honest and sublime. The elevation of tragedy cannot achieve its goal by modern naturalistic or even romantic means. The essay is a careful analysis of the tragic concept and treatment by modern writers. O'Neill seeks nobility in man and the answer to life in life itself without resort to romantic escape, but he does not exalt to elevation of heroic tragedy, finding life muddled and leaving it that way.

135. Trilling, Lionel. Introduction to O'Neill, Eugene, *The Emperor Jones, Anna Christie, The Hairy Ape.* NY, The Modern Library, 1937, pp. vii-xix.
Trilling discusses these three plays as a part of O'Neill's over-all philosophical pattern. O'Neill is uncopied because he is in the tradition of *Lear* and *Faust*, and nobody else is interested in the same thing.

136. Untermeyer, Louis. *Makers of the modern world.* NY, Simon & Schuster, 1955. "Eugene O'Neill," pp. 662-668.
Brief biography in a collection of 92 biographies of men and women "who formed the pattern of our century."

137. Van Doren, Carl, ed., *The Borzoi reader.* NY, Garden City, 1938.
Reprints "Eugene O'Neill," by George Jean Nathan, from *Intimate Notebooks* (No. 96) pp. 590-603.

138. — — — —, and Mark Van Doren. *American and British literature since 1890.* NY, Century, 1925; 1939, pp. 102-107.

The first edition of this volume was one of the first American literature surveys to consider O'Neill worthy of discussion. The treatment, however, is very broad.

* 139. Waton, Harry. *The historic significance of Eugene O'Neill's Strange Interlude.* NY, Worker's Educational Institute, 1928.

Originally a lecture delivered at the Rand School, NY, May 18, 1928. It is truly an astonishing document, showing the play to reflect "great, historic changes taking place in the life of mankind." The soliloquies show our double lives — that shown to the world, and that suppressed unhealthily — as well as how man has suppressed woman. Every character is a symbol of profound social significance. Nina is revolutionary woman; Leeds is the fossil priest-professor; Gordon is revolutionary hero who, like Jesus, dies young; the crippled soldiers are downtrodden masses; Darrell is modern science and crude materialism; and so on and on.

140. Whipple, Thomas K. *Spokesmen: Modern writers and American life.* NY, Appleton, 1928. XI, "Eugene O'Neill," pp. 230-253.

The essay is based on Whipple's *New Republic* article of 21 January 1925 (No. 390). O'Neill is seen as a writer of tragedy based on his own attitude that life is a matter of spiritual frustration — probably the tragedy of America as well. *BROWN* is his best play because it is not a tragedy of desolation, but of great poetry.

141. White, Arthur Franklin. *The plays of Eugene O'Neill.* Cleveland, Western Reserve Univ., Studies by Members of the Faculty, Bulletin Vol. 26, No. 8, August, 1923.

A pamphlet of historical interest as the first scholarly study of O'Neill's plays. It is rare, and not readily available in most libraries.

142. Wilde, Percival. *The craftsmanship of the one-act play.* NY, Crown, 1951.

Comprehensive guide to the creation of successful one-act plays through all the elements of composition. O'Neill's short plays are frequently used to illustrate pertinent points.

143. Wilson, Edmund. *Shores of light.* NY, Farrar & Strauss, 1952. "Eugene O'Neill and the naturalists," pp. 99-104.
Two brief essays discussing mainly *APE* and *CHILLUN.* He finds O'Neill at home most when he is writing in the vernacular.

* 144. Winther, Sophus Keith. *Eugene O'Neill: A critical study.* NY, Random House, 1934.
An excellent study of O'Neill's dominant ideas in relation to the modern industrial age, written when he was still considered a practicing playwright. Highly favorable, without eulogy. The whole O'Neill canon is considered as a unit, and discussed in terms of moral and social philosophy. It bears comparison with Skinner's *Poet's Quest* (No. 123) and contrast with Geddes' *Melodramadness* (No. 47).

145. Woollcott, Alexander. *The portable Woollcott.* NY, Viking, 1946.
Reprints Woolcott's review of *ELECTRA* from *While Rome Burns* (No. 147).

* 146. –– – –. *Shouts and murmurs.* NY, Century, 1922. Ch. XI, "Eugene O'Neill," pp. 144-170.
Woollcott was not an O'Neill admirer, but steers a neutral ground in his first major article about the playwright. He finds O'Neill the "most interesting playwright of the new generation," always vigorous, always somber, but undisciplined.

147. –– – –. *While Rome burns.* NY, Viking, 1934, 1940, pp. 288-291.
Prints a review of *ELECTRA.*

148. Young, Stark. *Immortal shadows.* NY, Scribner's, 1948.
Reprints these essays:
"The Great God Brown," *New Rep.*, 10 Feb. 1926 (No. 1066).
"Eugene O'Neill's new play," *New Rep.*, 11 Nov. 1931 (review of *ELECTRA*) (No. 1493).

"O'Neill and Rostand," *New Rep.*, 21 Oct. 1946 (review of *ICEMAN*) (No. 1202).

149. Zabel, Morton D., ed. *Literary opinion in America.* NY, Harper's, 1937, 1951.
Reprints the following essays:
Fergusson, Francis, "Eugene O'Neill," *Hound and Horn*, Jan-Mar. 1930 (No. 246).
Young, Stark, review of *ELECTRA*, *New Rep.*, 11 Nov. 1931, (No. 1493).

GENERAL REFERENCES — PERIODICALS

INTRODUCTION

This is a list of important articles about Eugene O'Neill the man and the artist, which have appeared in domestic periodicals up to the end of 1959. It is arranged within the limits explained below.

I. CONTENTS. Certain restrictions have been made in the type and treatment of the material.

1. Only articles of a critical or biographical nature deemed worthy of study have been included. This eliminates numerous items in which O'Neill is mentioned merely in passing, or which otherwise contribute little or nothing to O'Neill scholarship.

2. All items are concerned with O'Neill and/or his works in general. All references dealing primarily with the individual plays, such as opening night reviews and subsequent discussions in newspapers and periodicals, are included under the heading INDIVIDUAL PLAYS.

3. Because it has been impossible to assemble every single item about O'Neill from every possible publication, sources are limited as follows:

a. Only domestic publications, with rare exception, have been consulted.

b. Because of comparative ease of access through the New York Public Library, only New York newspapers have been consulted. Important articles from other city newspapers found in various clipping collections and special bibliographies may occasionally appear.

c. Primary sources for periodical references have been the several indexes: Reader's Guide, International Index, Essay and General Literature Index, and so on. Other special indexes and bibliographies, such as the Dramatic Index, have been employed as well (see Sources Consulted).

Library clipping collections have frequently yielded loose articles from periodicals not regularly indexed. These have been included whenever their importance warrants.

II. MECHANICS. The general pattern follows standard bibliographical practices, but departs on occasion as shown below. The order of information for each entry is as follows:

1. Author in alphabetical order. Title is used if author is unknown; no entry appears under "Anonymous."

2. Article title in "quotation marks." Library of Congress catalogue card procedure is followed by capitalizing only first words and proper nouns.

3. Periodical title, often abbreviated, *in italics*. Consult abbreviation list (p. 177) for complete titles.

4. Volume, date, and page.

a. Periodicals other than newspapers include, wherever possible, full information in this manner:

48 (21 Oct. 1946) 71

Some references were obtained from library collections of loose clippings, identified by title and date only. In these few instances ascertaining exact volume and page numbers was frequently impractical because of time limitations or impossible because of unavailability of the original source.

Please Note: If periodical reference covers more than one page, inclusive pages are indicated only if they are consecutive. Those articles covering several pages scattered throughout the periodical are located by the first page on which the item appears. No attempt has been made to enumerate all consecutive pages. Again, practical consideration has been the governing factor. A more uniform reference is obtained by avoiding the confusion of multiple numbers or the indefinite abbreviation, *ff.*

b. Newspaper references indicate date only. Because of frequent differences among various editions of the same paper and because of the general unavailability of newspapers other than the New York *Times*, it was considered impractical to indicate column or page. The exception is the *Times*. Its index and uniform edition on file in most libraries permit full information. All references indicate date, section (Sunday edition only), page and column in this manner:

25 Jan. 1921, II, 1:3

5. Cross reference information. This includes reprints in books and other publications. Most of the cross references are listed elsewhere in this bibliography.

6. Brief annotation concerning the contents of the entry, occasionally including an evaluation of the item as a piece of O'Neill scholarship. Frequent cross references are made to other items within the bibliography for comparison and contrast of material.

NOTE: Entries of more than routine interest or of special significance are marked with an asterisk (*) in the left margin. All of O'Neill's plays are spelled out in *CAPITAL LETTERS*. An abbreviated form is often used to save space: *e.g.*, *ICEMAN* for *THE ICEMAN COMETH; DESIRE* for *DESIRE UNDER THE ELMS*, and so on.

150. Agee, James. "Ordeal of Eugene O'Neill." *Time*, 48 (21 Oct. 1946) 71.

Review of O'Neill's life and works upon opening of *ICEMAN*. Agee sees O'Neill as our greatest craftsman, rather than a dramatist.

* 151. Alexander, Doris M. "Eugene O'Neill as social critic." *Am. Quar.*, 6 (Winter 1954) 349-363.

An extended analysis of O'Neill's criticism of modern society, including facts from earliest plays like *SERVITUDE* and *APE*, through *BROWN, MARCO, INTERLUDE*, and *DAYS WITHOUT END*, as well as *AH, WILDERNESS!*. Miss Alexander finds O'Neill's criticism cancels itself out because of his condemnation of all society and his rejection of all solutions to make it better.

152. — — — —. "Eugene O'Neill: The Hound of Heaven and the Hell Hole." *Mod. Lang. Q.*, 20 (Dec. 1959) 307-314.

Well documented thesis that *SERVITUDE, WELDED*, and *DAYS WITHOUT END* are all based on O'Neill's fear of love and his fascination with Thompson's "Hound of Heaven," which he delighted in reciting to all comers in Greenwich Village's Golden Swan bar, known as the Hell Hole.

153. Anderson, John. "Eugene O'Neill." *Th. Arts,* 15 (Nov. 1931) 938-942.
An appreciation of O'Neill's powers. He is first important dramatist to contend with shifting values of modern life.

154. Andrews, Kenneth. "Broadway, our literary signpost." *Bookman,* 53 (July 1921) 407-417.
JONES is the best argument against those who lament the passing of the "palmy days and their great tragedians." *JONES, DIFF'RENT,* and *HORIZON* show we are beginning to think in the theatre.

155. — — — —. "Broadway, our literary signpost." *Bookman,* 57 (April 1923) 191.
O'Neill and the Guild are encouraging producers to give better plays. O'Neill makes us think, which is something new.

156. Anshutz, Grace. "Expressionistic drama in the American theatre." *Drama,* 16 (April 1926) 245.
O'Neill is the best expressionistic writer in his welding of the external and internal — the body and the spirit — so harmoniously.

157. Atkinson, Brooks. "After all these years." NY *Times,* 12 Oct. 1941, IX, 1:1.
Atkinson wonders why more of O'Neill is not revived, though he realizes that many plays are beyond revival.

158. — — — —. "Dramatist of the sail and the sea." NY *Times,* 3 May 1931, VIII, 1:1.
The earthy, emotional characters of *APE, JONES, DESIRE* are better than those of O'Neill's recent confused experimentation.

159. — — — —. "Ennobel-ing O'Neill." NY *Times,* 22 Nov. 1936, XI, 1:1. [Reprinted as "O'Neill gets the Nobel prize," in Atkinson's *Broadway scrapbook,* NY, Theatre Arts, 1947, pp. 52-55 (No. 2).]

The award is one of the most cheering things of otherwise depressing theatre season. It was awarded fairly, to a man whose accomplishments merited it.

160. — — — —. "Eugene O'Neill." NY *Times*, 20 Jan. 1952, II, 1:1.
Atkinson praises the revivals of *ANNA CHRISTIE* and *DESIRE* and expresses sorrow for O'Neill's 25-year limbo.

161. — — — —. "Eugene O'Neill." NY *Times*, 13 Dec. 1953, II, 5:1.
Eulogy to a giant who has been dropped from the earth, a great spirit and a great dramatist. No one like him before, none like him now.

❖ 162. — — — —. "Feuding again." NY *Times*, 25 Apr. 1948, II, 1:1.
Reply to the anonymous "Counsels of Despair" (No. 204) from London *Times*. Atkinson attempts to point out O'Neill's greatness, showing how this "peevish" London writer lost sight of what was behind the plays. Atkinson successfully attacks the obvious weakness in the article by pointing out that the writer's prejudice and illogical reasoning are not based on what O'Neill has done, but on the critic's own ideas of what he should have done.

163. — — — —. "Head man in the drama." NY *Times*, 19 Aug. 1951, II, 1:1.
Only an improvident theatre such as ours today would neglect this man who has written the finest dramatic literature we have.

164. — — — —. "King of tragedy." NY *Times*, 28 Mar. 1954, II, 1:1.
Inquires why America does not recognize its own great master whose plays, regardless of one's personal opinion, have become accepted as the works of a man struggling with higher things.

165. — — — —. "O'Neill's finale." NY *Times*, 12 May 1957, II, 1:1.
A brief look at the current revival with especial reference to *JOURNEY* and *MISBEGOTTEN*.

166. — — — —. "O'Neill off duty." NY *Times*, 8 Oct. 1933, X, 1:1.

Informal interview finds O'Neill a different, more human person, relaxed and capable of laughing "without brilliant provocation," apparently having abandoned much of his earlier style of tragedy.

167. "Author." *New Yorker*, 31 Dec. 1927.

Brief discussion of the "quiet young man" sitting alone at rehearsals of his plays. Some "intimate notes" designed to alter the picture of O'Neill's morose pessimism.

168. Bab, Julius. "Eugene O'Neill — as Europe sees America's foremost playwright." *Th. Guild Mag.*, 9 (Nov. 1931) 11-15.

O'Neill is the most vigorous personality among all playwrights known to Europe, says Bab, and deserves at least some immortality for his tragedy of the proletariat.

169. Baker, George Pierce. "O'Neill's first decade." *Yale Rev.*, ns, 15 (July 1926) 789-792.

Review of O'Neill's first ten years by his erstwhile teacher. Now at middle of his career, says Baker, O'Neill should develop his material more imaginatively.

170. Band, Muriel S. "O'Neill is back." *Mayfair*, Oct. 1946, p. 66.

Report of the press conference before *ICEMAN*, with O'Neill's views concerning America's failings.

* 171. Basso, Hamilton. "The tragic sense." *New Yorker*, 24 (28 Feb. 1948) 34; 24 (6 Mar. 1948) 34; 24 (13 Mar. 1948) 37.

The most extensive item to appear in any periodical, this typical *New Yorker* "profile" is written in straightforward reportorial style, without criticism or evaluation of O'Neill or his work. Part I gives a good account of the playwright's background, in many ways better than what Clark supplies in his several editions of *The Man and His Plays* (No. 21). Part II lists and discusses all the plays. Part III deals with O'Neill's more recent life and closes with an interview expressing many of his personal views about his own work and the theatre. Basso makes the first announcement that the multi-play cycle, *A TALE OF POSSES-SORS SELF-DISPOSSESSED*, had been destroyed.

* 172. Bentley, Eric. "Trying to like O'Neill." *Kenyon Rev.*, 14 (July 1952) 476-492. [Reprinted in Bentley's *In search of theatre*, NY, Knopf, 1953 (No. 3).]

Having been asked to assist in directing the German language version of *ICEMAN*, Bentley thought he began to see some good points in O'Neill's work. But the period of "liking" was soon over, for O'Neill's great intentions are never realized, says Bentley, and he achieves less the more he attempts, with his characters blown up in size by cultural and psychological gas. The final conclusion is, however, that if one dislikes O'Neill he actually dislikes our age, of which O'Neill is the representative. This essay, together with Krutch's introduction to *Nine Plays* (No. 69), is a widely quoted criticism.

173. "Big run for O'Neill's plays." *Life* 42 (24 June 1957) 108.

Illustrations from the many revivals and adaptations in current popularity, such as *LONG DAY'S JOURNEY, MISBEGOTTEN, POET*, and the musical version of *ANNA CHRISTIE, New Girl in Town*.

174. Bird, Carol. "Eugene O'Neill — the inner man." *Theatre*, 39 (June 1924) 8.

This interview at the Provincetown Playhouse has particular interest because of its extended presentation of O'Neill's defense of his continued writing of the down-and-out.

175. Blackburn, Clara. "Continental influences on Eugene O'Neill's expressionistic drama." *Amer. Lit.*, 13 (May 1941) 109-133.

If "expressionistic drama" had been left out of the title the article would become clearer. Miss Blackburn finds many of O'Neill's plays have considerable Swedish and German influence. Carl Dahlstrom's "norms" for expressionism are used as points of departure, often much too literally. For instance, the simple battle of the sexes displayed by Nina and Darrell in *INTER-*

LUDE is seen as "expressionism." Miss Blackburn frequently mistakes mere similarity for influence.

176. Bodenheim, Maxwell. "Roughneck and romancer." *New Yorker*, 3 (6 Feb. 1926) 17-18.

The first *New Yorker* "profile" (see Basso's 3-installment version, No. 171) regrets O'Neill's apparent change from the prober of lower world rowdies and adventurers to more "highbrow" world of Mencken and Nathan.

177. Bowen, Croswell. "The black Irishman." *PM*, 3 Nov. 1946.

The main discussion centers around O'Neill's loss of faith early in life and his failure to regain it. Some good pictures of New London home and the O'Neill family. Most of the material here is available in earlier articles elsewhere. (See also Bowen's *Curse of the Misbegotten*, No. 8.)

178. Boyd, Ernest. "A great American dramatist." *Freeman*, 3 (6 July 1921) 404-405.

O'Neill's great ability is to create mood and atmosphere and great characters at expense of plot.

179. Boynton, Percy H. "American authors of today: X. The drama." *Eng. Jour.*, 12 (June 1923) 407-415.

This long treatment of the history of American playwriting concludes with a discussion of O'Neill as the man who embodies so much of modern theatrical and dramatic history in his own story.

* 180. Breese, Jessie M. "Home on the dunes." *Country Life in America*, 45 (Nov. 1923) 72-76.

Detailed description of O'Neill's unique residence on Cape Cod's Peaked Hill Bars, including five excellent photographs of its interior and exterior.

181. Brock, H. E. "O'Neill stirs the gods of the drama." NY *Times*, 15 Jan. 1928, V, p. 9.

Discussion of this amazing young man who commands audiences to do as he likes.

182. Brown, Ivor. "American plays in England." *Am. Merc.*, 33 (Nov. 1934) 315-322.

An attempt to explain why O'Neill is not generally accepted in England. The English have an idea of America which O'Neill does not present, and he is therefore ignored.

183. Brown, John Mason. "All O'Neilling." *Sat R. Lit.*, 29 (19 Oct. 1946) 26. [Reprinted as "Moaning at the bar," in Brown's *Seeing more things*, NY, Whittlesey House, 1948 (No. 13).]

Combined review of *ICEMAN* and discussion of O'Neill's past work, which has always shown unmistakable courage and the single theme of the relationship of man to the universe.

184. — — — "American tragedy." *Sat. R. Lit.*, 32 (6 Aug. 1949) 124-127. [Reprinted in Brown's *Still seeing things*, NY, McGraw-Hill, 1950, pp. 185-195 (No. 14).]

The need for tragedy today, in its exaltation of Man, is great. O'Neill sensed it, and despite shortcomings and lack of language, did exalt man, finding happiness not in the happy ending but in the tragic concept of the greater nobility of man. All of his plays have been in the Greek and Elizabethan concept of tragedy.

185. — — — —. "Eugene O'Neill, 1888-1953." *Sat. R.* 36 (19 Dec. 1953) 26-28.

Regardless of how high he aspired and how low he fell, O'Neill was never afraid to face and attack any theme he felt would forward his tragic theme. Wonder expressed that America, the land of laughter, should put forth the only major modern tragic writer.

186. — — — —. "The present day dilemma of Eugene O'Neill." NY *Post*, 19 Nov. 1932.

In his greatest victories, O'Neill has met defeat in his inability to keep in contact with the type of play he originally conceived, turning now from rough life of sea to the drawing room of Freud and Jung. Brown finds O'Neill's essay on masks in the *Spectator* (see Non-Dramatic O'Neill 1932) hard to take. It seems to mark the decline of a great original power.

187. Brustein, Robert. "Why American plays are not literature." *Harpers*, 219 (Oct. 1959) 167-172.

O'Neill is included in a discussion of the serious shortcomings
of American literary drama, including such aspects as O'Neill's
own "inarticulacy."

188. Burton, Katherine. "Aldous Huxley and other moderns." *Cath. Wld.*, 139 (Aug. 1934) 552-556.

This article on *Brave New World* includes discussion of
O'Neill's ideas about machine worship.

189. Carb, David. "Eugene O'Neill." *Vogue*, 68 (15 Sept.
1926) 100.

O'Neill's position as our first dramatist comes from his daring to
be himself and a sense of theatre unequalled by contemporaries.

190. Carpenter, Frederic I. "The romantic tragedy of
Eugene O'Neill." *Coll. Eng.*, 6 (Feb. 1945) 250-258.

Carpenter regards O'Neill's belief in the unattainably perfect
life as basically romantic. *LAZARUS, INTERLUDE, ELECTRA*
discussed as a trilogy showing the development in O'Neill's
attitude from the assertion of romantic perfection, through the
inability to gain it, to the tragic despair in failure. (See Carpenter's book, No. 19.)

191. Cerf, Bennett. "Three new plays." *Sat. R. Lit.*, 29
(23 Feb. 1946) 26.

Discussion of some of O'Neill's projected plays.

*   192. Cerf, Walter. "Psychoanalysis and the realistic
drama." *Jour. of Aesthetics & Art Criticism*, 16 (Mar. 1958)
328-336.

Taking Laurents' *A Clearing in the Woods* and O'Neill's
JOURNEY, Cerf attempts to show that modern realism cannot
successfully convey "psychoanalytically guided retrospection"
and that the impact of a play like *JOURNEY* is not good drama
because in this retrospect there is no place for Aristotle's "perip-
ity," or sudden turn, so essential to good drama.

193. Churchill, Allen. "Portrait of a Nobel prize winner as a bum." *Esquire* 47 (June 1957) 98-101.
Popular review of the influences behind O'Neill from the earliest days as a waterfront derelict until his death.

194. Clark, Barrett H. "Eugene O'Neill, a chapter in biography." *Th. Arts,* 10 (May 1926) 325-326.
Excerpts from Clark's first edition of *Eugene O'Neill* (No. 21).

195. Clurman, Harold. "O'Neill revived." *New Rep.* 126 (4 Feb. 1952) 22-23.
O'Neill is an artist of deep personal feeling and a playwright of high order, despite certain lacks as a writer.

196. Cole, Lester, and John Howard Lawson. "Two views on O'Neill." *Masses and Mainstream,* 7 (June 1954) 56-63.
Discussion of whether or not O'Neill has merit in view of Marxist criticism.

197. Coleman, Alta M. "Personality portraits: No. 3. Eugene O'Neill." *Theatre,* 31 (April 1920) 264.
This is the first acknowledgement given this "suddenly acclaimed" young writer by Arthur Hornblow's *Theatre* magazine, the "prestige" stage publication of its day. The article is a review of facts about O'Neill's life and writings.

198. Colum, Mary M. "Drama of the disintegrated." *Forum,* 94 (Dec. 1935) 358.
O'Neill brings his characters to life; they have disintegrated, but cling to sanity. Compared to these, Shaw's characters are mere abstractions.

199. Conrad, Lawrence H. "Eugene O'Neill." *The Landmark,* 11 (July 1929) 413-416.
Whatever it is O'Neill is trying in the theatre, it is of tremendous significance.

*   200. Cook, Jim. "A long tragic journey." NY *Post,* 2 Dec. 1956.
The important part of this brief sketch of O'Neill's life is an

interview with his first wife, the former Kathleen Jenkins, now Mrs. George Pitt-Smith of Little Neck, L.I. She lived with O'Neill for only a few days and in this article cannot recount much of their brief life together, although she does wonder why she is not even mentioned in *LONG DAY'S JOURNEY*. The article also includes some material on O'Neill's son Shane, whose dissolute life in many ways paralleled that of his father. (See Life Chronology.)

201. Cooper, Grace. "Laurel wreaths." NY *Telegraph*, 9 Oct. 1927.

Review of pertinent but well-known facts of O'Neill's life and some comments on *DYNAMO* and *INTERLUDE*.

202. Corbin, John. "The one-act play." NY *Times*, 19 May 1918, IV, 8:1.

This is the earliest "critical" reference to O'Neill in the *Times*. Discussing the demise of the Washington Square Players, Corbin states that one of their "highest results" was the introduction of O'Neill's one-act plays.

203. – – – –. "O'Neill and Aeschylus." *Sat. R. Lit.*, 8 (30 Apr. 1932) 693-695. [Reprinted in Walter, Erich A., ed., *Essay annual*, NY, Scott, Foresman, 1933, p. 159.]

Corbin believes a possible reason for O'Neill's decline of creative powers can be found in his increased interests in technical stunts and morbid psychology. *ELECTRA* is not Aeschylus, and even Freud would disapprove of this exploration of the mental underworld.

* 204. "Counsels of despair." *Times Lit. Supp.* (London), 10 Apr. 1948, pp. 197-199.

Written after publication of *ICEMAN* in London. One of the most bitter and devastating attacks on O'Neill's plays ever to be published, ranking far beyond Geddes' "melodramadness" (No. 47) or Kemelman's "highbrow melodrama" (No. 285). The anonymous author finds O'Neill juvenile, puerile, contemptuous of fellow man, of church and society, obsessed with undisciplined emotions and jejune opinions, regarding human beings without love. The award of the Nobel Prize was "capricious."

205. Cowley, Malcolm. "Eugene O'Neill, writer of synthetic drama." *Brentano's Book Chat*, 5 (July-Aug. 1926) 17-21.
Account of O'Neill's Hell Hole days, of which Cowley himself knew. Review of O'Neill's attempts to break from the conventional forms. Does not approve of these later tendencies as in *BROWN*.

206. — — — —. "A weekend with Eugene O'Neill." *Reporter*, 17 (5 Sept. 1957) 33-36.
Intimate glimpses of O'Neill's domestic life at Brook Farm, Ridgefield, Conn., in 1923.

207. Crawford, Jack. "Eugene O'Neill: A Broadway philosopher." *Drama*, 12 (Jan. 1922) 117.
O'Neill is shown as a man with a philosophy, literary courage and originality. Crawford does not seem quite sure whether or not O'Neill's philosophy is intentional.

208. Crichton, Kyle. "Mr. O'Neill and the iceman." *Collier's*, 118 (26 Oct. 1946) 18.
A popular entertaining interview in O'Neill's NY apartment prior to *ICEMAN*. Writer finds O'Neill "less like a ghost than would be imagined."

209. Cummings, Ridgley. "Hail, sailor, and farewell." *Am. Mer.*, 78 (May 1954) 45-46.
Upon hearing of O'Neill's death, this writer tells how it felt when he himself was a bum on the waterfront and how he enjoyed reading O'Neill's plays.

210. "Curse of the misbegotten." *Look*, 23 (12 May 1959) 57-58.
Brief discussion upon appearance of Bowen's book (No. 8).

211. Dale, Alan. "On the rebound back to Broadway, with its bad plays, from 'cult' pieces." NY *American*, 12 Mar. 1922.
Dale strongly attacks plays like *FIRST MAN* and *STRAW*, with their "slice of life, birth, death, and tuberculosis. Why not portray cirrhosis of the liver, or stage a post-mortem?"

*   212. De Casseres, Benjamin. "Eugene O'Neill — from Cardiff to Xanadu." *Theatre*, 46 (Aug. 1927) 10.

O'Neill's friend and vigorous champion outlines several aspects of O'Neill's ideas. De Casseres' praise is highly eulogistic and must be taken with reservation.

*   213. — — — —. "Eugene O'Neill — a vignette." *Popular Biography*, 1 (April 1930) 31-38.

A eulogy, rather than a vignette, showing O'Neill as a man who has been to hell, whose life is an epic of will.

214. — — — —. "The psychology of O'Neill." *Arts & Dec.*, 35 (Oct. 1931) 82.

A summation of O'Neill's apparent psychological themes. The most moving and lasting are to be found in *LAZARUS*, while all are summed up in *ELECTRA*.

*   215. — — — —. "The triumphant genius of Eugene O'Neill." *Theatre*, 47 (Feb. 1928) 12.

Extravagant, hysterical praise for *INTERLUDE, MARCO, LAZARUS*. "The genius of O'Neill evolves naturally, rhythmically, and masterfully like a colossal symphony."

216. De Polo, Harold. "Meet Eugene O'Neill, fisherman." *Outdoor America*, 6 (May 1928) 5-8.

Informal account of Maine fishing trip with O'Neill and wife.

217. de Pue, Elva. "The tragedy of O'Neill." *The Figure in the Carpet*, No. 4, May 1928, pp. 18-25. (Known as *Salient* after this issue.)

The shortcomings of recent O'Neill plays come from deficient language, a proneness to repetition, and a lack of the real unexpectedness, richness and glamor of life.

218. Deutsch, Helen, and Stella Hanau. "Flashlights of theatrical history — The old Provincetown." *Th. Guild Mag.*, 8 (Aug. 1931) 20-21; 8 (Sept. 1931) 30.

Brief passages concerning early days at MacDougal Street from the book, *The Provincetown* (No. 29).

219. — — — —. "When the Provincetown group began."
Drama, 21 (June 1931) 3.
Excerpts from first chapter of *The Provincetown* (No. 29).

* 220. De Voto, Bernard. "Minority report." *Sat. R. Lit.,*
15 (21 Nov. 1936) 3. [Reprinted as "Monte Cristo in modern
dress" in De Voto's *Minority report,* Boston, Little, Brown, 1943,
pp. 190-197 (No. 30).]
Sharp disagreement not only with the Nobel award but with
the recognition of O'Neill as a great dramatist. By De Voto's
standards, O'Neill has given us only great theatre, never great
drama.

221. Dobree, Bonamy. "The plays of Eugene O'Neill."
Southern Rev., 2 (Winter 1937) 435-446.
This English critic analyzes O'Neill's style and finds the playwright unable to overcome adolescent emotions. Despite great
powers, fate is never inevitable, and too obviously man-made.

222. Downer, Alan S. "Eugene O'Neill as poet of the
theatre." *Th. Arts,* 35 (Feb. 1951) 22-23.
Poetry of theatre is not necessarily the poetry of the printed
word, as evidenced by the patterns and rhythms of O'Neill.

223. Doyle, Louis F. "O'Neill redivivus." *America* 98 (2
Nov. 1957) 137-138.
Reviewing O'Neill's past in view of his popular revival, Doyle
finds only *JONES* and *APE* great drama. He deplores the later
autobiographical plays, defends the elder James O'Neill as one
who really knew theatre, which the son did not. Finds O'Neill's
final critical status, like Shaw's, undecided.

* 224. Driver, Tom F. "On the late plays of Eugene O'Neill."
Tulane Dr. Rev., 3 (Dec. 1958) 8-20.
Believing O'Neill does not write true tragedy as Krutch and
Nathan see it, Driver chooses *JOURNEY, ICEMAN* and *POET*
to show that O'Neill's later mood was a combination of Romanticism and Stoicism. He disagrees with O'Neill's assertion that
life is merely an inevitable progression toward death, but he

feels the grandeur and imagination of O'Neill makes the rest of our theatre "petite and timid."

225. Eastman, Fred. "Eugene O'Neill and religion." *Christ. Cent.*, 50 (26 July 1933) 955-957.

In Eastman's opinion, O'Neill will not become immortal as a great dramatist until he achieves a religious viewpoint. The preaching against sin and the devil never seems to recognize the help of higher grace.

226. Eaton, Walter Prichard. "The American drama flowers: Eugene O'Neill as a great playwright." *World's Work*, 53 (Nov. 1926) 105-108.

With the publication of Clark's *Eugene O'Neill* (No. 21) Eaton believes O'Neill has achieved major status as the first contributor to a native dramatic literature.

   *   227. — — — —. "The hermit of Cape Cod." NY *Her-Trib.*, 8 Jan. 1928.

A highly favorable critical appraisal of O'Neill's "natural rebellion" against theatrical convention. O'Neill is compared somewhat in extravagance to Emerson and Thoreau.

   *   228. — — — —. "O'Neill: New risen attic stream?" *Amer. Scholar*, 6 (Summer 1937) 304-312.

A discussion of O'Neill's approach to good and evil and his plays in the Greek tradition, especially *DESIRE*. Eaton makes the interesting point that *ELECTRA*, most Greek in form, is possibly less Greek in spirit than many others.

229. — — — —. "Where is the American theatre going?" *World's Work*, 52 (Aug. 1926) 461-465.

While American drama exhibits no special direction, O'Neill's sincerity as a sensitive artist shows some indication of a tendency toward the spiritual.

230. — — — —. "Why America lacks big playwrights." *Theatre*, 32 (Dec. 1920) 346.

Success of *HORIZON* shows our lack of playwrights of real

individualism, because the public generally approves only the "popular" writer.

231. Enander, Hilma. "Eugene O'Neill — his place in the sun." *Theatre*, 43 (Jan. 1926) 7.

This critic finds it difficult to evaluate the man and the plays separately, but has no doubt that O'Neill has elements of greatness which will put American drama in its proper place.

232. Engel, Edwin A. "Eugene O'Neill's long day's journey into light." *Mich. Alum. Quar. Rev.* 63 (1957) 348-354.

Taking *ICEMAN, JOURNEY* and *MISBEGOTTEN*, Engel shows how O'Neill has faced himself and his past in his last plays to show he has at last given "love an ascendancy over peace" (the peace of death) and reveals that the "sickness of today" at which he always stated his plays were digging was, in reality, his own sickness.

233. ———. "The theatre of today: Eugene O'Neill." *Chrysalis*, 6 (1953) No. 9-10, pp. 3-11.

A general review of O'Neill's entry into the writing of American drama.

234. Ervine, St. John. "Is O'Neill's power in decline?" *Theatre*, 43 (May 1926) 12.

Ervine finds indications of decline in O'Neill's reduction of his people to absolute bestiality. (See rebuttal by Frank H. Freed, No. 249.)

235. ———. "Literary taste in America." *New Rep.* 24 (6 Oct. 1920) 144-147.

An article on American poets, novelists and other writers by this famous Irish dramatist. O'Neill and the Cape Cod group are "trying to create an American drama that cannot be mistaken for any other than an American drama."

* 236. ———. "Mr. Eugene O'Neill." *Observer* (London) 31 Oct. 1926, p. 15.

Reviewing *BROWN* and others, along with Clark's *Eugene O'Neill* (No. 21), Ervine states O'Neill will not be an accomplished dramatist and live up to his tremendous ability until he stops being a faddist and settles down to a definite style. Ervine's attitude differs markedly from those who praise O'Neill for *refusing* to be a faddist.

237. — — — —. "Our playwrights as Europe sees them." *Theatre*, 43 (Feb. 1926) 12.
This discussion of the negligible influence of American plays in Europe shows that O'Neill has started no new movement in technique, despite his familiarity overseas.

238. "A Eugene O'Neill miscellany." NY *Sun*, 12 Jan. 1928.
An interview which gives a few of O'Neill's personal reactions to his own favorite plays.

239. "Eugene O'Neill, newest of the Guilders." *Van. F.*, 29 (Nov. 1927) 73.
Upon O'Neill's first production by the Guild, this article offers brief comment as he returns from Bermuda for the production of *MARCO*.

240. "Eugene O'Neill talks of his own plays." NY *Her-Trib.*, 16 Nov. 1924.
Anonymous interviewer tells of O'Neill's opinions on expressionism and his determination to use it in order to get his message across.

241. "Eugene O'Neill's teacher." NY *Times*, 12 Dec. 1936, 18:4.
Report of O'Neill's Nobel prize acceptance speech which gives credit to Strindberg. (O'Neill did not go to Stockholm himself.)

*   242. Fagin, N. Bryllion. "Eugene O'Neill." *Antioch Rev.*, 14 (March 1954) 14-26.
An evaluation of O'Neill shortly after his death looks at the overexaggerated praise he received at first and the undervalued reputation of later years. Reviewing many of the plays, Fagin determines that O'Neill, while imperfect, can still be powerfully disturbing in this generation.

* 243. — — — —. "Eugene O'Neill contemplates mortality." *Open Court*, 45 (April 1931) 208-219.

This periodical is devoted to "the science of religion, the religion of science, and the extension of the religious parliament idea." Fagin finds that O'Neill has a positive approach to the question of what life is; namely that it is a matter of endless continuity and no death. (Most critics, of course, are disturbed by O'Neill's *lack* of positive approach.)

244. — — — —. "'Freud' on the American stage." *Ed. Th. Journ.* 2 (Dec. 1950) 296-305.

Discussion of themes from *Suppressed Desires* to *Cocktail Party*. O'Neill found to be preoccupied with morbid psychological "obsession" from *DIFF'RENT* to *ICEMAN*.

245. "Fellow student thought O'Neill 'very likable.'" NY *Her-Trib.*, 9 Jan. 1927.

Facts about O'Neill's early experience in Baker's class. Compare this with John Weaver's account (No. 386).

* 246. Fergusson, Francis. "Eugene O'Neill." *Hound and Horn*, 3 (Jan.-March 1930) 145-160. [Reprinted in Zabel, Morton, ed., *Literary opinion in America*, NY, Harpers, 1937, 1951 (No. 149).]

Ferguson criticizes O'Neill for his inability to make his characers a true part of the play alone, because of being too closely identified with O'Neill himself. This article is one of the most widely cited essays on O'Neill up to this time.

247. Fiskin, A. M. "The basic unity of Eugene O'Neill." *Writers of Our Years*, Univ. of Denver Studies in Humanities, No. 1, 1950 (no further issues) p. 101.

An attempt to relate all of O'Neill's plays up to *ICEMAN* as parts of a consistent artistic viewpoint, mainly that of Being and Becoming. Plays fall into three groups: obsession, view of the universe involving a naturalistic mysticism, and the human beings in action within the metaphysical system set up.

248. Fleisher, Frederic. "Strindberg and O'Neill." *Symposium*, 10 (Spring 1956) 84-93.

Carefully documented account of Strindberg's influence on O'Neill in subject matter, dramatic style, themes, and so forth. Plays, dialogue compared to show resemblances. General conclusion, however, is that O'Neill was not as influenced by Strindberg as he was by Nietzsche.

249. Freed, Frank H. "Eugene O'Neill in the ascendant." *Theatre*, 44 (Oct. 1926) 30.

A rebuttal to St. John Ervine's assertion of O'Neill's decline (No. 234). Freed maintains that tremendous effect of *BROWN* has everything in it which Ervine desires in a good play.

250. Frenz, Horst. "Eugene O'Neill in France." *Books Abroad*, 18 (Spring 1944) 140-141.

Brief review of O'Neill's success in France.

251. — — — —. "Eugene O'Neill in Russia." *Poet Lore*, 49 (Autumn 1943) 241-247.

Review of the popularity of American writers in Russia, such as Twain and O'Neill. O'Neill himself liked the Russian productions of *DESIRE, CHILLUN*, and others.

252. — — — —. "Eugene O'Neill's plays printed abroad." *Col. Eng.*, 5 (March 1944) 340-341.

Frenz's list of foreign publication in *Bulletin of Bibliography* is better (No. 253).

253. — — — —. "A list of foreign editions and translations of Eugene O'Neill's dramas." *Bulletin of Bibliography*, 18 (1943) 33-34.

A listing of the major foreign editions of O'Neill's plays.

254. Gassner, John. "Eugene O'Neill: The course of a modern dramatist." *Critique: Critical Rev. of Th. Arts* 1 (Feb. 1958) 5-14.

In light of the revived interest in O'Neill, Gassner reviews his artistic career in an attempt to evaluate his position as a modern dramatist. Gassner concludes that no other dramatist of this century has approached O'Neill's "dark and disturbing impressiveness."

255. — — — —. "Homage to Eugene O'Neill." *Theatre Time*, 3 (Summer 1951) 17-21.

Considerable disappointment at the lack of interest of the younger theatre generation in this man who wrestled with demons instead of pigmies. This survey of O'Neill's work attempts to give him the stature that Gassner thinks a writer of his passion deserves.

256. — — — —. "There is no American drama." *Th. Arts*, 36 (Sept. 1952) 24-25.

The "new critics" says Gassner, insisting on comparison of American dramatic effort to that of Europe, find little in our modern drama. This is a sterile approach, he concludes.

257. Geddes, Virgil. "Eugene O'Neill." *Th. Arts*, 15 (Nov. 1931) 943-946.

A typical Geddes approach to O'Neill — strongly negative. (See his pamphlets, Nos. 47 and 48.) The plays have no real dramatic sense but make use of the devices of the bad dramatist in tricks of the theatre which do not convey dramatic emotion.

258. Gelb, Arthur. "O'Neill's hopeless hope for a giant cycle." NY *Times*, 29 Sept. 1958, II, 1:4.

Factual account of the development of the ideas for *TALE OF POSSESSORS* upon the opening of *POET*, the only play of the cycle to survive suitable for production.

259. Gierow, Karl-Ragnar. "Eugene O'Neill's posthumous plays." *World Th.*, 7 (Spring 1958) 46-52.

The director of the Stockholm Royal Theatre discusses the Cycle and its contents and O'Neill's plans which never materialized. Also revealed for the first time are facts concerning O'Neill's nervous trembling which had afflicted him most of his life and which was definitely not Parkinson's disease, as commonly assumed.

260. Gold, Michael. "Eugene O'Neill's early days in the old 'Hell-Hole'." *Sunday Worker*, 27 Oct. 1946.

This is a "party line" report of *ICEMAN*, which Gold had not even seen. The play, he says, attempts to give our youth "musty flavor of our more recent literary past."

261. Granger, Bruce Ingham. "Illusion and reality in Eugene O'Neill." *Mod. Lang. Notes,* 73 (March 1958) 179-186.
Extended evidence from most of the plays to show how O'Neill consistently discussed his belief that the dilemma of modern man involves his inability to get order out of chaos without illusion, which in turn incapacitates him for meaningful action.

262. Grant, Neil F. "The American theatre in England." *Atlantic,* 137 (Feb. 1926) 418-423.
O'Neill is mainly responsible for the rise in literary value of American plays in England. Grant sees American influence increasing, a somewhat different view from St. John Ervine (No. 237) who finds no influence whatever.

263. Grauel, George E. "A decade of American drama." *Thought,* 15 (Sept. 1940) 398-419.
In a review of the 1930's O'Neill is discussed as one who "sees conjunction of spiritual forces in the problem of evil," with *DAYS WITHOUT END* as climactic in its stormy, emphatic final assertion.

264. Groff, Edward. "Point of view in modern drama." *Mod. Dr.,* 2 (Dec. 1959) 268-282.
O'Neill briefly discussed with Miller in section entitled "Point of View in the Drama of the Inner Life."

265. Gump, Margaret. "From ape to man and from man to ape." *Ky. For. Lang. Quar.* 4 (1957) 177-185.
APE discussed along with items by Huxley, Kafka, and others, as a part of literary comment on man's often ape-like qualities and tendencies.

266. Halasz, George. "Crowds fame into 40 years." *Brook. Eagle,* 25 March 1928.
Newspaper supplement article on O'Neill's life and fame, acquired in so short a time.

267. Halline, Allan Gates. "American dramatic theory comes of age." *Bucknell Univ. Studies,* 1 (June 1949) 1-11.
O'Neill leaves something to be desired in proportion and comprehensiveness.

268. Halman, Doris F. "O'Neill and the untrained playwright." *Writer,* 40 (July 1928) 215-217.
Miss Halman gives firm warning to aspiring writers that O'Neill's genius transcends, rather than benefits by, theatrical tricks. They cannot be used to cover a shoddy plot.

❋   269. Hamilton, Clayton. "A shelf of printed plays." *Bookman,* 41 (Apr. 1915) 182.
Under "Playwrights of Promise" Hamilton writes the only known review of O'Neill's first book, *THIRST and Other One Act Plays.* He finds the favorite mood is horror. (Hamilton, a friend of the O'Neill family, had urged James O'Neill to finance publication of this book.)

❋   270. Hamilton, Gladys. "Untold tales of Eugene O'Neill." *Th. Arts,* 40 (Aug. 1956) 31-32.
Recollections of the youthful O'Neill written by Mrs. Clayton Hamilton. She describes him at New London in 1914-1915 as the inarticulate, unobtrusive young man who did not wish his silences disturbed. Quotations from O'Neill's letters to Hamilton show gratitude for his help and guidance, especially because Hamilton urged James O'Neill to send his son to Harvard.

❋   271. Hansford, Montiville M. "O'Neill as the stage never sees him." *Boston Transcript,* 22 March 1930.
Hansford lived with O'Neill for several years during the writing of *BROWN, INTERLUDE,* and *LAZARUS.* He admits the almost impossible task of presenting the man on paper. His report is one of the better personal recollections and avoids the pitfalls of "explaining" O'Neill through childhood influences and social backgrounds.

272. "Haunting recollections of life with a genius." *Life,* 45 (25 Aug. 1958) 55-56.
Ten pictures of O'Neill and his family from Agnes Boulton's

own collection, printed at time of publication of *Part of a Long Story* (No. 7). Comments by Miss Boulton make this a valuable collection hitherto unavailable.

273. Hawthorne, Hildegarde. "The art of Eugene O'Neill." NY *Times,* 13 Aug. 1922, III, 7:1.
Miss Hawthorne is impressed by O'Neill's originality and power, although she sees a note of hysteria in his work. He has been too long with sick people.

*   274. Hayward, Ira N. "Strindberg's influence on Eugene O'Neill." *Poet Lore,* 39 (Winter 1928) 596-604.
Comparison of styles in language, character, technique between the two playwrights. The language of *BROWN* and *FOUNTAIN* is poetic, according to Hayward, a view not widely shared with others.

275. Helburn, Theresa. "O'Neill: An impression." *Sat. R. Lit.,* 15 (21 Nov. 1936) 10.
Personal impressions by this Guild member who places O'Neill on a parallel with Lindbergh in his courage, conviction and strength, and desire to be alone, the "lone eagle" in his profession.

276. Henderson, Archibald. "Two moderns." *Va. Quar. Rev.,* 5 (Jan. 1929) 133-136.
Discussion of Shaw, past his zenith; O'Neill, the emotional adventurer; and Pirandello, the fantastic intellectual, as top men in the drama today.

*   277. Hofmannsthal, Hugo von. "Eugene O'Neill." *Freeman,* 7 (21 Mar. 1923) 39-41. Translated by Barrett H. Clark.
An important article by a distinguished Viennese poet and playwright who presents some strong indictments against much of O'Neill's material. He finds first acts good and last acts weak, heading toward a climax that is already expected.

278. Isaacs, Edith J. R. "Meet Eugene O'Neill." *Th. Arts,* 30 (Oct. 1946) 576-587. [Reprinted in Gilder, Rosamond, ed., *Theatre Arts anthology,* NY, Theatre Arts Books, 1950, pp. 168-176 (No. 49).]

Mrs. Isaacs reflects on the present interest in O'Neill after 12 years. His early plays were the "trumpet blare" that broke the walls of resistance.

279. — — — —. "The Negro in the American theatre." *Th. Arts*, 26 (Aug. 1952) 492-543.
The entire issue is devoted to this topic. Includes illustrations and general remarks about *JONES* and *CHILLUN*.

280. Janney, John. "Perfect ending." *Am. Mag.*, 117 (Apr. 1934) 38.
Popular account of O'Neill's life and personality.

281. Jones, Carless. "A sailor's O'Neill." *Revue Anglo-Americaine*, 12 (Feb. 1935) 226-229.
Portrayal of the working seaman is accurate and real, if at times restrained. Atmosphere is much better than character.

282. Kalonyme, Louis. "O'Neill lifts curtain on his early days." NY *Times*, 21 Dec. 1924, IV, p. 7.
Report of O'Neill's life as reflected in plays of the sea.

° 283. Karsner, David. "Eugene O'Neill at close range in Maine." NY *Her-Trib.*, 8 Aug. 1926.
In his interview at O'Neill's summer home in Maine, Karsner finds it impossible to describe what is behind the man and his work. This is an interesting and valuable account of a personal visit, which does not become sentimental in the manner of Merrill's account (No. 310).

284. Katzin, Winifrid. "The great God O'Neill." *Bookman*, 68 (Sept. 1928) 61-66.
Imaginary conversation between Eustace Jones, American critic, and Achille Pasivite, New York correspondent of a French journal. Jones worships O'Neill, finds little fault. Pasivite finds no masterpieces, and seems to get the better of the argument.

° 285. Kemelman, H. G. "Eugene O'Neill and the highbrow melodrama." *Bookman*, 75 (Sept. 1932) 482-491.
An extremely hostile and ill-conceived attack on all of O'Neill's

plays as "violent and unbalanced melodrama." Kemelman sets up and annihilates O'Neill's characters, action, dialogue and experimentation as the work of a writer lacking any dramatic talent whatsoever. Kemelman is in a forest-trees predicament, as he makes little effort to find any value whatever in O'Neill's work. Instead he violently attacks many of the obvious shortcomings which, in themselves and out of context, are admitted faults. Mere tabulating of deaths and murders, or listing the number of loose women is not valid criticism. Compared to this broadside, the opinions of Geddes (No. 47) and Salisbury (No. 113) are mild dissensions.

* 286. Kemp, Harry. "Out of Provincetown: A memoir of Eugene O'Neill." *Theatre*, 51 (April 1930) 22-23.

Harry Kemp, a "vagrom poet" and an original Provincetown Players member, wrote this recollection of the early days on Cape Cod and at MacDougal Street. O'Neill is painted as a very human and entertaining friend. Main shortcoming of the article is its lack of specific dates to identify important events.

287. Kerr, Walter. "He gave it to 'em, boy." NY *Her-Trib.*, 14 April 1957.

An attempt to determine what made O'Neill great, assuming Pulitzer prize will go to LONG DAY'S JOURNEY. (Similar item in Kerr's *Pieces at Eight*, NY, Simon and Schuster, 1957, p. 120, No. 65.)

288. – – – –. "The test of greatness." NY *Her-Trib.*, 25 Aug. 1957.

Kerr attempts to determine if O'Neill is permanent, and gives a reluctant "No." It is only his personal power that still holds us.

289. Kinne, Wisner Payne. "George Pierce Baker and Eugene O'Neill." *Chrysalis*, 7 (1954) No. 9-10, pp. 3-14.

A report of Baker's position as O'Neill's teacher at Harvard. Reprints three letters from O'Neill to Baker: two application letters of July, 1914, and a letter of 1919, before production of *HORIZON*, thanking Baker for past help.

290. Kommer, Rudolf. "O'Neill in Europe." NY *Times*,

9 Nov. 1924, VIII, 2:1. [Reprinted in Greenwich Village Playbill No. 2, Season 1924-1925.]

A valuable article on the poor reception of *ANNA CHRISTIE* in Berlin, condemning some of the inexcusable blunders such as the insertion of Anna's suicide.

* 291. Krutch, Joseph Wood. "Eugene O'Neill, the lonely revolutionary." *Th. Arts*, 36 (Apr. 1952) 29-30.

Like many American greats — Poe, Hawthorne, Melville — O'Neill is alone in his work, apart from the "spirit of the age." O'Neill's work with tragedy, which no one else attempted, kept him from successful communication with the mass of his audience.

292. — — — —. "The meaning of the modern drama. III — The American tradition." *Nation*, 141 (18 Sept. 1935) 320-323.

In this series of four articles, Krutch discusses the "classical" and "revolutionary" plays as developed in his *American Drama Since 1918* (No. 68). The public is now ready for the "liberal point of view" represented by Rice, Howard, Anderson, and O'Neill.

293. — — — —. "O'Neill the inevitable." *Th. Arts*, 38 (Feb. 1954) 66-69.

In Krutch's opinion, whatever you may think of O'Neill you cannot discuss American drama in the 20th century without him. As the drama had its obligatory scene, O'Neill is the obligatory subject.

* 294. — — — —. "O'Neill's tragic sense." *Amer. Schol.*, 16 (Summer 1947) 283-290.

Krutch discusses the outstanding shortcomings and the equally outstanding merits of O'Neill's works in an effort to see why, after 30 years of writing, O'Neill can still command an audience to do as he wishes. Matters of intuition, sincerity, and skills as tragic writer are mentioned to show how this man is either praised or damned, never considered in between.

* 295. — — — —. "The rediscovery of Eugene O'Neill." NY *Times*, 21 Oct. 1956, VI, pp. 32-34.

After two decades of neglect, O'Neill may now be in the position to be rediscovered and reappraised by a new generation. No artist can be accurately evaluated in his own time, and if O'Neill survives this test, he will have the marks of permanent greatness.

296. – – – –. "Ten American plays that will endure." NY *Times*, 11 Oct. 1959, VI, pp. 34-35.
INTERLUDE and *LONG DAY'S JOURNEY* are chosen along with *Streetcar Named Desire, Green Pastures, Oklahoma!* and others as likeliest American plays to last through posterity.

297. Kutner, Nanette. "If you were daughter to Eugene O'Neill." *Good Housekeeping*, 115 (Aug. 1942) 26.
An "intimate glimpse" of O'Neill as a father, told by daughter Oona, age 17, whose cafe society life was intensely disliked by the parent.

298. Landauer, Bella C. "The international O'Neill." *Am. Book Collector*, 2 (1932) 55-56.
Gives complete list of foreign performances from Moscow to Berlin and Tokyo.

299. Lardner, John. "O'Neill's back." *Look*, 16 (26 Feb. 1952) 4.
Brief, admiring welcome to the revivals of *DESIRE* and *CHRISTIE*, plus a report of O'Neill's love of sports during his stay in south of France.

300. Lewisohn, Ludwig. "Eugene O'Neill." *Nation*, 113 (30 Nov. 1921) 626.
Lewisohn was never one to praise O'Neill. In this accurate evaluation of the writer's early faults, he states that O'Neill must learn to stop interfering with fate if he is to create memorable plays and not merely memorable fragments.

301. Lindley, Ernest K. "Exile made him appreciate U.S., O'Neill admits." NY *Her-Trib.*, 22 May 1931.
Interviewed on his return from France, O'Neill gives some personal viewpoints on the European theatre.

302. Lovell, John, Jr. "Eugene O'Neill's darker brother."
Th. Arts, 32 (Feb. 1948) 45-48.
By presenting the Negro on equal terms with white, O'Neill
portends of a brighter future for stage treatment of the Negro.

* 303. Loving, Pierre. "Eugene O'Neill." *Bookman*, 53 (Aug.
1921) 511-520.
This is one of the earliest long journalistic treatments of the
rising O'Neill. It is a generally favorable account, written by a
personal friend. Each play briefly analyzed in an attempt to
discover influences of Conrad, Strindberg, etc., and possible
trends.

* 304. McCardell, Roy L. "Eugene O'Neill: Son of Monte
Cristo born on Broadway." NY *Telegraph Sunday Mag.*, 19 Dec.
1920.
A long article about O'Neill's life and early plays. The first
important item to appear in a New York Sunday supplement.

305. McClain, John. "O'Neill cometh back." NY *Jour-Am.*,
12 Oct. 1956.
With the current revival in interest, McClain reviews O'Neill's
background and early stage experiences.

306. Macgowan, Kenneth. "O'Neill as stage director." NY
Post, 18 Dec. 1926.
O'Neill's producing partner gives examples of the demands
which most O'Neill plays make on stage effects.

307. — — — —. "O'Neill in his own plays." NY *Times*, 9
Jan. 1927, VII, 2:7.
Brief discussion by O'Neill's partner concerning matters of
O'Neill's life as reflected in the plays.

308. — — — —. "The O'Neill soliloquy." *Th. Guild Mag.*,
Feb. 1929.
A discussion of the evolution of the O'Neill technique from
the earliest plays like *WELDED* through *INTERLUDE*.

309. Mayo, Thomas F. "The great pendulum." *Southwest
Rev.*, 36 (Summer 1951) 190-200.

Tracing the swing from romance to rationalism and back in the history of western civilization, Mayo finds O'Neill's early "ruthless dissection of emotions" part of the rationalism of 20's, and *DAYS WITHOUT END* and *ICEMAN* part of the swing to romanticism of 30's and 40's.

*   310. Merrill, Charles A. "Eugene O'Neill." *Equity Mag.*, Aug. 1923, pp. 26-29.

An interesting report of an interview at O'Neill's Cape Cod home, which presents a sentimental picture of cozy domesticity and of peaceful isolation from the world. Merrill creates an image of a man extraordinarily eager to return to Ireland, a facet of O'Neill's personality no other commentator ever seems to have discovered. Compare with Karsner's interview in Maine (No. 283) and Cowley's report of a weekend in Connecticut (No. 206).

311. Miller, Jordan Y. "Eugene O'Neill's long journey." *Kansas Mag.*, 1958, pp. 77-81.

O'Neill's enigmatic character and his reluctance to be anything but a devoted playwright discussed in a general review of his life and plays in view of the revived interest in his works.

312. — — — —. "The Georgia plays of Eugene O'Neill." *Georgia Rev.*, 12 (Fall 1958) 278-290.

O'Neill's decline into romanticism and ultimate disappearance from the American stage for more than a decade are traced through the two plays sent to NY from Georgia, *AH, WILDERNESS!*, and *DAYS WITHOUT END.*

313. Mollan, Malcolm. "Making plays with a tragic end; an intimate interview with Eugene O'Neill, who tells why he does it." Phila. *Public Ledger*, 22 Jan. 1922.

One of the most widely, quoted articles of its type. O'Neill asserts he will write happy endings only when he finds the right kind of happiness.

314. Morehouse, Ward. "The boulevards after dark: Four hours from Paris in his French chateau Eugene O'Neill is writing American drama." NY *Sun*, 14 May 1930.

Report of O'Neill's life in France, including description of his love for speed in a 100 mph French sports car.

* 315. Morrill, M. M. "Eugene O'Neill's shack." *Drama*, 20 (Apr. 1930) 203.
An overdramatic discussion of O'Neill's home at Peaked Hill Bars. This writer is firmly convinced its desolation is the only kind of atmosphere O'Neill could happily live in (a view obviously disproven within a short time). Three pictures of the home are included.

316. Moses, Montrose J. "A hopeful note in the theatre." *North Am. Rev.*, 234 (Dec. 1932) 528-535.
O'Neill is one of those who is bringing new hope to the theatre.

317. — — — —. "The 'new' Eugene O'Neill." *North Am. Rev.*, 236 (Dec. 1933) 543-549.
The O'Neill legend is shattered somewhat by *AH, WILDERNESS!*. Does it represent a new O'Neill? Moses is not sure.

318. — — — —. "New trends in the theatre: IV. American." *Forum*, 73 (Jan. 1925) 83-87; 73 (Feb. 1925) 231-237.
Moses observes that O'Neill's treatment of the Negro was formerly impossible on the commercial stage. O'Neill also has the quality of soul which is not detected in other modern American playwrights.

319. Motherwell, Hiram. "O'Neill — what next?" *Stage*, 12 (Aug. 1935) 28-30. [Reprinted in Walter, Erich A., ed., *Essay annual*, NY, Scott, Foresman, 1936, p. 202.]
After a year's silence from O'Neill, Motherwell speculates if he will emerge as perhaps the diagnostician and prophet of individualism in the social order.

* 320. Mullet, Mary B. "The extraordinary story of Eugene O'Neill." *Am. Mag.*, 94 (Nov. 1922) 34.
The best article to appear in a popular magazine up to this date, discussing O'Neill's plays and personal philosophy. It recognizes O'Neill's successes as a new force in the theatre.

321. Nathan, George Jean. "The American dramatist." *Am. Merc.*, 17 (Aug. 1929) 500-505.

In a review of the accomplishments of all modern American dramatists, Nathan finds O'Neill the leader, a first rate dramatist, despite his failures.

322. — — — —. "The bright face of tragedy." *Cosmopolitan*, 143 (Aug. 1957) 66-69.

More personal recollections, designed to remove the idea that O'Neill was always gloomy. Many stories of his youth. Nathan reveals that O'Neill fought all his life against the nervous trembling which eventually incapacitated him. (See Gierow's explanation of this affliction, No. 259.)

323. — — — —. "The case of Eugene O'Neill." *Am. Merc.*, 13 (Apr. 1928) 500-502.

Stinging attack in the Nathan manner on the critics who praise O'Neill's early amateur works and condemn the later ones, like *MARCO* and *INTERLUDE*.

324. — — — —. "The Cosmopolite of the month." *Cosmopolitan*, 102 (Feb. 1937) 8.

As a close friend for 20 years, Nathan attempts to debunk the common idea of the gloomy introvert by giving facts about O'Neill's personal life which show him the happiest most contented practitioner of *belles-lettres*.

325. — — — —. "Eugene O'Neill — Intimate portrait of a Nobel prizewinner." *Rev. of Rev.*, 95 (Feb. 1937) 66-67.

O'Neill shown as lover of detective stories, sports, garden work, as opposed to the common depressing picture of him.

326. — — — —. "Many are called and two are chosen for the dramatic hall of fame." *Cur. Op.*, 69 (Aug. 1920) 201-202.

George Jean Nathan chooses George Ade and O'Neill as top American playwrights. O'Neill chosen not for what he has done, but for what he has tried and failed to do. Nathan was the earliest important critic to recognize O'Neill's potential. *LONG*

VOYAGE HOME and *ILE* had already been published in Nathan and Mencken's *Smart Set* magazine.

327. — — — —. "O'Neill." *Van. F.*, 41 (Oct. 1933) 30.
After years of restiveness O'Neill has found calm and tranquility. Nathan also shows how he has been a severe O'Neill critic while remaining a close friend.

328. — — — —. "O'Neill: A critical summation." *Am. Merc.*, 63 (Dec. 1946) 713-719.
Critical appraisal of O'Neill as writer, taking all plays in chronological order. Nathan cites some of Eric Bentley's criticism from *Playwright as Thinker* (No. 4) to show lukewarm British reception.

329. — — — —. "The recluse of Sea Island." *Redbook*, 65 (Aug. 1935) 34. [Reprinted in Nathan's *The theatre of tho moment*, Knopf, 1938, pp. 196-207 (No. 102).]
More of Nathan's revelation of intimate facts about O'Neill as a man. Many pictures from the plays.

330. Neuberger, Richard L. "O'Neill turns west to new horizons." NY *Times*, 22 Nov. 1936, VIII, p. 6.
Purely reportorial account of an interview, relating well-known facts about his life, etc. Portrait and scenes from *APE, CHRISTIE, AH, WILDERNESS!* and *INTERLUDE.*

331. Norton, Elliot. "Conscience and a touch of the poet." Boston *Post*, 2 May 1954.
An attempt to show why O'Neill uses New England almost exclusively for settings, mainly because of the "laconic, volcanic, soul searching people" whose conscience is "uneasy, accusing, and relentless."

332. "Notes on rare books." NY *Times*, 18 Nov. 1928, IV, 29:1.
An attempt to review Benjamin De Casseres' poem, "Anathema! Litanies of Negation" to which O'Neill wrote the introduction. O'Neill is out of his element in this introduction, says the anonymous critic, who finds himself unable even to finish the poem itself.

333. "O'Neill as actor is recalled by one who saw him in '17." NY *Her-Trib.*, 17 Mar. 1929.

Report of O'Neill's few stage appearances in early Provincetown days.

[*] 334. "O'Neill goes mildly pirate, etc." *House & Garden*, 65 (Jan. 1934) 19-21.

Description and six excellent photographs of Casa Genotta, Sea Island Beach, Georgia.

335. "O'Neill in Paris." NY *Times*, 18 Nov. 1923, VIII, 2:8.

This report of O'Neill's Paris failures, especially *JONES*, gives some interesting examples of the complete misunderstanding of the French critics.

336. "O'Neill, 'shy, dark boy' bold master of modern drama." *Newsweek*, 2 (19 Aug. 1933) 16-17.

A general news report concerning O'Neill's life and current activities upon completion of *DAYS WITHOUT END* and *AH, WILDERNESS!*

337. "O'Neill's future." *Drama*, Oct.-Nov., 1921.

O'Neill may become spoiled by the praise heaped upon him, but so far he has not. He occupies a "seat which has long been empty."

338. Pallette, Drew B. "O'Neill's A Touch of the Poet and his other last plays." *Ariz. Quar.*, 13 (Winter 1957) 308-319.

All of the later plays, starting with *AH, WILDERNESS!*, are reviewed as parts of O'Neill's changed aproach of more individualized characters instead of Freudian representatives and a tone of compassion for the "damaged" human being. *POET* is a synthesis of the various elements of all the others.

[*] 339. Parks, Edd Winfield. "Eugene O'Neill's symbolism." *Sewanee Rev.*, 43 (Oct.-Dec. 1935) 436-450.

Attempting to analyze the poor critical reception of *DAYS WITHOUT END*, Parks goes into a complex explanation of O'Neill's symbols and philosophy. Parks' main theme, apparent amidst frequently unclear digressions, is that O'Neill has consistently overused symbols, employing them as the reason for the play itself. An interesting contrast to Skinner's viewpoint in "poet's quest" (No. 123), because Parks sees no continuity of philosophy at all.

* 340. Peck, Seymour. "Talk with Mrs. O'Neill." NY *Times*, 4 Nov. 1956, II, 1:6.

A rare interview with O'Neill's widow, in which she describes the background of *LONG DAY'S JOURNEY* and the eventual destruction, page by page, of the entire cycle, *A TALE OF POS-SESSORS SELF-DISPOSSESSED*. Some other interesting personal revelations, including O'Neill's initial doubts concerning their life in a French chateau.

* 341. Peery, William. "Does the buskin fit O'Neill?" *Univ. of Kansas City Rev.*, 15 (Summer 1949) 281-287.

Taking O'Neill's statement of his goal in writing tragedy plus a good general definition of what tragedy should offer, this article makes a telling case for those who would prove that, through lack of nobility of character, O'Neill never really achieved true tragedy.

342. Phelps, William Lyon. "Eugene O'Neill, dramatist." NY *Times*, 19 June 1921, III, 17:2.

Phelps sees O'Neill as one of the "rarest birds" in America — an American dramatist. "He may well become of international significance."

343. Prideaux, Tom. "Most celebrated U.S. playwright returns to theatre." *Life*, 21 (14 Oct. 1946) 102-104.

A well illustrated popular account of life and plays.

344. "Prof. Baker advises writers for stage." NY *Times*, 7 Mar. 1926, I, 13:1.

Speaking before League for Political Education, O'Neill's old professor praises his ex-student, whose poetry in his soul is just beginning to be seen.

345. "The proletariat of the sea." NY *Call*, 6 July 1919, Mag. Sec., p. 10.

This workingman's paper, to which O'Neill had at one time contributed some poetry, finds favor in his treatment of the laboring man at sea, deprived of the human relationships of the landsman.

* 346. Quinn, Arthur Hobson. "Eugene O'Neill, poet and mystic." *Scribner's,* 80 (Oct. 1926) 368-372.
Reprints this chapter from 1927 ed. of Quinn's *History* (No. 110).

347. — — — —. "Modern American drama II." *Eng. Jour.,* 13 (Jan. 1924) 1-10.
O'Neill's tragedies meet the highest test of being "spiritually exalted."

348. — — — —. "The real hope for the American theatre." *Scribner's,* 97 (Jan. 1935) 30-35.
O'Neill's later plays discussed in light of their contribution to the hope of the American theatre.

349. — — — —. "The significance of recent American drama." *Scribner's,* 72 (July 1922) 97-108.
A long discourse on the rising value of American drama, including details about all major writers. O'Neill is unique in his sincerity, integrity, subject matter, volume and success of plays in three years.

350. Rahv, Phillip. "The men who write our plays." *Am. Merc.,* 50 (Aug. 1940) 463-469.
O'Neill is the single exception to the fact that no American creative writer of the first rank has used drama as a natural means of expression.

351. Randel, William. "American plays in Finland." *Am. Lit.,* 24 (Nov. 1952) 291-300.
This brief factual review starts with 1900 and indicates that O'Neill is a "most respected" dramatist in Finland.

352. Reniers, Percival. "If I were you." *Theatre,* 41 (Apr. 1925) 12.

"A dialogue between Eugene O'Neill and Owen Davis — overheard in the imagination." They discuss writing about the hard New England life.

353. Riddell, John. "Strange interview with Mr. O'Neill." *Van. F.*, 30 (May 1928) 86.
Parody of O'Neill's style in a dialogue between O'Neill and his own inner voice.

354. Royde-Smith, Naomi. "Eugene O'Neill." *Forum*, 76 (Nov. 1926) 795-796.
It is time O'Neill stops being a Conrad and Maupassant and starts being "our one and only Eugene O'Neill."

355. Sayler, Oliver M. "The artist of the theatre." *Shadowland*, 49 (Apr. 1922) 66. [Reprinted in *Theatre Arts*, June 1957, p. 23.]
"A colloquy between Eugene O'Neill and Oliver M. Sayler." Discusses playwright as an artist not only *in* but *of* the theatre.

356. — — — —. "Our awakening theatre." *Century*, 102 (Aug. 1921) 514-524.
O'Neill may yet be able to blend the old realism and the new theatre into a successful combination.

357. — — — —. "The real Eugene O'Neill." *Century*, 103 (Jan. 1922) 351-359.
Sayler attempts to explain this man who is already a kind of legend. It is too early, says Sayler, to mark him as our greatest, but his background enables him to bring forth essential tragedy of life.

358. — — — —. "Seeking a common denominator to Andreieff, Pirandello, O'Neill." NY *Her-Trib.*, 26 Apr. 1931.
The native writing of these 3, says Sayler, transcends national limits.

* 359. Sergeant, Elizabeth Shepley. "O'Neill: The man with a mask." *New Rep.*, 50 (16 Mar. 1927) 91-95. [Reprinted in *Fire Under the Andes*, NY, Knopf, 1927 (No. 116).]

An attempt to analyze the mask O'Neill wears in life. Compare this discussion with O'Neill's revelation of his own family life in *LONG DAY'S JOURNEY.* This critic explains O'Neill's plays in terms of childhood rebelliousness against parental autocracy and the need for the "lovely distant mother" who was never there when wanted. Many of the interpretations of O'Neill's later behavior are much closer to the truth than was probably recognized at the time. No other contemporary critic pursued this line of thinking.

360. Sisk, Robert F. "Eugene O'Neill disgusted with opposition to stage art." NY *American*, 29 May 1927.
Admiration expressed that O'Neill has maintained his ideals and has written what he wanted, despite opposition of those who would discourage true stage art.

361. Skinner, Richard Dana. "O'Neill and the poet's quest." *North Am. Rev.*, 240 (June 1935) 54-67.
Excerpts from Skinner's book, *Eugene O'Neill: A Poet's Quest* (No. 123).

362. Slochower, Harry. "Eugene O'Neill's lost moderns." *Univ. Rev.*, 10 (Autumn 1943) 32-37.
His characters often being "masochistic products of modern rationalistic self-probings" they never find any release or resting place, live in a closed world, their doom foreshadowed.

363. Smith, Winifred. "Mystics in the modern theatre." *Sewanee Rev.*, 50 (Jan.-Mar. 1942) 35-48.
General discussion of all mystics, including O'Neill, Sherwood, and Hemingway.

364. Smyser, William L. "A temporary expatriate again views Broadway." NY *Times*, 1 July 1928, VIII, 1:4.
A returning traveler points out that much of O'Neill's technique is really gleanings from what Europe long since discarded.

❋   365. Stamm, Rudolph. "The dramatic experiments of Eugene O'Neill." *Eng. Stud.*, 28 (Feb. 1947) 1-15.
Interesting survey covering O'Neill's main phases from one-

acts to *DAYS WITHOUT END*. To one unfamiliar with O'Neill it is somewhat misleading because the "phases" of atmosphere, emotional struggle, and split personality do not follow in chronological order. Conclusion is that most plays are admirable experiments.

366. — — — —. " 'Faithful realism': Eugene O'Neill and the problem of style." *Eng. Stud.*, 40 (Aug. 1959) 242-250.

This European critic is convinced that after rejecting the unsatisfactory experiments of his plays before 1934, O'Neill at last found his own consistent style in *ICEMAN, JOURNEY*, and *MISBEGOTTEN; i.e.*, a belief in a Puritanical view of life as worse than death, portrayed in a style of "faithful realism" in scene and language.

367. — — — —. "The Orestes theme in three plays by Eugene O'Neill, T. S. Eliot and J. P. Sartre." *Eng. Stud.*, 30 (Oct. 1949) 244-255.

ELECTRA, Family Reunion, and *The Flies* diagnosed carefully in terms of the concept of guilt and sin in Orestes story. O'Neill finds no purification or liberation therein, which the others definitely do.

368. Steinhauer, H. "Eros and Psyche: A Nietzschean motif in Anglo-American literature." *Mod. Lang. Notes*, 64 (Apr. 1949) 217-228.

Convincing partial explanation of *BROWN* and meaning of *LAZARUS* in terms of Nietzschean philosophy on evils of sex-repression, plus certain aspects of *ELECTRA* in the same vein.

369. Stevens, Thomas W. "How good is Eugene O'Neill?" *Eng. Jour.*, 26 (Mar. 1937) 179-186.

Attempt to evaluate O'Neill in light of his Nobel prize. The contribution of each major play is discussed as seen by Puff and Sneer of Sheridan's *Critic*. The decision determines that he cannot be judged from literary standards, and many no better than he have received the award.

*   370. Straumann, Heinrich. "The philosophical background of the modern American drama." *Eng. Stud.*, 26 (June 1944) 65-78.

A brief but excellent analysis of O'Neill's place in modern American literature from an objective European viewpoint. American drama is classified into three schools: empirico-pragmatic, historical, and ethico-religious. O'Neill achieves greatest success in combination of all in *ELECTRA*. Straumann finds all of these groups evident to varying degress in all O'Neill's plays.

371. Sullivan, Frank. "Life is a bowl of Eugene O'Neills." *Golden Bk.*, 18 (July 1933) 60-62.

A parody on O'Neill's style, presenting the struggles of the General Baddun family.

372. Sweeney, Charles P. "Back to the source of plays written by Eugene O'Neill." NY *World*, 9 Nov. 1924.

Report of brief interview with O'Neill before production of *DESIRE*, revealing where he got the ideas of many of his plays.

373. Tapper, Bonno. "Eugene O'Neill's world view." *Personalist* (Univ. of So. Cal. School of Philosophy), 18 (Winter 1937) 40-48.

INTERLUDE and *ELECTRA* taken as examples of O'Neill's world view, determining the manner in which he has diagnosed the "sickness of today."

374. Taylor, Joseph R. "The audacity of Eugene O'Neill." *Jour. of Expression*, 3 (Dec. 1929) 209-212.

A run-down of O'Neill's "rule-breaking" that brought him success.

375. Towse, J. Ranken. "A word of warning to Eugene O'Neill." NY *Post*, 18 Mar. 1922.

Towse's opening night reviews of *FIRST MAN, APE, STRAW* were not particularly favorable, and *APE* was roundly condemned. He therefore warns O'Neill that he must not give way to the broad and easy "path of sensationalism" or use the abnormal merely to point up general propositions.

376. Trask, C. Hooper. "Eugene O'Neill in Berlin." NY *World*, 4 Jan. 1925.

Discussion of minimum success of *APE, JONES* and *ANNA CHRISTIE.*

❀   377. Trilling, Lionel. "Eugene O'Neill, a revaluation." *New Rep.*, 88 (23 Sept. 1936) 176-179. [Reprinted in Cowley, Malcolm, ed., *After the genteel tradition,* NY, 1937, pp. 127-140 (No. 28).]
Although Trilling is no great admirer of O'Neill, he regards the playwright's artistic efforts worthy of attention and therefore of criticism. In this excellent survey he contrasts the "surrender" of *DAYS WITHOUT END* to O'Neill's more typical great force in affirming the power and hope of life by saying, "O'Neill has crept into the dark womb of the mother church and pulled the universe in with him."

378. "Trouble with Brown." *Time,* 62 (7 Dec. 1953) 77-78.
Obituary, review of life and works. He may not have achieved his tragic view, but few tried so hard as he.

379. Vernon, Grenville. "Our native dramatist comes into his own." *Theatre,* 41 (May 1925) 20.
O'Neill is not yet the great American dramatist, says Vernon, but in imagination and courage he represents the great hope in native playwriting. This article contains an interesting photograph of O'Neill at age 8, sitting on a rock, pad and pencil in hand.

❀   380. Vorse, Mary Heaton. "O'Neill's house was shrine for friends." NY *World,* 11 Jan. 1931.
Written by the owner of the famous wharf which saw the first production of an O'Neill play, *BOUND EAST FOR CAR-DIFF* in 1916, Miss Vorse relates in detail the collapse of the Peaked Hill Bars cottage during a storm.

381. Watts, Richard, Jr. "Can O'Neill do wrong or not?" NY *Her-Trib.*, 17 Mar. 1929.
Criticism which condemns O'Neill for lack of "intellect" and use of "tricks" is invalid, says Watts, who argues that good use of theatrical tricks is a perfectly valid step for any playwright.

382. — — — —. "Difficulty in staging plays is no concern of Mr. O'Neill." NY *Her-Trib.,* 8 Jan. 1928.

A catalogue of the almost impossible demands O'Neill makes on actor and stage designer with his written directions, but admitting they come from a knowledge of the theatre and a desire to blend all the arts into one.

383. — — — —. "Realism doomed, O'Neill believes." NY *Her-Trib.,* 5 Feb. 1928.

Quotes O'Neill's belief that realism as we know it is doomed, though not necessarily in the style of *INTERLUDE.*

384. — — — —. "A visit to Eugene O'Neill, now of Arcady." NY *Her-Trib.,* 8 June 1930.

Report of an interview at O'Neill's chateau at Villa Mimosas, France. Watts wonders how the lovely home and easy life will affect O'Neill works yet to come. Compare this with Morrill's view concerning O'Neill's home on Cape Cod (No. 315).

385. Weaver, John V. A. "Eugene O'Neill and Pollyanalysis." *Van. F.,* 16 (July 1921) 43.

Weaver maintains that the "Pollyannas" who attack O'Neill have only one real complaint — his lack of pity for his characters.

* 386. — — — —. "I knew him when. . ." NY *World,* 21 Feb. 1926.

Weaver was O'Neill's classmate in Baker's English 47 at Harvard. This informative report is one of the few such personal reminiscences in existence. Weaver is unhappy to find that the "swashbuckling" O'Neill he knew has now disappeared.

387. Welch, Mary. "Softer tones for Mr. O'Neill's portrait." *Th. Arts,* 41 (May 1957) 67-68.

The actress who played the original Josie in the first abortive production of *MISBEGOTTEN* writes of her experiences trying out for the part and acting under O'Neill's supervision. Some interesting glimpses into O'Neill's personality not long before his death.

388. Welsh, Robt. G. "Behind the scenes." NY *Telegram*, 24 Feb. 1922.
Some interesting background material on O'Neill's life.

389. Wenning, T. H. "Dead man triumphant." *Newsweek*, 49 (17 June 1957) 65-68.
General review of life and works by the magazine's theatre editor in view of the widely popular O'Neill revival.

390. Whipple, Thomas K. "The tragedy of Eugene O'Neill." *New Rep.*, 41 (21 Jan. 1925) 222-225.
This writer sounds a different note in his analysis. While most critics observe that O'Neill's characters are far beyond the identity of the audiences which view them, Whipple believes their tragedy of frustration in modern society is ours as well.

391. Wiegand, Charmion von. "The quest of Eugene O'Neill." *New Theatre*, Sept. 1935. p. 12.
Lengthy detailed analysis of all plays, showing that O'Neill's quest for his "long lost innocence" has gotten him nowhere. Strongly leftish article condemns O'Neill as the "poet" of the decadent American petty bourgeois, whose audience is fast dwindling. (Compare with Skinner, No. 123.)

392. Winchell, Walter. "Portrait of a playwright." NY *Mirror*, 13 June 1957.
Facts and information about O'Neill's life and personality, quoting Nathan and others.

° 393. Winther, Sophus Keith. "Strindberg and O'Neill: A study of influence." *Scand. Stud.*, 31 (Aug. 1959) 103-120.
The best study of Strindberg's influence on O'Neill, going much farther in matters of artistry and philosophy than either Hayward (No. 274) or Fleisher (No. 248). Winther is convinced that Strindberg and Nietzsche were far more important to O'Neill than Freud and Jung throughout his entire creative life.

394. Wolfson, Lester M. "Inge, O'Neill, and the human condition." *South. Sp. Jour.*, 22 (Summer 1957) 221-232.
Comparison of Inge's "often deftly slick" treatment of the

isolated, lonely individual with O'Neill's "deadly earnest" portrayals in *ICEMAN, MISBEGOTTEN*, and *JOURNEY*. Wolfson finds *JOURNEY* a tragedy of near-Shakespearean quality.

395. Woodbridge, Homer E. "Eugene O'Neill." *South Atl. Quar.*, 37 (Jan. 1938) 22-35. [Reprinted in Hamilton, W. B., *Fifty years of the South Atlantic Quarterly*, Durham, N.C., Duke Univ. Press, 1952, pp. 258-271 (No. 55).]

A tendency toward melodrama, and an inability successfully to mix symbol, naturalism, and melodrama deprive much of O'Neill's work of great success. An interesting analysis of each play in light of this opinion.

396. Woollcott, Alexander. "The rise of Eugene O'Neill." *Everybody's*, 43 (July 1920) 49.

Mainly a review of his life and explanation of strength of plays.

397. Young, Stark. "Eugene O'Neill." *New Rep.*, 32 (15 Nov. 1922) 307-308.

Young hopes O'Neill gets out from the burden of the fairly limited world he has created and goes on to find his own truth in the complex nature of life.

398. — — — —. "Eugene O'Neill: Notes from a critic's diary." *Harper's*, 214 (June 1957) 66.

Some interesting facts about Young's personal acquaintance with O'Neill revealed in notes from 1923 to 1956.

INDIVIDUAL PLAYS

INTRODUCTION

This portion of the bibliography has been designed to present a clear picture of the tenor of O'Neill criticism as seen in the reviews of individual plays. To do so most effectively the following entries have been arranged in a somewhat arbitrary fashion which, it is sincerely hoped, offers the best possible system for the purpose in mind.

To establish the precise pattern of criticism throughout O'Neill's lifetime and during his posthumous revival would demand a strict chronological listing of each article, regardless of the play under discussion, the writer of the article, or the periodical source. This might be interesting, but it would be tedious to assemble and beyond practical use. On the other hand, to present the accumulated opinions of each individual critic would demand a straight alphabetical listing by author. This would force a large number of anonymous items to be grouped together without meaning and would prevent determining the attitude of the critics as a whole toward any one play. Grouping articles together by periodical title would offer many of the same problems. In this fashion one could easily enough follow the opinions of Brooks Atkinson, John Mason Brown, Joseph Wood Krutch, the *Saturday Review* or *Theatre Arts*, but the cumulative reaction to each play by those who saw it or by the magazines that reviewed it could not be clearly delineated.

The best method would seem to be the inclusion of all critical references under the title of the individual play, and for practical purposes to list the plays in alphabetical, rather than chronological, order. This has been the basis for the more than 1400 references in this section.

Once the items are assembled under the play title, the most appropriate order of presentation again becomes a problem. Several plays were published before they were produced; some died on the road; and others tried out and then entered

New York. Many were revived, some with more success than when first presented. Frequently periodicals have discussed the plays long after they first opened, and scholarly journals, such as the literary quarterlies, have often published studies of individual plays with no relationship to their publication or presentation dates. Again, a strict alphabetical listing of opinion by author or title under the individual plays would not successfully indicate the interesting pattern of developing criticism. In the hope that the most satisfactory compromise has been found to meet the objective for which the bibliography was designed, the entries in this portion are listed in the following manner:

1. BOOK. In a very few instances, as in the case of *LONG DAY'S JOURNEY INTO NIGHT* or *MARCO MILLIONS*, the published version appeared before the play was actually staged. These were reviewed somewhat irregularly, generally by literary commentators rather than drama critics. Reviews of published versions that have been located are therefore presented as the first series of entries. Column headings appear in this fashion:

LONG DAY'S JOURNEY INTO NIGHT

Book — 1956

followed by entries in alphabetical order by author or title. Periodicals are indicated with volume and page when known. Dates will include month and day but not year because of the designated date in the heading.

2. ROAD TRYOUTS. O'Neill would not ordinarily permit his plays to be given road tryouts and preferred to open "cold" in New York. A few, however, did open out of town. Reviews of these tryouts form the second group of entries. Opinions from local newspapers (Pittsburgh, Atlantic City, Boston, and others) form the bulk of the entries. Infrequently a New York newspaper comment is also listed. Column headings appear in this fashion:

AH, WILDERNESS!

Opening night reviews — Pittsburgh Tryout
Newspapers of 26 Sept. 1933

followed by entries in alphabetical order by author or title. Newspaper titles are given but dates are not included because of designated date in the heading.

3. OPENING NIGHTS. In the great majority of cases, opening night reviews are the first listed entries. There are a few matters in this connection which must be explained.

a. New York critics generally ignored the plays of the openly avowed "art" theatre of the Provincetown Players during its first years. The group made no effort to attract them and it was considered more of a "club" than an important theatre. Therefore, most of O'Neill's early one-act plays were reviewed only spasmodically, except for those given by the Washington Square Players, the "little" theatre which actively competed with Broadway and invited the major newspaper and magazine critics to attend. Even *THE EMPEROR JONES* in 1920, after Washington Square had become the Theatre Guild, did not receive its full complement of reviews.

b. In the case of the one-act and a few other full-length plays, reviews often came some days after the play opened. In this case, there will be a series of entries grouped together as opening *run* reviews, with several different dates.

c. The number of newspapers has been purposely restricted. Certain clipping collections, particularly the Provincetown scrapbooks in the New York Public Library and O'Neill's own newspaper clipping service scrapbooks at Yale, contain reviews from newspapers throughout the United States, often reproduced from wire service releases. These have been omitted. Other less known newspapers from the New York metropolitan area, such as the Newark *Evening News* and the various Brooklyn papers, reviewed the plays, but these papers are difficult for the average reader to find and the reviews themselves appear in clipping collections and other sources in highly irregular fashion. Therefor, opening night (or run) reviews and all subsequent reviews have been restricted to New York City (*i.e.*, Manhattan Island) dailies plus the Brooklyn *Eagle*. A page by page search of each of these journals was instituted in the New York Public Library in order to locate all possible reviews. Those found are included here. If a review is omitted it is because that particular newspaper did not review the play, it was no longer (or not yet) publishing at the time, or for some reason was unavailable in the Public Library newspaper collection.

Column headings appear in these two fashions:

AH, WILDERNESS!

Opening night reviews — New York Newspapers of 3 Oct. 1933

followed by entries in alphabetical order by author or title. *Please Note:* The date is always the day *following* the first performance. Newspaper titles are given but dates are not included because of designated date in the heading.

DESIRE UNDER THE ELMS

Opening run reviews — New York Newspapers of 12 to 15 Nov. 1924

followed by entries in alphabetical order by author or title. Newspaper titles are given and month and day included. Year is omitted because of designated date in the heading.

4. OTHER REVIEWS. Subsequent reviews and discussions in magazines and quarterlies and in newspapers themselves on drama pages or Sunday supplements are included in the next heading. Trade dailies, such as *Women's Wear Daily, The Wall Street Journal,* or *Variety,* were often several days late in their opening night reviews. These are included here to avoid confusion with the conventional opening night reviews of the large dailies. (On the occasions when these papers printed their

reviews on the same day as the regular papers they are, of course, included.) When volume of material under this category warrants, it is broken down by year or group of years. Column headings appear in this fashion:

ANNA CHRISTIE

Other reviews and criticism
1921

followed by entries in alphabetical order by author or title. Periodical titles, often abbreviated, follow with volume, date and page when known. Year is omitted because of designated date in the heading.

1922

followed by entries in the same manner. In some case, years have been condensed as follows:

AH, WILDERNESS!

Other reviews and criticism
1933

followed by subsequent heading

1934-1936

Entries will then contain complete dates to distinguish their chronological position.

5. REVIVALS. When the revivals warrant, as they generally do, they are included under a separate listing, with entries treated in the same manner. Column headings appear in this fashion:

AH, WILDERNESS!

Opening night reviews — Revival — New York
Newspapers of 3 Oct. 1941

followed by entries in the same fashion as before.

6. FURTHER REVIEWS. Subsequent reviews and criticism are treated in the same manner as those following opening nights.

NOTE: To achieve the cumulative opinion of any one critic, consult the index, which lists each reviewer in alphabetical order and the plays he has reviewed. Also, be sure to consult the editorial comments that accompany any unusual listing of entries. These comments appear in various appropriate spots under the individual plays.

It can readily be seen that this arrangement is unorthodox. It does, however, supply at a glance the immediate reaction of the important professional critics (1) to each separate production of an O'Neill play immediately after it opened; (2) to the subsequent reconsideration by the same reviewers or by others, and (3) to the revivals which were often attempted. The general chronological order is maintained within this framework, and the user of this bibliography can determine, by placing each play in its chronological order of production, the whole order of development of the professional critic's attitude toward this vigorous and mystifying new playwright, or their subsequent distress or exaltation at the plays of his later years.

The general MECHANICS of this section — order of presenting the material — follow the same system used under the preceding section, GENERAL REFERENCES — PERIODICALS. Only the New York *Times* entries contain page and column number. Other papers have date only. Magazine entries contain full information concerning volume, date and page if known, but as in the case of those in the previous section, certain information is lacking because of the impossibility or impracticality of locating it. Consult the introduction to the Periodical section for full details.

AH, WILDERNESS!

The title will be punctuated as O'Neill intended: *Ah, Wilderness!*
Variants within different reviews will be disregarded.

Opening night reviews — Pittsburgh Tryout
Newspapers of 26 Sept. 1933

399. Gaul, Harvey. "O'Neill, Cohan share spotlight in
world premiere at Nixon." Pitt. *Post Gazette.*
It is Cohan's piece; long arid stretches need trimming.

400. Parry, Florence F. "Wherein the boy Penrod grows
older under the new and nostalgic pen of Eugene O'Neill."
Pitt. *Press.*
Negative report; not a play, but a series of unmatched scenes
strung together; old O'Neill is much preferred.

401. Seibel, George. "O'Neill world premiere of Ah,
Wilderness! hit at Nixon." Pitt. *Sun Telegraph.*
Praise for O'Neill's ability to restrain and condense.

Opening night reviews — New York
Newspapers of 3 Oct. 1933

402. Allen, Kelcey. "Ah, Wilderness! O'Neill play, is bright
comedy." *W. W. Daily.*
General account of play's subject, showing that O'Neill can
write in a lighter vein.

403. Anderson, John. "Humor flows from O'Neill pen."
NY *Jour.*
High praise for charm and vivacity, "affectionate, indulgent,
and tear-stained humor."

404. Atkinson, Brooks. "In which Eugene O'Neill recaptures the past . . ." NY *Times*, 28:2.
O'Neill now on level where he can talk to all of us; highest

recommendation, even with evidence of the commonplace and hackneyed.

405. Brown, John Mason. "George M. Cohan in Eugene O'Neill's comedy." NY *Post*.
Praise for cast, production, and O'Neill's laying aside the tragic mask.

406. Gabriel, Gilbert. "Ah, Wilderness!" NY *Amer*.
Comedy of recantation as well as recollection; the play is "paradise enow."

407. Garland, Robert. "Laughs, tears in Ah, Wilderness!" NY *Wor-Tel*.
Enthusiastic praise for all elements of play and production.

408. Hammond, Percy. "Ah, Wilderness!" NY *Her-Trib*.
Dismissed as little more than sentiment; Cohan is better than the script.

409. Lockridge, Richard. "Ah, Wilderness! . . . is offered by the Theatre Guild." NY *Sun*.
O'Neill is just plain folks after all.

410. Mantle, Burns. "Ah, Wilderness! — and George Cohan." NY *News*.
Praise for Cohan; play fits the groove of American family life as it is currently being presented in drama.

411. Pollock, Arthur. "Eugene O'Neill writes a gentle, kindly play." Brook. *Eagle*.
O'Neill has gone through his own revolution and likes the world a bit more.

412. Winchell, Walter. "Cohan triumphs at Guild theatre in O'Neill hit." NY *Mirror*.
Eventful night, abundance of delight; "chords of emotion played with skill, dignity and good taste."

Other reviews and criticism
1933

413. Adams, Franklin P. "The conning tower." NY *Her-Trib.*, 2 Oct.
Best O'Neill play ever seen; worth "50 Interludes and dozen Electras."

414. "Ah, Wilderness!" *Variety*, 10 Oct.
Admirable start for Guild; helps enliven new season.

415. "Ah, Wilderness!" NY *Wor-Tel.*, 13 Oct.
This editorial regards O'Neill's experiments as a good thing, but the writer is delighted with this play's turn toward gentleness and simplicity.

416. Bolton, Whitney. "Geo. M. Cohan is THE THING in O'Neill's Ah, Wilderness!" NY *Morn. Teleg.*, 4 Oct.
Not great, but extremely satisfying, the skilled trickery of good theatre. Cohan is a better actor than O'Neill is a playwright.

417. Bowen, Stirling. "E. O'Neill and G. Cohan." *Wall St. Jour.*, 5 Oct.
A folksy play, full of nostalgia, which brings together in O'Neill and Cohan two foremost virtuosi of observation and showmanship in this generation.

418. "Broadway boy." *Time*, 22 (9 Oct.) 26.
"Human, kindly, sure drawn" picture of home life.

419. Burr, Eugene. "Ah, Wilderness!" *Billboard*, 45 (14 Oct.) 16.
Strongly negative report; most of the play is trite, full of stage tricks. Written by anybody else it would have been thrown out. (Burr, however, finds the beach love scene one of the theatre's "most lovely," while many other critics condemned it.)

420. Caldwell, Cy. "To see or not to see." *New Outlook*, 162 (Nov.) 42.
Charming, tender, thoroughly delightful.

421. Corbin, John. "O'Neill backs and fills." *Sat. R. Lit.*, 10 (28 Oct.) 217.

A new facet of O'Neill's genius, but with the same preoccupation with deadly sin.

422. Eaton, Walter Prichard. "Eugene O'Neill changes style and mood." NY *Her-Trib.*, 22 Oct.

O'Neill proves he can write a normal play and please the masses; smiling, tender, simple treatment of subject.

423. Gabriel, Gilbert. "Personal element." NY *Amer.*, 5 Oct.

Gabriel draws some tenuous parallels between O'Neill's early life and the play's events.

424. Garland, Robert. "Finds subtle change in outlook of O'Neill." NY *Wor-Tel.*, 5 Oct.

Garland likes this best of any O'Neill.

425. – – – –. "Hails O'Neill play for wit and daring." NY *Wor-Tel.*, 9 Oct.

Extensive quotes from Clayton Hamilton's high praise; the kind of play nobody previously dared write or produce in this "over-wearied world."

426. – – – –. "Hokum that assays at humanity." NY *World*, 3 Nov.

O'Neill and Mae West both use hokum and both succeed.

427. "Garment of repentance." *Lit. D.*, 116 (28 Oct.) 24.

"The family scenes strike one as things overhead rather than lived or truthfully imagined."

428. "Guild's new O'Neill play escapes dullness with Cohan." *Newsweek*, 2 (7 Oct.) 29.

"Moonlight and soft roses in old New England" which do not stand up very well without the stars and splendid supporting cast.

429. Hammond, Percy. "The theaters." NY *Her-Trib.*, 8 Oct.

Cohan keeps the play from being completely boring. He has been good in many bad plays, "among the worst of which is Ah, Wilderness!"

430. Isaacs, Edith J. R. "Good plays a plenty." *Th. Arts,* 17 (Dec.) 908-909.
Not much of a play, but merely conventional comedy.

431. Jordan, Elizabeth. "Mr. O'Neill soft pedalled." *America,* 28 Oct., p. 89.
This critic does not admire O'Neill's usual plays and is happy to see this one. She concludes that if his recent marriage was the cause of his change, his wife is a public benefactor and should be awarded Pulitzer and Nobel prizes.

432. Krutch, Joseph Wood. "Mr. O'Neill's comedy." *Nation,* 137 (18 Oct.) 458-459.
Charming humor, pleasant entertainment, written about sentiment instead of passion.

433. Lockridge, Richard. "Requiescat in pace?" NY *Sun,* 7 Oct.
Hope expressed that the change in O'Neill will not remove one of the most exciting reasons for going to the theatre by becoming ordinary, unexciting, conventional.

434. Mantle, Burns. "Mister O'Neill changes a few spots." NY *News,* 15 Oct.
Attempts to explain the change in O'Neill, tracing back some of his personal history. It is to O'Neill's credit that he should have written this play.

435. Nathan, George Jean. "A turn to the right." *Van. F.,* 41 (Nov.) 66.
Proof O'Neill can write comedy as well as serious material. Nathan is glad he can work in a conventional medium.

436. "Old man O'Neill, and others." NY *Her-Trib.,* 5 Oct.
This review of published version warns that if this is a changed

O'Neill, we may soon expect a satire on "serious young Freudian of yesteryear."

437. "O'Neill relaxes." *Stage,* 11 (Nov.) 7-9.
Large double page picture of dinner scene, with brief review. O'Neill has put people you are drawn to on stage just because you love them.

438. "O'Neill turns to simple folk." NY *Post,* 11 Oct.
Mainly discusses the ease with which the play was composed in six weeks.

439. Skinner, Richard Dana. "Ah, Wilderness!" *Commonweal,* 18 (27 Oct.) 620. [Reprinted as "A note on Eugene O'Neill," in Skillin, Edward S., ed., *The Commonweal reader,* NY, Harpers, 1949, pp. 80-83 (No. 124).]
More than just Tarkington; O'Neill is looking into his own soul as he pauses on a difficult journey.

440. Wyatt, Euphemia Van R. "A great American comedy." *Cath. Wld.,* 138 (Nov.) 214-215.
No more tender plea could be made for the Pope's Encyclical on Marriage than this play, written in keeping therewith by Catholic O'Neill. (In reality, O'Neill did not practice his religion after his childhood.)

441. Young, Stark. "Variegated hits." *New Rep.,* 76 (18 Oct.) 280.
Some effect lost by O'Neill's lack of gift for true words and living speech rhythm. The basic appeal is still O'Neill.

1934-1936

442. "Ah, Wilderness!" *Th. Arts,* 18 (May 1934) 390.
The published version, while gracious, nostalgic, and trivial, loses much without Cohan.

443. Brandt, George. "Ah, Wilderness!" *Rev. of Rev.,* 89 (Feb. 1934) 39.

"Booth Tarkington sort of tenderness."

444. Eaton, Walter Prichard. "The drama in 1933." *Am. Schol.*, 3 (Winter 1934) 96-101.
Reviewing the season, Eaton hopes O'Neill has not departed from his gropings into the human spirit.

445. Gilbert, Douglas. "Did the Nobel judges consider O'Neill's Ah, Wilderness!?" NY *Wor-Tel.*, 14 Nov. 1936.
A play not to be taken lightly; more rational than any of O'Neill's others.

446. Wyatt, Euphemia Van R. "O'Neill and his miracle." *Cath. Wld.*, 138 (Mar. 1934) 729.
This play is a "sincere confession of faith" and forecasts the "miracle" of the later *DAYS WITHOUT END*.

Opening night reviews — Revival — New York Newspapers of 3 Oct. 1941

447. "Ah, Wilderness!" *W.W. Daily.*
Has lost none of its flavor and charm; welcome to excellent production.

448. Anderson, John. "Ah, Wilderness! revived by Guild." NY *Jour-Am.*
Enduring comedy; never reaches the sentimental or slushy.

449. Atkinson, Brooks. "Eugene O'Neill's Ah, Wilderness! restaged." NY *Times*, 26:2.
Welcomes return; still a play of great pleasure, "never more enchanting."

450. Brown, John Mason. "Ah, Wilderness! remains tender and enjoyable." NY *Wor-Tel.*
Even better than the original, despite Cohan's absence.

451. Coleman, Robert. "Ah, Wilderness is again a hit." NY *Mirror.*

One of the best scripts from the master's pen. It has heart, decent sentiment, literate humor.

452. Kronenberger, Louis. "The Miller family stands the test." *P.M.*
More sentiment than Tarkington, without the gentility.

453. Lockridge, Richard. "O'Neill's Ah, Wilderness! is revived." NY *Sun.*
Better than the original.

454. Mantle, Burns. "Ah, Wilderness! is happily revived." NY *News.*
Expertly written play, intelligently revived.

455. Pollock, Arthur. "O'Neill's Wilderness pleasingly revived." Brook. *Eagle.*
Still a pleasant comedy; O'Neill's insight into character is apparent.

456. Waldorf, Wilella. "Theatre Guild's revival series begins with Ah, Wilderness!" NY *Post.*
Measures up in every respect to the original, and there is even some improvement. Still provides a tender and amusing picture of family life.

457. Watts, Richard, Jr. "O'Neill revival." NY *Her-Trib.*
Enchanting picture of a lost decade, despite some dawdling.

Other reviews and criticism
1941

458. "Ah, Wilderness!" *Commonweal*, 34 (17 Oct.) 613.
Fresh as the day it was written; Guild is to be thanked for reviving it when the theatre needs spiritual awakening.

459. "Ah, Wilderness!" *Variety*, 8 Oct.
"Least exciting" of Guild's proposed revivals.

460. "Ah, Wilderness! revival is season's best play." *Life*, 11 (3 Nov.) 59-61.
Mainly pictures of the revival, small amount of text.

461. Cooke, Richard P. "O'Neill revival." *Wall St. Jour.*, 4 Oct.
Refreshing reminder that there are still some good plays in existence, though its open and unabashed sentiment lacks what we call "pace" today.

462. Freedley, George. "Guild presents poignant revival of Eugene O'Neill's Ah, Wilderness!" NY *Telegraph*, 4 Oct.
Eight years have not dimmed the success of this play.

463. Gibbs, Wolcott. "Ah, Wilderness!" *New Yorker*, 17 (11 Oct.) 47.
Full of cliches; less to believe in than even a Tarkington story.

464. Gilder, Rosamund. "Candles that light the way — Broadway in review." *Th. Arts*, 25 (Dec.) 867-868.
Mellowed with age; still has basic quality of Americana appropriate in these times.

465. Kronenberger, Louis. "Wanted: Six grade B playwrights." *P.M.*, 12 Oct.
A minor play, but not a false one. Kronenberger pleads for more plays of this type, about ordinary good people. The theatre should stop its search for new Ibsens and Chekhovs and concentrate on some good adult plays on a level with good magazine fiction.

466. Krutch, Joseph Wood. "The fires of spring." *Nation*, 153 (18 Oct.) 381.
Better than original. The play is typical of O'Neill in dealing with "hard virtues vs. the soft ones."

467. Lockridge, Richard. "Footnote on Ah, Wilderness! and the way of life it celebrates." NY *Sun*, 18 Oct.
Improved in quality; paints life as basically good and a way of life all but forgotten at this time.

468. Warner, Ralph. "Theatre Guild revival reveals the true O'Neill." *Daily Worker,* 7 Oct.
Welcomes the revival of this lovable family.

469.   Wyatt, Euphemia Van R. "The drama." *Cath. Wld.,* 154 (Nov.) 212-213.
Thoroughly recommended revival.

ALL GOD'S CHILLUN GOT WINGS

Opening night reviews — New York
Newspapers of 16 May 1924

470.   "All God's Chillun Got Wings proves a poignant drama." *W. W. Daily.*
The more it is understood, the less virulent will be the criticism. Powerful, somber, and poignant, probing into the human soul and ferreting out truths of its dark recesses. Probably better as a treatise than a play.

471.   Broun, Heywood. "All God's Chillun Got Wings." NY *World.*
A "downstroke" in O'Neill's uneven career; tiresome problem play about sanity and insanity. Some of the characters' reactions are not very clear.

472.   Corbin, John. "All God's Chillun Got Wings." NY *Times,* 22:3.
"A painful play" which, if left alone, would not have received the attention it got.

473. Hammond, Percy. "The mayor interferes a little bit with All God's Chillun Got Wings." NY *Her-Trib.*

Plays better than it reads, but without significance one way or another.

474. Mantle, Burns. "Fitful fevers attack drama." NY *News*.

A dull drama, but sincere; sometimes exciting, but never inspiring. Nobody will go back twice.

475. "New O'Neill play and the mayor." NY *Post*.

It would be a good one-act play and does not rank with O'Neill's best. The second act climax is the O'Neill of *JONES*, going straight to the heart. The landscape is wreckage, but it is breathtaking.

476. Pollock, Arthur. "All God's Chillun." Brook. *Eagle*.

Not a play to arouse great enthusiasm. O'Neill can be heard explaining and expounding most of the evening, for it is mainly exposition. Affectation still persists in the Provincetown, and O'Neill is not free of it.

477. Welsh, Robert G. "James (*sic*) O'Neill's Negro play." NY *Telegram and Eve. Mail*.

From the standpoint of a situation drawn out to its conclusion, one of the most "appealingly moral" plays.

478. Woollcott, Alexander. "All God's Chillun Got Wings." NY *Sun*.

Strange, wanton, largely unbelievable tragedy in which the antagonist is a taboo. The author is too much in evidence, pushing his characters into a trap and weeping for them. It is something tried, but missed.

Other reviews and criticism
1924

479. Bjorkman, Edwin. "Plays and playmakers." *Outlook*, 137 (11 June) 238.

Reviewing published version of this and *WELDED*, finds both worth reading, with shortcomings hard to define.

480. Carb, David. "To see or not to see." *Bookman,* 59 (July) 582.

Many faults, but stabs "as only great tragedy can stab."

481. Corbin, John. "Among the new plays." NY *Times,* 18 May, VII, 1:1.

In a rather surprisingly blunt assertion of white superiority over the Negro, Corbin pleads for a sane attitude toward the play, judgment of which will be by those who see it and by the play itself.

482. Gruening, Ernest. "The wings of the children." *Th. Arts,* 8 (July) 497-498.

Has O'Neill poignancy, vigor, honesty, but race issue should be more clear-cut without the abnormalities.

483. Hornblow, Arthur. "Mr. Hornblow goes to the play." *Theatre,* 39 (July) 15.

The "tremendous theme" (which Hornblow does not define) lamely handled; Provincetown Players add nothing to their laurels.

484. Kantor, Louis. "O'Neill defends his play of Negroes: All God's Chillun." NY *Times,* 11 May, IX, 5:2.

Presents O'Neill's defense of this and *APE* as nothing but the treatment of problems of the individuals involved. He advocates nothing, merely presenting what is in the problem itself. Race prejudice is not O'Neill's concern.

485. Lewisohn, Ludwig. "All God's Chillun." *Nation,* 118 (4 June) 664.

Race prejudice idea brings O'Neill new heights "hitherto inaccessible to him." Symbolic character, almost Greek.

486. Metcalfe, J. S. "Stage miscegenation." *Wall St. Jour.,* 17 May.

The obvious strain of showing "realism" in relationship between white and Negro prevents the play from becoming real. Dramatic values are lost in the obvious racial basis of the play. (This critic makes the interesting suggestion that white actor in blackface, or Negro in whiteface would have eliminated much of the difficulty.)

487. Nathan, George Jean. "The theatre." *Am. Merc.*, 2 (May) 113-114.
Done with sincerity and intelligence, if overly sketchy. The violent attacks on the play all miss the point.

488. Wilson, Edmund. "All God's Chillun and others." *New Rep.*, 39 (28 May) 22.
One of best things about race prejudice and one of best O'Neill.

489. Woollcott, Alexander. "All God's Chillun etc." NY *Sun*, 20 May.
Lesser O'Neill; compromises realism of the past with lack of persuasion; highly improbable situation in the first place.

1932

490. Rice, Elmer. "Sex in the modern theatre." *Harpers*, 164 (May) 665-673.
In a discussion of aspects of sex and sex taboos on the modern stage, Rice finds this play an "only moderately successful attempt" to deal honestly with the problem of miscegenation.

THE ANCIENT MARINER

Opening night reviews — New York
Newspapers of 7 Apr. 1924

491. Allen, Kelcey. "New plays at Provincetown Playhouse." *W. W. Daily.*
Impressively done. Flawless stage lighting, but the whole thing drags terribly.

492. Broun, Heywood. "The Ancient Mariner." NY *World*.
Base metal from a cracked test tube in the Provincetown lab.
The ballad is now dreary recitation.

493. "Coleridge, Moliere and O'Neill on Provincetown
bill." NY *Post*.
Even with the O'Neill assist, Coleridge as theatrical entertainment is under serious handicap. Neither narrative drama nor
dramatic narrative. The weird imagery came through from time
to time, but it was not sustained.

494. Corbin, John. "A new Provincetown playbill." NY
Times, 15:5.
Less grewsome and thrilling than the poem as read.

495. Vreeland, Frank. "Ancient Mariner made vivid even
for schoolboys." NY *Her-Trib*.
It is so vivid, fresh and heart stirring that schoolboys will go
home and start memorizing it. The production has all the beauty
one has suspected of being in the poem. Dramatic fire has been
drawn down to it.

496. Welsh, Robert G. "Classics and Provincetown." NY
Telegram & Eve. Mail.
Skillfully arranged as sort of a dramatic monologue. Students
of the stage will find much to discuss here.

497. Woollcott, Alexander. "Coleridge and Eugene
O'Neill." NY *Sun*.
More a charade than anything else; Coleridge comes out
second best.

Other reviews and criticism
1924

498. Canfield, Mary Cass. "The Provincetown Playhouse
takes a chance." *Ind. & Week. R.*, 112 (10 May) 259.
"Almost comes off," but offering no comment on O'Neill's con-

tribution this critic states she does not know the amount of O'Neill's own effort.

499. "The chorus as used in the Ancient Mariner." NY *Sun*, 23 Apr.
Anonymous critic comments on the part of the chorus, which was used without any choral training.

500. "Coleridge and O'Neill." NY *Times*, 13 Apr., VIII, 1:4.
Reprints portion of MS to show the adaptation. Some stage directions are actual lines from the poem. A drawing of scenery is on p. 2.

501. Corbin, John. "The playboys of Macdougal street." NY *Times*, 13 Apr., VIII, 1:2.
Force of the poem shrinks to the size of the Provincetown stage. The producers are fooling around, getting nowhere.

502. Hornblow, Arthur. "Mr. Hornblow goes to the play." *Theatre*, 39 (June) 19.
Ponderous and dull despite artistic background effects. The poem is destroyed; production wearisome, far from entertaining.

503. Macgowan, Kenneth. "Crying the hounds of Broadway." *Th. Arts*, 8 (June) 357-358.
A beautiful and significant form which is what is important, having nothing to do with the poem itself.

504. Metcalfe, J. S. "Playing theatre." *Wall St. Jour.*, 8 Apr.
A strong suggestion of the kind of theatre children would put on at home before a curtain hung in a doorway; it is not art. Those who have forgotten the poem's dreariness will find it recalled here. "O'Neill's pretentious experiment seems hardly worth the hard work wasted on it."

505. Nathan, George Jean. "The theatre." *Am. Merc.*, 2 (June) 243-244.
No scenery or lighting will remove the fact that this needs a writer. Too much an attempt at literal interpretation.

506. "Plays and players." *Town and Country*, 81 (1 May) 48.

A very thrilling experience.

507. Pollock, Arthur. "About the theatre." Brook. *Eagle*, 13 Apr.

One of the most interesting of the week's productions. The Provincetown players are always a step ahead of the Guild, being daring instead of dainty.

508. Woollcott, Alexander. "The Ancient Mariner." NY *Sun*, 12 Apr.

Reminiscent of a charade by children in the back parlor.

ANNA CHRISTIE

ANNA CHRISTIE was originally conceived as a play about the old barge captain, Anna's father, and was named both *CHRIS CHRISTOPHERSON* and merely *CHRIS*. Under the latter title it was given a tryout tour in Atlantic City and Philadelphia before being withdrawn for major revisions. Because *CHRIS* has never been published and because it is the play from which *ANNA CHRISTIE* emerged, the few notices it received are included here from No. 509 to 523. *ANNA CHRISTIE* begins with No. 524.

Tryout reviews — CHRIS
Atlantic City and Philadelphia
Miscellaneous reviews of March 1920

509. Bronte, C. H. "Chris and the modernist school." Phil. *Pub. Ledger*, 21 Mar.

O'Neill discussed in relation to modern ideas of realism. This unsuccessful piece cannot be dismissed.

510. Casseboom, Will, Jr. "A masterly play at the Apollo."
Newspaper unidentified on NYPL clipping. Apparently an Atlantic City paper of 9 Mar.
Not a masterpiece, but masterly piece of writing; the tragedy
of life.

511. "Chris." *Dram. Mir.*, 81 (27 Mar.) 577.
Slim plot, very little action.

512. "Chris." Phil. *Bulletin*, 16 Mar.
Hardly enough story for a good one-act.

513. "Chris a new play by Eugene O'Neill." Phil. *Record*,
16 Mar.
Worthy of serious attention in character and dialogue, but
it is more of a short story expanded into a play than an
original play.

514. "Chris a sea play, is Conrad on stage." Phil. *Eve.
Ledger*, 16 Mar.
Little or no action or plot, like a staged Conrad story.

515. "Chris at Broad." Phil. *Inquirer*, 16 Mar.
Draggy, dreary play helped by excellent dialogue, though
even that is tedious at times.

516. "Chris at the Apollo tonight." Apparently Atlantic
City *Union*, 8 Mar., but source and date on NYPL clipping are
not clear.
The story's climax is told with "unerring art."

517. "Chris sailor play at Broad." Phil. *Press*, 16 Mar.
Suggestions of Conrad. We should recognize the talent in
this new writer.

518. "Lounger in the lobby." Phil. *Press*, 21 Mar.
The young writer is feeling his way, has defective sense of
drama, but talent for character and atmosphere.

519. Martin, Linton. "Dramaless drama." Phil. *North American*, 22 Mar.

The overemphasis on art and atmosphere nearly omits the play.

520. — — — —. "Novel note struck in Eugene O'Neill's Chris." Phil. *North American*, 16 Mar.

A novel note in playwriting. Everything is here for the success of a play but the play itself, which is a "colossal failure" because it is dramaless.

521. "Saline zephyrs blow through O'Neill's play." Atlantic City *Daily Press*, 9 Mar.

The play is a surprising comedy which everybody seemed to enjoy, but this critic lost interest in the conflict between the man and the sea after Act III.

522. "Sea story Chris by Monte Cristo's son." Phil. *Pub. Ledger*, 16 Mar.

Little feeling of theatre. Play is not engrossing; real drama comes too late.

523. "Seafaring folk as they really are." Phil. *Record*, 21 Mar.

Loses intensity in happy ending, but play is the work of a "realist with poet's vision."

*Opening night reviews — New York
Newspapers of 3 Nov. 1921*

524. "Anna Christie at Vanderbilt." NY *Telegram*.
A hit, promising to repeat former O'Neill success.

525. "Anna Christie has its premiere." NY *Sun*.
Unconventional play dwindles to conventional happy ending, but still proves O'Neill can write 3-act play.

526. "Anna Christie is sordid and sad." *Journal of Commerce*.

Falls short of great play; dialogue far out of proportion to action.

527. "Anna Christie new triumph for O'Neill." NY *Journal*.
Great promise for future successes.

528. Dale, Alan. "Anna Christie is offered at the Vanderbilt." NY *American*.
Nothing comes through the oleaginous, permeating fog, and there's nothing worth coming through anyway. Better to have presented the fog without either O'Neill or Anna Christie.

529. De Foe, Louis V. "Another grim O'Neill drama." NY *World*.
Performance makes this production worth seeing; shows keen imagination and ability of this yet immature artist.

530. "Drab life of the sea in O'Neill's Anna Christie." NY *Herald*.
Not worthy of O'Neill's ability. Too much "realism"; needs something more. Fantastic to have the sea as the protagonist.

531. Hammond, Percy. "Anna Christie, by the acrid O'Neill." NY *Tribune*.
Recommended for "veracious picture of some interesting characters in interesting circumstances."

532. Kaufman, S. Jay. "Round the town." NY *Globe*.
Good play, despite repetition and happy ending.

533. Macgowan, Kenneth. ". . . A notable drama notably acted." NY *Globe*.
No American drama has searched its portion of life as this does. Power and humor; notable in vision, writing, acting.

534. Mantle, Burns. "Anna Christie, vivid drama." NY *Mail*.
Whatever your opinion, it is finest piece of O'Neill writing, sheer realism "stripped to its ugly vitals."

535. Marsh, Leo A. "Anna Christie at the Vanderbilt."
NY *Telegraph.*
O'Neill's claim to fame could rest with this alone. Continuing
vitality despite apparent compromise in happy ending.

536. Pollock, Arthur. "Anna Christie." Brook. *Eagle.*
At last produced as O'Neill should be; a play of real persons.
Happy ending comes naturally out of the plot.

537. Torres, H. Z. "Anna Christie a triple triumph." NY
Commercial.
End result somewhat unhappy because of ugliness and mor-
bidness of the story, despite brilliant writing.

538. Towse, J. Ranken. "Anna Christie." NY *Post.*
"Incredible" happy ending is "disastrous." The play promises
more for the future than is presently achieved.

539. Woollcott, Alexander. "The new O'Neill play." NY
Times, 22:1.
Mark of imagination. Much better than most current plays.

Other reviews and criticism
1921

540. Allen, Kelcey. "Anna Christie superbly played drama
of the sea." *W. W. Daily,* 4 Nov.
Ranks with the best of several seasons.

541. "Anna Christie." NY *Clipper,* 16 Nov.
Too literal a transfer from life; too much gloom, commonplace dialogue.

542. "Anna Christie." *Drama Calendar,* 21 Nov.
As fine a play as American theatre has yet produced.

543. "Anna Christie." *Variety,* 11 Nov.
While most critics are lyrical in praise of Pauline Lord, this
one finds her very ordinary, using stock mannerisms.

544. "Anna Christie at the Vanderbilt Theatre." *Town Topics*, 10 Nov.
Does not cohere; more of shreds and patches than a unified whole.

545. Benchley, Robert. Untitled review. *Life*, 78 (24 Nov.) 18.
Miss Lord's performance better than the play, but it is still one of the season's most important productions.

546. Boyd, Ernest. "Mr. O'Neill's new plays." *Freeman*, 4 (7 Dec.) 304.
The ending is the worst anti-climax in the theatre, after one of the most tremendous third acts ever written.

547. Castellun, Maida. "Anna Christie thrilling drama, perfectly acted, with a bad ending." NY *Call*, 4 Nov.
Ending not a blunder but a crime; 3½ acts have the quality of greatness.

548. — — — —. "The plays that pass — the season's climax." NY *Call*, 6 Nov.
Reiteration of praise; "the spark of divine fire."

549. Darnton, Charles. "Anna Christie human flotsam." NY *World*, 4 Nov.
Chris is the main character, Anna merely a "barnacle on the paternal hulk." Treatment of character is the most important aspect.

550. Dawson, N. P. "Books in particular." NY *Globe*, 23 Dec.
This writer, who "knows nothing about the theatre anyway," does not find the ending of the published version sentimental.

551. Hackett, Francis. "After the play." *New Rep.*, 29 (30 Nov.) 20.
Essentially a hoax, full of fantasy. To become great, O'Neill must use people for their effectiveness as they are.

552. "How Joseph Conrad influenced O'Neill." NY *Eve. Telegram,* 16 Nov.

This critic finds interesting parallels between O'Neill and Conrad by quoting their common idea toward the sea.

553. Kaufman, S. Jay. "Anna Christie." *Dram. Mir.,* 84 (12 Nov.) 701.

Simple story and theme played upon by a great artist; honest, not stooping to theatrical effect for its own sake.

554. "The O'Neill irony." NY *Herald,* 6 Nov.

"None of the works of the O'Neill theatre is so destitute of imagination as Anna Christie."

555. Parker, Robert Allerton. "An American dramatist developing." *Ind. & Week. R.,* 107 (3 Dec.) 235.

O'Neill is in the literary class of those who continually create anew. This has some of his most exalted moments.

556. — — — —. "Deeper notes in the current drama." *Arts & Dec.,* 16 (Dec.) 110.

This play, despite its faults, is preferable to most of the technically perfect, but superficial, offerings.

557. Pollock, Arthur. "About the theatre." Brook. *Eagle,* 6 Nov.

Play not so significant as earlier works, but excellent staging brings out the best, more than in any other O'Neill play.

558. Seldes, Gilbert. "The theatre." *Dial,* 71 (Dec.) 724-725.

Conclusion and "happy ending" unsatisfactory; O'Neill surrenders to a certain amount of theatricality.

559. "A triumph for Eugene O'Neill and Pauline Lord." NY *Review,* 5 Nov.

Questionable ending; deep ethical significance in play.

560. Whittaker, James. "O'Neill has first concrete heroine." NY *News,* 13 Nov.

For the first time characters surmount environment; O'Neill denies the sea its prey as in earlier works.

561. Woollcott, Alexander. "Second thoughts on first nights." NY *Times,* 13 Nov., VI, 1:1.
Despite faults (last act) "hardened with theatrical alloy" and should be seen again and again.

562. — — —. "Second thoughts on first nights." NY *Times,* 25 Dec., VI, 1:1.
Comment on O'Neill's letter to editor (see Non-Dramatic O'Neill 1921) defending the "happy" ending. Woollcott informs O'Neill that he, O'Neill, should not have been surprised at the public reaction to it.

1922

563. "Anna Christie." *Cur. Op.,* 72 (Jan.) 57-66.
Retells the plot, with some critical comment from New York press. Well illustrated.

564. Bone, David W. "The sea across the footlights." NY *Times,* 15 Jan., III, p. 3.
This member of the British merchant marine finds that the character and atmosphere of the sea as the sailor knows it is now shown for the first time on the stage.

565. Eaton, Walter P. Untitled comment. *Freeman,* 11 Jan.
The main aspects that puzzle the O'Neill audience are: sympathy for actually unsympathetic characters, poetry in brutal dialogue, grim naturalism that attracts.

566. Hammond, Percy. "The theaters." NY *Tribune,* 28 May.
Justifies the award of the Pulitzer Prize; the play meets the specifications.

567. Hornblow, Arthur. "Mr. Hornblow goes to the play." *Theatre,* 35 (Jan.) 29.

A youthful interest in tragedy is shown by this play. It blunders at times, but has some unforgettable scenes and good character delineation.

568. Macgowan, Kenneth. "Anna Christie." *Th. Arts,* Jan. [Reprinted in Hewitt, Barnard, *Theatre USA,* NY, McGraw-Hill, 1959, pp. 337-338 (No. 56).]
"The most searching and the most dramatically consistent study in realism that our playwrights have produced."

569. — — — —. "Anna Christie." *Vogue,* Jan.
O'Neill's most mature play yet. Finest first act ever written by an American. Clear, vigorous pictures of life in the characters.

570. Pearson, Edmund L. "New books and old." *Independent,* 109 (19 Aug.) 78.
On reading the published version, this critic cannot understand the "extravagant praise" the play has received.

Opening night reviews — City Center Revival — New York Newspapers of 10 Jan. 1952

571. Atkinson, Brooks. "Anna Christie." NY *Times,* 33:1.
Still a play of vitality. Tumultous and elemental, with honest and dramatic characters. It is part of our American theatre heritage.

572. Chapman, John. "A fine O'Neill play in a grand revival." NY *News.*
After 30 years it still stands the test because "when it was made it was made right."

573. Colby, Ethel. "Revival of Anna Christie reveals O'Neill still packs a potent punch." *Journal of Commerce.*
One of the best O'Neill's, still has a fascination.

574. Coleman, Robert. "Anna Christie welcome revival at the City Center." NY *Mirror.*
Comparison of Lord and Holm in the roles.

575. Dash, Thomas R. "Anna Christie." *W. W. Daily.*
Because of valid, well drawn characters, play is not dated.
It is basically a comedy.

576. Hawkins, William. "Anna Christie back — why not
sooner?" NY *Wor-Tel. & Sun.*
Great stature and power; O'Neill's theme "crystal clear."

577. Kerr, Walter. "Anna Christie." NY *Her-Trib.*
Still "seaworthy," but "shipping light" because characters not
presented as O'Neill demanded; too much comic emphasis.

578. McClain, John. "Anna Christie." NY *Jour-Am.*
Celeste Holm is as good as Garbo or any of the rest.

579. Sheaffer, Louis. "Only 'Anna' herself disappoints in
City Center O'Neill revival." Brook. *Eagle.*
Still effective; flavorsome, true dialogue.

580. Watts, Richard. "Revival of O'Neill's Anna Christie."
NY *Post.*
Still has emotional power and atmosphere, "brute intensity."

Other reviews and criticism
1952

581. "Anna Christie." *Time*, 59 (21 Jan.) 73.
This production stresses the age and O'Neill's "adolescence."
Wasn't one of his good plays anyway.

582. "Anna Christie." *Variety*, 16 Jan.
"Somewhat dated" but still of power and "compelling drama."

583. Beyer, William H. "The state of the theatre: Classics
revisited." *School & Society*, 75 (16 Feb.) 107.
"An unfortunate production."

584. Bolton, Whitney. "An interesting, vigorous version of
Anna Christie." NY *Telegraph*, 11 Jan.
Still touching and at times witty; age has affected it a little.

585. Brown, John Mason. "Dat ole Davil and a hard God."
Sat. R. Lit., 35 (16 Feb.) 32-34.
Irony rather than tragedy; still moving and effective.

586. Gibbs, Wolcott. "Two from way back." *New Yorker,*
27 (2 Feb.) 48.
"One of the most engagingly absurd works in the English
language" but still effective theatre, on a "primary level."

587. Kerr, Walter. "New generation gets two looks at
O'Neill." NY *Her-Trib.*
Revaluation of the revival (including *DESIRE*) finds *ANNA
CHRISTIE* the more read and genuine play.

588. — — — —. "The stage — Anna Christie." *Commonweal,*
55 (25 Jan.) 399.
Still has a strong ring.

589. Krutch, Joseph Wood. "Anna Christie." *Nation,* 174
(26 Jan.) 92.
While "dated" as any play of another time is "dated" this
still has strength of its own.

590. — — — —. "The strange case of Anna Christie." NY
Her-Trib., 6 Jan.
Explanation of why the public liked and O'Neill disliked
this early play, clearly indicating the completely opposite views
of playwright and playgoer.

591. Nathan, George Jean. "Mr. Nathan goes to the play."
Th. Arts, 36 (Mar.) 70.
Better than the original, which is not saying much.

592. "O'Neill shines again." *Life*, 32 (4 Feb.) 82.
Pictures of Celeste Holm in City Center revival and June
Havoc on Celanese Theatre TV performance.

593. Watts, Richard, Jr. "Those two plays by Eugene
O'Neill." NY *Post*, 27 Jan.
Praise for revival of this and *DESIRE*.

594, Wyatt, Euphemia Van R. "Anna Christie." *Cath. Wld.*, 174 (Mar.) 462-463.
Agrees this is not one of O'Neill's best.

BEFORE BREAKFAST

Search through the files of major New York newspapers could not reveal a single report of the Provincetown's third bill, 1 December 1916, which included this play. The first references appear after the revival of 5 March 1929, when *BEFORE BREAKFAST* was given on the same bill with Vergil Geddes' *The Earth Between.*

*Opening night reviews — Revival — New York
Newspapers of 6 March 1929*

595. Allen, Kelcey. "Before Breakfast." *W. W. Daily.*
Evidence even in this apprentice work that O'Neill would develop into the incorrigible experimenter.

596. Anderson, John. "Before Breakfast." NY *Journal.*
Flimsy and artificial; so tedious as to seem longer than *INTERLUDE.*

597. Atkinson, Brooks. "The McDougal street blues." NY *Times,* 33:1.
O'Neill a glutton when he composed this interlude of domestic horror.

598. "Before Breakfast, short O'Neill play, produced in Village." NY *Her-Trib.*
The least of all O'Neill plays currently showing.

599. "The Earth Between in the Village." NY *News.*

"Mary Blair played Eugene O'Neill's *Before Breakfast* as a curtain raiser. She played it for half an hour."

600. Gabriel, Gilbert. "Incest and other dark drama down MacDougal street way." NY *American.*
Little service is rendered O'Neill in doing this.

601. Garland, Robert. "Before Breakfast." NY *Telegram.*
Miss Blair "did wonders with a role which called for no less a star than Harpo Marx with a skirt on."

602. Littell, Robert. "The play." NY *Post.*
Moderately effective. Does not like the intrusion of the disembodied hand.

603. Lockridge, Richard. "Some dramatic episodes." NY *Sun.*
This critic's hair stood on end only mildly.

604. Pollock, Arthur. "The theatre." Brook. *Eagle.*
No need to see this twice.

Other reviews and criticism
1929

605. "Before Breakfast." *Arts and Dec.*, 81 (May) 104.
Powerful, but tricky in construction.

606. Clark, Barrett H. "Eugene O'Neill and the Village experiment." *Drama*, 19 (29 Apr.) 200.
"It is not an impressive work."

607. Ervine, St. John. "Greenwich gloom." NY *World,* 7 Mar.
A monologue misnamed a play; mostly bunk.

608. Littell, Robert. "Broadway in review." *Th. Arts*, 13 (May) 334.
Insistent, clumsy *tour de force*, not well written.

609. Riley, Wilfred J. "Before Breakfast." *Billboard*, 41 (16 Mar.) 49.
Ineffective and incoherent; O'Neill at his worst.

BEYOND THE HORIZON

Opening matinee reviews — New York Newspapers of 4 Feb. 1920

610. Broun, Heywood. "Beyond the Horizon by O'Neill a notable play." NY *Tribune*. [Reprinted in Moses and Brown, *The American theatre as seen by its critics, 1752-1934*, NY, Norton, 1934 (No. 89).]
Signs of clumsiness because the young man has not mastered the tricks of his trade, but deserves attention; significant and interesting.

611. Darnton, Charles. "Beyond the Horizon close to life." NY *Eve. World*.
"A real play with real people"; the writer should go far.

612. "Eugene O'Neill's tragedy played." NY *Herald*.
O'Neill's fame will be vastly increased. Profoundly moving and human story, although unnecessarily long and formless.

613. Marsh, Leo A. "Beyond the Horizon stirring drama." NY *Telegraph*.
"This new American tragedy is one of the best New York has been fortunate enough to see in many a season."

614. "O'Neill play is a tragedy of misery." *Journal of Commerce*.
Shouldn't be missed; one of season's great plays.

615. Towse, J. Ranken. "Beyond the Horizon." NY *Post*.
"Uncommon merit and definite ability" though shambling and unnecessarily gloomy.

616. "Tragedy of great power at Morosco." NY *World*.
Great power from psychological study of character; much promise for this young writer. A real event in intellectual theatre.

617. Welsh, Robert G. "Bitter, ironic strength in Beyond the Horizon." NY *Telegram*.
Masterpiece; because of its type and subject it may not be popular.

618. Woollcott, Alexander. "Beyond the Horizon." NY *Times*, 12:1.
O'Neill is a gifted writer; the play is so full of meat the rest of season's offerings look like so much meringue.

Other reviews and criticism
1920

619. "An 'American tragedy'." *Lit. D.*, 64 (28 Feb.) 33.
This item summarizes other reviews, mainly NY *World*.

620. "Better days for the theatre." NY *Post*, 21 Feb.
Considerable accomplishment that so young a man could write such a play and draw audiences; the theatre is showing a healthy reaction.

621. "Beyond the Horizon." *Dram. Mir.*, 82 (14 Feb.) 258.
"Fine sense of the theatre," with much promise in the mood of Synge, Chekhov.

622. "Beyond the Horizon." *Independent*, 101 (13 Mar.) 382.
Powerful play, weak construction.

623. "Beyond the Horizon a frank tragedy, is very interesting." NY *Clipper*, 68 (11 Feb.) 21.

Strong in human appeal, frankly a tragedy. The writer has promise.

624. "Beyond the Horizon is presented at matinee." NY *News Record*, 6 Feb.
The essence of tragedy; we await further writings of this man.

625. "Beyond the Horizon one of season's real successes." NY *Review*, 26 Feb.
Proof that American public will support a tragedy of their own soil.

626. Bishop, John Peale. "At last an American tragedy." *Van. F.*, June.
Great, within narrowness of the *genre*. Perhaps it could be better as a novel.

627. "Broadway banter." *Town Topics*, 12 Feb.
Greatness is here; our first modern native tragedy, and it must not fail.

628. Broun, Heywood. "Books." NY *Tribune*, 29 Mar.
The published version deserves much praise, but it is immature in spots, showing false tragedy.

629. — — — —. "The heroine may die and the play still live." NY *Tribune*, 15 Feb.
A long discussion of "rule breaking" in modern drama (such as the death of the leading character) uses this play as a striking example.

630. Dale, Alan. "With Alan Dale at the new plays." NY *American*, 8 Feb.
The slow acting pace is sharply criticized, but the play is of "sterling merit."

631. Eaton, Walter Prichard. "Eugene O'Neill." *Th. Arts*, 4 (Oct.) 286-289.
Judging by this first major play and some of O'Neill's others,

this young writer is spiritually thin, but with organic form so necessary to true works of art.

632. "Eugene O'Neill's Beyond the Horizon is one of the great plays of the modern American stage." NY *Call*, 5 Feb., p. 4.
Overpowering with realism and naturalness, devoid of theatricalism but great in drama. It is memorable drama; the writer has great promise for the future.

633. "Eugene O'Neill wins fame." NY *Telegraph*, 31 Mar.
An explanation of who this suddenly popular writer is.

634. Firkins, O. W. "Beyond the Horizon." *Weekly Rev.*, 2 (21 Feb.) 185-186.
O'Neill has slipped and fallen in the transfer from one act to three.

635. Hamilton, Clayton. "Seen on the stage." *Vogue*, 1 Apr. [Reprinted in Hamilton's *Seen on the stage*, NY, Holt, 1920 (No. 54).]
He will write better plays if he steers clear of theatres.

636. Hornblow, Arthur. "Mr. Hornblow goes to the play." *Theatre*, 31 (Mar.) 185.
A tragedy that could happen anywhere, but Hornblow wonders why the intelligent man married the clod of a woman.

637. James, Patterson. "Beyond the Horizon." *Billboard*, 21 Feb.
Uncommonly fine play about real people; beauty, tenderness, faithfulness to artistic ideal.

638. Kaufman, S. Jay. "Round the town." NY *Globe*, 1 Mar.
If O'Neill keeps this up he will become the American Ibsen.

639. Lewisohn, Ludwig. "An American tragedy." *Nation*, 110 (21 Feb.) 241-242. [Reprinted in Hewitt, Barnard, *Theatre USA*, NY, McGraw-Hill, 1959, pp. 332-333 (No. 56).]
Establishes American kinship with the stage of the modern world.

640. McElliot. "Eugene O'Neill's new tragedy is most pathetic." NY *Illus. News,* 11 Feb.
"It is art, and it is life, but it hurts intolerably."

641. Macgowan, Kenneth. "America's best season in the theatre." *Th. Arts,* 4 (Apr.) 91.
Just as powerful and sturdy as the one-acts were, but could be perhaps shorter, getting the doom "over with."

642. — — — —. "Eugene O'Neill writes a fine, long play." NY *Globe,* 7 Feb.
Extraordinary ability in stretching the theme out; gets down to emotional roots, shows real power.

643. Mantle, Burns. "A fine performance of a fine play." NY *Mail,* 5 Feb.
True sense of theatre; much promise for future in this tragedy, which should hearten those interested in serious drama.

644. Metcalfe, J. S. "Beyond the Horizon." *Life,* 75 (19 Feb.) 332.
Before "placing the crown of greatness" on O'Neill's head, we had better wait to see if he can write further tragedy without the great gloom shown here.

645. Nathan, George Jean. "Beyond the Horizon." *Smart Set,* April.
Praise from this magazine which first printed O'Neill's early works.

646. Pollock, Arthur. "About the theater." Brook. *Eagle,* 6 Feb.
Not as good as some of the one-acts, but at his worst O'Neill is far better than most current drivel and this is not his worst.

647. Untitled discussion in column on drama. *Freeman,* 17 Mar.
Not native in form and tone, because naturalism and tragedy are foreign to us, but the theme is universal.

648. Woollcott, Alexander. "The coming of Eugene O'Neill." NY *Times*, 8 Feb., VIII, 2:1.

One of the real plays of our time. At times impracticable and loose, but a tragedy of the misfit which in mood and austerity has seldom been written in America even half so good.

649. "Words versus situations." NY *Sun*, 19 Mar.

Richard Bennett, star of play, discloses great admiration for way O'Neill can use words alone to bring his idea.

650. "A 'worthwhile' drama." NY *Sun*, 5 Feb.

Discriminating theatregoers will put this bleak but poignant tragedy on their select list.

1921-1926

651. Macgowan, Kenneth. "1920 saw great progress in the American theatre both in plays and acting." NY *Globe*, 15 Jan. 1921.

This and *JONES* are two of the most important plays of an encouraging season.

652. Ridge, Lola. "Beyond the Horizon." *New Rep.*, 25 (5 Jan. 1921) 173-174.

The published version is good drama, but short of being a great play because of "theatre consciousness" of playwright. He is "too anxious a father to his brood."

653. Shipp, Horace. "Conviction and the drama." *Eng. Rev.*, 42 (May 1926) 701-703.

Despite "realism" the play fails because the writer seems to follow too many rules and predestines his characters.

Opening night reviews — Revival — New York Newspapers of 1 Dec. 1926

654. Anderson, John. "The Actor's theatre revives O'Neill's Beyond the Horizon." NY *Post*.

It has withstood the years well; a rich and engrossing evening. Its early, naive approach in its strict sorrow is still vivid and compelling. For all its creakiness its blunt impact on the feelings is tremendous.

655. "Beyond the Horizon is seen here again." NY *Times*.
Still fine and engrossing; an almost perfect tragedy. It has lost none of its power.

656. "Beyond the Horizon staged in revival." NY *American*.
Its realism never tires; the intensity holds the audience. The revival is befitting the play's power and beauty.

657. Gabriel, Gilbert. "Recalling the early O'Neill." NY *Sun*.
Still one of the great contributions to our American drama. It is full of vigor, simplicity, fierce sincerity.

658. Garrick. "An O'Neill revival." NY *Journal*.
Still stands out as one of the finest American dramas of all time. Seems infinitely better than when first produced.

659. Hammond, Percy. "Beyond the Horizon revived skillfully by the Actors' Theatre." NY *Her-Trib*.
Even better in its production than the original.

660. Mantle, Burns. "Beyond the Horizon food for the O'Neills." NY *News*.
Still an eloquent drama of frustration.

661. Osborn, E. W. "Beyond the Horizon." NY *World*.
One of O'Neill's finest. There is a feeling of being cleansed rather than of sorrow on leaving the theatre.

662. Zimmerman, Katharine. "Actors' Theatre revives Beyond the Horizon." NY *Telegram*.
Still strong and unimpaired by its age.

Other reviews and criticism
1926-1927

663. "Beyond the Horizon." Brook. *Eagle*, 2 Dec. 1926.
Distinguished production, although O'Neill's plays are "always something of a penance to witness." It is about average O'Neill.

664. "Beyond the Horizon, O'Neill's tragedy of soil, born at sea." NY *Her-Trib.*, 5 Dec. 1926.
O'Neill explains how he came to creat Robert.

665. Brown, John Mason. "The gamut of style." *Th. Arts*, 11 (Feb. 1927) 86.
One of our "starkest" plays, showing signs of age.

666. Clark, Barrett H. "Dirty plays and dirty minds." *Drama*, 17 (Feb. 1927) 136.
The season's review finds this one of O'Neill's minor efforts.

667. Harkins, John. Untitled article. NY *Telegram*, 5 Dec. 1926.
Still O'Neill's best; a play of great dramatic moments.

668. Krutch, Joseph Wood. "A note on tragedy." *Nation*, 123 (15 Dec. 1926) 646-647.
After giving a clear definition of what tragedy is now and has been, Krutch then praises *HORIZON* because it comes closer to the real thing than other modern plays.

669. Leland, Gordon. "Beyond the Horizon." *Billboard*, 38 (11 Dec. 1926) 9.
Improved with age; shows O'Neill's great ability in tragic drama. It is not depressing; one actually feels refreshed.

670. Stengel, Hans. "Beyond the Horizon." NY *Telegraph*, 5 Dec. 1926.
Whatever else O'Neill has done he has never come nearer greatness. He is best in his love of soil, but loses much in flights of symbolism.

DAYS WITHOUT END

Opening night reviews — Boston Tryout
Newspapers of 28 Dec. 1933

671. Crosby, Edward H. "Mr. O'Neill drama at Plymouth."
Boston *Post*.
A strange play.

672. Eager, Helen. "Eugene O'Neill's new play in first
performance at the Plymouth theatre." Boston *Traveler*.
A fascinating and absorbing evening with this sombre
serious drama.

673. Holland, George. "Eugene O'Neill's new play has
masterpiece possibilities." Boston *American*.
More than a love story: that of the soul sold to the devil.
Ridges as Loving should make New York critics "delirious."

674. Hughes, Elinor. "O'Neill play has world premiere
here." Boston *Herald*.
On dangerous ground; O'Neill now the affirmer instead of
the denier.

675. "In new vein the new play from O'Neill." Boston
Transcript.
O'Neill's "Faust." He writes, reborn, out of his inner life.

676. "Premiere performance of Days Without End."
Boston *Globe*.
Typically O'Neill; a little more baffling than usual.

Opening night reviews — New York
Newspapers of 9 Jan. 1934

677. Allen, Kelcey. "Days Without End, O'Neill's new
play, here." *W. W. Daily*.

A work of exceptional strength and characterization; the speeches are vigorous and strikingly written, but it is mainly for the serious theatre goer.

678. Anderson, John. "Guild makes fine production of work in which author delves into religion." NY *Journal*. [Reprinted in Moses and Brown, *The American theatre as seen by its critics, 1752-1934*. NY, Norton, 1934 (No. 89).]
Fundamental error in making faith an intellectual process that can be touched through words. Confusing, florid, ornamentally phony.

679. Atkinson, Brooks. "Days Without End." NY *Times*, 19:1.
A bad play, written as if O'Neill had never written a play before. Lacks size, imagination, vitality and knowledge of human character.

680. Brown, John Mason. "The play." NY *Post*.
Tedious and artificial, one of O'Neill's feeblest. Split infinitive of a hero. Conclusion so trite that without the O'Neill name the play would not have been tolerated.

681. Gabriel, Gilbert "Days Without End." NY *American*.
Nothing can make it good; true miracle is that it got produced at all.

682. Garland, Robert. "O'Neill's drama is certain to mean many things to many people." NY *Wor-Tel*.
Sophomoric; told in the most awkward manner possible.

683. Hammond, Percy. "Days Without End." NY *Her-Trib*.
Signs of showmanship, but Hammond is not sure just what the play is.

684. Lockridge, Richard. "O'Neill's miracle play." NY *Sun*.
Not his best, but shows O'Neill as the poet seeking God.

685. Mantle, Burns. "Back to the soul with O'Neill." NY *News*.
"A thrill for the true religionist."

686. Pollock, Arthur. "Days Without End." Brook. *Eagle.*
Many audiences will listen devoutly. The Guild has a valuable
piece of theatrical property.

687. Sobel, Bernard. "Eugene O'Neill's new play." NY
Mirror.
Outmoded theme; masks have lost poignancy and novelty.

Other reviews and criticism
1934

688. Anderson, John. "Defenders rally to O'Neill play."
NY *Journal,* 20 Jan.
Having spoken twice against the play (Nos. 678 and 689),
Anderson reports on those who favor it, including the secular
press. He still maintains, however, that it is not a matter of faith
but of analyzing the playmaking itself.

689. — — — —. "O'Neill's interest in religion." NY *Journal,*
12 Jan.
A review of the aspects of O'Neill's interest in religious themes
from *FOUNTAIN* and *MARCO* through *DYNAMO* and *DAYS
WITHOUT END.*

690. Atkinson, Brooks. "On Days Without End." NY
Times, 14 Jan. IX, 1:1.
This criticism is clear in its analysis of O'Neill's failure to
reach exhilaration and spiritual exaltation needed for the theme.
Language, expression and story all fail to gain the heights.

691. Bolton, Whitney. "Mr. O'Neill has not taken holy
orders, but new play misses fire." NY *Telegraph,* 10 Jan.
Befuddled concept of religion and sophomore philosophy.
Diffuse, immature, completely lacking in O'Neill's usual authority.

692. Bowen, Stirling. "The O'Neill drama." *Wall St. Jour.,*
11 Jan.
O'Neill has not changed, as *AH, WILDERNESS!* suggested,

but in plays of this type he keeps alive the idea that drama can be art in the classic sense, infused with imagination.

693. Brown, John Mason. "Mr. O'Neill and his champions." NY *Post,* 22 Jan.
This article prints quotations from some of the more violent attacks by the clergy on the lay critics. Brown tries to show that professional criticism was not against the theme but against O'Neill's presentation.

694. — — — —. "O'Neill's interest in the agents controlling the fate of his characters in Days With End." NY *Post,* 15 Jan.
Brown reviews many plays in which God or Fate becomes a vitally interested, directly interfering personification in O'Neill's plays. *DAYS WITHOUT END* fails miserably to achieve any solution, and it is something that has bothered O'Neill since the days of *THIRST.*

695. Burr, Eugene. "Days Without End." *Billboard,* 46 (20 Jan.) 17.
The truly religious should be offended. The play has no real relation to fundamental realities. Blind, groveling faith; a bad play.

696. Caldwell, Cy. "Days Without End." *New Outlook,* 163 (Feb.) 48-49.
Morbid inspection of the human soul. The weird and lugubrious "Siamese twins" are not real stuff. "Spiritual indigestion."

697. Corbin, John. "Psyches without end." *Sat. R. Lit.,* 10 (20 Jan.) 419.
Much of theatrical value here.

698. "The critics and Days Without End." *Commonweal,* 19 (26 Jan.) 357-358.
Because critics are unable to recognize faith as a worthwhile subject they will not see this as a good play, although it is probably one of O'Neill's most important works.

699. "Critics out of their element." *Cath. Wld.,* 138 (Feb.) 513-517.

Lay critics are not qualified to criticize a play of this type without understanding the religious experience it portrays. This article is not, however, typical of the hysterical attack made by many of the clergy as shown in Brown's article (No. 693).

700. "Days Without End." *Lit. D.*, 117 (10 Feb.) 17.
Summary of professional and clerical criticism.

701. "Days Without End." *Newsweek*, 3 (20 Jan.) 34.
The play suggests a high school debate.

702. "Days Without End." *Th. Arts*, 18 (May) 390.
Confused, pedestrian, no better as a book than as a play.

703. Donnelly, Rev. Gerard B., S.J. "O'Neill's new Catholic play." *America*, 50 (13 Jan.) 346.
Magnificently Catholic play in characters, story and mood. Priest is "noblest priest in the history of the modern theatre." Defies Broadway tradition; O'Neill at last heading toward the light.

704. Eastman, Fred. "O'Neill discovers the cross." *Christ. Cent.*, 51 (7 Feb.) 191-192.
"O'Neill's greatness has begun. May they be Days Without End."

705. Eaton, Walter Prichard. "Days Without End." NY *Her-Trib.*, 11 Feb.
This play dispels fears that O'Neill was becoming "normal." It is one of his weaker works.

706. Fergusson, Francis. "Mr. O'Neill's new play." *Am. Rev.*, 2 (Feb.) 491-495.
There is no more Christianity in this than in *DYNAMO* or *CHILLUN*. It is like all the others and has all the same faults. "It is not about a conversion; it is Mr. O'Neill's debate with himself about a man like Mr. O'Neill who is writing a novel about *another* man like Mr. O'Neill, who is toying with the Idea of the conversion of Mr. O'Neill."

707. Gabriel, Gilbert. "As to Mr. O'Neill's latest Guild drama." NY *American*, 21 Jan.
Churchly in theme and well meant, but it is pretentious, wordy, and childishly indignant, like nursery blocks clumsily raised.

708. Garland, Robert. "Jesuit editor hails O'Neill miracle play." NY *Wor-Tel.*, 12 Jan.
Extended quotations from Donnelly's article (No. 703).

709. — — — —. "O'Neill miracle play of shopworn fabric." NY *Wor-Tel.*, 10 Jan.
A stingingly sarcastic review; doubts the play's sincerity, finds it a shoddy specimen, and "holy hokum."

710. Hammond, Percy. "Mr. O'Neill's experiment with masks and faces." NY *Her-Trib.*, 14 Jan.
Mainly a protest against the unnecessary alter-ego.

711. Isaacs, Edith J. R. "Parents and other people — Broadway in review." *Th. Arts*, 18 (Mar.) 167.
Must not confuse bad play with religion. It is dull, pedestrian, unconvincing in every aspect.

712. Krutch, Joseph Wood. "The sickness of today." *Nation*, 138 (24 Jan.) 110-111.
After an unpromising first act, the play shows good theatre, but it is one of O'Neill's least successful plays. Does not solve today's sickness, but merely shows how "primitive religious instinct" survives.

713. Lockridge, Richard. "Quest Without End." NY *Sun*, 20 Jan.
A review of the play's religious aspects. The play challenges as it was meant to, but it is unsafe to assume O'Neill is now converted.

714. Mantle, Burns. "An illuminating winter for the first dramatist." NY *News*, 21 Jan.
A serious and intelligent play.

715. March, Michael. "A book critic disagrees with the drama critics." Brook. *Citizen*, 17 Jan.

Strong rebuttal to comments by the critics, whom March accuses of bigotry and prejudice. The play is of great importance, showing O'Neill's sincerity in his theme.

716. "The mask and the face." NY *Times*, 7 Jan., X, 2:5.

Mainly quotes from O'Neill "Memo on Masks." (See Non-Dramatic O'Neill 1932.)

717. Motherwell, Hiram. "Days Without End." *Stage*, 11 (Feb.) 16-18.

Not about religion, but about one man's experience in his own problem of personal salvation. Illustrated with four excellent pictures.

718. Nathan, George Jean. "L'amour et — mondieu." *Van. F.*, 42 (Mar.) 42.

One of poorest and dullest things O'Neill has written.

719. − − − −. "Whither?" *Van. F.*, 42 (June) 49-50.

This O'Neill failure was notable among several others during the season.

720. Skinner, Richard Dana. "Eugene O'Neill's next play." *Commonweal*, 19 (5 Jan.) 273.

It may be his most important play.

721. − − − −. "Can religious plays succeed?" *Commonweal*, 19 (23 Feb.) 469.

Skinner realizes other professional critics did not think the play truly dramatic, and he shows why he thinks it is. This is one of the most rational criticisms which appeared in a religious journal.

722. − − − −. "Days Without End." *Commonweal*, 19 (19 Jan.) 327-329.

Culmination of every play O'Neill has written, fitting the sequence of his work. John Loving's struggle will live among the great poetic and religious creations of world literature.

723. Wyatt, Euphemia Van R. "A modern miracle play."
Cath. Wld., 138 (Feb.) 601-602.

Clumsy, and not his masterpiece, but "it is the cry of a man"
with O'Neill baring his poet's soul to God.

724. Young, Stark. "Days Without End." *New Rep.*, 77
(24 Jan.) 312.

Dramatic skeleton good; writing bad, though it does have
theatrical and spiritual creation.

1935-1956

725. Cajetan, Brother. "The pendulum starts back." *Cath.
Wld.*, 140 (Mar. 1935) 650-656.

This play is one of the most outstanding examples of the swing
back to Christian tradition in literature.

726. Eastman, Fred. "O'Neill's drama of Christian hope."
Christ. Cent., 73 (15 Aug. 1956) 950-951.

Eastman asks us to take note of the one play of hope which
O'Neill wrote as we come to a reappraisal of his life in view
of *LONG DAY'S JOURNEY*. (See Eastman's original review,
No. 704.)

727. Geier, Woodrow. "O'Neill's Miracle play." *Religion
in Life*, 16 (Autumn 1947) 515-526.

In Christian terms Loving's redemption is very pleasing.

DESIRE UNDER THE ELMS

Opening run reviews — New York
Newspapers of 12 to 15 Nov. 1924

728. Broun, Heywood. "Desire Under the Elms." NY *World,* 12 Nov.
Despite some faults which he enumerates, Broun finds this towers high and could be O'Neill's best work.

729. Dale, Alan. "Desire Under the Elms." NY *American,* 14 Nov.
Strenuous vein of morbidity presumably presented seriously. So much could be funny — and isn't.

730. "Desire Under the Elms an outspoken drama." *Journal of Commerce,* 12 Nov.
This review does little more than sketch out the story.

731. Gabriel, Gilbert. "Desire Under the Elms." NY *Telegram,* 12 Nov.
Some vivid and great moments, such as bedroom scene, but play slumps into repugnance in last two scenes.

732. Habersham, Stanton. "Another O'Neill offering at the Greenwich Village." NY *Graphic,* 13 Nov.
"An unnecessary subject most impressively handled." Crude and vulgar dialogue.

733. Hammond, Percy. "Mr. O'Neill's Desire Under the Elms is the best of his pleasing tortures." NY *Her-Trib.,* 12 Nov.
Hammond always leaves an O'Neill play glad he is not one of the people involved.

734. Mantle, Burns. "O'Neill's new play is lustful and tragic." NY *News,* 14 Nov.

Should be seen by all who praise foreign drama and by all students of drama. Go prepared for lust, infanticide, sin.

735. Metcalfe, J. S. "The slums of New England." *Wall St. Jour.*, 15 Nov.

O'Neill makes use of new freedom to create interesting drama, and this is faithful reproduction of New England at its most degraded. He is showing the daring for which he is known, but he will be admired only when he stops working in this field.

736. "Mr. O'Neill runs aground on a bleak New England farm." NY *Post*, 12 Nov.

Sterile bit of realism, mistaking crudity for power.

737. Niblo, Fred, Jr. "New O'Neill play sinks to depths." NY *Telegraph*, 12 Nov.

"A gruesome, morbid" play, as real to life as a sewer. "Anyone who cares anything about the theatre cannot approve . . . or disapprove in silence."

738. "O'Neill wins new somber laurels in latest drama." W. W. *Daily*, 12 Nov.

The gloom is deepened by pathos and horror and tragic irony. Its realism is lit by sympathy and a grim authentic poetry throughout.

739. Osborn, E. W. "Desire Under the Elms." NY *World*, 14 Nov.

This play is very effective in its "relentless realism," making it better than the disliked *ANNA CHRISTIE* or *APE*.

740. "Shades of O'Neill." Brook. *Eagle*, 12 Nov.

Much of the material from the sea plays is now on a New England farm, which is not necessarily good. It is unentertaining; the more O'Neill's genius repeats itself, the more ingenious it appears. Nobody can paint yellow sin more gleaming white than O'Neill.

741. Woollcott, Alexander. "Through darkest New England." NY *Sun*, 12 Nov.

Criticizes the "fake" dialect and "ugly" climax.

742. Young, Stark. "Eugene O'Neill's latest play." NY *Times,* 12 Nov., 20:7.
O'Neill has written nothing with more qualities of realism, poetry and terror than this.

Other reviews and criticism
1924

743. Benchley, Robert. "Two ways." *Life,* 84 (11 Dec.) 18.
Up to a point O'Neill's finest, after which it becomes phony and ends in "a blaze of green fire."

744. "Desire Under the Elms." *Time,* 4 (24 Nov.) 12.
People will object because they won't believe life can be so brutal.

745. Edba. "Desire Under the Elms." *Variety,* 19 Nov.
Written in his best style; depth of story and characterization are typical O'Neill.

746. Howard, Sidney. Letter to the editor. NY *Times,* 14 Dec., VIII, 4:1.
A true tragedy, which can be compared only with *Macbeth* in practically every aspect.

747. Krutch, Joseph Wood. "The God of stumps." *Nation,* 119 (26 Nov.) 578. [Reprinted in Hewitt, Barnard, *Theatre, USA,* NY, McGraw-Hill, 1959, pp. 360-362 (No. 56).]
This criticism attempts to get to the basis of O'Neill's plays; there is something in his nature that makes him "brother to tempest." If this quality is recognized and then overlooked, there are great compensations in this play.

748. Nathan, George Jean. "The Kahn-Game." *Judge,* 87 (6 Dec.) 17.
May not be better than others he has done, but better than most being done nowadays.

749. "Plays and players." *Town and Country*, 81 (1 Dec.) 58.

A concentration of realism, rather than realism itself; elemental life and passion is presented in the spirit of blank verse.

750. RML. "Desire Under the Elms." *New Rep.*, 41 (3 Dec.) 44.

Exterior is stark and tragic, but interior, like the setting, is huddled and confused.

751. Skinner, Richard Dana. "Decay 'under the elms.'" *Commonweal*, 1 (17 Dec.) 163.

Once the theme is accepted the play is worked out with often masterful intensity. The theme of decay, however, demands challenge.

752. Young, Stark. "Acting in Eugene O'Neill." NY *Times*, 7 Dec., VIII, 5:1.

On the surface it may seem realistic, but it is actually on the edge of poetry and a tremendous task for the actor.

1925

753. Bromfield, Louis. "The New Yorker." *Bookman*, 60 (Jan.) 621.

This simple and terrible story on fine level of Greek tragedy is best analysis of witch-burning Puritans yet done; better than *Scarlet Letter*.

754. "The censored audience." *Nation*, 120 (1 Apr.) 346.

Attacks those who come to this to see a "dirty" play, or who go to one approved by the "play jury" because it must be "clean."

755. Crawford, J. R. "Desire Under the Elms." NY *World*, 26 Apr.

Book review. "His creative passion almost sufficient to bridge those gaps of somewhat pedestrian writing."

756. Eaton, Walter Prichard. "Desire Under the Elms." NY *Her-Trib.*, 24 May.

Book review. Crude and elemental tale elevated toward poetry. Fails as great work of art because of too much emotion and theatricality.

757. Garland, Robert. "Eugene O'Neill and this big business of Broadway." *Th. Arts,* 9 (Jan.) 3-16.
At his most "O'Neillian" and in ways one of his finest plays, going his own way completely apart from the big business of Broadway.

758. Hornblow, Arthur. "Mr. Hornblow goes to the play." *Theatre,* 41 (Jan.) 22.
Powerful enough by an ordinary writer, but must be judged differently because O'Neill demands different standards. Fails mainly because he gives in to the designer's art.

759. Krutch, Joseph Wood. "Drama — Summary I." *Nation,* 120 (10 June) 672-673.
Thanks to the producers, apart from the "commercial managers," we have such masterpieces as this.

760. — — — —, "Drama — Summary II." *Nation,* 120 (24 June) 724.
Most "fundamentally important" of the season's major plays.

761. — — — —. "Establishing a new tradition." *Nation,* 120 (7 Jan.) 22-23.
This play shows that writers no longer must have thesis plays but can proceed with the assumption that these subjects are already understood by audience.

762. Nathan, George Jean. "By the dawn's early light." *Arts & Dec.,* 22 (Jan.) 76.
The play lifts above all contemporary playwriting, but still lags after first half.

763. — — — —. "The theatre." *Am. Merc.,* 4 (Jan.) 119.
Reads better than it acts. O'Neill does not define difference between real intensification and overexaggeration.

764. Seldes, Gilbert. "The theatre." *Dial*, 78 (Jan.) 82.
Outstanding fault is failure to make us believe in murder of baby.

765. Skinner, Richard Dana. "Decay and flowing sap." *Ind. & Weekly R.*, 114 (10 Jan.) 51.
O'Neill will not be great until he is able to let light of finer things come into his soul; not a tragedy because nobody is on a height to fall, and everybody is on one level and rots there.

766. Whipple, Leon. "Two plays by Eugene O'Neill." *Survey*, 53 (1 Jan.) 421-422.
Fails in its attempt to cross the abyss between realism and romanticism with bridge of symbolism.

767. Woollcott, Alexander. "Desire Under the Ellums." *Van. F.*, 23 (Jan.) 27.
"A mad play, my masters," but still the kind that will be read long after other contemporary work has been forgotten.

768. Wyatt, Euphemia Van R. "Eugene O'Neill on Plymouth rock." *Cath. Wld.*, 120 (Jan.) 519-521.
An unclean play and unhealthy scenes, with no healthy idea behind it.

1926-1928

769. "Desire Under the Elms." *Dial*, 80 (Jan. 1926) 70.
O'Neill is a much better dramatist than a literary man. Plays should carry their own emotion instead of having it written into them.

770. Van Druten, John. "The sex play." *Th. Arts*, 11 (Jan. 1927) 23-27.
Plea for treatment of sex as Elizabethans regarded it — incidental and universal. This play is a sex play in the theme of physical desire, which is unobjectionable enough.

771. Watts, Richard. "Regarding Mr. O'Neill as a writer for the cinema." NY *Her-Trib.*, 4 Mar. 1928.

Presents a synopsis of O'Neill's own film scenarios for *DESIRE* and *APE*, neither of which were produced. They are much altered from the stage versions.

Opening night reviews — ANTA Revival
New York — Newspapers of 17 Jan. 1952

772. Atkinson, Brooks. "At the theatre." NY *Times*, 23:4.
It may turn out to be the greatest play written by an American; the design of a masterpiece.

773. Chapman, John. "Desire Under the Elms remains powerful, if just a leetle quaint." NY *News*.
A first class revival, but it seems a shade fancy and self-conscious.

774. Coleman, Robert. "ANTA puts on O'Neill's Desire Under the Elms." NY *Mirror*.
Makes a lot about people not worth it; a literary *Tobacco Road*.

775. Hawkins, William. "Desire Under the Elms revived." NY *Wor-Tel. & Sun*.
Praise for this stark, hard play of elemental, overblown passions.

776. Kerr, Walter. "Desire Under the Elms." NY *Her-Trib*.
Well worth seeing.

777. McClain, John. "A powerful drama, highly recommended." NY *Jour-Am*.
Still a good play, powerful drama.

778. Sheaffer, Louis. "O'Neill's Desire soundly revived." Brook. *Eagle*.
A play of uncommon stature, with no show of age.

779. Watts, Richard, Jr. "The tragic power of Eugene O'Neill." NY *Post*.
Play of overwhelming elemental power and almost em-

barassing intensity, still one of the distinguished works of modern stage.

Other reviews and criticism
1952

780. Beyer, William H. "The state of the theatre: Classics revisited." *School & Society,* 75 (16 Feb.) 106-107.
Incredible that this powerful play has not been produced more.

781. Bolton, Whitney. "Desire Under the Elms comes alive again as ANTA project." NY *Telegraph,* 18 Jan.
The original attitude that this was a play of strong and eloquent statement of man's fate still remains today.

782. Brown, John Mason. "Dat ole davil and a hard god." *Sat. R. Lit.,* 35 (16 Feb.) 32-34.
Still retains its strength and intensity; achieves tragic grandeur.

783. Cooke, Richard P. "Another O'Neill." *Wall St. Jour.,* 18 Jan.
It seems a bit heavy-handed, with a lack of conviction. Elemental passions often come close to parody, and O'Neill's "potent magic" does not come across.

784. "Desire Under the Elms." *Newsweek,* 39 (28 Jan.) 83.
Recognizable symbols of classic tragedy are here.

785. "Desire Under the Elms." *Time,* 59 (28 Jan.) 44.
A play neither realistic nor tragic, but clumsily in between.

786. "Desire Under the Elms." *Variety,* 23 Jan.
A classic in its own right which years have failed to dim.

787. Gibbs, Wolcott. "Desire Under the Elms" *New Yorker,* 27 (26 Jan.) 53.
At times coming close to parody, it is still one of America's few classics.

788. Kerr, Walter. "Desire Under the Elms." *Commonweal*, 55 (1 Feb.) 423.
A play that should be revived; characters so human it is difficult to present them.

789. — — — —. "New generation gets two looks at O'Neill." NY *Her-Trib.*, 26 Jan.
A revaluation of the revival (including *ANNA CHRISTIE*) finds the characters in *DESIRE* are "mere figures," behaving in unnatural rhythms against a cosmic background.

790. Nathan, George Jean. "Desire Under the Elms." *Th. Arts*, 36 (Mar.) 70-71.
Comes off pretty well, all considered.

791. "O'Neill shines again." *Life*, 32 (4 Feb.) 82-84.
Pictures from revival, text is generally approving.

792. Watts, Richard. "Those two plays by Eugene O'Neill." NY *Post*, 27 Jan.
Praise for the revival. Possibly O'Neill's mightiest play.

793. Wyatt, Euphemia Van R. "Desire Under the Elms." *Cath. Wld.*, 174 (Mar.) 464.
Stylized form of this production better than original.

1958-1959

794. Conlin, Matthew T. "The tragic effect in Autumn Fire and Desire Under the Elms." *Mod. Drama*, 1 (Feb. 1959) 228-235.
Compares *DESIRE* with the successful *Autumn Fire* by T. C. Murray, both plays of 1924 concerning May-December marriages destroyed by father-son conflicts. *DESIRE* is less a tragedy because of its failure to evoke pity for the protagonist in the play's "painful nihilism."

795. Gelb, Arthur. "At the roots of O'Neill's Elms." NY *Times*, 2 Mar. 1958, II, 5:3.

In light of the coming motion picture version, Gelb shows how much of the original play came out of O'Neill's own background, including the "autobiographical" sketch of Cabot — taken in many points from his own life and that of his father, James O'Neill.

DIFF'RENT

Opening run reviews — New York
Newspapers of 28-31 Dec. 1920

796. "A new O'Neill play." NY *Globe*, 31 Dec.
The conclusion is hard to stomach because it is brutal and bitterly nauseating but "true enough, God pity us." It is hoped O'Neill goes more toward the vein of *JONES* than continuing this way.

797. "New O'Neill play produced." NY *Tribune*, 28 Dec.
A brief notice of the opening, without comment.

798. "O'Neill's latest play presented by the Provincetown players." NY *Sun*, 31 Dec.
It is not a pleasant play, but written with the strength and subtlety that stamp O'Neill as a leading playwright. Well worth seeing; front rank O'Neill.

799. "Provincetown players offer second bill." NY *Commercial*, 31 Dec.
A reaction must have set in after success of *JONES* for this play and its companion piece represent a poor bill.

800. Towse, J. Ranken. "The play." NY *Post*, 29 Dec.
Relentless, ironic, sometimes gripping tragedy; intense drama.

801. "Two plays on programme." NY *World*, 28 Dec.
The play was warmly received. O'Neill is a fine drawing card
for the Provincetown organization.

802. Woollcott, Alexander. "A new O'Neill play." NY
Times, 29 Dec., 8:1.
Despite O'Neill's seeming lack of interest at the end, this
will cause attention because of the great power of dramatic
dialogue.

Other reviews and criticism
1921

803. Broun, Heywood. "Diff'rent comes to Broadway at
the Selwyn." NY *World*, 1 Feb.
O'Neill obviously does not know about what he is writing.
O'Neill, a new Puritan of the theatre, finding man basically evil.

804. — — — —. "Grey gods and green goddesses." *Van. F.*,
16 (Apr.) 33.
Broun complains against these "real" plays which are not art.
True artist cannot be neutral and cannot be the scientist that
O'Neill tries to be in this play of sex starvation.

805. Castellun, Maida. "'Diff'rent' . . . is true but not
good drama." NY *Call*, 14 Jan.
Interesting sex psychology study; hero dies of "O'Neillitis"
which is instinct for violent death rather than one from character
or situation.

806. "Diff'rent." *Dial*, 70 (June) 715.
Brief book review.

807. "Diff'rent." NY *Independent*, 105 (12 Feb.) 153.
A problem play "well written but amateurishly played."

808. "Diff'rent." *Th. Arts*, 5 (Oct.) 334-335.
Book review. "A backward step."

809. "Diff'rent." *Variety*, 4 Feb.

Should never have been written; until O'Neill gets restraint he should not be permitted to write again. Theatre should not be used as a chamber of horrors.

810. Firkins, O. W. "Drama." *Weekly Rev.*, 4 (2 Mar.) 207-208.

Feeling of strangulation; curious rather than serious.

811. ————. "Plays for the reader." *Weekly Rev.*, 4 (25 June) 406-407.

O'Neill is still not the master of the long play.

812. "Fresh horrors in Diff'rent brought from the Village." NY *Herald*, 1 Feb.

A clinical case; the move uptown is not successful.

813. "Greenwich Village cannot keep away from Broadway." NY *Review*, 5 Feb.

"Incisive study in the seamy side of human nature."

814. Hornblow, Arthur. "Mr. Hornblow goes to the play." *Theatre*, 33 (Apr.) 261.

Curious, if interesting.

815. James, Patterson. "Diff'rent." *Billboard*, 22 Jan.

Savage, true, brutal, told without faltering.

816. Kaufman, S. Jay. "Round the town." NY *Globe*, 17 Jan.

Greater than *JONES*; hope expressed it will move uptown.

817. Krutch, Joseph Wood. "Diff'rent." *Bookman*, 52 (Feb.) 565.

Brief book review along with *JONES*.

818. Macgowan, Kenneth. "The centre of the stage." *Th. Arts*, 5 (Apr.) 102.

"Utterly of the theatre in the best sense" but questions if O'Neill is at his best here.

819. "Provincetowners put on Diff'rent, a really great play." NY *Clipper*, 68 (5 Jan.) 19.
Best he has done to date; vitality far superior to *JONES*.

820. Sayler, Oliver M. "Eugene O'Neill master of naturalism." *Drama*, 11 (Mar.) 189-190.
High, almost blind praise for a great naturalistic play, one of O'Neill's best and perhaps best of any American writer.

821. VSGL. "Diff'rent." *New Rep.*, 26 (25 May) 386.
Unfavorable review, together with *JONES* and *STRAW*.

Opening night reviews — Provincetown Revival
New York — Newspapers of 11 Feb. 1925

822. "Diff'rent." NY *World*.
It rings in a strange key "that will sound in your sleep."

823. "Diff'rent's revival at Provincetown players." NY *Telegram & Mail*.
Emma Crosby is probably the most enraging feminine creature a playwright ever conceived. O'Neill was not in a happy mood.

824. "Diff'rent revived." Brook. *Eagle*.
Passing notice that "Mary Blair is the starved old maid."

825. "Double bill excellently presented at the Provincetown." NY *Post*.
The acting is praised; the production is by-passed.

826. "O'Neill's Diff'rent revived." NY *Times*, 19:2.
Not in the best O'Neill tradition.

827. "Triumph of the Egg played at Provincetown." NY *Her-Trib*.
Mary Blair effectively plays the lead in this specimen of O'Neill grimness.

Other reviews and criticism
1925

828. Brown, John Mason. "Halfway theatre." *Th. Arts,* 9 (May) 291.
Brief mention of revival in a "discouraging" season.

829. "Diff'rent." *Drama Calendar,* 23 Feb.
This clinical analysis of abnormal people does not rise to the element of poetry as does some O'Neill.

830. "Diff'rent." *Time,* 5 (23 Feb.) 13.
One of the most unpleasant plays in our literature.

831. Littell, Robert. "Three shades of black." *New Rep.,* 42 (4 Mar.) 45.
The marionettes on strings never become individualized characters.

832. Skinner, Richard Dana. "O'Neill and Anderson." *Commonweal,* 1 (4 Mar.) 466.
O'Neill a prisoner of his own feelings, and the gloom and decay deprive the tragedy of any power.

833. Young, Stark. "Mary Blair in Diff'rent." NY *Times,* 1 Mar., VII, 1:2.
A "moving and unforgettable" performance.

Opening night reviews — Federal Theatre
Revival — New York — Newspapers of 26 Jan. 1938

834. Brown, Herrick. "Diff'rent." NY *Sun.*
Worth doing. Full of closely knit action and well-drawn characters.

835. "Early O'Neill." NY *Times,* 26:4.

Worth study and revival, but O'Neill of 1921 is not the O'Neill of 1938.

836. "Eugene O'Neill's Diff'rent at Maxine Elliott theatre."
NY *Wor-Tel*.
Theme seems old fashioned; does not ring true to contemporary dramatic reasoning.

837. Francis, Robert. "O'Neill revival." Brook. *Eagle*.
Performance brings significance and power to this early work.

838. Waldorf, Wilella. "Federal theatre troupe in O'Neill's Diff'rent." NY *Post*.
Welcome relief from the more pretentious O'Neill of recent years.

DYNAMO

Opening night reviews — New York
Newspapers of 12 Feb. 1929

839. Allen, Kelcey. "Whir of Dynamo electrifies audience of O'Neill admirers." *W. W. Daily*.
A veritable anthology of O'Neill drama; everything so typical of him. Stirring and provocative, and actually reverent and pious; the most dynamic of O'Neill's plays.

840. Anderson, John. "Dynamo has premiere." NY *Journal*.
Digs around roots of the big question about what is God with nothing more than a toothpick. No passionate sincerity and blazing vision. Too hysterical and sensational — no more important religious matter than that of Hottentot.

841. Atkinson, Brooks. "God in the machine." NY *Times*, 22:1.

The play is a center of controversy, but with much strength and breadth. "At last he seems to have gotten his drama in harmony with the universal theme he is freely developing."

842.   Bolton, Whitney. "O'Neill's machine-god." NY *Telegraph.*
Incoherent disappointment. Nobody else could match thoughtful and sympathetic first act — best part of the play. One cannot completely condemn on first visit because many overtones come out in later visits.

843. Gabriel, Gilbert. "Eugene O'Neill salutes our god of the machine with new play, Dynamo." NY *American.*
A disappointment; the scheme only intermittently comes alive. Settings more eloquent than the play.

844. Garland, Robert. "Eugene O'Neill's Dynamo displayed in 45th Street." NY *Telegram.*
O'Neill "shook his fist at God and blew kisses in the general direction of electricity. Each of the gestures seemed a wee bit childish." Self consciously profound, phoney.

845. Hammond, Percy. "The Theatre Guild in Eugene O'Neill's slow and startling Dynamo." NY *Her-Trib.*
This amusingly bitter criticism finds little to recommend. Asides are crutches, play at times ludicrous, "frequently raving."

846. Littell, Robert. "The Theatre Guild presents Dynamo." NY *Post.*
Second-rate O'Neill. Goes into "often foolish neomysticism" with a "silly and dull" last act.

847. Lockridge, Richard. "Mr. O'Neill's Dynamo." NY *Sun.*
Sophomoric, O'Neill fumbling whatever intentions he had.

848. Mantle, Burns. "Dynamo throbs with mystery." NY *News.*
An indeterminant drama meeting with mixed reception.

849. Osborn, E. W. "Dynamo." NY *Eve. World.*

Applause sounded symbolically like a question mark. Not a satisfactory play — began better than it ended.

850. Pollock, Arthur. "Dynamo." Brook. *Eagle.*
A play of hardly any importance, sleazy and quick compared to *STRANGE INTERLUDE.*

851. Winchell, Walter. "In the Einstein manner." NY *Graphic.*
Incoherent, listless, a bore, will not survive.

Other reviews and criticism
1929

852. Anderson, John. "About Great God Conc, his new play and Mr. Broun." NY *Journal,* 16 Feb.
This is "unconscionable bunk" from one who takes himself so seriously he doesn't recognize how bad he is.

853. Atkinson, Brooks. "Concluding a dramatic cycle." NY *Times,* 17 Feb., IX, 1:1.
In this play O'Neill has completed the cycle started by Ibsen; *i.e.,* the return to plays of a general instead of a specific nature.

854. Bellamy, Francis R. "The theatre." *Outlook,* 151 (27 Feb.) 331.
Departs too far from reality, but O'Neill at his worst remains "more provocative and interesting than most others at their best."

855. Benchley, Robert. "Dynamo." *Life,* 93 (8 Mar.) 24.
"Nobody who could write this play is above being kidded." Now convinced that *BROWN* and *INTERLUDE* were as bad as they seemed.

856. Bolton, Whitney. "By easy stages." NY *Telegraph,* 17 Feb.
A general review of the first O'Neill decade, including some of Heywood Broun's comments on O'Neill and on *DYNAMO.*

857 Boyd, Ernest. "Eugene O'Neill and others." *Bookman*, 69 (Apr.) 179-180.
O'Neill's capacity is projecting simple, elemental emotions, but in treating ideas he is dramatically lost.

858. Brackett, Charles. "Essays in the sublime and the ridiculous." *New Yorker*, 6 (23 Feb.) 27.
Pretentious rant.

859. Broun, Heywood. "It seems to me." NY *Telegram*, 14 Feb.
This review sharply attacks the poor criticism which enables O'Neill to become more than he actually is. This play is not tragedy.

860. Carb, David. "Dynamo." *Vogue*, 73 (30 Mar.) 61.
Intemperate outpouring of adolescence; boring, flatulent, maudlin.

861. Clark, Barrett H. "O'Neill's Dynamo and the Village experiments." *Drama*, 19 (Apr.) 201.
A refusal to write off O'Neill as "lost," despite his unimpressive result as thinker and prophet.

862. Colum, Padriac. "Dynamo." *Dial*, 86 (Apr.) 349-350.
Whatever possessed O'Neill to write it? Insists on thinking in the philosophy of the day-before-yesterday.

863. De Casseres, Benjamin. "Broadway to date." *Arts & Dec.*, 30 (Apr.) 72
If he had continued the play in the souls of his characters instead of the electric plant, would have been a different story to tell.

864. "Dynamo." *Variety*, 13 Feb.
Not the best he has written, but the inspiration of a poet. Terrific, moving and agitating, will probably be a resounding success.

865. Ervine, St. John. "The Greenwich Village atheist prepares to meet his God." NY *World*, 13 Feb.

O'Neill is killing the poet in himself determining to be intellectual. A plea to cease before it is too late.

866. — — — —. "Mr. O'Neill takes a toss." NY *World*, 24 Feb.
Undeniably juvenile. O'Neill is a dramatic poet "who perversely imagines himself a philosopher." This long column by a critic not given to O'Neill praise, discusses O'Neill's difficulties, and asks not to condemn him in this piece alone, in view of his tremendous efforts otherwise.

867. Gabriel, Gilbert. "Opening Nights." NY *American*, 17 Feb.
Reviewing the play at a later date Gabriel admits that it is a bad attempt on a mighty subject, although other critics have missed the point of its drama of frustration.

868. Garland, Robert. "Eugene O'Neill's Dynamo and what the critics say." NY *Telegram*, 14 Feb.
Summary of statements from major critics.

869. Gould, Bruce. "O'Neill faw down, go boom!" *Wall St. News*, 14 Feb.
O'Neill has been living beyond his intellectual means and this finds him bankrupt. He has redramatized a drama dramatized a hundred times all ready.

870. Hammond, Percy. "Mr. O'Neill, an unfair iconoclast." NY *Her-Trib.*, 17 Feb.
Unfair to electricity and public utilities — such things don't happen in power houses. An amusing but telling attack against the artificial uses to which O'Neill puts his power house and his people.

871. Hansen, Harry. "Dynamo." NY *World*, 19 Oct.
Review of book.

872. Hornblow, Arthur. "The editor goes to the play." *Theatre*, 49 (May) 45.
Shocks O'Neill followers by intellectual ineptitude.

873. Jordan, Elizabeth. "Plays of early spring." *America,* 30 Mar.
"Annoyingly childish," often ridiculous, most of it too unpleasant to discuss.

874. Krutch, Joseph Wood. "Epitaph I." *Nation,* 128 (29 May) 655-656.
Krutch admits that as a critic he was one of few who found this play interesting.

875. — — — —. "The virgin and the dynamo." *Nation,* 128 (27 Feb.) 264.
An attempt to explain O'Neill's point, as a man on an individual quest for the meaning of existence.

876. Littell, Robert. "The land of the second best." *Th. Arts,* 13 (Apr.) 245-247.
When O'Neill makes mistakes he makes big ones. Full of crudity, unconscious caricature, muddy oratory.

877. — — — —. "Two on the aisle." NY *Post,* 16 Feb.
In discussing O'Neill the Thinker and O'Neill the Artist, Littell finds a real issue in who is to rescue the artist from the thinker. O'Neill does not think through his profound thoughts. Passages from Adams' *Education* on "The Dynamo and the Virgin" are quoted to show O'Neill is not a thinker.

878. Macgowan, Kenneth. "Eugene O'Neill's new play." *Van. F.,* 31 (Feb.) 62.
If used often enough the asides may become standard in our theatrical conventions.

879. — — — —. "O'Neill's new play Dynamo to be presented by the Theatre Guild." NY *Post,* 9 Feb.
In this preview, Macgowan warns that the play, though about religion, is not comforting, and would be banned in fundamentalist religious areas.

880. "Machines and motives." *Psychology Mag.,* Apr.

Obscurity need not enter — may be avoided by realizing O'Neill deals in symbols.

881. Mantle, Burns. "The Messrs. O'Neill and Ibsen. Dynamo both irritates and mystifies." NY *News*, 17 Feb.
A plea not to judge the whole trilogy on basis of this play. No interested person can afford to miss it, especially those seeking what O'Neill actually is.

882. "Mr. O'Neill and the audible theatre." NY *Times*, 3 Mar., VIII, 4:6.
An explanation of O'Neill's viewpoints toward the use of the definite rhythm of sound as an important part of theatrical art.

883. Moses, Montrose J. "Eugene O'Neill searches for God." *Rev. of Rev.*, 79 (Apr.) 158.
Nothing particularly new being said, but it is done "dynamically and with mad frenzy."

884. Nathan, George Jean. "Judging the shows." *Judge*, 96 (9 Mar.) 18.
Crude, childish, trivial; a dud.

885. — — — —. "A non-conductor." *Am. Merc.*, 16 (Mar.) 368-373.
Reprints complete stage directions from Act I, with some condensed dialogue, to show how ridiculous the play becomes. In science and philosophy O'Neill is lost.

886. "The new Dynamo as seen by O'Neill." NY *World*, 27 Jan.
Excerpts from some of O'Neill's letters to the Guild concerning his ideas, such as the emphasis upon sound and the insistence that the cast visit an actual power station.

887. "O'Neill wrestles with God." *Lit. D.*, 100 (2 Mar.) 21-22.
Evidence from most reviews that O'Neill was "thrown in the first round."

888. Pollock, Arthur. "Mr. O'Neill gets excited again in Dynamo." Brook. *Eagle,* 17 Feb.

Under the impression he is to be taken seriously, O'Neill takes himself seriously. Mistakes excitement for thought.

889. Riley, Wilfred J. "Dynamo." *Billboard,* 41 (23 Feb.) 47.

Must await the rest of the proposed trilogy before a decision is made.

890. Ruhl, Arthur. "Second nights." NY *Her-Trib.,* 17 Feb.

A detailed review of the many symbols and the general approach O'Neill uses — aimed at showing how preposterous and outlandish the whole play is.

891. Shipley, Joseph T. "Dyna-Might." *New Leader,* 15 Feb.

Distinct advance technically beyond *INTERLUDE.* The expressed thoughts are effective; a bold replacement of speech.

892. — — — —. "Dynamolatry." *New Leader,* 1 Mar.

O'Neill can reach power, but perhaps his misdirection of aim keeps this from being poetry; he has gone astray.

893. Skinner, Richard Dana. "Eugene O'Neill's Dynamo." *Commonweal,* 9 (27 Feb.) 389-390.

Not about world sickness, but about O'Neill's own.

894. Watts, Richard. "Literary ancestor of Dynamo." NY *Her-Trib.,* 24 Feb.

Interesting review of other literary uses of the machine as in *Frankenstein, RUR, Processional,* and others.

895. Wellman, Rita. "In and out of town." *Town & Country,* 83 (15 Mar.) 58.

An arrogant experiment that does not come across.

896. Wyatt, Euphemia Van R. "Plays of some importance." *Cath. Wld.,* 129 (Apr.) 80-82.

O'Neill is the loser in his clenching with a tremendous theme.

897. Young, Stark. "Dynamo." *New Rep.*, 58 (27 Feb) 43-44.
Significant as a "personal document" showing what can mean so much to O'Neill.

THE EMPEROR JONES

*Opening run reviews — New York
Newspapers of November 1920*

898. Broun, Heywood. "Emperor Jones gives chance for cheers." NY *Tribune*, 4 Nov.
Extreme praise for O'Neill's great value.

899. Castellun, Maida. "O'Neill's Emperor Jones thrills and fascinates." NY *Call*, 10 Nov.
Provincetown players give the most thrilling evening of their theatrical lives. Vivid imagination, relentless power; a rare feast for lovers of the true drama.

900. Macgowan, Kenneth. "Emperor Jones an extraordinary drama of imagination." NY *Globe*, 4 Nov.
High praise for this new drama designed for the new stagecraft.

901. Mantle, Burns. "Plays, players and playwrights." NY *Mail*, 6 Nov.
"A weird tragedy, this one." It does not cheer, because it leaves one cheerless, lacking O'Neill's promising distinction of text evident in other plays. Some traces of simple eloquence.

902. "Provincetown players stage remarkable play." Brook. *Eagle*, 9 Nov.
"Admirable piece of dramatic craftsmanship."

903. Rathbun, Stephen. "Provincetown players stage a brilliant bill." NY *Sun*, 6 Nov.

One of the noteworthy events of the season, both in depth and power.

904. Towse, J. Ranken. "The play." NY *Post*, 3 Nov.

O'Neill knows how to communicate the feelings of character to the audience. Typical of little theatre experiments, and O'Neill took the chance of being a trifle ridiculous in this one.

905. Woollcott, Alexander. "The new O'Neill play." NY *Times*, 7 Nov., VII, 1:3.

The "as yet unbridled" O'Neill has strength and originality so far unequaled in the American theatre.

During November and most of December 1920 *THE EMPEROR JONES* continued in the tiny Greenwich Village theatre of the Provincetown Players. By popular demand it was moved uptown into a larger theatre, the Selwyn, on 27 December, and thence to the Princess on 29 January 1921. Reviews continued to appear, and many critics who had missed it downtown wrote their opinions after seeing it in the Broadway house. Others, who had seen it earlier, reviewed it again. Later in 1921 various publications of the play, in the same volume with *DIFF'RENT* and *THE STRAW* and in separate editions, were also discussed in periodical columns. To simplify matters, all reviews and criticism after November 1920 and through 1921 are placed together.

Other reviews and criticism
1920-1921

906. "Amusement notes." *W. W. Daily*, 28 Dec. 1920.

The move uptown is an improvement because action flows more quickly without the long waits between scenes.

907. Castellun, Maida. "The Emperor Jones at the Selwyn repeats its success with Charles Gilpin." NY *Call*, 30 Dec. 1920.

Still unusual and thrilling.

908. Dale, Alan. "Emperor Jones artistically staged; appeals to fancy." NY *American,* 28 Dec. 1920.
Somewhat unique, somewhat impressive, somewhat artistic, could be improved with some comedy.

909. "The Emperor Jones." *Dial,* 70 (June 1921) 715.
Brief book review. *JONES* reads well, in spite of its essentially pictorial character.

910. "The Emperor Jones." *Independent,* 105 (8 Jan. 1921) 33.
A "sensation."

911. "The Emperor Jones." *Th. Arts,* 5 (Oct. 1921) 334-335.
Book review. *JONES* is "brilliant and forward looking."

912. "The Emperor Jones." *Variety,* 14 Jan. 1021.
Genuine tragedy, mixed with the "cynicism of youth."

913. "Emperor Jones at Selwyn." NY *Sun,* 28 Dec. 1920.
The transfer from Greenwich Village is an improvement.

914. "Emperor Jones uptown." NY *Herald,* 28 Dec. 1920.
Few pictures of terror are so engrossing as this.

915. Firkins, O. W. "Eugene O'Neill's remarkable play, The Emperor Jones." *Weekly Rev.,* 3 (8 Dec. 1920) 567-568.
Literary and theatrical, rather than dramatic; highly imaginative, possibly a profound piece of work.

916. — — — —. "Plays for the reader." *Weekly Rev.,* 4 (25 June 1921) 606.
Book review. O'Neill is not yet the master of the long play. A sense of theatre and honesty should be helpful in the future.

917. Gilliam, Florence. "The Emperor Jones." *Quill,* Nov. 1920, pp. 24-26.
The production could have been smoother.

World, 4 June 1921.
918. Harrison, Hubert H. "The Emperor Jones." *Negro*

It is aimless to criticize this play because it "does not elevate the Negro," since it could have been written about any race anywhere.

919. James, Patterson. "The Provincetown players." *Billboard*, 14 Dec. 1920.
"One of the pitiably few compensations of the season."

920. Lewisohn, Ludwig. "Native plays." *Nation*, 112 (2 Feb. 1921) 189.
Power and promise, though visions of the Negro seem to have been carefully selected rather than leaping from "creative necessity."

921. Macgowan, Kenneth. "The new season." *Th. Arts*, 5 (Jan. 1921) 5-7. [Reprinted in Gilder, Rosamond, ed., *Theatre Arts anthology*, NY, Theatre Arts Books, 1950, pp. 592-594 (No. 49); and in Hewitt, Barnard, *Theatre USA*, NY, McGraw-Hill, 1959, pp. 333-335 (No. 56).]
A new and untheatrical power, with rhythmed beauty; genius and imagination are evident.

922. "More room improves The Emperor Jones." NY *World*, 28 Dec. 1920.
Vigor and charm of Gilpin stood out stronger and the characters are more convincing with the move.

923. Moses, Montrose J. "O'Neill and the Emperor Jones." *Independent*, 105 (12 Feb. 1921) 158-159.
Mainly a discussion of the one-act play as a dramatic form and O'Neill's use of it, especially in this play.

924. "Not as others are, but still worth it." *Outlook*, 126 (22 Dec. 1920) 710-711.
Remarkable, despite severe shortcomings in drama and staging.

925. "Provincetown bill best thing they've done for long time." NY *Clipper*, 68 (24 Nov. 1920) 19.
Highly interesting, although O'Neill is not great. It is not certain whether he is better than Cohan or Walter.

926. Sayler, Oliver M. "Delving into the sub-conscious." *Freeman*, 24 Nov. 1920.
Success is limited because of O'Neill's plunge into the field of Negro psychoanalysis.

927. VSGL "The Emperor Jones." *New Rep.*, 26 (25 May 1921) 420.
Book review. It is better not to read *JONES* if you liked it on the stage.

928. Whyte, Gordon. "Provincetown players." *Billboard*, Nov. 1920 (exact date undetermined).
About the best of O'Neill so far.

Opening night reviews — Paul Robeson revival
New York — Newspapers of 7-9 May 1924

929. "The Emperor Jones." NY *World*, 7 May.
Robeson is almost as good as Gilpin.

930. "The Emperor Jones reappears at the Provincetown with a new emperor." NY *Post*, 7 May.
On the whole worthily presented. One comes away with a new respect for O'Neill's dexterity.

931. "The Emperor Jones revived." NY *Times*, 7 May, 18:1.
The play instead of the player seems to hold the audience.

932. "Paul Robeson wins fame in O'Neill play." NY *Telegram & Mail*, 7 May.
High praise for Robeson's interpretation.

933. Pollock, Arthur. "The Emperor Jones." Brook. *Eagle*, 8 May.
The revival is praised, as is Robeson's interpretation.

934. "Provincetown theatre — The Emperor Jones." NY *American*, 9 May.

Completely satisfying, but there is a "bridge of difference" between Robeson and Gilpin.

935. Vreeland, Frank. "Bayoo they cry as Robeson rages in The Emperor Jones." NY *Her-Trib.*, 7 May.
High praise for the performance.

936. Woollcott, Alexander. "The Emperor Jones revived." NY *Sun*, 8 May.
Recommended without reservation.

THE EMPEROR JONES was revived twice in 1926, once by the Provincetown Theatre, 15 February, and once by the Mayfair Theatre, 10 November. Both starred Gilpin. Newspaper reviews, when they appeared, still maintained their high praise, and were so repetitive as to be of little value here. Moss Hart, who played Smithers in the Mayfair production, describes his experiences in some detail in *Act One*. Periodicals outside of New York gave these other revivals only random mention. One other opinion, however, is worth noting, and is included below.

937. Shand, John. "The Emperor Jones." *New Statesman*, 25 (19 Sept. 1925) 628-629.
O'Neill is basically a one-act dramatist and should not attempt something beyond his scope. This will never be a famous play because a good idea is spoiled by the wrong treatment.

THE FIRST MAN

Opening night reviews — New York
Newspapers of 6 March 1922

938. Allen, Kelcey. "The First Man produced." *W. W. Daily*.
Well written, but far too morbid to succeed.

939. "Another O'Neill play on Grand Street." NY *Telegram.*
Distinct departure; keen satire, one of O'Neill's best.

940. "Convocation of woe in The First Man, O'Neill's
new play." NY *Tribune.*
A murky play; it is hard to recognize O'Neill. "The name of
Eugene O'Neill's star is Wormwood."

941. Dale, Alan. "The First Man, Eugene O'Neill's play
staged." NY *American.*
The theatre is out of place in such painful and morbid exhibits.

942. DeFoe, Louis V. "Another play by O'Neill." NY
World.
"Grimly humorous satire" on contemporary human traits; not
O'Neill's best.

943. "Eugene O'Neill's study in morbid paternity." NY
Globe.
A strain between O'Neill and theme; hardly an O'Neill play
at all.

944. "First Man presented at Neighborhood Playhouse."
NY *Sun.*
No glory here; should stick to the sea which is his best friend.

945. Mantle, Burns. "O'Neill's The First Man." NY *Mail.*
Repetitious, lacks convincing detail.

946. Marsh, Leo A. "New O'Neill play a morbid drama."
NY *Telegraph.*
Modern play with primitive theme; O'Neill still is able to
write well about human frailties.

947. Reamer, Lawrence. "First Man . . . is a gloomy
suburban story." NY *Herald.*
Should never have been produced; nothing new in the theme.

948. Torres, H. Z. "Latest O'Neill opus a drama of gestation." NY *Commercial.*

No dramatic or literary excuse for this revolting and abhorrent treatment of gestation.

949. Towse, J. Ranken. "Eugene O'Neill's latest play." NY *Post*.
Signs of ability and inventive mind; what good is here is obstructed by violence and exaggeration.

950. Woollcott, Alexander. "The new O'Neill play." NY *Times*, 9:2.
Reiterative, clumsy, rubbishy language.

Other reviews and criticism
1922

951. Andrews, Kenneth. "Broadway, our literary signpost." *Bookman*, 52 (May) 284.
"Revives one's shaken faith in the author" after the *HAIRY APE*. Powerful and well rounded.

952. Baury, Louis. "Mr. O'Neill's new plays." *Freeman*, 5 (3 May) 184-185.
O'Neill must learn responsibility of his art and stop wallowing in words.

953. Castellun, Maida. "Eugene O'Neill misses his mark." NY *Call*, 8 Mar.
Badly constructed, overwritten, far from a good play. This critic points up the interesting fact that this is the first time in a play that a man instead of a woman has shown he does not want children.

954. "The First Man." Brook. *Eagle*, 7 Mar.
O'Neill on unfamiliar ground, but still a very good play.

955. "The First Man." *Drama Calendar*, 13 Mar.
Not up to O'Neill's rest, but shows ability to write comedy scene and to handle more than two or three people in his dialogue.

956. "The First Man." *Town Topics*, 9 Mar.
Personal rancor, missing the form of art; ill-written melodrama.

957. "The First Man new O'Neill play at the Playhouse."
NY *Clipper*, 15 Mar.
Distasteful, badly acted, worse O'Neill language than usual.

958. Hopkins, Mary Alden. "First Man at the Neighborhood Playhouse." *Greenwich Villager*, 11 Mar.
This critic tries hard to find something to praise, but is not convincing. Says we must understand what O'Neill is doing, etc.

959. Hornblow, Arthur. "Mr. Hornblow goes to the play."
Theatre, 35 (May) 308.
Stretches to the straining point the obligation to be "truthful" about life. Some dramatic effectiveness, but not much more.

960. Macgowan, Kenneth. "Broadway at the spring." *Th. Arts*, 6 (July) 182.
Shallow and arbitrary.

961. Whittaker, James. "O'Neill vents his gorge in The First Man." NY *News*, 18 Mar.
Rampant and arrogant pessimism.

THE FOUNTAIN

Opening night reviews — New York
Newspapers of 11-14 Dec. 1925

962. Allen, Kelcey. "O'Neill's The Fountain leaps to geyser heights of fantasy and romance." *W. W. Daily*, 11 Dec.
Gushes, tumbles, and drops, like a fountain. Smothered with scenery, throwing sprays of condensed prose, colorful and dull.

Reminds one of Rostand; Cyrano always seems to be peeking out somewhere.

963. Anderson, John. "New O'Neill play at the Greenwich Village theatre." NY *Post,* 11 Dec.
"Desire under the palms." Beautifully, often brilliantly written, lit with genuine poetic imagination and literary craftsmanship. Faults are poor construction, too many jerky tableaux, lack of cumulative interest.

964. Coleman, Robert. "Author explains play." NY *Mirror,* 14 Dec.
More pageant than play; feast for eyes, lean diet for ears.

965. Dale, Alan. "The Fountain." NY *American,* 12 Dec.
Without O'Neill's program notes it would have been impossible to gain the slightest idea what the play was meant to be.

966. Gabriel, Gilbert. "De Leon in search of his spring." NY *Sun,* 11 Dec.
"Trial by scenery"; probably should not have been produced. Overly wordy, out-talking its aspirations.

967. Hammond, Percy. "Eugene O'Neill's The Fountain; a large romance done in a small way." NY *Her-Trib.,* 11 Dec.
Perhaps all right as a book, but it suffers from lack of elbow room in production. Needs too many of O'Neill's program explanations.

968. Metcalfe, J. S. "The first Florida boom." *Wall St. Jour.,* 12 Dec.
O'Neill has discovered Ponce de Leon and embalmed him. One feels that George Cohan, Anne Nichols and others can claim rights as dramatists if O'Neill does so with this one. "A large section of Mr. O'Neill's most enthusiastic followers will be disappointed . . . It is a perfectly clean play."

969. Mr. O'Neill seeking romance." NY *Times,* 11 Dec., 26:1.

Unwieldy; climactic scenes too brief. O'Neill is still brooding on human beings caught in the web of existence.

970. Pollock, Arthur. "Plays and things." Brook. *Eagle,* 11 Dec.
Structurally faulty, and O'Neill demands a Reinhardt production in his scenery. Some scenes are fluent, but dogged, and the romance seems amateurish.

971. Vreeland, Frank. "Te Deum and tedium." NY *Telegram,* 11 Dec.
Too many pauses; it meditates too much. It is an obvious play which lays bare O'Neill's weaknesses.

972. Woollcott, Alexander. "The Fountain." NY *World,* 11 Dec.
Never uninteresting, but almost never alive. O'Neill fails for the first time to create real characters.

THE FOUNTAIN received only one production and was never revived. Many reviews did not appear until several weeks after the 11 December 1925 opening, so for this reason all reviews and criticism after 14 December are combined in a single group.

Other reviews and criticism
1925-1926

973. Atkinson, Brooks. "New O'Neill aspects." NY *Times,* 20 Dec. 1925, VII, 3:1.
Attempting poetical history, O'Neill leaves his best medium of "morbid realism" behind. This is neither realism nor drama.

974. Barretto, Larry. "The New Yorker." *Bookman,* 62 (Feb. 1926) 704-705.
Fantasy is not O'Neill's forte. A fantastic, over-long tale.

975. Benchley, Robert. "Art work." *Life,* 86 (31 Dec. 1925) 18.

O'Neill's morbid realism preferable to this boring play.

976. Brown, John Mason. "The director takes a hand." *Th. Arts*, 10 (Feb. 1926) 77.
Full of inequalities; long winded and tiresome.

977. Carb, David. "Seen on the stage." *Vogue*, 67 (1 Feb. 1926) 60-61.
Maundering play, arousing no emotions. Here shuffles instead of strides.

978. Clark, Barrett H. "The new O'Neill play and some others." *Drama*, 16 (Feb. 1926) 175.
The romantic is unfamiliar to O'Neill, but he surprises critics who do not realize he is an idealist and a poet.

979. Eaton, Walter Prichard. "Masks and mysticism." NY *Her-Trib.*, 16 May 1926.
Published version reads extremely well despite failure as play.

980. Freeman, Donald. "A mid-season dramatic mixture." *Van. F.*, 25 (Feb. 1926) 118.
"Enriching and glamorous experience" despite certain failures in writing.

981. Gillette, Don Carle. "The Fountain." *Billboard*, 37 (19 Dec. 1925) 10.
"It interests but it does not stir; it pleases but it does not impress."

982. H.J.M. "The theatre." *New Yorker*, 1 (19 Dec. 1925) 17.
Questions how long O'Neill can be considered great with this and plays such as *WELDED* and *ALL GOD'S CHILLUN*.

983. Hornblow, Arthur. "Mr. Hornblow goes to the play." *Theatre*, 43 (Feb. 1926) 4a.
The scenery conceals much of what the play is about.

984. Kalonyme, Louis. "Delectable mountain of current drama." *Arts & Dec.*, 24 (Feb. 1926) 66.
Shows some greatness in O'Neill, despite over-production.

985. M.W. "The play." *Commonweal*, 3 (23 Dec. 1925) 189.
Though a good portent that O'Neill may achieve his search for beauty and truth, the play itself is vague and dull.

986. Nathan, George Jean. "O'Neill's latest." *Am. Merc.*, 7 (Feb. 1926) 247-249.
Much rewriting has ruined it, but it still shows O'Neill as our greatest native writer.

987. "Plays and players." *Town and Country*, 81 (1 Jan. 1926) 43.
Lusterless, formless and windy; prodigious, talky bore.

988. Seldes Gilbert. "The theatre." *Dial*, 80 (Feb. 1926) 168-169.
Interesting play, produced with passion and beauty.

989. Sisk. "The Fountain." *Variety*, 16 Dec. 1925.
Moments of dash killed by slow movement; not a popular success.

990. Young, Stark. "The new O'Neill play." *New Rep.*, 45 (30 Dec. 1925) 160-161.
A beautiful mood, new to O'Neill, but unequal to the demands the style places on words.

GOLD

*Opening night reviews — New York
Newspapers of 2 June 1921*

991. Allen, Kelcey. "Eugene O'Neill's drama Gold acted at Frazee theatre." *W. W. Daily.*
Worth seeing if you like your drama strong.

992. Broun, Heywood. "Gold at Frazee shows O'Neill below his best." NY *Tribune.*
Slow, conventional beginning, with the O'Neill sign in last act.

993. Dale, Allen. "Artistic moments in Gold at the Frazee." NY *American*
Curious symbolism, but too close to 10-20-30 melodrama.

994. De Foe, Louis V. "New O'Neill play Gold is shown." NY *World.*
Moments of genuine drama, lacks effectiveness of his others.

995. "Eugene O'Neill's Gold tells a weird tale." NY *Times,* 14:2.
Interesting, but "curiously unconvincing" play; not up to standard.

996. "Eugene O'Neill's new play Gold not without alloy." NY *Herald.*
Too many "chunks of gloom" falling on the stage.

997. "Gold." NY *Sun.*
Over long; not among his best.

998. "Gold a triumph for Willard Mack." *Jour. of Comm.*
O'Neill seems unable to pen one light idea or pleasant thought.

999. Macgowan, Kenneth. "Eugene O'Neill's Gold disappoints in spite of many distinctions." NY *Globe.*

"Conceived in a bigger way than executed," but strength shows even in inadequate presentation.

1000. Mantle, Burns. "A new O'Neill tragedy." NY *Mail*.
Approaches *JONES* in study of conscience-driven fear, but with less of the novelty.

1001. Marsh, Leo A. "Gold opens at Frazee theatre." NY *Telegraph*.
Looking for entertainment, don't go to this; full of O'Neill's "morbid vein" and shivers and shudders.

1002. "O'Neill's Gold not glittering." NY *Telegram*.
Has power, but lines are blurred and uncertain; O'Neill deliberation becomes labored mannerism.

1003. Pollock, Arthur. "Another O'Neill play." Brook. *Eagle*.
Hard to determine its aim; much of aimless nothingness.

1004. Torres, H. Z. "Willard Mack glitters in Gold." NY *Commercial*.
Thrilling tale of adventure and crime, suffers from repetition and halted action.

1005. Towse, J. Ranken. "Gold." NY *Post*.
Crude melodrama; feeble play at best.

1006. "Willard Mack scores in new drama." NY *Journal*.
Praise for acting, offers no criticism of play.

Other reviews and criticism
1921

1007. Andrews, K. "Gold." *Bookman*, 53 (Aug.) 528-530.
O'Neill forgets his story between Acts I and IV, ends with his strange fire at his best.

1008. Benchley, Robert. "Gold — and some forty-niners." *Life*, 77 (16 June) 876.

Clumsy, resembles something Benchley (by own admission) might have written. Drought-provoking play.

1009. "Eugene O'Neill's Gold is a drama of greed and gloom, plus symbolism." NY *Call*, 3 June.
Much repetition and discussion, enough to irritate the spirit.

1010. Firkins, O. W. "Gold." *Weekly Rev.*, 4 (18 June) 584-585.
Two extraordinarily good first acts, but plot is abandoned and instead of Stevenson we have Conrad, the plot merely being towed into port.

1011. "Gold." *Independent*, 105 (18 June) 633.
It is not up to O'Neill's best.

1012. "Gold." *Lit. Rev. of NY Eve. Post*, 8 Oct., p. 74.
Gives hope of better things in the future.

1013. "Gold." *Variety*, 10 June.
A big failure without merit; talky, balky, tiresome, impossible.

1014. "Gold O'Neill's new play interesting but far from writer's best." NY *Clipper*, 69 (8 June) 19.
Almost 10-20-30 melodrama, but still more interesting than general run.

1015. Hornblow, Arthur. "Mr. Hornblow goes to the play." *Theatre*, 35 (Aug.) 97.
Much force of expression but this is tedious, reiterative, banal.

1016. Kaufman, S. Jay. "Gold." *Dram. Mir.*, 83 (11 June) 1001.
Chaos when O'Neill writes conventional melodrama.

1017. — — — —. "Seen on the stage." *Vogue*, 15 Sept.
As vivid and vital a first act as any American has ever written; play is ruined by acting and production.

1018. Lewisohn, Ludwig. "Drama." *Nation*, 112 (22 June) 902.

Seem to have heard all this before. Interesting comment by this critic who places O'Neill second to Susan Glaspell as our leading writer.

1019. "O'Neill's Gold proves to be an impressive play." NY *Review*, 4 June.
In some ways O'Neill's most impressive play.

1922

1020. Boyd, Ernest A. "Shorter notices." *Freeman*, 4 (4 Jan.) 406.
Book review. Prefers this to *WHERE CROSS IS MADE*, because of more wild elemental force.

1021. "Gold." *Cath. Wld.*, 114 (Jan.) 555.
More dramatic than literary value.

1022. "The truth of O'Neill's technic." *Dramatist*, 13 (Jan.) 1095-1097.
O'Neill must learn the rules of playwriting like everybody else.

THE GREAT GOD BROWN

Opening night reviews — New York
Newspapers of 25 Jan. 1926

1023. Allen, Kelcey. "Great God Brown by O'Neill unique." *W. W. Daily*.
The transfer of personality is unacceptable and far-fetched Expressionism and symbolism must have some relationship to the sphere of logic; there is mask switching to the point of strangulation. A laboratory experiment not good for the theatre.

1024. Anderson, John. "Another O'Neill play comes to town." NY *Post*.

O'Neill has ventured everything and achieved a superb failure. It is more than the stage can hold; O'Neill's fall from the heights of dramatic imagination is "brilliant and thrilling." The play eventually drowns magnificently in the seething theories of the writer.

1025. Atkinson, Brooks. "Symbolism in an O'Neill tragedy." NY *Times*, 26:1. [Reprinted in Durham & Dodds, *British and American plays, 1830-1945*, NY, Oxford, 1947 (No. 34).]

Acknowledging what O'Neill is trying to do, Atkinson refuses to be bothered by the fact the play is not always clear; what O'Neill does is more important than what he does not do.

1026. Coleman, Robert. "God Brown tedious." NY *Mirror*.

Ineffective and tedious psychological study. Despairing dirge of puzzled pessimist.

1027. Gabriel, Gilbert. "All God's chillun got masks." NY *Sun*.

O'Neill does not write for popularity but for posterity. One will remember the play, whatever he thinks of it. Gabriel's admiration is "hot but troubled" for O'Neill's most poetic and penetrating play.

1028. "Great God Brown opens at Greenwich Village." NY *Graphic*.

Strength and beauty of lines, but you will go home mystified and bored.

1029. Marsh, Leo. "O'Neill's latest pure experiment." NY *Telegraph*.

A clinical experiment.

1030. Metcalfe, J. S. "A plea in defence." *Wall St. Jour.*

The masks hinder instead of help, making some speeches seem laughable. O'Neill is no longer the great dramatist of realism and low-life characters.

1031. Osborn, E. W. "The Great God Brown." NY *World.*
The unexepected is again introduced and spells wonderful, though there is some symbolic running wild in the last act.

1032. Pollock, Arthur. "The Great God Brown." Brook. *Eagle.*
Very little critical comment; mainly plot review.

1033. Vreeland, Frank. "The masked marvel." NY *Telegram.*
O'Neill at both his best and his worst.

Other reviews and criticism
(With two exceptions all dates are 1926)

1034. Anderson, John. "O'Neill the realist turns mystic." *Lit. Rev. of NY Eve. Post,* 10 Apr., p. 2.
O'Neill is still handicapped by his tools of the theatre, but he is also still an impressive dramatist.

1035. Anschutz, Grace. "Masks, their use by Pirandello and O'Neill." *Drama,* 17 (Apr. 1927) 201.
An interesting comparison of the two styles. Pirandello may do better through character portrayal alone, than through use of actual masks.

1036. Atkinson, Brooks. "Ibsen and O'Neill." NY *Times,* 31 Jan., VII, 1:1.
The two writers have much in common in emotional sensitiveness and philosophy, dealing with things that are not quite what they seem. Ibsen can be understood, but in this play O'Neill is on the verge of becoming unintelligible.

1037. Barretto, Larry. "The New Yorker." *Bookman,* 63 (Apr.) 213.
"O'Neill has come a cropper while riding on a brave quest."

1038. Benchley, Robert. "So deep!" *Life*, 87 (11 Feb.) 20.
Last half unintelligible jumble, but it probably reads well.

1039. Bogdanoff, Rose. "Masks, their uses, past and present." *Drama*, 21 (May 1931) 21.
O'Neill's use of the mask is the finest in modern theatre, as much a part of the play as the lines themselves.

1040. Brown, John Mason. "Doldrums of midwinter." *Th. Arts*, 10 (Mar.) 145-146.
In an otherwise dull season, this comes as utterly different experiment. Fine for two acts, then confusion.

1041. Carb, David. "The Great God Brown." *Vogue*, 67 (15 Mar.) 106.
"Subtly conceived symbolic tragedy, finely imagined, written with glowing loveliness. It fails to succeed only because of a physical device."

1042. Clark, Barrett H. "Fin de saison on Broadway." *Drama*, 16 (May) 289-290.
Hopes Pulitzer Prize is awarded to this play.

1043. — — — —. "High spots in a dull season." *Drama*, 16 (Mar.) 212.
Highest development of O'Neill's genius we have seen. Like all poets, he writes ahead of us.

1044. Eaton, Walter Prichard. "Masks and mysticism." NY *Her-Trib.*, 16 May.
The reading text may be clearer, but the absence of masks loses emotion.

1045. Gillette, Don Carle. "The Great God Brown." *Billboard*, 38 (6 Feb.) 43.
Audiences must be educated to O'Neill more slowly; he is given in too big doses. This is "glorious confusion."

1046. "The Great God Brown." *Drama Calendar*, 8 (1 Feb.) 1.

Has partly succeeded in "externalizing" the process of spiritual rebirth, and should be praised for it.

1047. "The Great God Brown." *Outlook*, 143 (26 May) 151.
Tragic allegory. The characters attain stature.

1048. "Great God Brown and other plays." *Dial*, 81 (Aug.) 175.
Most people over 40 would look at this with amused tolerance of the rebellion against life.

1049. "Great God Brown — Another grotesque conundrum." *Dramatist*, 17 (July) 1307-1309.
This review is almost unbelievably narrow and unimaginative, calling the play a drama "for dumb Doras," about an architect who masquerades as his dead rival and fails.

1050. G.W.G. "Goat Song, Great God Brown and other crashing symbols." *New Yorker*, 1 (6 Feb.) 26.
Some of the finest writing of O'Neill's career; underneath the "foam" of the masks lies the "nutritious fluid of a deeply digested idea."

1051. Hornblow, Arthur. "Mr. Hornblow goes to the play." *Theatre*, 43 (Apr.) 18.
The mask exchange in late scenes is piffle. Nothing in the play outside of some utterly incomprehensible hocus-pocus.

1052. Kalonyme, Louis. "Dramatica Dionysiana." *Arts and Dec.*, 24 (Mar.) 62.
O'Neill's greatest achievement to date. This critic finds no confusion in mask switch, sees it as an "inevitable and integral step."

1053. Krutch, Joseph Wood. "Review of the season." *Nation*, 122 (16 June) 675.
One of O'Neill's most moving and most chaotic plays.

1054. — — — —. "The tragedy of masks." *Nation*, 122 (10

Feb.) 164-165. [Reprinted in Hewitt, Barnard, *Theatre USA*, NY, McGraw-Hill, 1959, pp. 363-364 (No. 56).]

Never a more powerful or confused O'Neill play. Confusion perhaps because O'Neill is too close to subject; it masters him as much as he masters it.

1055. Macgowan, Kenneth. "The mask in drama." Brook. *Eagle*, 30 Jan.

Discussion of differences between O'Neill and the Greeks.

1056. — — — —. "The mask in drama." *Greenwich Playbill* No. 4, Season 1925-1926.

Points out this is the first modern play making direct use of the mask, using it for character change instead of physical or emotional change.

1057. Mantle, Burns. "Great God Brown fascinating mystery." NY *News*, 26 Jan.

Difficult play to follow, but one of most gripping tragi-comedies. Will stand as one of O'Neill's greatest messages.

1058. Nathan, George Jean. "The Theatre." *Am. Merc.*, 7 (Apr.) 503-504.

Richly imagined, brilliantly articulated, has power of conviction and dialogue of profundity seldom equalled in native drama.

1059. "Plays and players." *Town and Country*, 81 (15 Feb.) 60.

Jerkily written, pretentious, masks clumsy and annoying, the theme better to be treated by European writers.

1060. Quinn, Arthur Hobson. Letter to editor. NY *Times*, 21 Feb., VII, 2:6.

Calls attention to this profound study as worthy of support.

1061. Sisk. "Great God Brown." *Variety*, 27 Jan.

He has hit on something almost great in the masks — but not quite.

1062. Skinner, Richard Dana. "Blossoms in arid dust." *Ind. & Weekly* R., 116 (6 Mar.) 275.

Approval for masks, but audiences may not follow everything. O'Neill at his best. He is laying bare his own life, an opinion Skinner further develops in *Poet's Quest* (No. 123).

1063. — — — —. "The play." *Commonweal*, 3 (10 Feb.) 384. O'Neill emerges from the swamp of despair and shows faith in resurrection. A notable play; O'Neill capable of "lofty vision."

1064. Smith, Geddes. "Three mirrors." *Survey*, 56 (1 Apr.) 43.
"Heavy with implications . . . sometimes clear, sometimes muddled, always insistent."

1065. Wyatt, Euphemia Van R. "Plays of some importance." *Cath. Wld.*, 122 (Mar.) 805-807.
If O'Neill is not a mystic, he is as close as any contemporary American. The play is a subtle study of the hide and seek men play with their lives and souls.

1066. Young, Stark. "The Great God Brown." *New Rep.*, 45 (10 Feb.) 329-330. [Reprinted in Young's *Immortal Shadows*, NY, Scribners, 1948 (No. 148).]
Some unequal writing, but a feeling of great groping of life behind the play. Some effective use of masks.

*Opening night reviews — Revival — New York
Newspapers of 7 Oct. 1959*

1067. Aston, Frank. "Great God Brown reopens at the Coronet." NY *Wor-Tel. & Sun*.
Everyone deserves praise for courage in the revival; the difficulties of performance are beyond most people. Masks are clumsy, but play is harrowing, engrossing, rewarding.

1068. Atkinson, Brooks. "Theatre: O'Neill's Great God Brown." NY *Times*, 48:1.
As avante garde as any play of Beckett or Ionesco. In form there is nothing today more modern; memorable characters in a fascinating fantasy. Whether or not it is a "success" is pedantic.

O'Neill's power of introspection is magnetic, for he writes about permanent ideas.

1069. Chapman, John. "O'Neill's Great God Brown an impressive theatrical curio." NY *News*.
Nothing is any more clear now than ever. Perhaps a great work, but it seems now to be a curio.

1070. Coleman, Robert. "Great God Brown not O'Neill at best." NY *Mirror*.
O'Neill's mind and soul were in ferment. In seeking faith he had little interest in clarity. Appealing for students, not for regular playgoers.

1071. Dash, Thomas R. "Great God Brown confusing but stirring." *W. W. Daily*.
Beckett & Ionesco are "rank amateurs" in the bewitched, bothered, and bewildered kind of play compared to this. Still confusing after 33 years, the last scene being a "charade of fakery," fatuous and ludicrous.

1072. Kerr, Walter. "Great God Brown." NY *Her-Trib*.
Seems to have been written when O'Neill's energy was near exhaustion. Poor characters rob it of any cumulative force. Neither poetry nor people swell to any size. Seems dry as sand.

1073. McClain, John. "A well-acted puzzler." NY *Jour-Am*.
"A mess of dried shaving-cream" well performed, challenges anyone to dig out its meaning. McClain questions: "Why must good theatre be so oblique, so different?"

1074. Watts, Richard. "O'Neill's drama of men and masks." NY *Post*.
At times can be nothing short of maddening. Probably a failure, but a failure of genius. Third act philosophy is too much. Disturbing beauty, final confusion, but still a work of dramatic art.

Other reviews and criticism
1959

1075. Atkinson. Brooks. "Great God Brown." NY *Times,*
18 Oct., II, 1:1.
Absolute standards of excellence mark this a failure, although
O'Neill fascinates and enthralls with his attempt. The Phoenix
production meets with high approval, but O'Neill is too far
beyond his audience by the third act. None the less, it is a
major theatre work, full of O'Neill's indomitability and tragic
insight.

1076. Berkelman, R. "O'Neill's everyman." S. *Atl. Quar.,*
58 (Fall) 609.
This is a 20th century Everyman's journey through life.
Brown and Dion are one person, and the women combine in
Everywoman as well. The play is not, however, O'Neill's best.

1077. Bolton, Whitney. "O'Neill play has areas of confusion." NY *Telegraph,* 8 Oct.
The last act can become clownish. We are never sure whether
the masks are good or bad, but the fact O'Neill tried is a
tribute anyway.

1078. Brustein, Robert. "O'Neill's adolescent talkathon."
New Rep., 141 (Oct. 19) 29.
Despite talk and abstractions, the play shows O'Neill's greatness was in his probing of character instead of his hazy views
of the universe. Too many undeveloped themes make it incoherent, and the play cannot hold us now.

1079. Clurman, Harold. "Theatre." *Nation,* 189 (24 Oct.)
259-260.
A crucial American tragedy in its portrayal of the incomplete-
ness of American civilization as it focuses on the individual.
For all his faults, O'Neill is our most important dramatist because he is more truly relevant to the American people.

1080. Cooke, Richard P. "O'Neill's maskers." *Wall St.
Jour.,* 8 Oct.

Poetic jumble. Seems old fashioned and literary, still bearing the marks of an unsuccessful experiment.

1081. Gelb, Arthur. "An epitaph for the O'Neills." NY *Times*, 4 Oct., II, 1:1.

A review of the play as an epitaph for his family of father, mother, and brother, all lost within the previous five years. This play therefore begins a lifelong evaluation of O'Neill's relationship to them, culminating in *LONG DAY'S JOURNEY*. The article points up interesting parallels between the play's characters and the real people O'Neill knew.

1082. "The Great God Brown." *Th. Arts*, 43 (Dec.) 88.

There is more immediacy and impact than in the original. The masks are not dated, and they illustrate more than ever O'Neill's anger and grief.

1083. Hobe. "Great God Brown." *Variety*, 14 Oct.

Remains one of O'Neill's important works; engrossing, challenging, uneven, a milestone in his career. The masks, while still novel, require more than most audiences will give.

1084. "Into the shadows again." *Newsweek*, 54 (19 Oct.) 80.

It is still valid as an experiment. The philosophy is sometimes inspired, but confusing. A difficult but compelling play.

1085. Lewis, Theophilus. "The Great God Brown." *America*, 102 (31 Oct.) 139-140.

It is not O'Neill's most impressive, but probably his most fascinating work. It is good to see a revival of this challenging play.

1086. "Old play in Manhattan." *Time*, 74 (19 Oct.) 56.

Prolix and banal, as heavy with fog as it is lacking in flesh. The production is not good. Some vivid tricks, but the "gaudy orchestration" merely emphasizes the music's hollowness.

1087. Rhodes, Robert E. "A brilliant revival." *Newsday*, 14 Oct.

Just as absorbing, stimulating, and effective as ever, regardless of time.

1088. Tynan, Kenneth. "O'Neill in embryo." *New Yorker,* 35 (17 Oct.) 131.
A fascinating evening. The end, however, is in the "soggy realm" of bad fantasy and cannot be accepted.

1089. Watts, Richard. "A maddening and fascinating play." NY *Post,* 18 Oct.
Still disturbing as it was when first produced. A magnificent failure because of the confusion. It is impossible to strike a balance between its great virtues and its great defects.

THE HAIRY APE

Opening night reviews — New York
Newspapers of 10 Mar. 1922

1090. "Hairy Ape a logical tragedy." NY *World.*
Similar to but not as good as *JONES* because of less articulate human note.

1091. Hammond, Percy. "Hairy Ape shows Eugene O'Neill in a bitter and interesting humor." NY *Tribune.*
An "interesting thing," the best since *ANNA CHRISTIE.*

1092. Macgowan, Kenneth. "Eugene O'Neill sets a new mark in The Hairy Ape." NY *Globe.*
Welcome to a tremendous new drama form, "extraordinarily challenging."

1093. Mantle, Burns. "The Hairy Ape." NY *Mail.*
A better play than *JONES* because of better mood, more intimate contact with the modern world.

1094. Reamer, Lawrence. "Hairy Ape, new O'Neill play, an impressive study of life." NY *Herald*.

General praise. Downfall of *JONES* more effective than fall of this "feeble giant."

1095. Towse, J. Ranken. "Eugene O'Neill's latest effort." NY *Post*.

In his vigorous attack on the play's "juvenile appeal to ignorance and passion" Towse sees ominous foreboding for O'Neill's future. One of the strongest dissents among a minority of the critics who did not like the play. Towse finds the play worthless, and assigns it social and economic aspects which O'Neill probably never intended.

1096. Welsh, Robert G. "Behind the scenes." NY *Telegram*.

Expressive and weird; does not do well in the shift from realistic beginning to "fantasy" of the second part.

1097. Woollcott, Alexander. "Eugene O'Neill at full tilt." NY *Times*, 18:2.

"Monstrously uneven" but O'Neill towers above the milling mumbling crowd of contemporary playwrights.

Other reviews and criticism
1922

THE HAIRY APE moved from the crowded Provincetown stage to the Plymouth theatre uptown on 17 April 1922. Several newspapers sent their critics to review it again, and their comments are included below.

1098. Andrews, Kenneth. "Broadway our literary signpost." *Bookman*, 55 (May) 284.

The play is like a "badly written editorial in the 'Call.'"

1099. "As to the Hairy Ape." NY *Star*, 22 Apr.

Ending is inevitable, very natural. A vivid play.

1100. Baury, Louis. "The Hairy Ape." *Freeman*, 5 (19
July) 449.
Baury replies to Kantor (No. 1123) and denies that *APE* has
been categorized as completely expressionistic.

1101. — — — —. "Mr. O'Neill's new plays." *Freeman*, 5
(3 May) 184-185.
This and *FIRST MAN* are failures. O'Neill must learn responsibilities of his art and cease "wallowing in mere words."

1102. — — — —. "On reply to Mr. Block." *Freeman*, 5 (14
June) 330.
Sharp reply to Block's letter (No. 1104). Baury shows respect
for O'Neill but feels *APE* did not achieve greatness that modern
drama is capable of.

1103. Benchley, Robert. "The Hairy Ape." *Life*, 79 (30
Mar.) 18.
His most powerful thing yet.

1104. Block, Ralph. "The old order changeth." *Freeman*,
5 (31 May) 281-282.
Letter protesting Baury's approach (No. 1100) which seems
to assume there are rules and responsibilities an artist must follow, which this writer believes do not exist.

1105. Broun, Heywood. "The Hairy Ape." NY *World*,
2 Apr.
Interesting and gallant attempt that does not come off.

1106. — — — —. "It seems to me." NY *World*, 25 Apr.
In reply to an accusation that he did not give the play justice
as a social document, Broun states the artistic sense is lost when
the artist adopts a cause, and this is the case with O'Neill.

1107. — — — —. "It seems to me." NY *World*, 3 May.
Cites a letter from Michael Gold attacking Broun and his
"gang" for wanting sugar-coated stuff instead of this terrific
kind of play.

1108. Castellun, Maida. "The plays that pass — O'Neill's Hairy Ape a powerful tragedy of today." NY *Call*, 12 Mar.
One of his finest achievements; a powerful and shattering play.

1109. Dale, Alan. "Hairy Ape is presented at Plymouth." NY *American*, 19 Apr.
The audience should go to enjoy it for the new type play it is, and should forget the "bosh" about what it means.

1110. Darnton, Charles. "The Hairy Ape despair run amuck." NY *World*, 19 Apr.
Yank's bad liquor must be causing him bad dreams.

1111. Dawson, N. P. "Books in particular." NY *Globe*, 17 Apr.
O'Neill plows a very new and deep furrow in this one.

1112. Eaton, Walter Prichard. "The Hairy Ape." *Freeman*, 5 (26 Apr.) 160-161.
O'Neill is the writer of the future; no matter what one's opinion you cannot get away from it; whatever the symbols and interpretations, it is a tragedy.

1113. "The Hairy Ape." *Drama Calendar*, 20 Mar.
A great play, but makes one wince. Beautiful in bold directness and stark reality.

1114. "The Hairy Ape." NY *Post*, 22 Mar.
This editorial praises the play, which shows that the next decade in the theatre will be filled with admirable and surprising things.

1115. "The Hairy Ape." NY *Tribune*, 20 Apr.
O'Neill is a young genius and our greatest playwright, completely lacking in superficiality.

1116. "Hairy Ape at the Provincetown Playhouse." *Town Topics*, 16 Mar.
It should reach Broadway; if it does not it will be a disgrace.

1117. "Hairy Ape is O'Neill at best." NY *Journal*, 19 Apr.
Tremendous force and imagination.

1118. "The Hairy Ape, O'Neill play, is dull and tiresome."
NY *Clipper*, 70 (22 Mar.) 22.
Neither his best nor worst; interesting if you like O'Neill.

1119. "Hairy Ape — Undramatized sensation." *Dramatist*,
13 (July) 1117-1118.
"Brute force that goes nowhere."

1120. Hopkins, Mary Alden. "Hairy Ape at the Provincetown Theatre." *Greenwich Villager*, 11 Mar.
Not a criticism; merely reviews matters of staging.

1121. Hornblow, Arthur. "Mr. Hornblow goes to the play."
Theatre, 35 (May) 305.
"Towering accomplishment" brilliant, vitally poetic, apocalyptic
in message.

1122. James, Patterson. "Off the record." *Billboard*, 34
(15 Apr.) 18.
Violent, vitriolic attack comparing the play to swill wagons
and slaughter houses in its "realism" of staging and language.
This opinion is partner to Towse's (No. 1095) and Robbins'
(No. 1138) in its purely surfacy attitude. The critic is so hor-
ribly offended that he makes little effort to offer worthwhile
criticism.

1123. Kantor, Louis. "The Hairy Ape." *Freeman*, 5 (5
July) 402-403.
A letter to the editor differs with Baury's reply (No. 1100)
to Block's letter (No. 1104). Kantor says O'Neill is like the
"modernist movement" in Germany, which he does not identify.

1124. Levick, L. E. "Hairy Ape and the I.W.W. Marine
transport workers turn dramatic critics and praise O'Neill." NY
Call, 14 May.
Report of review in *Marine Worker*, which recommends the
play to its members.

1125. Lewisohn, Ludwig. "The development of Eugene O'Neill." *Nation*, 114 (22 Mar.) 349-350.
O'Neill cannot work freely within established drama forms, but this is his best and approaches his own true form.

1126. Macgowan, Kenneth. "Broadway at the spring." *Th. Arts*, 6 (July) 182.
Our first expressionist play and quite successful.

1127. — — — —. "Curtain calls." NY *Globe*, 13 Mar.
A sharp rebuttal to Towse (No. 1095), scolding "learned critics" who don't know a new form of drama when they see it.

1128. — — — —. "Hairy Ape uptown." NY *Globe*, 18 Apr.
Improved with the move from the Village; the same surging and exciting piece.

1129. — — — —. "The theatrical callboard." *Van. F.*, 18 (Apr.) 16 d.
This radically new play one of the big events of the season.

1130. "Mr. Brady's view of the season." NY *World*, 30 Apr.
It is part of a season that strives for the exceptional, bizarre, and shocking.

1131. Pearson, Edmund L. "New books and old." *Independent*, 109 (19 Aug.) 78.
Book review only. Gives feeling of being "deafening."

1132. Pemberton, Brock. "Mr. Pemberton goes to The Hairy Ape." NY *Globe*, 15 Mar.
Just back from Germany, writer finds "uncanny" similarities in comparison with Toller's *Masse Mensch*, though they are unlike in concept and execution.

1133. "A play to see." *Commerce and Finance*, 15 Mar.
"Not to see it is to have failed to have seen the best that American art has produced."

1134. Pollock, Arthur. "About the theatre." Brook. *Eagle,* 21 May.
Questions if we are to be confined to "sweet romances and banal detective plays" or if we will be permitted to encourage plays like *APE* so that America "may become articulate in the eyes of the artistic world."

1135. — — — —. "The Hairy Ape." Brook. *Eagle,* 12 Mar.
Enough realism ("imaginative realism") to make Belasco weep.

1136. "A portrait play." NY *American,* 20 Apr.
Notes O'Neill's insistence that the play is only about a man who does not "belong."

1137. Rathbun, Stephen. "Eugene O'Neill's Hairy Ape is one of the most vital plays of the season." NY *Sun,* 11 Mar.
Opposes O'Neill's "negative philosophy," but finds there is something here to think about.

1138. Robbins, R. "The I.W.W. on the stage." *Industrial Solidarity,* 8 Apr.
The critic of this labor periodical considers the play one of the most helpful and legitimate defenses of the I.W.W. position today. O'Neill has painted the inner tragedy of the proleterian soul.

1139. Sayler, Oliver M. "The Hairy Ape is a study in evolution of a play." NY *Globe,* 6 May.
This interesting account of the original idea for the play counts *JONES* as its "father."

1140. — — — —. "Our theatre at cross purposes." *Century,* 104 (Sept.) 748.
The season was a "patchwork of perversity," with O'Neill closest to whole garment.

1141. Seldes, Gilbert. "The Hairy Ape." *Dial,* 72 (May) 548-549. [Reprinted in Hewitt, Barnard, *Theatre USA,* NY, McGraw-Hill, 1959, pp. 338-340 (No. 56).]
Critic does not like shift from one framework to another.

1142. Towse, J. Ranken. "The Hairy Ape in new conditions." NY *Post*, 18 Apr.
Initial view (No. 1095) not changed; still a potboiler and melodramatic thriller without significance.

1143. Whittaker, James. "That horrible gorilla crushed the Hairy Ape." NY *News*, 16 Mar.
JONES was dissection of a reverting type; this is vivisection. Yank never had a chance, and O'Neill is not fair to him.

1144. Woollcott, Alexander. "Second thoughts on first nights." NY *Times*, 16 Apr., VI, 1:1.
General speculation on O'Neill's chances on Broadway in Plymouth Theatre, as opposed to success in Village.

1145. Young, Stark. "The Hairy Ape." *New Rep.*, 30 (22 Mar.) 112-113.
Whatever the opinion of the play or of O'Neill, this must be recognized as important in O'Neill's ability to free himself and carry through without impediment of event or convention.

1923-1934

1146. "The Hairy Ape." *Cath. Wld.*, 116 (Feb. 1923) 714.
The ape is a *tour de force*, an artificial product; fails in primary quality of convincingness.

1147. "The Hairy Ape." *Th. Arts*, 18 (Aug. 1934) 598.
O'Neill has caught the conflict of the individual and world around him more than anybody else.

1148. Johnson, Annette T. "The Hairy Ape." *Ind. & Weekly R.*, 110 (28 Apr. 1923) 282-284.
Some reflections on civilization's responsibility to all the "hairy apes."

1149. Macgowan, Kenneth. "Experiment on Broadway." *Th. Arts*, 7 (July 1923) 175-185.

A discussion of experimentation and expressionism includes this play.

1150. Robbins, R. "The emperor O'Neill." *Industrial Pioneer*, 2 (Jan. 1925) 26-27.
Labor (I.W.W.) publication praises O'Neill for creating real characters in an age of dramatic sham and counterfeit.

1151. Watts, Richard. "Regarding Mr. O'Neill as a writer for the cinema." NY *Her-Trib.*, 4 Mar.1928.
Synopsis of O'Neill's own film scenarios for *DESIRE* and *APE*, neither of which were produced. They are much altered from the stage versions.

HUGHIE

The following four references represent all the entries in *The Readers Guide* through 1959 plus the New York *Times Book Review*. The book apparently did not receive wide notice, and the play will not be important in the O'Neill canon until it is produced in the United States.

1152. Gelb, Arthur. "Dream and live." NY *Times*, 19 April 1959, VII, 5:3.
This reflects the same theme from many of the longer plays, namely that man must have his dreams in order to survive. The play, more of a short story, is a "compassionate, shattering character study."

1153. Hewes, Henry. "Short night's journey into day." *Sat. R.*, 41 (4 Oct. 1958) 27.
A report on the Stockholm production. "Top drawer O'Neill." The whole cycle of life has been put into forty-five minutes. The technique is Chekhovian.

1154. Krutch, Joseph Wood. "And now — Hughie." *Th. Arts,* 43 (Aug. 1959) 14-15.
A real addition to the canon, and unlike most posthumous works, a good one, showing perhaps O'Neill was reaching maturity of his powers. It is restrained and more compact than the longer plays, and the dialogue is better.

1155. Weales, Gerald. "Variation on an O'Neill theme." *Commonweal,* 70 (15 May 1959) 187-188.
Another illustration of O'Neill's theme of the need for life illusion. Impressive because it says so briefly what *ICEMAN* developed in such detail.

THE ICEMAN COMETH

*Opening night reviews — New York
Newspapers of 10 Oct. 1946*

1156. Allen, Kelcey. "The Iceman Cometh." *W. W. Daily.*
O'Neill's skilfull writing is here; it is vivid and dramatic, but has its dull moments. Its truthful dialogue seems unnecessarily profane, but the characters are real.

1157. Atkinson, Brooks. "Iceman Cometh has its world premiere." NY *Times,* 31:3.
One of O'Neill's best; over-long and garrulous, but he has heart of a poet.

1158. Barnes, Howard. "O'Neill — at long last." NY *Her-Trib.*
Striking plot twist of the characters facing their pipe dreams, but climax is disappointing. Excellent production does not remove confusion.

1159. Chapman, John. "Eugene O'Neill's Iceman Cometh great drama, wonderfully acted." NY *News.*
Magnificent drama, cuts the ordinary commercial theatre down to size.

1160. Coleman, Robert."The Iceman Cometh a terrific hit." NY *Mirror.*
Everyone urged to hurry and buy tickets.

1161. Cooke, Richard P. "New O'Neill play." *Wall St. Jour.*
A play more for people who think than for those who feel. Too long.

1162. Garland, Robert. "Iceman Cometh at Martin Beck." NY *Jour-Am.*
Combination of *Lower Depths* and old time vaudeville being put on simultaneously. Cannot find why O'Neill felt called to write it.

1163. Hawkins, William. "O'Neill's Iceman here at last." NY *Wor-Tel.*
O'Neill can bring poetic grandeur to these little people he knows so well.

1164. Morehouse, Ward. "The Iceman Cometh is power-ful theatre . . ." NY *Sun.*
Long winded, but has power and intensity, rich and vivid dialogue.

1165. North, Sterling. "Eugene O'Neill's turkey." NY *Post.*
Judging from reading version, "action draggeth, dialogue reeketh, play stinketh." North wonders how it ever got produced or published.

1166. Pollock, Arthur. "The Iceman Cometh." Brook. *Eagle.*
Over-long and too much repetition.

1167. Watts, Richard, Jr. "Eugene O'Neill's new play is powerful and moving." NY *Post.*
Too long and slow, still gives American theatre dignity and importance; moving, powerful, beautiful, eloquent, passionate.

Other reviews and criticism
1946

1168. "Applause in December." *Harper's Bazaar*, 80 (Dec.) 220-221.
Absorbing, disturbing, magnificently acted.

1169. Atkinson, Brooks. "Four hour O'Neill." NY *Times*, 20 Oct., II, 1:1. [Reprinted as "The Iceman Cometh" in Atkinson's *Broadway scrapbook*, NY, Theatre Arts, 1947 (No. 2).]
Our most dramatic dramatist; the play returns the theatre to its high estate.

1170. — — — —. "To be or not to be." NY *Times*, 27 Oct., II, 1:1.
Disputes the O'Neill premise that illusions must be kept to remain alive, but finds it one of O'Neill's best plays.

1171. Barnes, Howard. "The Iceman Cometh." NY *Her-Trib.*, 20 Oct.
This critic, after a few days' study, dissents, finding much of O'Neill's early power dissipated, and the curtain lines contrived.

1172. Bentley, Eric. "The return of Eugene O'Neill." *Atlantic*, 178 (Nov.) 64-66.
O'Neill must be judged far above regular Broadway standards. This evaluation by a critic not generally favorable toward O'Neill finds him less "terrific" than in *ELECTRA*, and less emotional than *INTERLUDE*, in many ways "cooler and steadier."

1173. "Broadway goes highbrow." *Life*, 21 (28 Oct.) 109-111.
Imperfect, but absorbing; reaffirms man's struggle toward dignity. Six very good production pictures accompany the article.

1174. Brown, John Mason. "All O'Neilling." *Sat. R. Lit.*, 29 (19 Oct.) 26. [Reprinted as "Moaning at the bar" in Brown's *Seeing more things*, NY, Whittlesey House, 1948, pp. 257-265 (No. 13).]

Blue pencil and shears needed to make it a better play, but there are fine examples of compassion, insight and theatricality that only O'Neill can bring.

1175. Bull, Harry. "The Iceman Cometh." *Town & Country*, Dec., p. 117.
This somewhat different review sees the theme as "the surviving need for violence in a peacetime world of artificial bourgeois convention."

1176. Chapman, John. "O'Neill brings new hope to the theatre." NY *News*, 20 Oct.
A frightening picture because it applies to all of us, drunk or sober. O'Neill's most profound work.

1177. Doyle, Louis F. "Mr. O'Neill's Iceman." *America*, 30 Nov., pp. 241-242.
This Catholic priest finds O'Neill a master playwright who falls short of being great because of his limitations in the field of thought. Keen disappointment that O'Neill's final solution is defeat.

1178. Eaton, Walter Prichard. "Habitués of Hope's saloon." NY *Her-Trib.*, 20 Oct.
Representative of nothing social or significant because the people are "self-made bums."

1179. Francis, Robert. "Time (4 hrs) goeth, as Iceman Cometh, reintroduces O'Neill." *Billboard*, 19 Oct.
O'Neill has not lost touch — each character meticulously developed, lusty, salty. He still packs a wallop.

1180. Freedley, George. "Iceman Cometh proves O'Neill is America's greatest dramatist." NY *Telegraph*, 11 Oct.
First rate O'Neill.

1181. — — — —. "Many brilliant performances given in O'Neill's The Iceman Cometh." NY *Telegraph*, 16 Nov.
The published version emphasizes even more so the great writer in O'Neill.

1182. Gibbs, Wolcott. "The boys in the back room." *New Yorker*, 22 (19 Oct.) 53-57.

Central theme of illusion very ordinary; ambiguity about ending shows O'Neill not the craftsman he should be. Not up to his best.

1183. Gilder, Rosamond. "Each in his own way." *Th. Arts*, 30 (Dec.) 684.

Despite unnecessary length and O'Neill's lack of humor, it still shows theatre is not just dumb show.

1184. Green, E. Mawby. "Echoes from Broadway." *Th. World.*, 42 (Dec.) 31-32.

Work of a genius, not talent; heavy and ponderous, but still monumental in stature that is rare in the theatre.

1185. Hawkins, William. "Iceman is long, but acting is superior." NY *Wor-Tel.*, 12 Oct.

Review of the fine performances, with some comment on O'Neill's attitude in the play.

1186. "The Iceman Cometh." *Variety*, 16 Oct.

"Bingo for the Theatre Guild"; a never to be forgotten play.

1187. Kronenberger, Louis. "Eugene O'Neill after 12 years." *PM*, 11 Oct.

O'Neill contributes nothing especially new to the dream idea.

1188. Krutch, Joseph Wood. "Drama." *Nation*, 163 (26 Oct.) 481-482.

Comparable in many ways to *The Wild Duck*, and contains more of O'Neill's sincerity, which removes him from any other playwright.

1189. McCarthy, Mary. "Dry ice." *Partisan Rev.*, 13 (Nov.-Dec.) 577-579. [Reprinted in Miss McCarthy's *Sights and spectacles, 1937-1956*, NY, Farrar & Strauss, 1956, pp. 81-88 (No. 76).]

O'Neill frankly cannot write. He is estranged from all influences and impressions, a man laughing in a square, empty room.

1190. Nathan, George Jean. "The Iceman Cometh, seeth, conquereth." NY *Jour-Am.*, 14 Oct.

The theatre is once more dramatically alive. Play approaches essential tragedy, and is far above any attempts by others in the intervening 12 years.

1191. "O'Neill's Iceman." *Newsweek,* 28 (21 Oct.) 92.

Too much of a good thing, though characters are developed with warmth and good humor.

1192. "O'Neill speaks." *Cue,* 19 Oct.

Like a slow motion magic trick; almost, but not quite, comes off.

1193. "The ordeal of Eugene O'Neill." *Time,* 48 (21 Oct.) 71.

As a drama, not much deeper than a puddle. This article is mainly about O'Neill, finding him not a great dramatist but our greatest dramatic craftsman.

1194. Pegler, Westbrook. "Sinks his sharp tongs in O'Neill's Iceman." NY *Jour-Am.,* 8 Nov.

The play never even starts — it is worse than a schoolgirl of 8 would write. Work is slapdash; nobody talks that much.

1195. Phelan, Kappo. "The Iceman Cometh." *Commonweal,* 45 (25 Oct.) 44-46.

The play is daring on its esthetic level, but must be judged by its level of content. This critic wishes O'Neill would definitely choose his God or gods, Devil or devils.

1196. Pollock, Arthur. "Edmond Rostand and Eugene O'Neill get the theater back on its feet." Brook. *Eagle,* 13 Oct.

With *Cyrano* and *ICEMAN* now playing there is much to praise in the theatre. Still there are times when the O'Neill play is quite a bore, but it is something that makes you think.

1197. Shipley, Joseph T. "Iceman cometh: Chill from the world of doom." *New Leader,* 19 Oct.

It is too sprawling. O'Neill is constantly struggling to integrate his theme.

1198. Single, E. A. "Eugene O'Neill, our foremost dramatist, returns triumphantly in Iceman." *Jour. Comm.*, 11 Oct.
O'Neill has lost none of his matchless skill in creating characters. Memorable experience in theatre going.

1199. Watts, Richard, Jr. "The controversies cometh over O'Neill's new play." NY *Post*, 19 Oct.
Watts takes sharp issue with North's book review (No. 1165) and sees the play even more tremendous as a book. O'Neill's philosophy is not so important as the humanity.

1200. Woolf, S. J. "Eugene O'Neill returns after 12 years." NY *Times*, 15 Sept., VI, p. 11.
Informal account of interview with O'Neill before play opening.

1201. Wyatt, Euphemia Van R. "Who against hope believed in hope." *Cath. Wld.*, 164 (Nov.) 168-169.
Horrid, brutal, unflinching, yet with piercing analysis, truth, and insight. Bears mark of great playwright.

1202. Young, Stark. "O'Neill and Rostand." *New Rep.*, 115 (21 Oct.) 517-518. [Reprinted in Young's *Immortal shadows*, NY, Scribners, 1948 (No. 148).]
General review of plot, scenery, acting; very little criticism.

1947-1953

1203. Alexander, Doris M. "Hugo of The Iceman Cometh: Realism and O'Neill." *Am. Quar.*, 5 (Winter 1953) 357-366.
Attempting to show that O'Neill's portrayal of Hugo was not the literary abstraction Bentley (No. 1172) and others thought, Miss Alexander proves conclusively through document and photograph that Hugo was the nearly literal translation of an O'Neill acquaintance, Hippolyte Havel. In conclusion, she shows the basic deficiency of the play because of its portrayal of a series of static characters.

1204 Arestad, Sverre. "The Iceman Cometh and the Wild Duck." *Scand. Stud.*, 20 (Feb. 1948) 1-11.

The two plays have much in common in exposing man's refusal to accept the truth as basis of life. Ibsen is optimistic, O'Neill pessimistic.

1205. Burke, Ed. "New York plays." *Player's Mag.*, 23 (Jan.-Feb. 1947) 58-59.

Some of the most penetratingly analytic writing on the stage in a long time.

1206. Dobree, Bonamy. "Mr. O'Neill's latest play." *Sewanee Rev.*, 56 (Jan.-Mar. 1948) 118-126.

This article, pursuing the question "Where is O'Neill taking us in this play?" concludes he uses more techniques of the novel than of the play.

1207. Gaynor, Leonard. "O'Neill's Iceman seen as ghost of Ibsen's Wild Duck." NY *Her-Trib.*, 2 Mar. 1947.

Comparison of many aspects of plot and theme. Ibsen is somewhat better because of the tragedy that he keeps pent up, while O'Neill's tragedy has occurred before the play begins.

1208. Gilder, Rosamond. "Broadway laurels." *Th. Arts*, 31 (June 1947) 16.

Not sufficiently above other O'Neill plays to merit the Pulitzer prize.

1209. Hopkins, Vivian C. "The Iceman seen through The Lower Depths." *Coll. Eng.*, 11 (Nov. 1949) 81-87.

Interesting comparison, showing why O'Neill is more negative in his conclusion that death is the only solution. Gorki becomes far more dramatic, despite his errors regarding the perfect society and revolution.

1210. Morgan, Frederick. "The season on Broadway." *Sewanee Rev.*, 55 (Apr. 1947) 344-346.

O'Neill treats nothing beyond the most crude and general level because his characters have lost all humanity. The play lacks good dialogue.

1211. Muchnic, Helen. "Circe's swine: Plays by Gorky and O'Neill." *Comp. Lit.*, 3 (Spring 1951) 119-128.

Excellent analysis of *Lower Depths* and *ICEMAN*, showing their wide divergence. Gorki maintains man is in an evil society; O'Neill maintains man himself is evil.

1212. Winther, Sophus. "The Iceman Cometh: A study in technique." *Ariz. Quar.*, 3 (Winter 1947) 293-300.

Detailed analysis of O'Neill's use of the paradox as an instrument of tragedy in character, action, settings.

Opening night reviews — Circle-in-the-Square Revival
New York — Newspapers of 9 May 1956

1213. Atkinson, Brooks, "O'Neill tragedy revived." NY *Times*, 38:1.

Major production of a major theatrical work. O'Neill achieves value on level with Ibsen, Gorki, Strindberg.

1214. Coleman, Robert. "O'Neill's Iceman deserveth revival." NY *Mirror*.

Eminently deserves revival, an absorbing cavalcade of humanity on the rack. O'Neill at his most interesting in plays about people he knew.

1215. Dash, Thomas R. "The Iceman Cometh." *W. W. Daily*.

Anticipates Becket's *Waiting for Godot*. We cannot identify with these people, so it is not good tragedy.

1216. Hawkins, William. "Circle cast revives Iceman." NY *Wor-Tel. & Sun*.

There is not one dull or indifferent moment. O'Neill is bitter but compassionate, and play reveals new, biting vividness.

1217. Kerr, Walter. "Iceman revived at Circle in the Square." NY *Her-Trib*.

The author's compulsive conviction is our own. Play is verbose, but built "like a drunken, somnambulistic dance." O'Neill is ready for reexamination and this revival should do it.

1218. McClain, John. "Iceman's message too elusive." NY *Jour-Am*.

O'Neill in one of his most depressed moods. Audience is in for a long haul.

1219. Watts, Richard, Jr. "The revival of O'Neill's Iceman." NY *Post*.

A pleasure and honor to see it again, the work of titanic power, quite possibly is O'Neill's finest drama. Deep insight into human heart, closer to *Godot* than to Gorky.

Other reviews and criticism
1956 (One entry dated 1958)

1220. Atkinson, Brooks. "Iceman returns." NY *Times*, 20 May, II, 1:1.

O'Neill essentially romantic, driven by a romantic dream. His characters are romantic, and heroes to themselves. This play ranks with *DESIRE* and *ELECTRA* as O'Neill in his greatest form.

1221. Day, Cyrus. "The Iceman and the bridegroom: Some observations on the death of O'Neill's salesman." *Mod. Drama*, 1 (May 1958) 3-9.

Asking if there is a more nihilistic play in drama, Day shows O'Neill's pessimistic anti-Christian approach through a correlation of Hickey with the Biblical bridegroom in Mark 25:5-6. Whole play points to man's destiny of awaiting Death and fulfillment through annihilation. Day shows some interesting parallels between the characters and the men and women surrounding Jesus at the time of his death.

1222. Gassner, John. "Broadway in Review." *Ed. Th. Jour.*, 8(Oct.) 224-225. [Reprinted in Hewitt, Barnard, *Theatre, USA*, NY, McGraw-Hill, 1959, pp. 479-481 (No. 56).]

A devastating and exhilarating experience.

1223. Gibbs, Wolcott. "Good old Hickey." *New Yorker*, 32 (26 May) 72-74.

The revival is better appreciated than the original because

its great length is expected and not a hindrance. All modern tragedies seem like soap operas compared with this.

1224. Hatch, Robert. "Theatre." *Nation*, 182 (26 May) 458.
O'Neill works with acid that eats deep. Leaves you glad you do not have to wrestle with a Hickey yourself.

1225. Hayes, Richard. "Waiting for Hickey." *Commonweal*, 64 (24 Aug.) 515-516.
Pain and personal upheaval is made into art by some inexplainable process. Main shortcoming is lack of any sense of possibility or of reality.

1226. Hewes, Henry. "Derelictical materialism." *Sat. R.*, 39 (26 May) 24.
In spite of obvious artificialities, it is a good production. The characters are "desperately real."

1227. "The Iceman Cometh." *Variety*, 16 May.
A brilliant study of self-delusion.

1228. Lewis, Theophilus. "The Iceman Cometh." *America*, 95 (June) 251.
An intellectual challenge. One cannot quite decide what O'Neill is saying, and we do not have to believe him.

1229. Mannes, Marya. "Theatre: A matter of style." *Reporter*, 14 (28 June) 35-36.
O'Neill makes all modern "realists" seem mannered, crude, and sterile. The play moves relentlessly toward Hickey's doom.

1230. Oppenheimer, George. "Long night's journey." *Newsday*, 25 May.
The stuff of which nightmares are made. Better than *Lower Depths;* a bitter play, reflecting O'Neill's bitter life.

1231. Wyatt, Euphemia Van R. "The Iceman Cometh." *Cath. Wld.*, 183 (July) 310.
The fact nobody leaves the play is some kind of proof of O'Neill's "haunted genius."

ILE

Reviews of first Greenwich Village production
1918

1232. Allen, Kelcey. "Fourth bill presented by Frank Conroy." NY *News Record,* 20 Apr.
Intensely dramatic, a fine piece of writing.

1233. "Art improves at Greenwich village theatre." NY *Herald,* 21 Apr.
Displays the start of skill and power in the young writer, "son of James O'Neill."

1234. Broun, Heywood. "Greenwich Village players." NY *Tribune,* 21 Apr.
Disapproval of making the wife go mad for no adequate reason. It shows lack of inventiveness.

1235. Gardy, Louis. Review of the Greenwich bill. NY *Call,* 22 May.
Biggest attraction on the bill; highly dramatic, if not always artistic.

1236. "Greenwich players in 3 new acts." Brook. *Eagle,* 19 Apr.
Nothing new here; *ILE* something of a *tour de force.*

1237. "Greenwich Village bill." NY *Telegram,* 19 Apr.
A grim little play with the writing better than the acting.

1238. "The Greenwich Village theatre." NY *Post,* 19 Apr.
A certain vigor, but too obvious as a shocker to have much value as realism.

1239. Hornblow, Arthur. "Mr. Hornblow goes to the play." *Theatre,* 27 (June) 356.
It's a mercy that the audience does not lose its mind also.

1240. "Ile." NY *Drama Mirror*, 78 (4 May) 620.
Typical of the young writer. Vigorously characterized, tense, cheerless.

1241. Mantle, Burns. "Greenwich Village players offer 3 short plays." NY *Mail*, 19 Apr.
Obviously theatrical, not so good as *IN THE ZONE*, but still this "son of James O'Neill" has gift of realism and characterization.

1242. "New bill at the Greenwich Village." NY *Globe*, 19 Apr.
Much interest in this man O'Neill. This play is the only one on the bill worthy of praise.

1243. "A new bill at the Greenwich Village." NY *Times*, 19 Apr., 13:3.
Not pleasant, but vigorously characterized; another of these sea plays "owed" to O'Neill.

1244. Sherwin, Louis. "New bill at the Greenwich Village." NY *Globe*, 19 Apr.
Young O'Neill arouses interest, seems to have promise. Wonder what he can do with a three-act.

1245. Smith, Agnes. Review of Greenwich Village bill. NY *Telegraph*, 19 Apr.
Written with some literary distinction. Effective if you like this sort of thing.

1246. "Village players present best bill." *Jour. Comm.*, 22 Apr.
ILE attracts most attention; morbid, depressing, strongly written.

1247. "Village theatre stirs patriotism." NY *Sun*, 19 Apr.
O'Neill's idealistic sense of drama is perhaps too idealistic because he pictures the actors carrying his work to the audience with the same refined sense of his own.

IN THE ZONE

Opening night reviews — New York
Newspapers of 1 Nov. 1917
(One magazine review dated 10 Nov.
also included)

1248. Block, Ralph. "The Washington Square players in 4 one-acters." NY *Tribune.*
Not the best play on the bill.

1249. "The Comedy opens season." NY *Sun.*
The play is tense, but not exciting as it could be because of early emphasis on comedy.

1250. Dale, Alan. "Worth while is new bill at Comedy." NY *American.*
The best of the bill; good idea and good thrills.

1251. "Four plays to start season for players." NY *Herald.*
Praise for realism; held audience well. Ingenious dramatic effects.

1252. "In the Zone." NY *Drama Mirror*, 77 (10 Nov.) 5-7.
Appealing and exciting; does not go off into melodrama.

1253. "In the Zone at the Comedy." NY *World.*
A significant play; effective realism of a Conrad.

1254. Mantle, Burns. "Washington Square Players present James O'Neill's son as a new playwright." NY *Mail.*
"This boy's first play . . . easily the best thing in the opening bill . . ."

1255. "New play bill from Washington Square." NY *Times,* 13:3.
Tense O'Neill sea play marks top of the evening; sense of tragedy.

1256. "New season of short plays at the Comedy . . ." NY *World*.
Dialogue out of all proportion to substance of play; does have a certain amount of real suspense.

1257. "Play season opens for Washington Square." NY *Sun*.
Much dialogue about the box could have been done away with.

1258. Sherwin, Louis. "The Washington Square players at the Comedy." NY *Globe*.
A young man capable of writing this has a marvelous gift. This play quite enough reason to go see the bill.

1259. "The Washington Square players." NY *Post*.
A clever thriller of the "sell" variety.

1260. "The Washington Square players at the Comedy." NY *Telegram*.
"A bit of human history which holds the interest and sympathy of the spectator."

1261. Wolf, Rennold. "Players begin Comedy season." NY *Telegraph*.
"Grim little story" most effective because of the unusual setting.

LAZARUS LAUGHED

This play is reviewed in its published form from Nos. 1262 to 1269. The Pasadena Playhouse production is included in Nos. 1270 to 1274. The Fordham University version begins with No. 1275.

Book

1262. Aiken, Conrad. "Lazarus Laughed." NY *Post*, 24 Dec. 1927.

Much that is fine; "pitched a little too high" and comes close to parody. Lacks humor, too serious and grandiose.

1263. Atkinson, Brooks. "Man's challenge to death in Lazarus Laughed." NY *Times*, 27 Nov. 1927, V, 5:1.
Akin to pre-reformation miracle and mystery plays, recovering some of the "primordial impulses of drama." Ranks with heroic poetry in its creative imagination.

1264. —— — —. "O'Neill again on the horizon." NY *Times*, 11 Sept. 1927, VIII, 1:2.
If he were not serious, poetic and forceful, this first act would be dismissed as "incohate, unwieldy figment of madness."

1265. Bjorkman, Edwin. "A dramatist of moods." NY *Sun*, 26 Nov. 1927.
The "big idea" is carried out "constructively, dramatically, picturesquely" within O'Neill's limitations. Masks go to verge of absurdity — maybe good on stage but superfluous in reading.

1266. Kalonyme, Louis. "Eugene O'Neill's dithyrambic Lazarus Laughed." *Arts & Dec.*, 27 (Sept. 1927) 68-69.
High praise for this "spiritually liberating dithyrambic poem which should convince all that O'Neill is no morbid pessimist."

1267. Krutch, Joseph Wood. "Beyond life." *Nation*, 126 (4 Jan. 1928) 19.
Whole idea of death being an illusion and permitting laughter is "so effectively bodied forth that it seems true so long as the play endures." Succeeds because of emotional ardor.

1268. Lustig, Norman. "Poetically dramatic." Brook. *Citizen*, 25 Dec. 1927.
Reviews the poetry and legends of this play with Masefield's "Tristan and Isolt." O'Neill seeks truth rather than beauty.

1269. Mumford, Lewis. "Lazarus laughs last." NY *Her-Trib.*, 20 Nov. 1927.
This review traces O'Neill's development from earliest plays to present, showing his treatment of human nature up to this arrival at a positive decision in affirmation of death.

Pasadena

1270. Hersey, F. W. "Lazarus Laughed." *Drama*, 18 (May 1928) 244-246.
Pictures of preparation for production and some actual scenes (pp. 242-243).

1271. Kehoe, M. E. "The amateur stage." *Theatre*, 48 (July 1928) 42-44.
Full page of illustrations of production and general review of the effort put into it.

1272. "Lazarus Laughed." *Rev. of Rev.*, 78 (Oct. 1928) 439-440.
Effectiveness of music discussed. It is possibly a great American opera. Pictures of production.

1273. Stechan, H. O. "Lazarus Laughed." *Billboard*, 40 (21 Apr. 1928) 11.
Reviewing Pasadena Playhouse production, this not unenthusiastic critic sees much real merit, but items like the laughter are monotonous.

1274. "The tributary theatre." *Th. Arts*, 12 (June 1928) 447-448.
3 pictures and brief review. Reports unanimous critical praise for the effort.

Fordham

1275. Atkinson, Brooks. "O'Neill's affirmation." NY *Times*, 9 Apr. 1948, 27:4.
Shallow, sophomoric, hortatory, unwieldy, practically unbearable theatre.

1276. Freedley, George. "Fordham ambitiously offers O'Neill Lazarus Laughed." NY *Telegraph*, 10 Apr. 1948.
Poor acting, monotonous performance mar the first New York production.

1277. Garland, Robert. "University players present O'Neill play." NY *Jour-Am.*, 9 Apr. 1948.
"Over-written, over-wrought, and frequently bombastic." Lazarus talks and talks and talks and the play stands still, or limps in "sophomoric circles."

1278. Hartung, Philip H. "Stage and screen." *Commonweal*, 48 (30 Apr. 1948) 674.
The substitution of the musical note for the laughter is approved. But the play is "biggest lemon" in all O'Neill works, worth forgetting immediately.

1279. Hawkins, William. "Lazarus Laughed — but very gloomily." NY *World-Tel.*, 9 Apr. 1948.
Requires almost superhuman, heroic efforts of even the best players. It is essentially literary.

1280. "Lazarus Laughed." *Variety*, 9 Apr. 1948.
Shows commercial impracticability of the play. As presented it is an ordeal for an evening in the theatre.

1281. Watts, Richard, Jr. "Fordham players in Lazarus Laughed." NY *Post*, 9 Apr. 1948.
Tedious, verbose, pretentious; written beyond a subject playwright could adequately handle.

1282. Wyatt, Euphemia Van R. "The drama." *Cath. Wld.*, 167 (June 1948) 64.
Slumps down into complete ineptitude and bathos.

Other reviews and criticism
1956

1283. Alexander, Doris M. "Lazarus Laughed and Buddha." *Mod. Lang. Quar.* 17 (Dec.) 357-365.
An attempt to clarify the character of Lazarus by a list of saviours "upon whom he has been modeled." He is Christian and Greek (Dionysus) as interpreted by Nietzsche, as well as a lot of Zarathustra. Buddha must be added to make the charac-

ter completely understandable because of his abstractness in time of family danger and the cool quality of his affections. A well documented article developing the entire thesis in Miss Alexander's typically scholarly fashion.

LONG DAY'S JOURNEY INTO NIGHT

Book — 1956

1284. Atkinson, Brooks. "Tragedy behind a tragic masque." NY *Times*, 19 Feb., VII, p. 1.
Prolix and repetitious, but written "by the mind of a great dramatist." Thoroughly absorbing and characteristic work.

1285. Breit, Harvey. "In and out of books." NY *Times*, 19 Feb., VII, 8:1.
An explanation of how the book was published by Yale instead of Random House.

1286. Clurman, Harold. "The O'Neills." *Nation*, 182 (3 Mar.) 182-183.
A valuable play; it does far more good released now than in the proposed 25 years.

1287. Fagin, N. Bryllion. "Remembrance of things past." *New Rep.*, 134 (5 Mar.) 20.
Despite some fog, rises to a poignant clarity which only the poet-dramatist can achieve.

1288. Hewes, Henry. "O'Neill and Faulkner via the abroad way." *Sat. R.*, 39 (20 Oct.) 58.
Like so many O'Neill plays, a work of desperation; abounds in arguments hashed and rehashed.

1289. Krutch, Joseph Wood. "Domestic drama with some difference." *Th. Arts,* 40 (Apr.) 89-91.
More than biography and domestic tragedy; it is modern tragedy of alienation or not belonging, and universal tragedy of search for the cause of our fates.

1290. "The last O'Neill tragedy." *Life,* 40 (12 Mar.) 93-99.
A general review of O'Neill's background and the play, together with some fine pictures of the Stockholm production and of the O'Neill family.

1291. Lewis, Theophilus. "Long Day's Journey." *America,* 95 (5 May) 141.
Impressive play, but not inspiring.

1292. Pickrel, Paul. "Unconventional memoirs." *Harpers,* 212 (Mar.) 96-97.
"It is as much an American tragedy as Dreiser's novel, and it has the power of Dreiser at his best."

1293. Prescott, Orville. "Books of the Times." NY *Times,* 20 Feb., 21:4.
O'Neill's tragic pessimism "is one of the most psychologically interesting of American literary problems." Not up to his best.

1294. Seldes, Gilbert. "Long Day's Journey into Night." *Sat. R.,* 39 (25 Feb.) 15-16.
Does not measure up to the tortured genius of O'Neill. Contains his usual weaknesses.

1295. Whichner, Stephen. "O'Neill's long journey." *Commonweal,* 63 (16 Mar.) 614-615.
Much of the mood of homelessness and helplessness of the early plays. Completely transcends biography. "If our definitions of tragedy do not fit this work, we should perhaps rethink our definitions."

Opening night reviews — New York
Newspapers of 8 Nov. 1956

1296. Atkinson, Brooks. "Theatre: Tragic journey." NY *Times*, 47:2.

"The American theatre acquires stature and size" with this play. The tragedy transcends the material facts.

1297. Chapman, John. "Long Day's Journey into Night a drama of sheer magnificence." NY *News*.

"Exploded like a dazzling skyrocket over the humdrum of Broadway theatricals." A most beautiful play; one of the great dramas of any time.

1298. Colby, Ethel. "Entertainment on Broadway." *Jour. Comm.*

A bitter drama. The script's indictment of the father is "incredible."

1299. Coleman, Robert. "O'Neill's last drama emotional dynamite." NY *Mirror*.

Needs editing; repetitious, yet fascinating. Sprawling, ruggedly chiseled monument "carved from granite." Never touches the heart, but excites admiration.

1300. Dash, Thomas R. "Long Day's Journey into Night." *W. W. Daily*.

Savagely incisive and harrowing, but does not rank with *IN-TERLUDE* or *ELECTRA*. The very nature of the work prevents catharsis or exaltation. Repeats and meanders exasperatingly.

1301. Donnelly, Tom. "A long journey but worth taking." NY *Wor-Tel. & Sun*.

Long and tortuous, but the ultimate effect is "tremendously powerful." Requires patience; early scenes come close to parody.

1302. Kerr, Walter. "Long Day's Journey into Night." NY *Her-Trib*. [Reprinted in Hewitt, Barnard, *Theatre USA*, NY, McGraw-Hill, 1959, pp. 481-482 (No. 56).]

Deliberately, masochistically harrowing, but it is an obligation for anyone who cares about the theatre. "It is a stunning theatrical experience."

1303. McClain, John. "Superb cast supplements O'Neill genius." NY *Jour-Am.*
One can never doubt its stature. "O'Neill makes today's playwrights look a little silly."

1304. Watts, Richard, Jr. "Superb drama by Eugene O'Neill." NY *Post.*
Magnificent and shattering. "Unmistakably" registers O'Neill's giant stature. Play gives the entire season stature.

Other reviews and criticism
1956-1959

1305. Appleyard, J. A. "Long journey's end." *America,* 96 (19 Jan. 1957) 452-454.
O'Neill, for all his sensitivity to human problems, is inarticulate and generally beyond his ability in most of his plays.

1306. Atkinson, Brooks. "One man's truth." NY *Times,* 3 Mar. 1957, II, 1:1.
While the "truth" of O'Neill's family is, of course, hard to determine, even from this play, there is obvious truth in the tensions and loyalties of family life. If it were merely autobiographical the play would not succeed as it has; there are other universal and tragic truths.

1307. — — — —. "O'Neill's journey." NY *Times,* 18 Nov. 1956, II, 1:1.
It is hard to determine if this is O'Neill's greatest, but it ranks with his finest. The end fulfills the tragic definition.

1308. Boulton, Whitney. "Long Day's Journey O'Neill at his best: Monumental play." NY *Telegraph,* 9 Nov. 1956.
The theatre grows up with this, reaching size and power of which it is capable. One of the most important plays in quarter of a century.

1309. Clurman, Harold. "Theatre." *Nation,* 183 (24 Nov. 1956) 466. [Reprinted in Clurman's *Lies like truth,* NY, Macmillan, 1958 (No. 25).]

A play everybody should see and admire.

1310. Cooke, Richard P. "Formation of a playwright." *Wall St. Jour.,* 9 Nov. 1956.

A strong play, weakened by length. It is difficult for the playgoer to assimilate it all. There is enough for a half-dozen family tragedies.

1311. Driver, Tom F. "Long and short of it." *Christ. Cent.,* 74 (20 Feb. 1957) 235.

It takes on artistic stature because it gradually reveals shape of a consistent view of human nature. Here is a picture of Fate which enables us to bear the hell these people are in.

1312. "Eugene O'Neill: A new phase." *Chrysalis,* 9 (1956) No. 5-6, pp. 3-13.

Reviews essence of the play and its place in O'Neill's work. Questions whether or not it is pessimistic or optimistic.

1313. Gassner, John. "Broadway in review." *Ed. Th. Jour.,* 9 (Mar. 1957) 43-44.

Great vibrancy of life. O'Neill makes most other modern writers seem miniscule.

1314. Gibbs, Wolcott. "Doom." *New Yorker,* 32 (24 Nov. 1956) 120.

Despite need of editing and the fact it is often "barbarously" written, it is impressive. It will not go down as a major contribution to the drama of our time.

1315. Hayes, Richard "A requiem for mortality." *Commonweal,* 65 (1 Feb. 1957) 467-468.

Spirals inward to the tragic fact; weaves a "seamless pattern of time, suffering, and nobility" typical of tragedy. Final wisdom and love elevates these people.

1316. Hewes, Henry. "O'Neill: 100 proof — not a blend."
Sat. R., 39 (24 Nov. 1956) 30-31.
It may be "the most universal piece of stage realism ever
turned out by an American playwright."

1317. Hobe. "Long Day's Journey." *Variety*, 14 Nov. 1956.
It may stand as O'Neill's finest play. Tremendous and inspiring;
an unforgettable theatrical experience.

1318. Krutch, Joseph Wood. "The rediscovery of Eugene
O'Neill." NY *Times*, 21 Oct. 1956, VI, pp. 32-34.
A review of O'Neill's artistry in an attempt to determine
whether or not he will remain in our literature after this revival
of interest. Concludes with a discussion of the tragic view as
shown in *LONG DAY'S JOURNEY.*

1319. Lerner, Max. "To face my dead at last." NY *Post*,
7 Jan. 1957.
". . . . no one, after seeing it, can be content again with anything less than the unflinching truth about his work, his world,
and himself."

1320. "Long Day's Journey into Night." *Th. Arts*, 41 (Jan.
1957) 25-26.
It is a play as well as frank autobiography and it commands
attention. It can lay claim as one of his finest works.

1321. "Long Day's Journey into Night." *Vogue*, 128 (15
Nov. 1956) 105.
Includes small picture of O'Neill family in New London.

1322. Mannes, Marya. "A dissenting opinion on the O'Neill
play." *Reporter*, 15 (13 Dec. 1956) 38-39.
A rare theatrical experience, but it is not a great play nor a
great tragedy. Too embarrassingly personal.

1323 ."New play in Manhattan." *Time*, 68 (19 Nov.
1956) 57.
May constitute his most substantial legacy to the American

stage. O'Neill has achieved more here by "stripping himself bare" than he did with masks.

1324. "O'Neill's youth on U.S. stage." *Life*, 41 (19 Nov. 1956) 123-128.
Several fine pictures of the play, and three of interior and exterior of the original home in New London.

1325. Oppenheimer, George. "The tragic truth." *Newsday*, 16 Nov. 1956.
There has been no family so haunted since Oedipus. But O'Neill never loses his love for his people. It is something to see for all its faults of being prolix, prosy, and montonous.

1326. Raleigh, John Henry. "O'Neill's Long Day's Journey and New England Irish-Catholicism." *Partisan Rev.*, 26 (Fall 1959) 573-592.
Interesting and detailed study of this play's autobiographical qualities as they reflect the traditions and the mores of American Irish-Catholics.

1327. Rubinstein, Annette. "The dark journey of Eugene O'Neill." *Mainstream*, 10 (Apr. 1957) 29-33.
In reviewing O'Neill's portrayal of his family, this article shows how the playwright has frequently written two plays at once — philosophic "false conclusion" and the artist's "truthful presentation." This play throws this contradiction into "startling relief."

1328. "Theatre notes." *English*, 12 (Spring 1959) 140.
Powerfully compelling. Not uplifting; an "orgy of accusation." Stark, excorciating.

1329. "Triumph from the past." *Newsweek*, 48 (19 Nov. 1956) 117.
Less a play than willful act of autobiographical catharsis. The mark of America's greatest living playwright even in death.

1330. Winther, Sophus Keith. "O'Neill's tragic themes: Long Day's Journey." *Ariz. Quar.*, 13 (Winter 1957) 295-307.

Important play because of the revelation of O'Neill's creative life. Father is symbol of evil, and home as a place of failure and death — items present in the most important of his other plays.

1331. Wyatt, Euphemia Van R. "Long Day's Journey into Night." *Cath. Wld.*, 184 (Jan. 1957) 306.
Sartre's Hell is less violent than this.

LOST PLAYS

Book Reviews — 1950

1332. Brown, John Mason. "Finders keepers, losers weepers; ugly business of publication of Lost Plays of Eugene O'Neill." *Sat. R. Lit.*, 33 (17 June) 28.
Resounding condemnation of the shoddy, if legal, practice of exploitation of unpublished MMS. No decent excuse for the publication over O'Neill's protest; the copyright laws should be changed.

1333. Clark, Barrett H. "Lost Plays of Eugene O'Neill." *Th. Arts*, 34 (July) 7.
Nothing much in these plays; cannot imagine them being produced.

1334. Colin, Saul. "Without O'Neill's imprimatur." NY *Times*, 18 June, VII, 4:3.
In discussion of other famous works published after death against writers' wishes, Colin finds these plays "extremely stageable."

1335. Eaton, Walter Prichard. "Young O'Neill." NY *Her-Trib.*, 25 June.

Publication of these "juvenile ineptitudes" is deplorable; they can cause O'Neill admirers only pain.

1336. Freedley, George. "Lost Plays of Eugene O'Neill." *Library Jour.*, 75 (15 June) 1048.
Crude and bathetic; for library collections only, though there is a spark of genius.

1337. Pollock, Arthur. "Guide for the young playwright." NY *Compass*, 7 June.
Plays are condemned as the floundering of an inept writer.

1338. R.H. "Lost plays of Eugene O'Neill." *New Rep.*, 123 (28 Aug.) 21.
Extraordinary workmanship. The plays are tightly organized.

1339. Wagner, Charles. "Books." NY *Mirror*, 18 June.
This should be welcomed because it fills in a chunk of the O'Neill mosaic never seen before. All of the plays have a "strange fascination."

1340. Watts, Richard, Jr. "The early sins of Eugene O'Neill." NY *Post*, 23 June.
The publication was a shabby deed, but O'Neill will not suffer.

MARCO MILLIONS

The published version is reviewed from No. 1341 to No. 1356. Reviews of the Theatre Guild production begin with No. 1357. Other reviews and criticism start with No. 1374.

Book

1341. Atkinson, Brooks. "Marco Polo as an American merchant prince." NY *Times*, 15 May 1927, III, 6:1.

Common vein of satire, but background and impulses are O'Neill.

1342. Canfield, Mary Cass. "The albatross afoot." *Sat. R. Lit.*, 4 (10 Sept. 1927) 102.
O'Neill's past writing of passion and "blasting sincerity" is likened to Emersonian "self-moved, self-absorbed" man or to Baudelair's albatross afoot.

1343. Eaton, Walter Prichard. "A cycle of Cathay." NY *Her-Trib.*, 29 May 1927.
Not a comedy, but the same O'Neill following the Gleam to far Cathay.

1344. Firkins, O. W. "O'Neill and other playwrights." *Yale Rev.*, 17 (Oct. 1927) 173-174.
Real stuff of drama is here, but questions why writers must go so far in their satire of America. Admiration for O'Neill's "refusal to be tethered by success."

1345. Garland, Robert. "Well, what of it?" NY *Telegram*, 23 May 1927.
"A swell Eugene O'Neill drama to stay away from."

1346. Gilder, Rosamond. "Theatre Arts bookshelf." *Th. Arts*, 11 (Sept. 1927) 724-725.
Gorgeous and far-flung pageant, a challenge to any producer. An allegory, with moral of definite interest and application.

1347. Krutch, Joseph Wood. "Marco the westerner." *Nation*, 124 (18 May 1927) 562-564.
Krutch likes the spiritual depth realized in both the "idealized Orientals" and the "shallow, bumptious complacency" of Marco.

1348. Macy, John. "O'Neill's wise and humorous Marco Millions." NY *World*, 22 May 1927.
Glorious satire, streak of burlesque, does not slide to farce.

1349. "Marco Millions." *Outlook*, 146 (29 June 1927) 292.
Some good poetry. O'Neill still is an "incorrigible mystic" but he can write satire.

1350. "Marco Millions — Theatric travelog." *Dramatist*, 18 (July 1927) 1341-1342.

No plot, no problem, no sequence. It is not a play; O'Neill's style "is not art, it's abortion."

1351. Nathan, George Jean. "O'Neill's new play." *Am. Merc.*, 8 (Aug. 1926) 499-505.

Long detailed review of plot. O'Neill is a man not unaware of sardonic humor even in most tragic drama, says Nathan, and in this play answers those who say he has no sense of humor.

1352. Roedder, Karsten. "The book parade." Brook. *Citizen*, 19 June 1927.

O'Neill's first bid for the library makes perfect transition from stage. In many respects his best play, a "perfectly constructed farce."

1353. Simon, Bernard "Some notes on Marco Millions." NY *Her-Trib.*, 22 May 1927.

A superb piece of literature which will depend much on the production for its effect.

1354. Untitled item. *New Yorker*, 28 May 1927.

The satire is superb, with lots of poetry and wisdom.

1355. Watts, Richard, Jr. "Marco Millions versus Marco Polo." NY *Her-Trib.*, 12 June 1927.

Instead of sympathy, this shows hatred of Polo. Watts wonders why he is made a "bumptious ass" and "clownish dolt."

1356. Whipple, Leon. "Scripts for the summer solstice." *Survey*, 58 (1 July 1927) 390.

"Bravura piece" which shows more sureness instead of the gropings of previous O'Neill. "Intellectual mastery of the material."

Opening night reviews — New York
Newspapers of 10-11 Jan. 1928

1357. Allen, Kelcey. "Marco Millions is poignant O'Neill satire." *W. W. Daily*, 10 Jan.
An eventful night in the theatre. The play is "corruscating satire, biting in irony, suffused with poetry, rich and dramatic."

1358. Anderson, John. "Marco Millions gorgeous spectacle." NY *Jour.*, 11 Jan.
Expansive, expensive, opulent, colorful and utterly beautiful. O'Neill in gayest mockery, almost lighthearted. Despite looseness and tiresome verbosity, it has poetic beauty in writing.

1359. Atkinson, Brooks. "Eugene O'Neill's gorgeous satire." NY *Times*, 10 Jan., 28:2.
It is a tragedy of emotion as well as satire.

1360. Cohen, Julius. "Marco Millions." *Jour. Comm.*, 11 Jan.
Masterpiece of writing. O'Neill was never more poetical or satirical.

1361. Coleman, Robert. "Marco Millions fine tragic play by Eugene O'Neill." NY *Mirror*, 11 Jan.
Amusing, heart-breaking, blending humor and grim drama, sympathetic and ironic. Prose soars to meet poetry. A fine play, flawless, without a single dull moment.

1362. Dale, Alan. "Marco Millions by Eugene O'Neill." NY *American*, 10 Jan.
Voluminous, sketchy, occasionally tiresome and "inordinately flimsy"; almost a travelogue with words. Never drab, but a sense of humor might have helped.

1363. Gabriel, Gilbert. "Marco Millions." NY *Sun*, 10 Jan.
The poetry raises it above being merely dramatic or undramatic. This has much strength and power.

1364. Hall, Leonard. "Theatre Guild presents its first Eugene O'Neill play." NY *Telegram*, 10 Jan.

O'Neill's uppercut to the "quivering jaws" of those who said he had no humor; it is a very comical creation.

1365. Hammond, Percy. "Marco Millions." NY *Her-Trib.,* 10 Jan.
Interesting satire; splendid and thoughtful burlesque.

1366. Higley, Philo. "New O'Neill play at Guild." NY *Telegraph,* 10 Jan.
If intended as a spectacle, then it succeeds. If a drama with dominant theme, then perhaps not. But much of it stirs impressively to life in stately, if wearisome, stride.

1367. "Immortal Marco." *Wall St. Jour.,* 11 Jan.
A complete delight; a beautiful play of infinite intent. Not often is such literary achievement so well treated, histrionically and pictorially.

1368. Littell, Robert. "Mr. O'Neill pillories a Venetian Babbitt." NY *Post,* 10 Jan.
O'Neill, taking a vacation from his post as our greatest playwright, is way below par, surprisingly "simple minded, obvious, foolish." Delights the eye, distracts the ear.

1369. Mantle, Burns. "Marco Millions impressive." NY *News,* 10 Jan.
The story is stimulating to the imagination. An unusual and altogether satisfying evening.

1370. Osborn, E. W. "Marco Millions." NY *World,* 10 Jan.
O'Neill's high mark up to this moment. Almost poetic in handling of Kukachin.

1371. Pollock, Arthur. "The Theatre Guild does a play by O'Neill at last." Brook. *Eagle.*
Worth "something less than the time" it takes to present it. Not one of his best. Could be said more easily, briefly, persuasively in simple 3-act play.

1372. Winchell, Walter. "O'Neill the clown. NY *Eve. Graphic.*

Pictorially gorgeous. O'Neill never so gay and kidding. For the most part unique and enchanting, an artistic if not prosperous achievement.

1373. Woollcott, Alexander. "Marco Polo of Zenith." NY *World*.
The Babbitt theme is now a little worn; this is an elaborate way of saying the same thing.

Other reviews and criticism
1928

1374. "After Babbitt what?" *Daily Worker*, 16 Jan.
Excellent satire, fourth rate poetry, excellent fun. But O'Neill really knows nothing about what makes up the modern business man. Despite faults, it should be seen.

1375. Atkinson, Brooks. "After the battle." NY *Times*, 22 Jan., VIII, 1:1.
Much of value, though it may not come across because O'Neill is not a wit and he cannot express his thoughts clearly.

1376. Benchley, Robert. "The prevalent scoffing." *Life*, 91 (26 Jan.) 19.
Splendid production hurt mainly by satire coming too late.

1377. Brackett, Charles. "Tears and spectacles." *New Yorker*, 3 (21 Jan.) 25.
Obvious, repetitious, dull. Others have taken the subject and done it much better.

1378. Brown, John Mason. "New York goes native." *Th. Arts*, 12 (March) 163-166.
More than a satire, for O'Neill never intended it to be just that. More nearly tragic in the disintegration of Marco.

1379. Carb, David. "Marco Millions." *Vogue*, 71 (1 Mar.) 82-83.

Does nothing, causes nothing to happen, is not even good theatre; it was not worth producing.

1380. Clark, Barrett H. "Eugene O'Neill and the Guild." *Drama*, 18 (Mar.) 169-171.
Reviews *MARCO* and *INTERLUDE* together, finding the former "minor."

1381. De Casseres, Benjamin. "Broadway to date." *Arts & Dec.*, 28 (Mar.) 62.
A "whack in the face" after reading the original. Production is much too heavy with too much caricature.

1382. "Digging for Marco Polo." Brook. *Eagle*, 8 Jan.
Interesting account of some of the historical points which O'Neill observes in the play.

1383. Farquhar, E. F. "Marco Millions." *Letters* (Univ. of Kentucky) 1 (Nov.) 33-40.
A provocative comment on the purpose behind writing "poetic" drama. This play, says Farquhar, is not poetry, but he approves of it more than plays like *GREAT GOD BROWN*, which "fuss and fume."

1384. Gabriel, Gilbert. "The boor of Venice." NY *Sun*, 16 Jan.
The play proves the possibility of singing freely, with tongue in cheek. Admiration for O'Neill power to "read into a curious and devious travelogue such living scorn and modern beauty."

1385. — — — —. "The newer O'Neill." *Van. F.*, 30 (Apr.) 52-53.
MARCO and *INTERLUDE* show that O'Neill is the most influential and contributive playwright America has yet produced.

1386. Gould, Bruce. "O'Neill takes a crack at Babbitt." *Wall St. News*, 12 Jan.
Thrilling beautiful production, but O'Neill "falls far." Stinging disappointment. Apparently a "slashing thoughtless attempt" to say his angry say about money mad people.

1387. Hammond, Percy. "Marco Millions a rich and sardonic extravaganza." NY *Her-Trib.,* 15 Jan.
Further comments upon reflecting back on the play.

1388. Houghton, William M. "East and west." NY *Sun,* 22 Apr.
It is important to behave as we are, rather than to put on appearances of another society; hence Polo's leaving Kukachin behind is approved.

1389. Krutch, Joseph Wood. "Marco Millions." *Nation,* 126 (25 Jan.) 104-105.
Great purity of outline with a "delicacy of execution." The other treatments of Babbitt theme now seem "raucous and dull."

1390. Leland, Gordon M. "Marco Millions." *Billboard,* 40 (21 Jan.) 10.
Can be called "hooey" or "tripe" or whatever; unpoetic, theatrically dull. Shaw does it much better.

1391. Mantle, Burns. "Mr. O'Neill writes a comedy." NY *News,* 15 Jan.
For once we would like to think of O'Neill as happy, and this play seems written without the burden of the cares of the world on his shoulder.

1392. "Marco Millions." *Variety,* 11 Jan.
Will add prestige to the Guild.

1393. "Marco Millions O'Neill's latest, done by Guild." NY *Review,* 14 Jan.
Satire obvious, humor not overly spontaneous or keen.

1394. "Marco Polo masquerading as Babbitt." *Lit. D.,* 96 (4 Feb.) 26-27.
Three illustrations. Some excerpts from press reviews.

1395. Nathan, George Jean. "Judging the shows." *Judge,* 94 (4 Feb.) 19.

"Uncommonly well-wrought play" adding luster to American drama.

1396. "O'Neill and his plays." NY *Times,* 8 Jan., VIII, 2:4.
Article traces history of development of the play plus a summary of O'Neill's past history with Provincetown and others.

1397. "O'Neill took few liberties with life of Marco Polo." NY *American,* 22 Jan.
Review of some of the historical facts which O'Neill made use of.

1398. Osborn, E. W. "The theatres." NY *World,* 14 Jan.
Osborn reviews some of the facts about Polo which O'Neill did and did not follow in constructing the play.

1399. Pollock, Arthur. "Eugene O'Neill and Marco Millions." Brook. *Eagle,* 15 Jan.
Because O'Neill is "bent on growing" instead of just developing naturally, his plays get longer and less comprehensible. Marco Millions is at times actually banal. Too wide and flat — he should try to make the point, rather than adorn it.

1400. Sayler, Oliver M. "The play of the week." *Sat. R. Lit.,* 4 (11 Feb.) 590.
Pales into insignificance beside Nina Leeds; could have been written with his left hand.

1401. Shipley, Joseph. "Babbitt Billions." NY *New Leader,* 14 Jan.
First act weakens it. O'Neill is too indignant about moderns to treat his theme well.

1402. Skinner, Richard Dana. "Marco Millions." *Commonweal,* 7 (25 Jan.) 986.
Little of dramatic importance, few moments of authentic drama, a "Strange Interlude" in the career of our premiere dramatist.

1403. Young, Stark. "Dilations." *New Rep.,* 53 (25 Jan.) 272-273.

Much promise of an extraordinary drama, but lacks delineation of satire and lyricism. The satire is spread over too wide a field.

MARCO MILLIONS was given a revival of 8 performances beginning 3 March 1930. New York newspapers reviewed the play, finding it very little different from the original.

A MOON FOR THE MISBEGOTTEN

Opening night reviews — Columbus, Ohio, Tryout
Newspapers of 21 Feb. 1947

1404. Kissel, Bud. "Two much conversation in A Moon for the Misbegotten." Columbus *Citizen*.
Cast wasted time on an unimportant play. Mostly conversation. Action occurs only when somebody picks up a bottle and drinks. Beautiful story to tell but too much time telling it, a *Tobacco Road* with an all Irish cast.

1405. McGavran, Mary V. "O'Neill lifts curtain on sympathetic drama." Columbus *Ohio State Journal*.
Represents all the art that is theatre, but it is not arty. Shows O'Neill talent for stripping the comic mask from life and revealing it naked and afraid.

1406. "New play by O'Neill opens in Columbus." NY *Times*, 16:2.
This "conventional" play is about "straightforward lust to obscure psychological complexes."

1407. Wilson, Samuel T. "A Moon for the Misbegotten has world premiere here." Columbus *Dispatch*.
Arresting and fine play. Third act has muted beauty, a tremendous emotional impact.

Other reviews and criticism, including published version
1947-1954

1407. Adams, Phoebe Lou. "The inner truth." *Atlantic,*
190 (Sept. 1952) 76.
Thoroughly interesting plot; more readable than most of
his works.

1409. Bentley, Eric. "Eugene O'Neill's pieta." *New Rep.,*
127 (4 Aug. 1952) 17. [Reprinted in Bentley's *The dramatic
event,* NY, Horizon Press, 1954, pp. 30-33.]
Will change nobody's views; not O'Neill's best or worst. Better
than some recent plays, so much the worse for recent plays.

1410. Carroll, Joseph. "A play Broadway could use." *Th.
Arts,* 36 (Sept. 1952) 6-7.
Scholars of theatre should take a new look at O'Neill. Other
writers may "approach his best or surpass his worst" but none
equal his achievements.

1411. Clurman, Harold. "Theater." *Nation,* 178 (8 May
1954) 409. [Reprinted in Clurman's *Lies like truth,* NY, Macmillan, 1958 (No. 25).]
Noting the success of *MOON* in Stockholm, Clurman reviews
O'Neill's status as an off-Broadway possibility.

1412. Darrach, Henry B. "Moon in Columbus." *Time,* 49
(3 Mar. 1947) 47.
Brief review of Columbus premiere, with feeling it is much
more impressive than *ICEMAN,* but needs much more work.

1413. Eaton, Walter Prichard. "A bookshelf premiere for
a play by Eugene O'Neill." NY *Her-Trib.,* 3 Aug. 1952.
Increasingly difficult to find a soul in the fumes of Bourbon;
not O'Neill's best and only he could or would have written it.

1414. Freedley, George. "A Moon for the Misbegotten."
Library Journal, 77 (Aug. 1952) 1307.
"Highly recommended."

1415. Jones, Johnny. "A Moon for the Misbegotten." *Billboard*, 1 Mar. 1947.
Usual O'Neill philosophy of frustration. Intricate play that should smooth itself out and do business.

1416. Krutch, Joseph Wood. "Genius is better than talent." *Th. Arts*, 39 (Oct. 1954) 22-23.
This general review finds the play to be an *ANNA CHRISTIE* with an unhappy ending. Lacking the facility of talent, O'Neill does have genius, which is probably better anyway.

1417. McCarthy, Mary. "The farmer's daughter." NY *Times*, 31 Aug. 1952, VII, p. 7.
Crude technique. Still exacts "homage" for its "mythic powers."

Opening night reviews — New York
Newspapers of 3 May 1957

1418. Atkinson, Brooks. "Theatre: O'Neill's last." NY *Times*, 21:2.
No stage production can solve the problems of the play which were evident when it first appeared. It is prolix and uneventful, lacking much of O'Neill's elemental power. A tired work.

1419. Chapman, John. "Wendy Hiller is magnificent in A Moon for the Misbegotten." NY *News*.
Without the impact of *JOURNEY*, but still a compelling piece of theatre; another beautiful O'Neill play.

1420. Dash, Thomas R. "A Moon for the Misbegotten." *W. W. Daily*.
It has all of the virtues and many of the vices of O'Neill's plays. A superb study of people tormenting themselves, spasmodic power, trenchantly realistic, but also overwritten. It is not one of his best.

1421. Donnelly, Tom. "A long night's moongazing." NY *Wor-Tel & Sun*.
The serious playgoer will want to see it, but it will be a labor

of love. O'Neill is close to smothering everything in a mass of tedium.

1422. Gilbert, Justin. "O'Neill play grim, uneven work." NY *Mirror*.

Alternately grubby and funny, grim and poetic. O'Neill's incandescence "barely flickers here and there."

1423. Kerr, Walter. "Moon for the Misbegotten." NY *Her-Trib*.

First half rattled and blathered, without mercy and without meaning. O'Neill seems to have lost his sense of the theatre, although last act is a superb "dance of death."

1424. McClain, John. "O'Neill opus long but fiercely great." NY *Jour-Am*.

Power and grandeur evident, the same fierce qualities of *JOURNEY*. Brings poetry to this squalid place, never losing control of understanding the characters.

1425. Watts, Richard, Jr. "Another moving O'Neill tragedy." NY *Post*.

Suffers from typical faults of length and lack of eloquence, but still moving and shattering. Haunting emotional experience, further proving O'Neill was a titan of the theatre.

Other reviews and criticism
1957

1426. Atkinson, Brooks. "O'Neill's finale." NY *Times*, 12 May, II, 1:1.

A minor work. Only fitfully alive; the tragic drive is missing. O'Neill's grand achievements were over when this was written.

1427. Colby, Ethel. "Entertainment on Broadway." *Jour. Comm.*, 6 May.

The need for condensation is a "glaring fault." Too much reiteration. Rich and vital though it is, it is not up to O'Neill's best.

1428. Cooke, Richard P. "O'Neill's last." *Wall St. Jour.*, 6 May.
Minor O'Neill with touches of greatness; lacks tragic inner fires of *JOURNEY*. The recital of drunken deeds is tiresome.

1429. Driver, Tom F. "Misbegotten." *Christ. Cent.*, 74 (22 May) 657.
O'Neill's loquacity has spun a good one-act play into four. Does not achieve nobility of vision seen in *ICEMAN* or *JOURNEY*. The valid, poignant theme needs lightness.

1430. Gibbs, Wolcott. "A tired Tyrone." *New Yorker*, 33 (11 May) 84.
It is hard to see how this will add much to O'Neill's reputation. His other plays, for all their verbosity, had something to say; this does not.

1431. Hatch, Robert. "Theatre." *Nation*, 184 (18 May) 446.
O'Neill is trying to lay the ghost of his brother. The truth in this play is very evasive; the ending rings false.

1432. Hayes, Richard. "The image and the search." *Commonweal*, 66 (30 Aug.) 541.
"Full of sucking guilt and reddened with whiskey." It does not demand audience response as much as endurance.

1433. Hewes, Henry. "Requiem for a roué." *Sat. R.*, 40 (18 May) 34.
There is too much time spent on trivial things, but it is still a memorable experience.

1434. Lewis, Theophilus. "A Moon for the Misbegotten." *America*, 97 (25 May) 270.
O'Neill is too long getting started. Many early scenes are written with the frenzy of a man who knew he did not have much longer to live.

1435. "A Moon for the Misbegotten." *Th. Arts*, 41 (July) 12-13.
Comparisons to *JOURNEY* and others are unfortunate, but

final impact is worth waiting for. Unhappily the rest of the play does not measure up to the last forty-five minutes.

1436. "More Eugene O'Neill." *Newsweek*, 49 (13 May) 70. O'Neill can no longer transport his characters to the pinnacle of tragedy. A minor work.

1437. "New play in Manhattan." *Time*, 69 (13 May) 91. Too much talk. Becomes a ghost of O'Neill's other plays. It is nothing to be remembered.

1438. Wyatt, Euphemia Van R. "A Moon for the Misbegotten." *Cath. Wld.*, 185 (July) 308-309. It is still too long, too much talk. There is a limitation to alcoholic values. It is sad to think that O'Neill's play is itself so sad.

THE MOON OF THE CARIBBEES

Because newspaper critics generally ignored the early productions of the Provincetown Players, there are only limited reviews of O'Neill's one-act plays. The following are the only two discovered in a search of the files of major New York newspapers.

1918

1439. Broun, Heywood. "Susan Glaspell and George Cook have bright one-act play." NY *Tribune*, 23 Dec. A disappointment in spite of the true dialogue and atmosphere. A pointless tale; Smitty is an uninteresting deep sea snob. The trouble is with the playwright, not the actors.

1440. "Greenwich Village sees new dramas a la Provincetown." NY *Herald*, 21 Dec.

The play is mainly just an interlude; the prelude and afterlude are left to the audience.

Book reviews
1919

The Moon of the Caribbees and Six Other Plays of the Sea was the first volume of O'Neill's plays to be published, other than the abortive *Thirst and Other One Act Plays* of 1914. These are some of the more important notices which it received.

1441. Broun, Heywood. "The Moon of the Caribbees." NY *Tribune*, 4 May.
O'Neill's very unusual talent is confirmed by these plays, which read well.

1442. Clark, Barrett H. "The plays of Eugene O'Neill." NY *Sun*, 18 May.
Our most promising young native playwright.

1443. "Eugene O'Neill's plays." NY *World*, 18 May.
Collection is not for weaklings; does not fear ugly truths. Breezy as a sea gale and realistic as a rocky shore.

1444. Leonard, Baird. "The Moon of the Caribbees." NY *Telegraph*, 17 May.
Pleasant to read, an exception to most published plays.

1445. "Mr. O'Neill's plays." NY *Sun*, 17 May.
These plays show a true theatrical gift.

1446. "The Moon of the Caribbees." *Dial*, 66 (17 May) 524.
Atmosphere of the stage production is still present in the printed version. Action halting; motivation commonplace.

1447. "The Moon of the Caribbees." NY *Globe*, 10 May.
Too many stage directions, but they read better than they act.

1448. "The Moon of the Caribbees." *Rev. of Rev.*, 60 (July) 112.

Should convince us that O'Neill has arrived; he is the Conrad of playwrights.

1449. "The Moon of the Caribbees." *Th. Arts,* 4 (20 Jan.) 80.
"No one has more completely mastered the technique of the one-act play." They read as well as they act.

1450. "Sea plays." NY *Post,* 30 Aug.
Much to gratify the admirers of theatrical thrillers.

1451. "Seven artisans and an artist." *Nation,* 108, (14 June) 948.
O'Neill's best gift is "hard and virile pathos." The introduction of women makes the plays lapse almost into melodrama; he presents them as merely romantic.

MOURNING BECOMES ELECTRA

Opening night reviews — New York
Newspapers of 27 Oct. 1931

1452. Allen, Kelcey. "Mourning Becomes Electra seethes with epic tragedy." *W. W. Daily.*
Magnificent tragedy of classic proportions; has quality as pitiless and remorseless as the original Greek.

1453. Anderson, John. "O'Neill's trilogy." NY *Journal.*
Unreserved praise for masterpiece with strength, clarity and unflagging intuition, putting flesh of modern psychology on the bare bones of impersonal Greek original. Play of "enduring greatness."

1454. Atkinson, Brooks. "Strange images of death in Eugene O'Neill's masterpiece." NY *Times,* 22:1.

Superb strength, coolness and coherence, much Greek but no slavish imitation. Cause of great rejoicing for O'Neill, Guild, drama.

1455. Brown, John Mason. "O'Neill's trilogy Mourning Becomes Electra presented at the Guild theatre." NY *Post*. [Reprinted in Brown's *Two on the aisle,* NY, Norton, 1938, pp. 136-242 (No. 15).]
Proof that the theatre is very much alive; rises above the "scrubby output of our present day theatre" like the Empire State Building above New York.

1456. Coleman, Robert. "Mourning Becomes Electra fascinates brilliant audience." NY *Mirror*.
It will cause a lot of controversy and be subject of much debate.

1457. Gabriel, Gilbert. "Mourning Becomes Electra." NY *American*.
A grand scheme grandly fulfilled. One of the dramatic masterpieces of the world today; O'Neill achieves new stature.

1458. Garland, Robert. "Eugene O'Neill turns out a masterpiece." NY *Wor-Tel*.
Bears out the promise of earlier plays.

1459. Hammond, Percy. "Mr. O'Neill blends Athens, New England, and Broadway in an exciting new tragedy." NY *Her-Trib*.
Easily applauded despite length. O'Neill to be congratulated.

1460. Lockridge, Richard. "Mourning Becomes Electra." NY *Sun*.
An implacable and unrelenting tragedy marking O'Neill's emergence as an artist in the theatre.

1461. Mantle, Burns. "Mourning Becomes Electra." NY *News*.
If we had to have the old story rewritten it was nice O'Neill did it.

1462. Pollock, Arthur. "Broadway sees New Eugene O'Neill play." Brook. *Eagle*.

May not be his most fascinating, but in many ways his best. O'Neill has grown wiser and calmer.

Other reviews and criticism
1931

1463. Atkinson, Brooks. "Tragedy becomes O'Neill." NY *Times*, 1 Nov., VIII, 1:1.

O'Neill's only masterpiece, but not a great play because of lack of nobility of character and appropriate language. One of "supreme achievements" of the modern theatre.

1464. Benchley, Robert. "Top." *New Yorker*, 7 (7 Nov.) 28. [Reprinted in Moses and Brown, *The American theatre as seen by its critics*, NY, Norton, 1934 (No. 89); and Oppenheimer, Louis, *The passionate playgoer*, NY, Viking, 1958 (No. 107).]

Grand, stupendous thriller, with the melodramatic hand of Monte Cristo much in evidence.

1465. Bolton, Whitney. "By easy stages." NY *Telegraph*, 1 Nov.

Five days after opening it is still possible to feel the impact of great tragedy.

1466. Bowen, Sterling. "The O'Neill play." *Wall St. Jour.*, 28 Oct.

Hard to place in the catalogue of O'Neill work. The first part is melodrama, the last is dilution. Instead of becoming tragic, the characters are merely exotic.

1467. Brown, John Mason. "Two on the aisle." NY *Post*, 28 Oct.

A widely quoted article reprinting many of the notes from O'Neill's working diary. Clark also includes excerpts in *European Theories of the Drama* (No. 22).

1468. Burr, Eugene. "Mourning Becomes Electra." *Bill-board*, 43 (7 Nov.) 17.
Written by any other man the play would have been taken as the misguided outpouring of an inferior writer. It is little more than a good three-act "meller."

1469. Canby, Henry Seidel. "Scarlet becomes crimson." *Sat. R. Lit.*, 8 (7 Nov.) 257-258. [Reprinted in Canby's *Seven years' harvest*, NY, Farrar & Rinehart, 1936, pp. 139-146 (No. 17).]
An excellent approach to modern decadence. The Greeks would not have liked the approach of the abnormal instance. But O'Neill has "consummate skill" as a writer which none can question.

1470. Chatfield-Taylor, Otis. "The latest plays." *Outlook*, 159 (11 Nov.) 343.
Argument about length and needed editing are unimportant beside the fact it is the most actable play of the year. Some performances that are rare experiences in the contemporary theatre.

1471. Clark, Barrett H. "Mourning becomes Electra." *Con-tempo* (Chapel Hill, N.C.), 1 (1 Dec.) 2.
Artful, skillful, magnificent, though it still does not represent the goal O'Neill has set up for himself.

1472. Eaton, Walter Prichard. "Powerful but not Greek." NY *Her-Trib.*, 22 Nov.
Not a Greek tragedy, though gripping, because of contemptible and small characters. O'Neill is as near classic as we can ask in modern drama.

1473. Evans, Harry. "Mourning Becomes Electra." *Life*, 98 (13 Nov.) 19.
Adds stature to the theatre, establishing O'Neill as the "leading dramatist of his time."

1474. Fergusson, Francis. "A month of the theatre." *Book-man*, 74 (Dec.) 440-445.
Bad taste shown in attempting to present a case history in

classical trappings and confusing psychological approach. The Greek values are not with us today.

1475. Garland, Robert. "Second thoughts on prophets, playwrights, the critics of Mourning Becomes Electra." NY *Wor-Tel.*, 29 Oct.
A review of the press comments shows American theatre is not dead.

1476. "Greece in New England." *Time*, 18 (2 Nov.) 34-38.
The significant straightforward treatment of the theme is good. Most of this review discusses O'Neill's background and the play.

1477. Jordan, Elizabeth. "Mr. O'Neill and others." *America*, 28 Nov.
Drawn as we are to morgues, or around accident victims, we want thrills, and this has them.

1478. Krutch, Joseph Wood. "Our Electra." *Nation*, 133 (18 Nov.) 551-552.
A great play, not "meaning" anything in sense of Ibsen or Shaw, but like *Hamlet* it means that human beings are great and terrible when in the grips of passion. One of the "very greatest works of dramatic literature" despite a lack of appropriate language.

1479. Lockridge, Richard. "Out of the show shop." NY *Sun*, 29 Oct.
The highest point O'Neill has reached; true art. He is now above his early faults, showing the theatre is not trivial.

1480. Mantle, Burns. "Yankee Electra releases a flood of superlatives — What next?" NY *News*, 1 Nov.
Reviews the critical reaction, wonders if there will not soon be a recession of praise. O'Neill treatment of Electra is a greater writing achievement than the original Greek, but it is probably not as great in character as *INTERLUDE*.

1481. Motherwell, Hiram. "Mourning Becomes Electra."

Th. Guild Mag., 9 (31 Dec.) 14-20. [Reprinted in Hewitt, Barnard, *Theatre USA*, NY, McGraw-Hill, 1959, pp. 387-390, (No. 56).]
This is a modern tragedy of psychology and shows need for shift of emphasis from Orestes to Electra in today's reliance on woman. An interesting counter to criticisms finding the play only a murder melodrama.

1482. "Mourning Becomes Electra." *Variety*, 1 Nov. (?)
Lusty, vigorous drama with more human emotional punch than any gang melodrama ever written. Never lets you out of its grip. Grim, horrifying, intensely absorbing.

1483. Nathan, George Jean. "The theatre of —" *Judge*, 21 Nov.
One of the most important plays in history of American drama. Monument not only to O'Neill but American Theatre as well.

1484. "O'Neill at top notch." *Lit. D.*, 111 (21 Nov.) 18-19.
Excerpts from other reviews, with two illustrations from original.

1485. "O'Neill's own story of Electra in the making." NY *Her-Trib.*, 8 Nov.
Excerpts from O'Neill's diary, first published by John Mason Brown in NY *Post*, 28 Oct. (No. 1467).

1486. Pollock, Arthur. "O'Neill does his finest work in Mourning Becomes Electra." Brook. *Eagle*, 29 Oct.
Beautiful play, showing O'Neill improved, no longer a faddist; more self-reliant than ever before.

1487. "Priscilla and Electra." NY *Times*, 31 Oct., 16:4.
Editorial comment; an amusing plea to leave poor old New England alone in its struggle with the Depression instead of accusing it of such horrors as here and in *DESIRE UNDER THE ELMS*.

1488. Ruhl, Arthur. "Second nights." NY *Her-Trib.*, 1 Nov.
Brief discussion of the effectiveness of play.

1489. Skinner, Richard Dana. "The play." *Commonweal*, 15 (11 Nov.) 46-47.

Emotions and artistic ability still not mastered enough to make O'Neill a great playwright, though this is his finest.

1490. — — — —. "What of the new season?" *Commonweal*, 26 (Aug.) 406.

Because O'Neill's future is important to our theatre, Skinner hopes forthcoming *ELECTRA* returns to the "rich intuition" of *BROWN*.

1491. Wellman, Rita. "In and out of town." *Town & Country*, 86 (1 Dec.) 46.

No softening element in the tragedy; like a New England boiled dinner the effect does not soon wear off.

1492. Wyatt, Euphemia Van R. "Agamemnon turned Puritan." *Cath. Wld.*, 134 (Dec.) 330-331.

Misses Olympus because of complete lack of human nobility and charity, without which human race would have long since perished.

1493. Young, Stark. "Eugene O'Neill's new play." *New Rep.*, 68 (11 Nov.) 352-355. [Reprinted in Zabel, Morton D., ed., *Literary opinion in America*, NY, Harpers, 1937, 1951 (No. 149); and in Young's *Immortal shadows*, NY, Scribners, 1948 (No. 148).]

The entire approach of Young's criticism is an objective discussion successfuly opposing those who would pick the play apart because of departures from the Greek. He finds modern additions "exhilarating."

1932

The road company, starring Judith Anderson, Walter Abel, and Florence Reed gave 16 performances starting 9 May 1932. New York critics reviewed it briefly, with little change in their original opinions.

1494. Atkinson, Brooks. "Tempest of the fates." NY *Times*, 22 May, VIII, 1:1.
Revaluation of the play upon return engagement finds it still tremendous, written "with the heat and fume of humanity."

1495. Brown, John Mason. "Two on the aisle." NY *Post*, 15 Apr.
Extensive quotes from St. John Ervine's criticism of O'Neill in London *Observer* (No. 234).

1496. Carb, David. "Seen on the stage." *Vogue*, 79 (1 Jan.) 56-57.
Abandoning tricks, O'Neill returns to characters about whom he can write at first hand. Majesty, dignity, tremendous sweep.

1497. Clark, Barrett H. "Aeschylus and Eugene O'Neill." *Eng. Jour.*, 21 (Nov.) 699-710.
This criticism is good to contrast to Feldman's article (No. 1518). Clark objectively compares the Greek pattern and O'Neill, making clear O'Neill used Aeschylus only where necessary in trying to show a modern idea in psychology in pattern of basic Greek sense of fate. It was ready-made story that did not need explaining.

1498. De Casseres, Benjamin. "Broadway to date." *Arts & Dec.*, 36 (Jan.) 52.
Most unique American play ever to be seen on the stage, some of O'Neill's greatest and mightiest characters, the culmination of all his work.

1499. "Electra revisted." *Th. Guild Mag.*, 9 (Mar.) 10.
Second visit shows more visual beauty and expression; a play for both eyes and ears.

1500. Fergusson, Francis. "Recalling the highlights." *Bookman*, 75 (June-July) 290-291.
Jones and Nazimova brought brilliance to a "stiff and pretentious monstrosity."

1501. Frederick, J. George. "Evening becomes intolerable." *Van. F.*, 37 (Jan.) 46-47.

A T.B.M. (tired business man) taken as guest expresses definite and adverse opinion that things like this do not make drama. A convincing case is made for the theatre of pure entertainment.

1502. Hutchens, John. "Greece to Broadway." *Th. Arts*, 16 (Jan.) 13-16. [Reprinted in Gilder, Rosamond, ed., *Theatre Arts anthology*, NY, Theatre Arts Books, 1950, pp. 619-622 (No. 49).]

For the first time O'Neill shows himself the great story teller in this horrific murder melodrama, having none of the uncertainty of former emotional writing.

1503. Kirstein, Lincoln. "Theatre chronicle." *Hound and Horn*, 5 (Jan.-Mar.) 280-282.

A "low high-water mark" of current theatre. Not a great play, not a tragedy, but given so much, one wants so much more.

1504. Knickerbocker, Frances Wentworth. "A New England house of Atreus." *Sewanee Rev.*, 40 (Apr.-June) 249-254.

Close comparison and contrast of Greek and O'Neill. Not great tragedy because Mannons are not great people and there is no "gleam of reconciliation."

1505. Krutch, Joseph Wood. "O'Neill again." *Nation*, 134 (17 Feb.) 210-211.

Defending his original enthusiastic response, Krutch finds the criticism against the psychoanalytical approach worthless, because it is merely explaining actions of the characters in a way we today can readily understand.

1506. "Mourning Becomes Electra." *Th. Guild Mag.*, 9 (Jan.) 2.

The one play you cannot walk out on or stop watching; O'Neill doing the thing he can do better than anything else.

1507. Nathan, George Jean. "Our premier dramatist." *Van. F.*, 37 (Jan.) 24.

Nathan attempts to show why O'Neill, except O'Casey, is the only living writer of English plays of any stature.

1508. — — — —. "Retrospect." *Van. F.*, 38 (June) 57.
A less important work than *STRANGE INTERLUDE.*

1509. Skinner, Richard Dana. "The play." *Commonweal*, 15 (6 Apr.) 636.
Reviewing the season, Skinner discusses the production and what O'Neill tries to do. The next great period of our writing will come when the feelings of O'Neill are harnessed into right direction.

1510. — — — —. "Some thoughts on O'Neill and Sophocles." *Commonweal*, 15 (3 Feb.) 386.
Almost nothing of Greek is in this because of failure to find substitute for fate.

1511. Smith, Althea E. "Mourning Becomes Electra." *Players Mag.*, 8 (Jan.-Feb.) 11.
Seeing is much different from reading; characters do not move one to pity on the stage. There is no faith transcending disaster, and we do not identify.

1512. Wyatt, Euphemia Van R. "The Theater weathers depression." *Cath. Wld.*, 135 (June) 336.
Despite a high price, this production brought the audience in and swept them into a world of imagination, which is art's function.

1935-1959

1513. Alexander, Doris M. "Capt. Brant and Capt. Brassbound: The origin of an O'Neill character." *Mod. Lang. Notes*, 74 (April 1959) 306-310.
Convincing argument that O'Neill "borrowed" Brant of *ELECTRA* directly from Shaw's Capt. Brassbound.

1514. — — — —. "Psychological fate in Mourning Becomes Electra." *PMLA*, 68 (Dec. 1953) 923-934.

Hamilton and Macgowan's 1929 *What is Wrong with Marriage* is shown as O'Neill's text in establishing his legitimate elements of psychological fate. The Puritan attitude toward love contributes about half; fate is completed by the Oedipus and Electra complexes handed down through parents to children in a vicious, never-ending circle.

1515. Asselineau, Roger. "Mourning Becomes Electra as a tragedy." *Mod. Dr.,* 1 (Dec. 1958) 143-150.
A carefully detailed analysis of the play, especially Lavinia, to show that O'Neill conceived a tragedy in the genuine classic sense, equal to if not surpassing the Greek, despite his lack of distinctive style.

1516. Barron, Samuel. "The dying theatre." *Harpers,* 172 (Dec. 1935) 108-117.
The theatre is dying because of narrow traditions unable to handle demands of modern drama. *ELECTRA* fails because of the limits of the stage.

1517. Battenhouse, Roy W. "Mourning Becomes Electra." *Christendom,* 7 (Summer 1942) 332-345.
An interesting and provocative analysis of the characters. O'Neill is writing variations on the one basic human ill, the "original" sin of insubordination to God, which can only end in dismal tragedy.

1518. Feldman, Abraham. "The American Aeschylus?" *Poet Lore,* 52 (Summer 1946) 149-155.
A lamentable failure, using theatrical tricks instead of drama to gain an "obscene" interpretation of Freud. Violently opposed to the entire play.

1519. Lecky, Eleazer. "Ghosts and Mourning Becomes Electra: Two versions of fate." *Ariz. Quar.,* 13 (Winter 1957) 320-338.
Both deal with the power of past over the present, including heredity, environment, and sexual conflict. The structure and

effect in both are, of course, different, and they are divergent as regards the future — *Ghosts* essentially optimistic, *ELECTRA* pessimistic.

THE ROPE

*Opening night reviews — Playwright's Theatre
New York — Newspapers of April-May 1918*

1520. Broun, Heywood. "Brilliant one-act play called The Rope Provincetown feature." NY *Tribune*, 29 Apr.
Glorious success among other neutral plays; finely imaginative story with surprising ending that comes without trickery.

1521. "Provincetown players give new playlets." NY *Clipper.*
A dramatic gem; the best of the works from this gifted author.

*Opening night reviews — Washington Square Players
New York — Newspapers of 14-15 May 1918*

1522. "Brace of new plays given at the Comedy." NY *Morn. World,* 14 May.
Ironic and vigorous; better than the companion piece by Susan Glaspell.

1523. Broun, Heywood. "Two new plays at the Comedy." NY *Tribune*, 14 May.
In the best vein of O'Neill.

1524. Dale, Alan. "Two new playlets at Comedy theatre." NY *American,* 14 May.

It may have been meant well, but you make of it what you like or don't like.

1525. Darnton, Charles. "The Rope." NY *Eve. World*, 14 May.
Admiration expressed for O'Neill's ability to draw character.

1526. Gardy, Louis. "The Rope put on at the Comedy." NY *Call*, 15 May.
A tremendous piece of rugged craftsmanship, carrying promise of future greatness. A terrifying spirit throughout.

1527. Mantle, Burns. "Washington Square players add a dose of tonic to their spring bill." NY *Mail*, 14 May.
Ugly but thrilling little drama; O'Neill's usual "fine, free active imagination."

1528. Sherwin, Louis. "Two new ones at the Comedy." NY *Globe*, 15 May.
Disappointing, not nearly as effective as others by O'Neill.

1529. "Three comedies and a drama." NY *Sun*, 14 May.
"A very original play."

1530. "Two new playlets instead of Salome." NY *Times*, 14 May, 11:5.
Has O'Neill vigor, lacking "singleness and bigness of motive" of his other better works.

1531. "Two new playlets on bill at Comedy." Brook. *Eagle*, 14 May.
The most striking and best of current bill; strength almost to brutality.

1532. "Two new plays at the Century (*sic*)" NY *Telegram*, 14 May.
Questionable taste at times, but good for those who like their drama straight.

1533. "Two new plays by Washington Square players."
NY *Herald,* 14 May.
Review of plot, no comment.

1534. "Two new plays given at Comedy." NY *Sun,* 14 May.
"Lamentably lacking in clearness and motive."

1535. "The Washington Square players." NY *Post,* 14 May.
A happy replacement for *Salome,* though it contributes nothing
much of dramatic value.

1536. "Washington Square players win new laurels." NY
Journal, 14 May.
Frank, direct, even brutal tragedy; its realism fairly makes the
audience gasp.

Other reviews and criticism
1918

1537. Hornblow, Arthur. "Mr. Hornblow goes to the play."
Theatre, 27 (June) 358.
O'Neill is a young playwright to be reckoned with, showing
much literary value.

1538. "The Provincetown Players." *Vogue,* 15 June.
Surprise at curtain is admirable, yet expected. Much talent for
the theatre in this young man.

1539. Untitled note in drama column. *Life,* 23 May.
In spite of repulsiveness, it does get a strong grip on the
interest.

1540. "Washington Square players." *Dram. Mir.,* 78 (25
May) 730.
The better of the two plays on the bill.

S. S. GLENCAIRN

The plays of the *Glencairn* cycle — *MOON OF THE CARIB-BEES, BOUND EAST FOR CARDIFF, IN THE ZONE,* and *THE LONG VOYAGE HOME* — were each produced separately during O'Neill's early career by both the Provincetown Players and the Washington Square Players. Only a few of the major New York newspapers sent their critics to the Provincetown, although the Washington Square productions were generally well covered. The four plays were later combined into the collective *S. S. GLENCAIRN.*

Opening night reviews — New York
Newspapers of 4 Nov. 1924

1541. Dale, Alan. "Cycle of plays offered at Province-town." NY *American.*
Little significance; too much of the unlovely and squalid.

1542. Four little O'Neill plays are revived." NY *Times,* 21:4.
This does not seem as good as the originals.

1543. Gabriel, Gilbert. "The S. S. Glencairn." NY *Telegram & Mail.*
Four stark, beautiful pictures of the sea and its men. They remain among the most affecting and poetical of O'Neill's plays. He has accomplished the music of the sea.

1544. Hammond, Percy. "S. S. Glencairn." NY *Her-Trib.*
"Honest relentless bits of humble sea life" told in the best O'Neill way.

1545. "Mr. O'Neill gets three hits and a foul ball." NY *Post.*
If you take your drama seriously here is a program to see. There is less salt, and more hokum than in his later plays, some of it too obvious.

1546. Pollock, Arthur. "Young Mr. O'Neill." Brook. *Eagle.*
These plays contain some of O'Neill's best work, but in view
of recent plays since they first appeared, they now seem tame.
But the force is still here, and they cut deep.

1547. "S. S. Glencairn." NY *World.*
Vivid pulsating drama.

Other reviews and criticism
1924-1925

1548. Hornblow, Arthur. "Mr. Hornblow goes to the play."
Theatre, 41 (Jan. 1925) 22.
A service to English speaking drama in presenting these.

1549. Nathan, George Jean. "O'Neill steams into port."
Judge, 87 (29 Nov. 1924) 10-11.
An excellent evening's entertainment.

1550. "S. S. Glencairn." *Drama Calendar,* 10 Nov. 1924.
This should forever cure any young boy who wishes to run
away to sea.

1551. "S. S. Glencairn." *Time,* 4 (17 Nov. 1924) 14.
Best thing on the current Provincetown bill.

1552. Sisk. "O'Neill's one acters." *Variety,* 12 Nov. 1924.
Though of little commercial value as plays, production is
excellent.

1553. Whyte, Gordon. "S. S. Glencairn." *Billboard,* 36
(15 Nov. 1924) 36.
"Welded into a fine show."

Opening night reviews — Provincetown Revival
New York — Newspapers of 10 Jan. 1929

1554. "Cast and forecast." NY *World.*
Brief notice of the revival of these "popular plays."

1555. "O'Neill's four plays of the sea revived." NY *Times*, 24:5.
Their vigor and freshness do not abate with the years.

1556. "O'Neill four sea episodes survive second revival." NY *Telegram*.
General praise for the revival.

1557. "O'Neill sea cycle at Provincetown." NY *American*.
Review of the play, no critical comment.

1558. "S. S. Glencairn." NY *Sun*.
Glad to see it back.

1559. "S. S. Glencairn at Provincetown playhouse." NY *Journal*.
Recreates all the rude power and tang of life of the early plays, which forecast O'Neill's later attainments. This far outweighs most current plays.

1560. "S. S. Glencairn here on return voyage; drab tale endures." NY *Her-Trib*.
Indelible picture of the dregs of human existence.

1561. "S. S. Glencairn revived here." NY *News*.
Brief notice of the revival.

1562. Waldorf, Wilella. "S. S. Glencairn." NY *Post*.
Decidedly worth the trip to see it.

Other reviews and criticism
1929

1563. Atkinson, Brooks. "Honor enough for everybody." NY *Times*, 27 Jan., IX, 1:1.
Warm praise. O'Neill's later works had roots in nature, sprang from the elemental.

1564. Ballantine, C. J. "Smitty of S. S. Glencairn." NY *World*, 6 Jan.
Tells of O'Neill's description of an actual young man, model of this character. (Note: Many critics at one time or another have identified O'Neill himself with Smitty.)

1565. Clark, Barrett H. "The real background of O'Neill in his S. S. Glencairn group." NY *Her-Trib.*, 10 Feb.
Discussion of the source material.

1566. "Down to the sea." NY *World*, 3 Mar.
Some references to the originals of the stage characters.

1567. "Four O'Neill plays on view." NY *Sun*, 11 Feb.
Mostly a review of O'Neill's past. He is in select group of writers with four plays running simultaneously.

1568. Lenz, Elita M. "S. S. Glencairn." *Billboard*, 41 (19 Jan.) 5.
"Lusty meat and ale of life"; wonderful evening of drama.

1569. Littell, Robert. "Brighter lights: Broadway in review." *Th. Arts*, 13 (Mar.) 172.
Stretches toward something "simple, elemental, fine" but achieves "sentimentality and crudity much too often."

1570. Nichols, Dudley. "Testing the play." NY *World*, 10 Feb.
Meets real test of good drama; true sweep of emotion.

1571. "O'Neill drew his gallery of sea characters from life." NY *Post*, 5 Jan.
This review of O'Neill's early life points out the sources.

1572. "O'Neill's one act plays." *Wall St. Jour.*, 16 Jan.
No parallel with these plays so far in the season.

1573. "S. S. Glencairn." *Commonweal*, 9 (23 Jan.) 349.
O'Neill at his best; moreso than when he is lost in the subconscious.

1574. "S. S. Glencairn." *Drama Calendar,* 5 Jan.
Grip of the scenes still holds; pulsating, tempestuous.

Opening night reviews — City Center Revival
New York — Newspapers of 21 May 1948

1575. Atkinson, Brooks. "At the theatre." NY *Times,* 21:2.
The acting makes these still fine sea plays. Honest realism
with the perspective of the poet. The modern American theatre
has nothing more genuine in its library.

1576. Barnes, Howard. "Smooth sailing." NY *Her-Trib.*
The mood becomes attenuated before the end, but there is
evidence of the flowering of great dramatic talent.

1577. Chapman, John. "O'Neill's S. S. Glencairn playlets
seem a bit quaint at City Center." NY *News.*
More interesting in history than in performance. The sailor
talk once seemed realistic, now seems stilted.

1578. Coleman, Robert. "S. S. Glencairn is top-flight
O'Neill." NY *Mirror.*
One of the finest contributions by the City Center. These plays
form an important page in the chronicles of the drama.

1579. Curril, George. "O'Neill's S. S. Glencairn still grips
an audience." Brook. *Eagle.*
There are anachronisms and inconsistencies, but the theme
still rings true.

1580. Dash, Thomas R. "S. S. Glencairn." *W. W. Daily.*
One can still see the writer in embryo, lacking technical skill
and dramatic proficiency.

1581. Garland, Robert. "Revival at City Center no credit
to O'Neill." NY *Jour-Am.*
Disapproval of the production.

1582. Hawkins, William. "Four O'Neill plays pale in City Center." NY *Wor-Tel*.
The sense of intimacy is lost. The serious mood cannot be conveyed in this large theatre.

1583. Morehouse, Ward. "Eugene O'Neill's S. S. Glencairn." NY *Sun*.
Curiously flat and unmoving. The theatrical realism of yesterday seems flat and tame here.

1584. Watts, Richard, Jr. "O'Neill's sea dramas done at City Center." NY *Post*.
These are now accepted as "classics" and much of the excitement and brightness have worn away. Other writers have come forward with more pungent dialogue, but they are worth seeing.

Other reviews and criticism
1948

1585. Atkinson, Brooks. "The tragic dream." NY *Times,* 30 May, II, 1:1.
A good revival. These plays are an authentic part of our literature of the stage, truly tragic in theme and beautifully executed in character.

1586. Beyer, William. "The state of the theatre." *School & Society*, 67 (26 June) 478.
"Tepid, contrived, routinely touching."

1587. Clurman, Harold. "O'Neill again." *New Rep.*, 118 (7 June) 27-29.
Good to see the classics of our literary heritage brought back, however inferior the production. O'Neill has given a lifetime of service in literature.

1588. Cooke, Richard P. "Early O'Neill." *Wall St. Jour.*, 24 May.
The moods of these early plays at times arc poignant and

dramatically interesting. At other times, they are lifeless and monotonous.

1589. Freedley, George. "Expert staging of O'Neill Glencairn." NY *Telegraph*, 23 May.
Nobody has done a better job of interpretation of the sea and its men than O'Neill.

1590. Gibbs, Wolcott. "Song and dance." *New Yorker*, 24 (29 May) 43-44.
The plays may have been something new when first produced, but they should now be relegated to the library.

1591. Nathan, George Jean. "A brief biography of American stage tars." NY *Jour-Am.*, 1 June.
They were amazingly popular because they presented for the first time in the drama the sea very close to reality.

1592. Phelan, Kappo. "S. S. Glencairn." *Commonweal*, 48 (4 June) 185.
The plays are hardly worth it any more.

1593. "S. S. Glencairn." *Variety*, 26 May.
More fragmentary drama compared to later works.

1594. Wilson, John S. "Four of O'Neill's early one-act plays." *PM*.

STRANGE INTERLUDE

*Opening night reviews — New York
Newspapers of 31 Jan. 1928*

1595. Anderson, John. "O'Neill's nine-act play opens." NY *Journ.*

Profound drama of subconscious. Ordeal by watered dialogue, sprawling, reckless waste — but still "profoundly engrossing." Bursts the seams of theatre in "stretching for deeper meaning and sharper truth." Passages of "soaring poetry," much "unwinking courage."

1596. Atkinson, Brooks. "Strange Interlude plays five hours." NY *Times*, 28:1.
Atkinson does not offer the high praise that others do, recognizing however that the unoriginal story is not as important as the technique of experiment. The asides are at times "the very stuff" of drama; at other times, used unwisely.

1597. Coleman, Robert. "Strange Interlude opens." NY *Mirror*.
Great day for faddists. "Long winded bark at the moon in nine fat acts." Tiresome, jerky, heavy-footed, obvious.

1598. Dale, Alan. "Strange Interlude." NY *American*.
The French would toss it off as a ribald farce. "A sordid mess"; "Pecksniffian outbursts," hysterical analysis of a psychopathic woman. "Six-hour bore."

1599. Gabriel, Gilbert. "Last night's first night." NY *Sun*.
This "magnificent" venture "cleaves the skyline of tomorrow." It is a "hewer of ways" in technique, and "enthralling" in theme.

1600. Hall, Leonard. "Eugene O'Neill is off on a huge and ambitious adventure." NY *Telegram*.
"One of the most astonishing adventures a stage ever held." ". . . great daubs of grays and browns and royal purples on a canvas the size of the side of a barn." Authentic genius.

1601. Hammond, Percy. "The theaters." NY *Her-Trib*.
Contains everything but brevity to make it an exciting evening in the theatre. Grand interlude for drama lovers who are patient and above average intelligence.

1602. Littell, Robert. "A great play." NY *Post*.

Greatest contribution to our stage, beside which all future plays in conventional style will seem flat and two dimensional.

1603. Mantle, Burns. "Strange Interlude nine acts." NY *News.*

Frankly biological. Solid gray in tone, slow-paced, repetitious, forbidding in length.

1604. "New O'Neill play worthy experiment." *W. W. Daily.*

Momentous and significant experiment in art and technique of dramaturgy. Wearisome to the layman, but attractive to the "epicurean." Less clumsy than masks of *BROWN.*

1605. Nichols, Dudley. "Strange Interlude." NY *World.*

Perhaps the most "important event in the present era of the American theatre." O'Neill catches not only a life but life itself; not just man and woman, but mankind.

1606. Pollock, Arthur. "Eugene O'Neill's nine-act play, Strange Interlude, proves fascinating." Brook. *Eagle.*

Fascinating as life itself. A novel written for the stage, but not a stunt. Sharply, beautifully written with a "bitterness and hard truth that hurts."

1607. Van Dycke, Thomas. "Nine-act O'Neill drama opens." NY *Telegraph.*

The most significant play O'Neill has written. Finest play yet written by an American, perhaps "most remarkable play of our generation." A monument in the history of American dramaturgy.

Other reviews and criticism
1928 (Two entries dated 1927 also entered)

1608. "Accounting for the popularity of O'Neill's nine-act drama." NY *Post,* 30 June.

Three factors may explain the play's popularity: desire to see something out of the ordinary, curiosity about what Guild and O'Neill had done to split the critics, and the possibility he wrote a great play.

1609.   Aiken, Conrad. "Strange Interlude." NY *Post*, 21 July. [Reprinted in Aiken's *Reviewer's ABC*, NY, Meridian Books, 1958, pp. 315-318.]

Book review. "Finest play by an American . . . ever seen on the stage."

1610.   Anderson, John. "Pieces of eight-thirty." NY *Post*, 3 Dec. 1927.

This report of the play before production calls it a "jawbreaking endurance contest" which has certain literary, perhaps poetic, qualities. "O'Neill spreads a vast and impressive net to catch a nuance" as he did in *GREAT GOD BROWN*.

1611.   Anthony, Luther B. "Strange Interlude, disease germs disseminated." *Dramatist*, 19 (Jan.) 1356.

Brief and strongly prejudiced attack against the play — suggests O'Neill's next step is dissemination of disease germs among audience.

1612.   Atkinson, Brooks. "Laurels for Strange Interlude." NY *Times*, 13 May, IX, 1:1.

The Pulitzer prize is approved, but the play is not great because of "cramping intrusion of the tenets of science." O'Neill has not ventured far enough into real tragedy to have written great drama here.

1613.   — — — —.   "Strange Interlude." NY *Times*, 5 Feb., VIII, 1:1.

Listing many faults in technique and philosophy, Atkinson none the less admits "when Mr. O'Neill is the black magician" nothing is boring and it is a very enjoyable evening.

1614.   Bellamy, Francis R. "Lights down." *Outlook*, 148 (22 Feb.) 304-305.

Not the last word in a new type drama, but the first, and O'Neill has given some of the most compelling drama ever witnessed.

1615.   Benchley, Robert. "All about Strange Interlude." *Life*, 91 (16 Feb.) 21.

Only O'Neill could make an audience stick through this kind of play. Highly important, maybe great, far from perfect.

1616. Brackett, Charles. "Not at their best." *New Yorker*, 3 (11 Feb.) 24.
An interesting stunt, four acts too long. Stream of consciousness cannot compare to Woolf or Joyce, and has much phony poetry.

1617. Broun, Heywood. "It seems to me." NY *World*, 1 Feb.
Broun points up the basic difficulty of getting all thoughts into words. Try as he might O'Neill can't really get the "lowest part of the iceberg" in.

1618. Brown, John Mason. "Intermission — Broadway in review." *Th. Arts*, 12 (Apr.) 237-240.
O'Neill taking himself as mystic seer is not so good, crystal ball in one hand, volume of Freud in another. But play is constantly interesting despite repetitions and asides.

1619. Carb, David. "The prize drama." *Vogue*, 72 (1 July) 62.
Play is above all else on the boards, but O'Neill's continued use of trick devices is bad. He is above such fiddle-faddle.

1620. — — — —. "Strange Interlude." *Vogue*, 71 (1 Apr.) 82-83.
O'Neill not a thinker or philosopher. His work on contrivance is both irritating and depressing. If he so continues it will be bad for him and calamity for American theatre.

1621. Cohen, Julius. "The Strange Interlude." *Jour. Comm.*, 1 Feb.
O'Neill's greatest; also greatest ever written.

1622. Dale, Alan. "Theatre and food cannot mix." NY *American*, 5 Feb.
"The unification of drammer and dinner is no more possible than that of oil and water." A biting attack on the whole matter of demanding that the audience eat during the play.

1623. De Casseres, Benjamin. "Broadway to date." *Arts & Dec.*, 28 (Apr.) 65.
Greatest play of the century; with *LAZARUS* it should make him a world figure. Nina is Eternal Woman in all respects.

1624. "The editor goes to the play." *Theatre*, Apr.
A masterpiece — it casts the hard and fast traditions on the scrapheap. O'Neill "shows the mechanism of the human soul under a microscope of verbal power and beauty." High praise for this "magnificent adventure into the guarded secret recesses of the mind."

1625. Gabriel, Gilbert. "Freud's first play." NY *Sun*, 5 Feb.
Successful with Freud for first time. Asides and soliloquies vital in probing of past lives, so much more important than what goes on at present.

1626. Gilder, Rosamond. "Plays bound and unbound." *Th. Arts*, 12 (May) 362.
"Surprising dramatic force." Asides bring us one step closer to the "springs of being."

1627. Gould, Bruce. "Suggestion for cutting O'Neill's Strange Interlude." NY *Post*, 12 Mar.
Reviewing the book, Gould finds the spoken thoughts do not intrude as much as on stage. But even in reading it is too long.

1628. Hall, Leonard. "O'Neill's drama is stirring up the playgoers this week." NY *Telegram*, 3 Feb.
Discussion of the way in which the play is affecting audiences, and the investigation into the matter of life which O'Neill attempts.

1629. Hammond, Percy. "Strange Interlude." NY *Her-Trib.*, 5 Feb.
"O'Neill has broken the drama's shackles and escaped from its prison more successfully than other fugitives from its many walls."

1630. Hope, Edward. "The lantern." NY *Her-Trib.*, 28 Feb.
Devotes full column to the futility of trying to put everything

down in the subconscious. Joyce failed, and so does O'Neill. Characters often speak obvious things that don't need speaking, though the play rises above "minor ineptitudes of technique."

1631. "In and out of town." *Town and Country*, 15 Feb.
"Richly wrought, handsome piece of pornography." A slow start, but by the end it is "incredibly fascinating." This critic sees Joyce and Proust as O'Neill's literary antecedents who stimulated him but whom he did not imitate.

1632. Jordan, Elizabeth. "Mr. O'Neill's dramatic 'stunt.'" *America*, 25 Feb.
The play would be infinitely clearer without the revelation of thought. O'Neill looks at humanity with jaundiced, red-rimmed, astigmatic eyes and sees abnormal people in abnormal situations.

1633. Krutch, Joseph Wood. "A modern heroic drama." NY *Her-Trib.*, 11 Mar.
Capable of doing on stage what novel could only do before; may start a new form. "Interesting, subtle, great, and also direct."

1634. — — — —. "Strange Interlude." *Nation*, 126 (15 Feb.) 192.
Does O'Neill say anything worth saying in such unusual technique? Krutch believes so, because he has made dramatic those elements of the novel heretofore forbidden to the stage.

1635. Leland, Gordon M. "Strange Interlude." *Billboard*, 40 (11 Feb.) 10.
Pretty much of a triumph all around, perhaps greatest play written by an American.

1636. Littell, Robert. "Two on the aisle." NY *Post*, 4 Feb.
No doubt it is the greatest contribution to our stage. This "brief expedition into the depths" of the play finds any simplified account of it difficult to write.

1637. Mantle, Burns. "A play that makes history." NY *News*, 5 Feb.
It will be parodied and kidded as a freak for some time, but

no doubt will become part of the Guild repertory. Cannot be compared with anything else ever written. Significant milestone in progress of drama. No matter what you think of it, it has significance.

1638. Moeller, Phillip. "Silences out loud." NY *Times*, 26 Feb., VIII, 4:7. [Reprinted in *Theatre Guild Quarterly*, 5 (Feb.) 9.]
Interesting account of many attempts tried and discarded in the establishment of correct procedure for delivering the asides.

1639. Nathan, George Jean. "The idea and comedy." *Am. Merc.*, 14 (May) 120.
Asides have gotten rid of infantile stage directions of 19th century which suggest sotto-voice asides, etc. The full and articulate speech is much to O'Neill's credit.

1640. — — — —. "Judging the shows." *Judge*, 94 (18 Feb.) 31.
One of his most important contributions to the American drama, which could have been written in no other way.

1641. — — — —. "O'Neill's finest play." *Am. Merc.*, 11 (Aug. 1927) 499-506.
A long synopsis of play before production with lament that O'Neill has not been properly produced before this time by the Guild. Finds play one of the most distinguished pieces of dramatic writing our stage has known.

1642. Osborn, E. W. "Strange Interlude." NY *World*, 21 Jan.
An amazing play. Cleverly conceived use of the soliloquy. Characters rounded out and full.

1643. — — — —. "The theatres." NY *World*, 4 Feb.
Comparison of the reading and acting versions. The play definitely becomes an acting play, because of the effect of the spoken asides.

1644. Pollock, Arthur. "Eugene O'Neill and Strange Interlude." Brook. *Eagle*, 5 Feb.

His finest drama, in which he is not so much a philosopher as a propagandist against life, which he finds is Hell.

1645. R. S. "Obsessions." *Wall St. Jour.*, 2 Feb.
The story is of questionable material for theatre; more for a mental clinic.

1646. "The rhyming reader." *Bookman*, 67 (Aug.) 692-693.
Amusing eleven-verse rhymed account of play, finding no real human being in entire work.

1647. Ruhl, Arthur. "Second nights." NY *Her-Trib.*, 19 Feb.
Deserves the attention it is getting as great news item, but there are many questions as to the value of technique and the fact everybody acts like "so many Freudian rats."

1648. S. M. W. "O'Neill's Strange Interlude is his supreme effort." NY *Review*, 31 Jan.
Clinches O'Neill's right to be called "most individual dramatist in America if not world." His success in defiance of tradition and rules "one of the greatest triumphs of individualism in the history of the theatre."

1649. Sayler, Oliver M. "The play of the week." *Sat. R. Lit.*, 4 (11 Feb.) 590.
A *tour de force* which may be over-praised too easily, or too easily dismissed. Encouraging to see the work of one who dares the unknown and forbidden.

1650. Seldes, Gilbert. "The theatre." *Dial*, 84 (Apr.) 348-351.
The merits are almost entirely spoiled by "technical infelicities." O'Neill too good a dramatist to have to use the asides.

1651. Seligman, Herbert J. "A diagnostic poet." NY *Sun*, 10 Mar.
This review of the printed version enters into considerable discussion of O'Neill's interest in diagnosing his characters. Regardless of how he does it, O'Neill is plumbing phases of American life with true theatricality, seriousness and profundity.

1652. Shipley, Joseph T. "Strange Interlude." *New Leader,* 11 Feb.

Unique experience not to be missed; a profound study of well-rounded characters. O'Neill's experiments are not within but are without the realms of conventional drama.

1653. Skinner, Richard Dana. "Strange Interlude." *Commonweal,* 7 (22 Feb.) 1098-1099. [Reprinted in Hewitt, Barnard, *Theatre USA,* NY, McGraw-Hill, 1959, pp. 371-374 (No. 56).]

Combination of novel and play makes a very interesting if not necessarily great drama.

1654. Sloan, J. Vandervoort. "Strange Interlude." *Drama,* 18 (May) 248.

A masterpiece comparable in "elemental quality" to Dostoievsky. The greatest play written by an American.

1655. "Strange Interlude." Brook. *Eagle,* 6 May.

By style and length O'Neill has shown in impressive way facts of our lives and the absence of meaning in much of our desires.

1656. "Strange Interlude." *Christ. Cent.,* 37 (7 June) 737.

Tremendous; has depth. Shows souls turned inside out.

1657. "Strange Interlude." *Independent,* 120 (31 Mar.) 315.

Brief book review. Asides legitimate, if unnecessarily long.

1658. "A Strange Interlude." *Psychology,* Mar., p. 53.

Mainly a review of the play's plot, but raising the question interesting to the psychologist concerning whether or not monagamy is instinctive and what can be done when one cannot live that way.

1659. "Strange Interlude." *Sat. R. Lit.,* 4 (3 Mar.) 641.

Book review. First truly successful drama using "double voice." New power; play becomes more articulate because of it.

1660. "Strange Interlude." *Theatre,* 47 (Apr.) 39-40.

Great days of the drama have returned; O'Neill makes us have reverence for the theatre.

1661. "Strange Interlude." *Time*, 11 (13 Feb.) 36-38.
Reviews the play act by act and gives brief background of O'Neill's life and career.

1662. "Strange Interlude." *Variety*, 1 Feb.
The best thing O'Neill has ever done, throwing much cold water on his disparagers.

1663. "Strangest interlude is one of indigestion." NY *Post*, 31 Jan.
Report on the difficulties of eating the evening meal between acts — and a comparison of the more efficient way the Germans do it when attending Wagner.

1664. Strunsky, Simeon. "About books, more or less: Miscellaneous." NY *Times*, 20 May, IV, p. 4.
Reviewing Pulitzer awards, finds interesting contrasts in length of the play and brevity of Wilder's *Bridge of San Luis Rey*. Play has something of the "trick" about it.

1665. "Three dimensional play." *Lit. D.*, 96 (25 Feb.) 26-27.
Realistic drama has received a body blow.

1666. Van Dycke, Thomas. "The make-up box." NY *Telegram*, 5 Feb.
Looking back on his previous comments about the significance of the play and the writer, this critic still feels O'Neill has made "the most significant contribution to the drama of America."

1667. Winchell, Walter. "Another Eugenic O'Neill baby." NY *Eve. Graphic*, 31 Jan.
Gripped, awed, fascinated for six episodes, grew cumbersome last 3. Acutely interesting, powerfully spellbinding, tense and breathless tragedy.

1668. Woollcott, Alexander. "Giving O'Neill till it hurts." *Van. F.*, 29 (Feb.) 48.
Subtitle: "Unofficial program notes for the most punishing of his plays." The Guild not having given any O'Neill up to now, insists on giving until it hurts.

1669. — — — —. "Mr. Hecht goes to Strange Interlude."
NY *World*, 14 May.
Extensive quotes from an unidentified Hecht writing about
his amazement at this "cultural shell game" with which Woollcott
agrees.

1670. — — — —. "Second thoughts on first nights — Strange
Interlude." NY *World*, 5 Feb.
Admiration for the impulse to write this, but finds no living
characters after the five hours of "resonant emptiness."

1671. Wyatt, Euphemia Van R. "Plays of some importance." *Cath. Wld.*, 127 (Apr.) 77-80.
Despite some unpleasantness, the work of a master dramatist,
written with sincere thought; an absorbing play.

1672. Young, Stark. "The new O'Neill play." *New Rep.*,
53 (15 Feb.) 349-350.
Whatever its shortcomings, an overwhelming milestone in
American theatre.

1929-1953

1673. Alexander, Doris M. "Strange Interlude and Schopenhauer." *Am. Lit.*, 25 (May 1953) 213-228.
Extremely convincing development of thesis that Schopenhauer
was followed almost completely and that Freudian psychology
is not the basis. If accepted, this does explain much of seemingly
pointless ending which so many critics disliked.

1674. Battenhouse, Roy. "Strange Interlude restudied."
Religion in Life, 15 (Spring 1946) 202-213.
Thorough and fresh analysis in terms of failure of individual
to find peace by natural conscience or scientific reason when
God has been rejected. Critic feels play bears restudying today.
Has an interesting set of speculations on possible symbolic mean-
ing of title itself, plus statement that much in the play satirizes
the American of its day.

1675. Garland, Robert. "O'Neill play's success has critics gasping." NY *Telegram*, 15 June 1929.

After sitting through it again, Garland observes that the "only thing wrong with O'Neill characters is they're crazy." Play is childish, obvious, unnecessarily disagreeable.

1676. Krutch, Joseph Wood. "The new American drama." *Nation*, 130 (11 June 1930) 678-679.

Instead of thesis plays which must be explained and contain a "point" the modern American writer as here aims at contemporary American life, making comedy and tragedy acceptable to contemporary audiences.

1677. Littell, Robert "Two on the aisle." NY *Post*, 30 Jan. 1929.

Criticizes O'Neill for his continual identifying characters with himself instead of standing aside. A contrast of this play with other earlier O'Neill shows how far he has come.

1678. McGuire, Harry. "Beyond Strange Interlude." *Drama*, 19 (Mar. 1929) 172.

Attempt by this admirer to show O'Neill's faith in life and living despite apparent almost nihilistic disillusion of the play.

1679. Malone, Kemp. "The diction of Strange Interlude." *Am. Speech*, 6 (Oct. 1930) 19-28.

An attempt to discover if O'Neill realism in language is consistent, reaching obvious conclusion he is as realistic as he wished to be.

1680. Philipps, Alice E. "Strange Interlude and the blah brotherhood." *Drama*, 19 (Mar. 1929) 174.

Based on reading only, takes sharp issue with creation of Nina as a woman, and with critics in general for praise of what to this critic is only an expression of sex.

1681. Shipp, Horace. "The x-rays up to nature." *Eng. Rev.*, 52 (Mar. 1931) 378-380.

"An amazing, a lovely and provocative play which must be seen by everbody who loves the theatre."

1682. Wynne, Stella. "The Strange Interlude." *Overland,* 87 (July 1929) 220.

Nina becomes the very ancient and primitive woman desiring to propagate the race.

THE STRAW

Reviews of the published version appear from No. 1683 to No. 1688. Reviews of the produced play begin with No. 1689.

Book

1683. Firkins, O. W. "Plays for the reader." *Weekly Rev.,* 4 (25 June 1921) 406-407.

O'Neill is not yet the master of the long play. A sense of theatre and honesty should be helpful in the future.

1684. Reniers, Percival F. "O'Neill's plays." *Lit. Rev. of NY Post,* 16 July 1921, p. 3.

Interesting, sincere, realistic; scenes of unquestioned dramatic skill.

1685. "The Straw." *Dial,* 70 (June 1921) 715.

Reviewed with *JONES. STRAW* is a less important work.

1686. "The Straw." *Th. Arts,* 5 (Oct. 1921) 334-335.

Strongly and truly written, with good character, but everybody is tied up too much with tuberculosis.

1687. V.S.G.L. "The Straw." *New Rep.,* 26 (25 May 1921) 386.

No half lights, no gray shades, nothing fragile and delicate. Constructed of 2x4's spiked together with O'Neill's reiterated emphasis.

1688. Woollcott, Alexander. "Second thoughts on first nights." NY *Times,* 8 May 1921, VI, 1:2.
Typical O'Neill, recognizable any place. Pure tragedy; a study of human misery, salted with irony.

Opening night reviews — New York
Newspapers of 11 Nov. 1921

1689. Allen, Kelcey. "Eugene O'Neill puts real vigor into The Straw." *W. W. Daily.*
Optimism makes it less bitter than *HORIZON* or *CHRISTIE;* well written dialogue and skillful characterization.

1690. Broun, Heywood. "It seems to me." NY *World.*
Last act "one of the most thrilling things our native theatre has ever known."

1691. Dale, Alan. "Tuberculosis dramatized in the latest play by Eugene O'Neill." NY *American.*
Parody of a play; O'Neill wasting his time on a subject nobody cares about seeing dramatized.

1692. Darnton, Charles. "The Straw human and moving." NY *World.*
Does not make this forbidding and gloomy; gives it saving quality of youth and hope. A memorable play.

1693. De Foe, Louis D. "O'Neill's triple extract of gloom." NY *World.*
Unbearable and strangely beautiful, superior quality but exceedingly lugubrious and depressing.

1694. "Eugene O'Neill's The Straw is gruesome clinical tale." NY *Sun.*
The sight of a tuberculosis sanitarium in full operation is not a good tonic. The play is a good example of "morbid Teutonic drama." The end hardly justifies the tubercular means.

1695. "Eugene O'Neill's The Straw profoundly impressive play." NY *Herald.*

Much could be made shorter, and though moving, it is a painful play.

1696. Hammond, Percy. "The Straw." NY *Tribune.*
O'Neill does not make use of any of the TB props for pity, yet manages to bring much new emotion to the viewer.

1697. Macgowan, Kenneth. "The Straw." NY *Globe.*
"A drama of character, uneven in emotion until last scene, when it surges into undeniable tragic power."

1698. Mantle, Burns. "The Straw a hopeful play." NY *Mail.*
More conventional than most O'Neill plays; surprisingly sympathetic.

1699. Marsh, Leo A. "Another O'Neill play presented."
NY *Telegraph.*
Striking study on subject of the strength of hope.

1700. "O'Neill scores new triumph in The Straw." NY *Journal.*
Written with great force; the interest of real life is in it.

1701. "The Straw." Brook. *Eagle.*
Not up to *ANNA CHRISTIE,* but still a play that should succeed.

1702. "The Straw by Mr. O'Neill." NY *Telegram.*
Every play assures O'Neill of a strong position, and this play proves him to be the most vital American dramatist.

1703. Towse, J. Ranken. "The Straw." NY *Post.*
Not the play admirers of O'Neill might have expected, but it is good realism and absorbingly interesting.

1704. Woollcott, Alexander. "Another O'Neill play." NY *Times,* 16:2.
Interesting and moving, with last scene having tragic irony and pathos seldom seen in the theatre.

Other reviews and criticism
1921-1922

1705. Andrews, Kenneth. "Broadway, our literary sign-post." *Bookman*, 54 (Jan. 1922) 463-464.
A new step in the as yet immature but developing O'Neill. He is able to weep with characters and feel their passions.

1706. Benchley, Robert. "The great plague." *Life*, 78 (8 Dec. 1921) 18.
Margalo Gilmore should recover because she is such a nice girl.

1707. Boyd, Ernest. "Mr. O'Neill's new play." *Freeman*, 7 Dec. 1921.
Depressing, unpleasant and vulgar.

1708. Broun, Heywood. "It seems to me." NY *World*, 12 Nov. 1921.
O'Neill's awareness that the greatness in tragedy lies in the struggle rather than defeat calls for praise.

1709. — — — —. "More moral victories." *Van. F.*, Jan. 1922.
Impossible to place O'Neill in any one category; in this play he sides with characters against fate.

1710. Crawford, Jack. "Broadway sheds tears." *Drama*, 12 (Feb. 1922) 152.
One of the first of the year's plays worthy of significance.

1711. De Foe, Louis V. "Our foremost apostle of woe." NY *World*, 20 Nov. 1921.
With continual emphasis on woe and depression, O'Neill's effectiveness and contribution may be limited.

1712. Hammond, Percy. "The theatres." NY *Tribune*, 20 Nov. 1931.
The play deals far more in troubles of the heart than the lungs.

1713. Hornblow, Arthur. "Mr. Hornblow goes to the play." *Theatre*, 35 (Jan. 1922) 31.

The production is a disappointment.

1714. Kaufman, S. Jay. "The Straw." *Dram. Mirror,* 84 (19 Nov. 1921) 737.
O'Neill's power does not ring as strong and ferocious as it could, but it is true, with a tremendous final scene.

1715. Macgowan, Kenneth. "The Straw." *Vogue,* Jan. 1922.
Not as well written or well knit as *CHRISTIE,* but tremendously moving at the end.

1716. — — — —. "Year's end." *Th. Arts,* 6 (Jan. 1922) 6.
A disappointment through production and no fault of the writer.

1717. Parker, Robert A. "An American dramatist developing." *Independent,* 107 (3 Dec. 1921) 230.
Lacks the interest and conviction of *ANNA CHRISTIE.*

1718. Reamer, Lawrence. "The Straw shows the effect of the sanitorium drama." NY *Herald,* 20 Nov. 1921.
O'Neill's promise may lead to great popularity uptown as well as down.

1719. "The Straw." *Town Topics,* 17 Nov. 1921.
From the standpoint of logic, integrity and soundness, it is O'Neill's best; ranks as a great American tragedy.

1720. "The Straw and its message." NY *Sun,* 18 Nov. 1921.
Dr. Lyman Fisk, eminent medical authority, sees a message of hope which is always important in medicine.

1721. "The Straw is play of hopefulness, pain, and death." NY *Clipper,* 16 Nov. 1921.
Merely plot review; little critical comment.

1722. "The Straw is repellant study in tuberculosis." NY *Review,* 12 Nov. 1921.
Seems mostly wasted effort; ugly subject is not embellished with art.

1723. "The Straw . . . remarkably well acted." NY *Call*, 23 Nov. 1921.

Despite the subject matter, play stands on its characterizations, which are extraordinary.

1724. Pollock, Arthur. "About the theatre." Brook. *Eagle*, 13 Nov. 1921.

No need to fear seeing it for its unpleasant subject, although it does not come off as well as could be hoped.

1725. Whittaker, James. "O'Neill's Straw compact history of girl's heart." NY *News*, 27 Nov. 1921.

Sanitorium used only to telescope an entire life and to indicate afflictions of a girl's heart.

THIRST

This play first appeared in O'Neill's initial venture into print called *Thirst and Other One Act Plays*, published in 1914 at the insistence of Clayton Hamilton. The entire expense was borne by James O'Neill. The Provincetown Players gave one performance of the play in 1916 at the Wharf Theatre during one of their summer series, but there is no record of any other production. The only printed review of the play was written by Hamilton soon after the book appeared.

1726. Hamilton, Clayton. "A shelf of printed plays." *Bookman*, 41 (April 1915) 182.

Under "Playwright of Promise" Hamilton states that the young writer has a knowledge of the sea, and that the plays have violent emotion.

A TOUCH OF THE POET

A select number of entries discussing the Stockholm production and the version published by the Yale University Press appear from No. 1727 to No. 1733. Opening night reviews begin with No. 1734.

Stockholm and Published Version
1957

1727. Atkinson, Brooks. "O'Neill's Poet." NY *Times,* 22 Sept. II, 1:1.
The book seems a temperate play after *JOURNEY;* it does not probe the "black corners of O'Neill's life." Although Melody somewhat overburdens the plot, it is vigorous and original and the characters come alive.

1728. Belair, Felix, Jr. "World premiere for O'Neill." NY *Times,* 7 Apr., II, 3:1.
A review of O'Neill's Stockholm reception and of the play's subject matter, "What is truth?" It is portraying O'Neill's conviction that those who are loneliest are the proudest, and in this play he has found entirely new characters to express what has been called his one obsession.

1729. Fleisher, Frederic. "A long day's journey into O'Neill." *New Rep.,* 136 (3 June) 21.
This review of the Stockholm production finds the play reminiscent of *The Wild Duck* in its destroying of the life-lies so typical of O'Neill.

1730. Hewes, Henry. "Self delusion in Stockholm." *Sat. Rev.,* 40 (13 Apr.) 24.
A distinguished and vital example of demon-driven dramaturgy. Even with its shortcomings it shows O'Neill's growth into this final great period.

1731. "The Iceman crumbleth." *Time,* 70 (30 Sept.) 102.
A distressingly flaccid play, but it still makes most Broadway productions seem stillborn, even it its published version.

1732. Krutch, Joseph Wood. "Eugene O'Neill's claim to greatness." NY *Times,* 22 Sept., VII, p. 1.
Another *ICEMAN* theme, a nihilistic *Wild Duck,* and it will not add to O'Neill's stature as did *JOURNEY.* Despite strong adverse criticism against him, O'Neill still draws audiences, and seldom is a writer given the second chance he now is. This review of O'Neill's present position offers a convincing case for his permanence in our theatre because, for all his lack of a facile style and his other major and obvious faults, he does communicate to the audiences which have always supported his plays in the past and which are apparently doing so once again.

1733. Seldes, Gilbert. "Small touch of genius." *Sat. Rev.,* 40 (21 Sept.) 21.
This reworking of old themes might just as well be left unproduced. *JOURNEY* had well developed characters, but this is only about a drunkard. O'Neill seems to have lacked conviction in this play.

Opening night reviews — New York
Newspapers of 3 Oct. 1958

1734. Aston, Frank. "Touch of Poet at Helen Hayes." NY *Wor-Tel. & Sun.*
Without much comment on the play, aside from its being a "garrulous, sardonic, clinical examination of a British major," this review praises the acting and production, particularly the performance of Helen Hayes.

1735. Atkinson, Brooks. "Theatre: Eugene O'Neill's A Touch of the Poet." NY *Times,* 23:2.
A recognizable O'Neill play in its characters and its illusions and pipe dreams though it is not typical in the lack of death at the end. Characteristically overwritten, full of O'Neill's bigness, bitterness, and hatred.

1736. Chapman, John. "Portman, Hayes and Stanley magnificent in Touch of the Poet." NY *News*.

O'Neill seems very much alive today; not a great O'Neill play, but makes much of contemporary theatre look pallid. "Once more Eugene O'Neill gives stature to the theatre."

1737. Colby, Ethel. "Entertainment on Broadway." *Jour. Comm.*

A lesser O'Neill, though nothing he ever wrote can be called a waste of time. Some brilliant dialogue and effective scene, but the over-all picture lacks marked effect.

1738. Coleman, Robert. "Touch of Poet magnificent." NY *Mirror*.

One of O'Neill's best. There are touches of O'Casey and Shaw, but it is genuine O'Neill, including as it does love, compassion and humor — a heart that is missing in many of his plays. It can be seen again and again.

1739. McClain, John. "O'Neill again proves he's incomparable." NY *Jour-Am*.

Even a lesser O'Neill play proves he is "majestically alone" in American theatre. Intensely created, full-dimensioned characters, though lack of sympathy weakens them. "Once more Mr. O'Neill makes everybody else look silly."

1740. Watts, Richard, Jr. "Eugene O'Neill's Touch of the Poet." NY *Post*.

The season takes on dignity and importance. Not quite what his others have been, but there is enormous power, compassion, and emotional impact. It is more than the revelation of character; it is a drama of America's formative years. A powerful, stirring, beautiful play.

1741. Whittaker, Herbert. "A Touch of the Poet." NY *Her-Trib*.

It may not rank with O'Neill's greatest, but it is worthy of them. The power of *JOURNEY* is evident here, and the collapse of Melody is set forth with force and brutality, hewn out of four compact acts.

Other reviews and criticism
1958 (two entries dated 1959)

1742. Atkinson, Brooks. "A Touch of the Poet." NY *Times*, 12 Oct., II, 1:1.
One of O'Neill's best, which takes skilled acting to bring out the vigorous internal life of the play. On its many levels of pessimism, savage quarrels and "boisterous theatricality" it is all O'Neill.

1743. Brustein, Robert. "Theatre chronicle." *Hudson Rev.*, 12 (Spring 1959) 96-98.
Actually a story of a hero divested of heroism and it has tragic possibilities. It shows O'Neill was improving as a dramatic draftsman with an authentic tragic theme.

1744. Cooke, Richard P. "Love and pride." *Wall St. Jour.*, 6 Oct.
Not upper-echelon O'Neill, but has unmistakable mark of craftsmanship and bears his trademarks of a "great flow of often wonderful words, . . . flashes of dark light."

1745. Dennis, Patrick. "Rake's progress." *New Rep.*, 139 (20 Oct.) 23.
Power and greatness abundantly evident. "A big evening of real O'Neill fireworks."

1746. Driver, Tom F. "Imagination in crisis." *Christ. Cent.*, 75 (26 Feb.) 252-254.
Perhaps our greatest crisis today is that of the imagination — the way man thinks of himself in relation to the world and his dreams. The published version suggests it is an age of meaninglessness because of man's lack of confidence in his ideas. In this play O'Neill is not negative, but merely skeptical.

1747. — — — —. "Kiss of death." *Christ. Cent.*, 75 (3 Dec.) 1401-1402.
The play greets the theatre like a kiss of death. If the theme is "the making of America" it does not fit the script as produced, for the production never focuses but is almost a parody of itself.

1748. Gelb, Arthur. "O'Neill's hopeless hope for a giant cycle." NY *Times*, 28 Sept., II, 1:3.

Upon the opening of *POET*, this informative article traces much of O'Neill's plans for the multi-play cycle, of which this play is the only surviving member.

1749. Hayes, Richard. "The music of old manners." *Commonweal*, 69 (7 Nov.) 151-153.

The defect is loss of grandeur, though one must admire the way O'Neill orchestrates and distributes his substance. It is not his best play.

1750. Hewes, Henry. "The playboy goes west." *Sat. R.*, 41 (18 Oct.) 56.

It glows "like a beautiful bridge" between the old fashioned theatrical conventions and the new love-filled O'Neill we are now discovering. The last act has some unforgettable moments.

1751. Hobe. "A touch of the poet." *Variety*, 8 Oct.

Second rate O'Neill but it should appeal to the box office. Diffuse, repetitious, somewhat old-fashioned in technique, but nobody can match its sheer theatricalism. Stunning emotional impact; a tremendous play.

1752. Krutch, Joseph Wood. "The O'Neill's on stage once more." *Th. Arts*, 42 (Oct.) 16-17.

It is more than a melodrama with a happy ending, because O'Neill had in mind more than just this play. Krutch assumes the entire *POSSESSORS* cycle was O'Neill's picture of his own family. It is better constructed than many of his plays.

1753. Lardner, John. "Irish pride and Mexican love." *New Yorker*, 34 (11 Oct.) 87.

Strident, sluggish, overmagnified people and an overly massive point of view. Compensations are found in intensity of purpose and honesty in writing.

1754. Lewis, Theophilus. "A Touch of the Poet." *America*, 100 (25 Oct.) 118.

A brief review offering "bravos" for those concerned with the production.

1755. McCarthy, Mary. "Odd man in." *Partisan Rev.*, 26 (Winter 1959) 100-106.
As in the case of many present-day plays this lacks both hero and villain, seen in *JOURNEY, Epitaph for George Dillon* or *Look Back in Anger*. Main characters alternate between brutality and seeking forgiveness, always needing a woman who "understands."

1756. Mannes, Marya. "A matter of motive." *Reporter*, 19 (13 Nov.) 37-38.
These are real people in real situations, held together in better structure than in *ICEMAN* or *JOURNEY*. O'Neill's purity of intent raises him above everybody else.

1757. "New play in Manhattan." *Time*, 72 (13 Oct.) 89.
The play has "centripetal force and centrifugal wastefulness, giant strength and giant sprawl." The characters are superior to the action, but it never gets the power of cumulative drama.

1758. "Once again the giant." *Newsweek*, 52 (13 Oct.) 112.
Middling-best O'Neill, but characteristic. It still charges the stage with electricity. "Another belated gift from the greatest."

1759. "A Touch of the Poet." *Th. Arts*, 42 (Dec.) 9-10.
Though a "mellow" O'Neill, it is still strong medicine and has considerable substance. It is not as forceful and convincing as *ICEMAN* or *JOURNEY*.

1760. "A Touch of the Poet." *Vogue*, 132 (15 Nov.) 105.
"Acerbates the nerves" with repetition in the early part, then "excites them" in the last half.

1761. Vidal, Gore. "Theatre." *Nation*, 187 (25 Oct.) 298-299.
The appeal is strong because of the element of Cornelius Melody in all of us. It is "human and gently wise," a contrast to the usual O'Neill.

1762. Watts, Richard, Jr. "Another triumph for Eugene O'Neill." NY *Post*, 12 Oct.

O'Neill can only be compared to his own work, and this is not quite *JOURNEY* or *ICEMAN*. It is not a minor work, either. Enormous force and impact. The American theatre is at its best again.

1763. Wyatt, Euphemia Van R. "A Touch of the Poet." *Cath. Wld.*, 188 (Dec.) 243-244.

The play leaves us wondering what came before and what followed in the cycle. Much is needed to understand this vigorous play.

WARNINGS

This play appeared in the small volume *Thirst and Other One Act Plays*, published in 1914 at the expense of James O'Neill. So far as is known, it has never received any important production, but one article appeared in 1936 and is listed below.

1764. Shklofsky, Bryna. "Eugene O'Neill and deafness." *Volta Review*, 38 (January 1936) 48.

This publication devoted to the teaching of the deaf relates the plot of this story of a ship's wireless operator who gradually loses his hearing. To this reviewer the play should be considered a tragedy.

WELDED

Opening run reviews — Baltimore Tryout
Newspapers of March 1924

1765. Clark, Norman. "New play by O'Neill at Auditorium." Baltimore *News*, 5 Mar.
Not in conventional dramatic form and the uncovering of human souls through conversation is not appealing.

1766. "Eugene O'Neill's latest drama here." Baltimore *Sun*, 4 Mar.
Motionless and wordy, though competent and dignified as is usual with O'Neill, but it probably will not succeed.

1767. Garland, Robert. "Welded fails to add to Eugene O'Neill's fame as author." Baltimore *American*, 9 Mar.
High strung and overly introspective, exasperating; strains our emotions and sense of humor.

1768. — — — —. "Welded is drama of married bondage." Baltimore *American*, 4 Mar.
"Provocative, earnest, not entirely convincing."

1769. "O'Neill play falls short of ideal upon its premiere." Baltimore *Post*, 4 Mar.
It is a disappointment.

1770. "Welded seen as probe of human soul." Baltimore *Sun*, 9 Mar.
An extensive article with dialogue excerpts showing how the play fails mainly because of our own failure to become interested in the characters.

Opening night reviews — New York
Newspapers of 18 March 1924

1771. Allen, Kelcey. "Latest O'Neill play Welded is study of marriage." *W. W. Daily.*
Reviews plot only.

1772. Corbin, John. "Romantic marriage." NY *Times*, 24:1.
Work of an original and distinguished playwright but the play is not up to the writer's ability.

1773. Gabriel, Gilbert. "Linked bitterness long drawn out in O'Neill's newest play." NY *Sun.*
True and wise and wearisome.

1774. Hammond, Percy. "Welded a lugubrious conversazione about life among the artists." NY *Tribune.*
Dull, uneventful, garrulous, about people in whom we have no interest.

1775. Mantle, Burns. "Welded intense but monotonous." NY *News.*
Uninspiring, repetitious, "written in a single doleful key."

1776. Osborn, E. W. "Welded." NY *Eve. World.*
Powerful first act, with anticlimactic ending.

1777. Sinnott, James P. "Welded a drama of married life." NY *Telegraph.*
Not much of a play, little but conversation; O'Neill falls from the heights of realism.

1778. Torres, H. Z. "Welded displays morbid tendency." NY *Commercial.*
O'Neill capable of better things; repetitious and dull, based on a pathological premise.

1779. Towse, J. Ranken. "O'Neill's Welded is disappointing." NY *Post.*

O'Neill befogs whatever he is trying to say and must learn the difference between power and sensationalism.

1780. "Welded." NY *World.*
For 2 acts as bold and true and well written a play as anything on the stage now.

1781. Welsh, Robert G. "Two chatty egotists." NY *Telegram & Mail.*
Characters created with skill and clear dialogue. A masterpiece with so few characters.

1782. Whittaker, James. "Eugene O'Neill's play shown at 39th Street." NY *American.*
Bilious cupid with poison arrows, a bull in this china shop of high society the same as in the grog shops of O'Neill's other plays.

1783. Woollcott, Alexander. "O'Neill's new play." NY *Herald.*
Perhaps O'Neill's integrity instead of incompetence is what makes this so prodigiously dull.

Other reviews and criticism
1924

1784. Benchley, Robert. "Three hot ones." *Life,* 83 (3 Apr.) 26.
Moves as if directed for slow-motion movie; very dull.

1785. Bjorkman, Edwin. "Plays and playmakers." *Outlook,* 137 (11 June) 238.
Brief review together with *CHILLUN.*

1786. Carb, David. "To see or not to see." *Bookman,* 59 (May) 332.
Poor acting and script which is not up to O'Neill standard; distressingly overwritten.

1787. Corbin, John. "Among the new plays." NY *Times*,
23 Mar., VIII, 1:1.
Characters are human but lack contact with normal experiences; play is uninspiring and dull.

1788. Gruening, Ernest. "The wings of the children." *Th.
Arts*, 8 (July) 497-498.
Harrowing, garish bathos and morbid melodrama; a wild and
maudlin night.

1789. Hammond, Percy. "Oddiments and remainders." NY
Tribune, 23 Mar.
Interesting only to those of similar temperament. Romance has
never been shown in so miserable a fashion.

1790. Hornblow, Arthur. "Mr. Hornblow goes to the play."
Theatre, 39 (May) 16.
O'Neill is not using his great dramatic gift; talky, morbid,
barren.

1791. Krutch, Joseph Wood. "Patterns." *Nation*, 118 (25
June) 743-744.
Reviews mainly *ALL GOD'S CHILLUN*.

1792. Lewisohn, Ludwig. "Pseudo-marriage." *Nation*, 118
(2 Apr.) 376-377.
A "new departure" as O'Neill once more starts his career over
again. The play is not thought out; becomes murky.

1793. Macgowan, Kenneth. "Crying the hounds of Broadway." *Th. Arts*, 8 (June) 357.
Brief review of season's offerings.

1794. — — — —. "Eugene O'Neill as realist." NY *Times*,
23 Mar., VIII, 2:6.
Being romantic instead of a realist, O'Neill wished to get
straight to the emotions and passions which realistic technique
could not have done, which is the reason for the style of dialogue
in this play.

1795. — — — —. "Seen on the stage." *Vogue*, 63 (15 May) 66-67.

Actually a piece of expressionistic writing instead of realism. More for experiments of Provincetown than Broadway.

1796. Metcalfe, J. S. "The need of segregation." *Wall St. Jour.*, 19 Mar.

A sharp attack against O'Neill and those of Greenwich Village who would sell wares like this as dramatic art or literature. Like the brothels of Tokyo, they should be segregated and perform without publicity. Plays of this type incite obscene thoughts and provoke ribald comment. There will be time enough to present O'Neill when he has written a decent piece.

1797. Nathan, George Jean. "Welded." *Am. Merc.*, 2 (May) 115-116.

Attempting a Strindberg, O'Neill has missed it completely. Full of "three-alarm dramaturgy" without point.

1798. Osborn, E. W. "The theatres." NY *Eve. World*, 22 Mar.

Further discussion of the play as a dramatic study of two characters.

1799. Pollock, Arthur. "About the theatre." Brook. *Eagle*, 23 Mar.

O'Neill still writes like a young man, refusing to be placed in a rut. The impression of this play is blurred.

1800. "Welded." *Variety*, 26 Mar.

Mostly a review of story, along with the assertion it will not run long.

1801. "Welded — luminous psychology of neurots." *Dramatist*, 15 (Apr.) 1208-1210.

Only play-going neurots of New York would go to this.

1802. Woollcott, Alexander. "O'Neill's new play Welded a melancholy stage study of quarrel of man and wife." NY *Sun*, 22 Mar.

WHERE THE CROSS IS MADE

These two reviews of the original Provincetown production are the only ones found in the New York Public Library.

1803. Broun, Heywood. "Provincetown players give fine thrill in sea play." NY *Tribune*, 23 Nov. 1918.
One of the best things O'Neill has done. Sweep of story has exceptional skill.

1804. "Only the captain's daughter stays sane." NY *Telegraph*, 23 Nov., 1918.
A good play to watch to enjoy sensation of going mad.

GRADUATE RESEARCH

O'Neill was a popular subject for graduate research during his lifetime, but by the end of 1959 the revival of interest in his works had not further prompted any extensive scholarly research. While masters' essays have formed the greater bulk of graduate investigation, it is nearly impossible to determine their total among the tremendous outpouring from the large number of institutions offering the degree. The subject matter and the extent of its treatment in most masters' theses is compartively superficial as well. On the other hand, doctoral dissertations have been more lasting contributions. Several, such as those by Doris Alexander, Doris Falk, and Edwin Engel, have formed the basis for further important publication. (See Nos. 38, 39, 151, 152.) The extent of doctoral research is also a simple matter to determine through the regularly published Dissertation Index.

Consequently, only PhD research has been listed below. None except Genevra Herndon's has been consulted. All are therefore listed without comment in alphabetical order.

Alexander, Doris M. "Freud and O'Neill: An analysis of *Strange Interlude*. New York University, 1952.

Bucks, Dorothy S. "The American drama of ideas, 1890-1929." Northwestern, 1944.

Burns, Sister M. Vincentia. "The Wagnerian theory of art and its influence on the drama of Eugene O'Neill." Univ. of Pennsylvania, 1943.

Dawson, Mary E. "The idea of tragedy in the contemporary American theater." Univ. of Iowa, 1945.

Engel, Edwin A. "Eugene O'Neill as a writer of tragedy." Univ. of Michigan, 1948.

Falk, Doris V. "Eugene O'Neill and the tragic tension." Cornell, 1952

Foster, Jacob Flavel. "The development of social criticism in the Broadway theatre during the inter-war period, 1919-1939." New York University, 1943.

Gallaway, Marian Hesse. "A composite study of the development of skills in plot construction by a group of living American dramatists." Univ. of Iowa, 1941.

Gould, Arthur S. "The idea of tragedy in modern American drama." Univ. of Michigan, 1948.

Hahn, Vera T. "The plays of Eugene O'Neill: A psychological analysis." Univ. of Louisiana, 1939.

Halline, Allan Gates. "Main currents of thought in American drama." Univ. of Wisconsin, 1936.

Herndon, Genevra. "American criticism of Eugene O'Neill, 1917-1948." Northwestern, 1948.

Kaucher, Dorothy J. "Modern dramatic structure." Univ. of Missouri, 1928.

Miller, Jordan Y. "A critical bibliography of Eugene O'Neill." Columbia, 1957.

Poag, Thomas Edward. "The Negro in drama and the theater." Cornell, 1943.

Redfern, Richard K. "A study of art structure in the American drama." Cornell, 1950.

Willoughby, Pearl Vivian. "Modern dramaturgy, British and American." Univ. of Virginia, 1928.

SOURCES CONSULTED

American Bibliography. Published as an annual supplement to PMLA.
An invaluable reference list, mainly of scholarly material, including new books and all important contributions in periodicals and journals.

Baker, Blanche M. *Dramatic Biblography: An annotated list of books on the history and criticism of the drama and stage and on the allied arts of the theatre.* NY, H. W. Wilson Co., 1933.
One of the basic reference books for any theatre library. General and specific subject matter; many cross references, well annotated.

————. *Theatre and Allied Arts.* NY, H. W. Wilson Co., 1952.
A smaller reference book based on the *Dramatic Bibliography,* and brought up to date.

Bibliographic Index. Edited by Dorothy Charles and Bea Joseph. NY, H. W. Wilson Co., 1945-1953.
The standard index to all bibliographies published in English.

The Book Review Digest. NY, H. W. Wilson Co. Published monthly.
Gives brief summaries of major books, together with short digests of leading reviews. At times it tends to favor some rather obscure publications, but still an excellent source of reference.

The Bulletin of Bibliography, Boston, F. W. Faxon. Published quarterly.
The journal devoted to pursuits of scholars in the field of bibliography. A primary source of current bibliographical information. Also lists magazines as they appear or cease publication. A separate section, "The Dramatic Index," appeared until the first quarter of 1953. It listed many articles about the drama in periodicals, but it was in many ways far from complete. (See below, *The Dramatic Index.*)

Catalogue of Copyright Entries: Books and Dramatic Works. Washington, Government Printing Office. Published annually.

A priceless help in determining names, dates and places. Much of the material on O'Neill's unpublished plays secured here.

The Cumulative Book Index. NY, H. W. Wilson Co. Published annually.

Regular listing of all the books in English in print.

Dramatic Compositions Copyrighted in the U.S., 1870-1916. Washington, Government Printing Office.

Two volumes separate from *Catalogue of Copyright Entries.* The same information is now contained in the regular catalogue.

The Dramatic Index. Boston, F. W. Faxon. Published annually.

Faxon's separate volume devoted to dramatic works and articles about them, based on the items in the *Bulletin of Bibliography.* The most complete single listing of its type, although not as comprehensive as it would at first seem. Unfortunately discontinued as a book after 1949.

The Education Index. NY, H. W. Wilson Co.

The companion index to *Reader's Guide, International Index,* etc.

Essay and General Literature Index. NY, H. W. Wilson Co.

Index of essays and other material of general literary interest to be found in anthologies and other published collections.

Firkins, Ina Ten Eyck. *Index to Plays, 1800-1926.* NY, H. W. Wilson Co., 1927. Supplement 1936.

A valuable source of basic information on full length plays.

Herndon, Genevra. *American Criticism of Eugene O'Neill, 1917-1948.* Ph.D. Dissertation, Northwestern Univ., 1948. Unpublished.

The text is a general review of major criticism, but the bibliography is very complete and was of considerable assistance in cross checking and amplifying this one.

Index to American Doctoral Dissertations. Ann Arbor, Michigan, University Microfilms, Published annually.

A cumulative index by subject matter (not individual topic) and author based on monthly publication, *Dissertation Abstracts.*

An Index to One-act Plays. Compiled by Hannah Logasa and Winifred Vcr Noey. Boston, F. W. Faxon. 1924, 1932, 1941, 1949.

The original volume and its supplements are a fine complement to the Firkins editions. Very complete in its field.

The International Index to Periodicals. NY, H. W. Wilson Co.

Companion to *Reader's Guide,* etc. Indexes foreign and scholarly periodicals not included in the more popular indexes.

Johnson, Merle De Vose, ed. *Merle Johnson's American First Editions,* Cambridge, Mass., Research Classics.

Published first in 1929, and in various editions up to 1947. Fourth edition, 1942, was revised and corrected by Jacob Blanck. Offers very little beyond the Sanborn and Clark O'Neill bibliography. A good reference for establishement of first editions, neatly and clearly arranged, but not as complete in information as might be desired.

Leary, Lewis, ed. *Articles on American Literature appearing in Current Periodicals.* Durham, North Carolina, Duke University Press, 1947.

The standard source of its type. Now revised, typed copy of which Mr. Leary permitted me to use in compiling this bibliography. An excellent source for scholarly and semi-scholarly entries. Cumulative listing from the same section in *American Literature.*

— — — —. *Doctoral Dissertations in American Literature 1933-1948.* Durham, North Carolina, Duke University Press, 1949.

Valuable source list of all such work compiled from quarterly listings in *American Literature*.

Leisy, E. E., and Jay B. Hubbell, eds. "Doctoral Dissertations in American Literature." *American Literature*, 4 (January 1933) 419-465.
Antecedent to the Leary compilation.

The New York Times Index. NY, The New York Times.
Published periodically during the year, and in annual volumes. A tremendous aid in establishing pertinent facts about current events.

Reader's Guide to Periodical Literature. NY, H. W. Wilson Co.
The standard periodical index.

Sanborn, Ralph, and Barrett H. Clark. *A Bibliography of the Works of Eugene O'Neill*. NY, Random House, 1931.
Only 500 copies were printed. Contains a careful collation of all texts to and including *DYNAMO*, with numerous plates illustrating variations within editions. Contains limited references to periodical, newspapers, and book articles (including separate books on O'Neill) and also contains a collection of little-known poems which O'Neill reluctantly gave permission to publish.

Schweitzer, Elizabeth L. *Eugene O'Neill: A Bibliography*. Wisconsin Library School, no date.
Typewritten copy consulted in New York Public Library. Often carelessly done, offers little except a listing of reviews of each play and a chronology of all first performances up to *DYNAMO*.

Theatre Collection, New York Public Library.
The Theatre Collection has no separate O'Neill collection, but it does have all of the scrapbooks and clipping collections kept by the Provincetown Players, much of which is in an alarming state of deterioration. (Two complete scrapbooks have been missing for many years.) The material is not filed for ready

reference, but requires tedious searching. The library's collections of theatre reviews were consulted for many of the newspaper reports included in this bibliography.

Thomson, Ruth Gibbons. *Index to Full Length Plays, 1926-1944.* Boston, F. W. Faxon, 1946.
Another valuable index to all plays.

University Collections
American Literature Collection, Yale University Library.
The large file of O'Neill's personal papers is not yet available to scholars, but there are many other items of value which may be consulted. All of O'Neill's scrapbooks compiled from the many clipping services to which he subscribed are available, and there are several boxes of loose material — photographs, pamphlets, and other newspaper items, all in a good state of preservation. The Theatre Guild scrapbooks may be consulted as well. The collection maintains an excellent card catalogue of all O'Neill material in the entire Library.

Landauer Collection, Baker Library, Dartmouth College.
The late Mrs. Bella Landauer turned over to Dartmouth her unique collection of programs of first night performances of O'Neill's foreign productions. Her collection of O'Neill letters is extremely valuable and helps close the gap existing by the restriction on the Yale material. There are also some books and galley proofs in this collection, but its main value is in the programs and the letters, which may be readily consulted.

O'Neill Collection, Princeton University Library.
This is the third major collection of O'Neill material although it is the smallest. It consists mainly of some manuscripts and a small group of letters. These may be consulted without restriction.

INDEX

The first series of figures following each index entry, or following each subheading of each entry, indicates *page numbers* and is printed in *Italic*. The second series of figures indicates *bibliography entry numbers* and is printed in *Roman*. Bibliography entries of particular interest or importance are marked with an asterisk (*).

Subheadings are self-explanatory. If no subheading appears following a major entry, it is to be assumed that the material is of general interest and cannot be successfully categorized. These items of general interest appear first, followed by the subheadings in alphabetical order, followed by the titles of Eugene O'Neill's plays, abbreviated according to the list which immediately follows this explanation.

Entries are arranged in the following patterns:

AUTHOR. All authors and/or editors of books, miscellaneous articles, and specific dramatic criticism of O'Neill's plays. A typical entry:

> Atkinson, Brooks, *70*, 157-158, 160-162*, 163-
> 165; interviews *25*, 166; Nobel prize 2, 159;
> AHW 404, 449; ANNA 160, 571; BB 597; etc.

Under Atkinson, therefore, will be found items of *general interest* on *page* 70 and in the bibliography under *numbers* 157-158, 160-162, and 163-165. Item number 162 is starred, and is of special importance. Material concerning interviews with O'Neill appears on *page* 25 under *number* 166 in the bibliography; the Nobel prize is discussed in bibliography entries 2 and 159. O'Neill's plays are treated in bibliography entries as indicated: AH, WILDERNESS! in numbers 404 and 449; ANNA CHRISTIE in numbers 160, 571; BEFORE BREAKFAST in number 597, and so on.

Editors of books which reprint items by other authors are indicated in this manner:

> Cowley, Malcolm, reprints Trilling 28; per-
> sonal reminiscences 205-206, 310; GGB 205

Dodds, John, reprints Atkinson (GGB) 34;
O'Neill's explanation GGB *169*, 34.

Cowley is editor of a volume which reprints an article of general
interest by Trilling, noted in bibliography entry number 28, and
is author of articles of a personal nature noted in numbers 205-
206 and 310 plus a review of THE GREAT GOD BROWN in
number 205. Dodds reprints a review of THE GREAT GOD
BROWN by Atkinson, number 34, and reprints O'Neill's own
explanation of the play, also discussed on page 169. All of the
reprinted items are, of course, listed under their original author
as well.

SUBJECT. 1) *Eugene O'Neill himself*. Because all of
O'Neill's plays are listed separately under their own titles,
O'Neill is entered as *subject* only. All headings and subheads
under his name are adequately explained, with frequent cross
references to further topics either under O'Neill, or in the main
listings.

2) *O'Neill's plays*. The plays appear in CAPITALS under
their own titles in the main listing, and are treated in this
manner:

DYNAMO, *63-64*, *66*, 88, 121*, 125, 201;
O'Neill's explanation *64;* production *152-153;*
publication *119-120,123, 125-126;* use of monologue-soliloquy *42*
    REVIEWS. NY opening 1929: 839-851;
    other 1929: 852-897

Thus on *pages* 63-64 and 66 will be found material of general
interest concerning the play DYNAMO, as well as in the
bibliography under numbers 88, 121, 125, and 201. Number 121
is starred because of its special interest. On page 64 appears a
discussion of O'Neill's explanation of the play; production information, including cast, appears on pages 152-153 and publication
of the play is discussed on pages 119-120, 123, and 125-126. The
monologue-soliloquy is discussed on page 42. Reviews of opening
night in 1929 are included in the bibliography from number 839
through 851, and subsequent reviews and discussion of the play
are included from number 852 through 897.

3) *Miscellaneous.* All other miscellaneous subject material, including names, titles, and subjects, not included in any other category.

TITLE. 1) *Books.* All books which pertain directly to O'Neill, contain significant material about him, or reprint articles concerning him or his plays are listed by their titles, uncapitalized, as in the bibliography, except for initial words and proper nouns. Typical entries:

> *After the genteel tradition,* reprints Trilling 28
> *American and British literature since 1890,* 138
> *Development of dramatic art, The,* GGB LAZ,
>   SI 131

These books contain, in order, a reprinting of an article of general interest by Trilling, bibliography number 28; an item of general interest, number 138; and a specific discussion of THE GREAT GOD BROWN, LAZARUS LAUCHED, and STRANGE INTERLUDE, number 131

2) *Periodicals.* Entries are treated similar to author entries, containing an indication of the type of material to be found under each periodical title. A typical entry:

> *American Mercury,* 209, 321, 323, 328, 350;
>   English productions 182; ALL GC 115, 487;
>   AM 505; etc.

This periodical contains items of general interest listed in the bibliography under numbers 209, 321, 323, 328, and 350. A discussion of English productions appears under number 182. ALL GOD'S CHILLUN GOT WINGS is discussed on page 115, and in the bibliography under number 487; THE ANCIENT MARINER has an entry under number 505, and so on.

NOTE: Periodical titles are fully capitalized to distinguish them from book titles, following the general pattern of indicating titles appropriately capitalized in the bibliography itself.

3) *Articles.* Only articles of *general interest* are listed and their contents are not generally noted. Article titles are included to enable the reader to locate some particular item by title if necessary, but more assistance will come from either the author or publication entry. Titles are indicated by quotation marks,

and are not capitalized except for initial words and proper nouns. Please note that specific reviews of the individual plays are *not* included. The reasons are many and obvious: the repetition of play title as the only title for newspaper reviews, or the repetition of column titles in other periodicals are the most immediately apparent reasons. Sheer volume of the number of reviews is another .No problem is really involved in finding specific articles about individual plays because they may be found by consulting the play titles and then the bibliography.

INDEX ABBREVIATIONS

AHW — AH, WILDERNESS
ALL GC — ALL GOD'S
CHILLUN GOT WINGS
AM — THE ANCIENT MARINER
ANNA — ANNA CHRISTIE
BB — BEFORE BREAKFAST
BH — BEYOND THE HORIZON
DAYS — DAYS WITHOUT END
DES — DESIRE UNDER THE
ELMS
DIFF — DIFF'RENT
DK — THE DREAMY KID
DYN — DYNAMO
EJ — THE EMPEROR JONES
FM — THE FIRST MAN
FOUNT — THE FOUNTAIN
GGB — THE GREAT GOD
BROWN
HA — THE HAIRY APE
ICE — THE ICEMAN COMETH
IN Z — IN THE ZONE
LAZ — LAZARUS LAUGHED
LDJ — LONG DAY'S JOURNEY
INTO NIGHT
LOST — Lost Plays of Eugene
O'Neill
MARCO — MARCO MILLIONS
MMIS — A MOON FOR THE
MISBEGOTTEN
MOON C — THE MOON OF
THE CARIBBEES
MOURN — MOURNING
BECOMES ELECTRA
NY — New York
SSG — S. S. GLENCAIRN
SERV — SERVITUDE
SI — STRANGE INTERLUDE
STRAW — THE STRAW
TALE — A TALE OF
POSSESSORS SELF-
DISPOSSESSED
TP — A TOUCH OF THE POET
WCM — WHERE THE CROSS
IS MADE

INDEX

ADDENDA

The following list represents a limited selection of major publications about O'Neill which have appeared since December 1959. These must, of necessity, remain unnumbered and unindexed, but their importance to O'Neill scholarship makes their entry in this publication imperative. Reviews of the three books are not normally included, and the several criticisms of the off-Broadway revival of *DIFF'RENT* have also been omitted.

BOOKS

Alexander, Doris. *The tempering of Eugene O'Neill*. NY, Harcourt, Brace & World, 1962.
A biographical study of the young O'Neill, ending with the award of his first Pulitzer Prize.

Cargill, Oscar, N. Bryllion Fagin, and William J. Fisher. *O'Neill and his plays*. NY, New York Univ. Press, 1962.
Nearly 100 articles are reprinted to show a wide variety of O'Neill criticism and opinion, including some of O'Neill's own remarks.

Gelb, Arthur, and Barbara Gelb. *O'Neill*. NY, Harper's, 1962.
A truly monumental volume of over 1000 pages, incorporating over five years' study of O'Neill's life and works. The most complete and authentic biography to date.

PERIODICALS

Adler, Jacob H. "The worth of Ah, Wilderness!" *Mod. Dr.*, 3 (Dec. 1960) 280-288.
Alexander, Doris M. "Eugene O'Neill and *Light on the path.*" *Mod. Dr.*, 3 (Dec. 1960) 260-267.
Arnett, B. M., and Nicola Chiaromonte. "Eugene O'Neill (1958)." *Sewanee Rev.*, 68 (Summer 1960) 494-501.

Chaitin, Norman C. "O'Neill: The power of daring." *Mod. Dr.*, 3 (Dec. 1960) 231-241.

Clurman, Harold. "At odds with gentility." *Nation*, 194 (7 Apr. 1962) 312.

Dahlstrom, Carl. "Dynamo and Lazarus Laughed: Some limitations." *Mod. Dr.*, 3 (Dec. 1960) 224-230.

Day, Cyrus. "*Amor fati*: O'Neill's Lazarus as superman and savior." *Mod. Dr.*, 3 (Dec. 1960) 297-305.

Engel, Edwin A. "O'Neill, 1960." *Mod. Dr.*, 3 (Dec. 1960) 219-223.

Falk, Signi. "Dialogue in the plays of Eugene O'Neill." *Mod. Dr.*, 3 (Dec. 1960) 314-325.

Frenz, Horst. "Notes on Eugene O'Neill in Japan." *Mod. Dr.*, 3 (Dec. 1960) 306-313.

Gelb, Arthur, and Barbara Gelb. "As O'Neill saw the theatre: Excerpts from his letters and interviews between 1920 and 1946." NY *Times*, 12 Nov. 1961, VI, p. 32.

— — — —. "Start of a Long day's journey, The." *Horizon*, 2 (March 1960) 25-40.

Hartman, Murray. "Desire Under the Elms in the light of Strindberg's influence." *Am. Lit.*, 33 (Nov. 1961) 360-369.

Hanzeli, Victor E. "The progeny of Atreus." *Mod. Dr.*, 3 (May 1960) 75-81.

Hicks, Granville. "O'Neill." *Sat. R.*, 45 (7 Apr. 1962) 16.

Hofmannsthal, Hugo von. "Eugene O'Neill." *Tulane Dr. Rev.*, 5 (Sept. 1960) 169-173.

Klavsons, Janis. "O'Neill's dreamer: Success and failure." *Mod. Dr.*, 3 (Dec. 1960) 268-272.

Krutch, Joseph Wood. "Why the O'Neill star is rising." NY *Times*, 19 Mar. 1961, VI, pp. 36-37.

Mayfield, John S. "Eugene O'Neill and the senator from Texas." *Yale Univ. Library Gazette*, vol. 35, pp. 87-93.

Nethercote, Arthur H. "The psychoanalyzing of Eugene O'Neill." *Mod. Dr.*, 3 (Dec. 1960) 242-256.

Pallette, Drew B. "O'Neill and the comic spirit." *Mod. Dr.*, 3 (Dec. 1960) 273-279.

Parks, Edd Winfield. "Eugene O'Neill's quest." *Tulane Dr. Rev.*, 4 (Spring 1960) 99-107.

Shawcross, John T. "The road to ruin: The beginning of

O'Neill's Long Day's Journey." *Mod. Dr.*, 3 (Dec. 1960) 289-296.

Waith, E. M. "Eugene O'Neill: An exercise in unmasking." *Ed. Th. Jour.*, 13 (Oct. 1961) 182-191.

Weissman, Philip. "Mourning Becomes Electra and the prodigal: Electra and Orestes." *Mod. Dr.*, 3 (Dec. 1960) 257-259.

Whitman, R. F. "O'Neill's search for a language of the theatre." *Quar. Jour. Sp.*, 46 (Apr. 1960) 153-170.

Winther, Sophus Keith. "Desire Under the Elms: A modern tragedy." *Mod. Dr.*, 3 (Dec. 1960) 326-332.

DISSERTATION

Raghavacharyulu, Dhupaty V. K. "The achievement of Eugene O'Neill: A study of the dramatist as seeker." Penn. 1959.